THE LESS DEVELOPED REALM:
A GEOGRAPHY OF ITS POPULATION

The Less Developed Realm:
A Geography of Its Population

GLENN T. TREWARTHA

Cartography by
Randall B. Sale
University of Wisconsin, Madison

John Wiley & Sons, Inc.
New York · London · Sydney · Toronto

To SARITA; Dan, Nan,
Mark and Susan

Errata for TREWARTHA, THE LESS DEVELOPED REALM: A GEOGRAPHY OF ITS POPULATION

Page 160. The map below replaces the one now shown as fig. 5.5

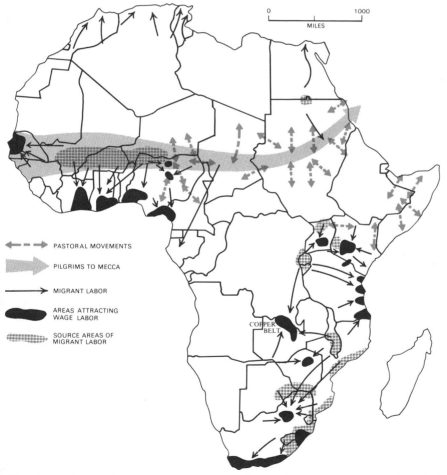

Fig. 5.5. Main migratory movements of population in Africa. Modified from maps by Grove, Prothero, and Dresch.

Page 360. The map below is a clearer presentation for fig. 12.2

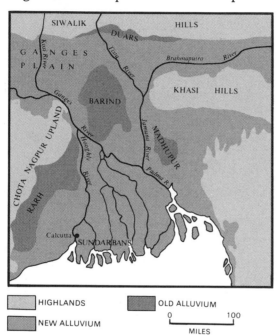

HIGHLANDS   OLD ALLUVIUM

NEW ALLUVIUM

0   100

MILES

Fig. 12.2. The lower Ganges-Brahmaputra delta region in India-East Pakistan. Note especially the extensive regions of older alluvium; also the Tista River.

Preface

A Geography of Population: World Patterns (Wiley, 1969) was the first of a conceived trilogy of books dealing with the earth's population geography. This is the second volume of the trilogy. Here the focus is on the earth's less developed realm: the spatial distribution features of its population (dynamic and static) involving both numbers and characteristics. Included are all of Africa; the tropical parts of Latin America (which, south of the Rio Grande, excludes only Argentina and Uruguay); and Asia (excluding the Asiatic part of the Union of Soviet Socialist Republics; Japan; and Israel). Much of the Introduction in *A Geography of Population: World Patterns* is also relevant to the present volume: *The Less Developed Realm: A Geography of Its Population*.

An attempt to fit the rudiments of the population geography of such an immense and varied realm into the dimensions of one modest-sized volume created unusual organizational difficulties. If a systematic, topical approach were used exclusively, for the whole realm or its individual continents, then the exceeding diversity would require a continual reference to regional exceptions. If, on the other hand, only an analysis of a host of individual regions were attempted, there arises the danger that the discussion would lack unity, would become repetitious, and would resemble a catalog.

My solution to this problem required a compromise. Introductory Chapter 1 provides an analytical unity through a survey of the less developed realm in its entirety. Features common to the realm are emphasized; yet the considerable variety of features is not neglected. In the remainder of the book, the three economically retarded continents are discussed individually. Both Latin America and Africa have separate introductory chapters (Chapters 2 and 5); in the case of Asia, where contrasting macroregions prevail, a few pages of prologue in Chapter 10 suffices. Each of the continental discussions is followed by chapters devoted to major individual regions, together with their subregions and even separate countries. The comparative element is emphasized.

The disparity in length of the discussions of the three continents is conspicuous; Asia's treatment represents forty percent of the book. This inequality is partially justified by the fact that Asia's population is more than three times as numerous as that of Latin America and Africa combined. In addition, Asia has four unusually populous countries (not including Japan), each with over 100 million inhabitants, and two of which—the supergiants mainland China and India—are of prime world importance. The more abundant literature on Asia's population likely also played a part.

Analysis of the spatial aspects of population numbers and characteristics within the economically less developed realm is made difficult by the scarcity and unrealiability of official data. This factor caused far greater reliance on estimates (official and otherwise), and on secondary sources in general than is desirable. It also resulted in greater inequalities in the in-depth analysis among individual regions and countries than might be expected. Their variable lengths of text are scarcely an indicator of relative importance.

It is regrettable that this book goes to press at the beginning of a new decade when recent censuses will shortly provide more up-to-date statistics. As it is, much of the statistical material used is for the early 1960's, and some is even for earlier dates.

GLENN T. TREWARTHA

Acknowledgments

The colleagues and associates who contributed time and advice in the preparation of this volume are so numerous that I can only thank them collectively; yet the gratitude expressed is no less sincere. However, I especially thank the colleagues who read substantial parts of the manuscript and made suggestions for improvement: Else Schmidt, who read the entire section on Africa and the introductory Chapter 1 covering the less developed realm as a whole; Roy Chung, who read not only Chapter 1 but also the chapters on Middle America, China, and Southwest Asia; Samuel Onakomiya of Nigeria, who scrutinized Chapter 5 on Africa in general and also Chapter 7 on West and Central Africa; Lucille Carlson, who covered the entire African part of the manuscript; S. P. Chatterjee of India, who scanned Chapter 12 on South Asia; Daniel F. Doeppers, who toiled over Chapter 11 on Southeast Asia; Narisimha Katary of India, who scrutinized Chapter 12 on South Asia; and Reece A. Jones, who read Chapter 2 on Latin America and Chapter 4 on South America.

G. T. T.

Contents

THE LESS DEVELOPED REALM:
A GEOGRAPHY OF ITS POPULATION

The Less Developed Realm: Population
Unity and Variety

A very meaningful dichotomy of the world's peoples and regions is one that separates them into the less developed (LD) and the more developed (MD) parts.[1] The LD realm includes the countries or regions that fail to provide acceptable levels of living for a large proportion of their populations, with resulting widespread poverty and material deprivation. Notice that such terms as less developed, underdeveloped, and backward refer especially to the economic conditions of a people; they do not necessarily imply cultural retardation, although profound differences in social organization between LD and MD populations usually do exist. LD human societies, then, are the ones that have been relatively unsuccessful in the struggle to earn a living. Unfortunately, this includes a large proportion of the earth's inhabitants, since it is estimated that the LD sector, which comprises 70–80 percent of the world's population, controls only 20 percent of the world's wealth. The causes for this situation are numerous and their interactions are notably complex. Underdeveloped countries vary greatly in size, geographic location, and magnitude and quality of natural resources. They also represent a wide range in national population numbers and densities. But one population feature they do seem to have in common—human settlement characteristically exists in the form of a few dense clusters whose growth has often benefited from historical and environmental advantages, although much more extensive surrounding areas are only thinly peopled or even uninhabited.

In most discussions of the earth's LD societies, it appears to be tacitly assumed that their people would be happier and better off if they could be pushed with all due speed out of their primitive ways of living and

---

[1] Among the other paired names used to designate this grand division are the following: developing versus developed; backward versus advanced; traditional versus modern; preindustrial versus industrial; and underdeveloped versus developed. These designations are used here somewhat interchangeably.

into the more imposing and complex industrial-scientific civilization best exemplified by Anglo-America and Northwest Europe. Indeed, the LD societies are clamoring loudly for aid in making a rapid escape from their bondage of scarcity and deprivation and for the advent of an economy of abundance like that of the MD countries, particularly the United States. Unfortunately, they are not aware that an economy of affluence and abundance, rooted in technology, is itself plagued by a host of negative features growing out of a surfeit of goods and wealth. Thus, in contrast to the poverty in machines characteristic of economically backward societies, more advanced countries suffer from a tyranny of machines and their ill effects on the environment.

The question of how complex, mechanized, and abundantly supplied with goods a society must be to permit the most favorable life possible for human beings has never been answered. The optimum conditions needed for the best life and greatest happiness are still unknown. Life as it is lived in the United States and Atlantic Europe is usually assumed to be the model that should be striven for, but the blessings of our mechanized, affluent Western society are far from being unmixed. We cannot help wondering whether there may not be some desirable halfway point between the crushing deprivation now prevalent in the LD realm and the glut of goods and wealth (and its associated worries and tensions) characteristic of our advanced mechanized societies. No one appears to know.

Perhaps the best single measure of the level of economic development is average per capita national income. Typical of LD regions are low average per capita production and, of course, low consumption as well. But even in those economically backward countries where per capita income is above average and on the increase, if the increment is not spread widely throughout the population strata so that the burden of widespread and crushing poverty is lightened, genuine economic improvement can scarcely be said to exist. The crucial test of economic advancement is not just expansion of national output, but rather the self-sustaining reduction of mass poverty.[2] Several of the oil-rich sheikdoms of the Near East illustrate the case of countries having large per capita national incomes but also grinding want.

But while meager average per capita productivity is characteristic of the LD countries as a class, there are still different degrees of underdevelopment, and the nations thus classified provide a production spectrum of considerable range. In a recent year, the countries with an average

[2] Jacob Viner, "The Economics of Development," in A. N. Agarwala and S. P. Singh (eds.), *Economics of Underdevelopment*, Oxford University Press, 1958.

per capita product below $100 represented somewhat more than half of the earth's population; the countries falling below $200 included about three fifths of it. Within the latter group is a vast proportion of the people of Asia and Africa and about half the population of Latin America.[3] By comparison, the non-Communist MD countries in that same year had an average per capita product of $1400. But in both LD and MD groups, the range of per capita national incomes forms a continuum.

Although the basic indicator of "less developed" stresses the fact of low per capita national production, there are other characteristics that are somewhat common to the group. It has been suggested, for example, that a country should probably be designated as underdeveloped if more than 50 percent of its gainfully occupied males are engaged in agriculture (including forestry and hunting). Such a country is still in the peasant-agriculture stage of development. By this definition, the LD world probably includes about three fourths of both the world's population and its habitable area.[4] That peasant agriculture sets only very general limits on the degree of crowding is suggested by the fact that the earth's LD countries characterized by that particular economy show an unusually wide range of average national population densities—from extremely low to remarkably high. At one end of the spectrum are crowded Java, India, and Nilotic Egypt, while at the opposite end are the relatively empty Amazon Basin, Sahara and Southwest Africa.

A list of other features common in various degrees to most of the LD realm includes the following: widespread poverty and misery (as suggested earlier), inadequate diets and low levels of health, high rates of illiteracy, high levels of fertility, relatively high but declining mortality, high and accelerating rates of population increase, age structures heavily weighted on young dependents, widespread unemployment and underemployment, a low proportion of industrial population to total population, scarcity of capital, and a low ratio of urban dwellers to total population. Also, the LD regions are overwhelmingly inhabited by non-European peoples with colored skins—the Negroid and Mongoloid strains. This feature sets them apart from the whites under whom they have been subjected to a long period of subservience and colonial rule. The experience has left them resentful, which continues to exacerbate the present relations between whites and coloreds. Notice also that the

[3] Simon Kuznets, "Population and Economic Growth," pp. 170–193 in *Population Problems, Proceedings of the American Philosophical Society*, Vol. 111, No. 3, June 22, 1967, Philadelphia, Pa., pp. 184–185.
[4] Kingsley Davis, "The Controversial Future of the Underdeveloped Areas," in Paul K. Hatt (ed.), *World Population and Future Resources*, American Book Co., Boston, 1952, p. 17.

peoples of traditional societies, having colored skins, are overwhelmingly concentrated in the tropical and subtropical latitudes.

Since World War II the increase in world food production has about kept pace with the increase in world population—exceeding it in the richer countries while lagging behind in the poorer ones. Two thirds of the earth's people live in countries where the national average diets are inadequate. These same diet-deficient countries have high population growth rates, exceeding 2.1 percent per year. By contrast, in the diet-adequate countries, growth is only about 1.3 percent per year.[5] A consequence of this imbalance is that an increasing share of the population increment in the LD realm has been sustained by shipments of food from the more affluent nations.

The recent spectacular success achieved in developing new varieties of high-yield wheats has caused the world's food outlook to temporarily appear a little brighter. But this so-called "green revolution" is only a stopgap, buying us 20 years or so in which to get the LD realm's population growth under control. It is not a cure.

Further aggravating the handicaps of LD countries is the large proportion of economically inactive persons in their populations. It has been estimated that people in the dependent age groups—preponderantly children 1–14 years of age, but also persons who are 65 and over—constitute 42–43 percent of the LD world's population, compared with 37–38 percent in the MD industrial world.[6]

VARIETY WITHIN THE LD REALM

An adequate understanding of the population problems of the LD continents and their individual countries requires not only a knowledge of their population similarities but also an awareness of the differences that prevail among them with respect to the degree to which they possess these various characteristics. Most emphatically, the LD countries cannot be regarded as a homogeneous group.

Continental Differences. Among the three LD continents of Asia, Africa, and Latin America, Asia is particularly noteworthy because of its much larger population. Some 76 percent of the earth's LD peoples

[5] Conrad Taeuber, "Population and Food Supply," pp. 73–83 in John D. Durand (ed.), *World Population, Annals of the American Academy of Political and Social Science,* Vol. 369, January 1967.

[6] Jan L. Sadie, "Labor Supply and Employment in Less Developed Countries," in John D. Durand (ed.), *World Population, Annals of the American Academy of Political and Social Science,* Vol. 369, January 1967, p. 123.

are in Asia, compared with only 14 percent in Africa and 10 percent in Latin America. This results in much higher population densities in Asia than in the other two continents, which is most significant when viewing their future development, since the obstacles to modernization in a peasant agricultural society are far more formidable where population is both vast and dense than where it is small and sparse or even moderate. In appraising the population problems of individual preindustrial countries, scale is of the highest importance. Thus, China's and India's gigantic numbers of human beings pose greatly different problems than do Peru's or Ceylon's far smaller numbers. Java's 75 million people are beyond help insofar as any solution by out-migration is concerned, even with empty lands not far away. The obstacles to moving nearly a million migrants a year, which is about the normal annual population increase in Java, appear insurmountable. A significant proportion of the labor force in populous peasant agricultural societies is surplus, economically speaking, since if these workers left, there would be no falling off in agricultural output. This condition, so prevalent in crowded parts of LD regions, is referred to as *hidden unemployment* or underemployment.

Of the three continents with predominantly traditional societies, Africa is by far the most backward and has the farthest to go before reaching the modern stage. A tribal organization of society still prevails in most parts of the continent. Asia and Africa do not differ greatly in their estimated per capita national incomes (about $128 and $123); Latin America's ($344) is two and one half to three times as high. An intensive garden agriculture, with emphasis on paddy rice, characterizes much of eastern and southern Asia. There, output per unit area of cultivated land is often high. More extensive types of cultivation, less efficient husbandry, and lower yields typify much of Latin America and Africa. Asia is a continent of ancient civilizations, far-reaching culture dispersions, and great empires—a land steeped in history and the seat of remarkable human accomplishments. This is much less true of Africa and Latin America. Racially and linguistically, of course, they are very different. Latin America is the only one in which Western languages and a Western culture prevails, while the proportion of the people with European origins is far higher. All of these contrasts create vastly different problems associated with the modernization process in each of the LD continents.

National Differences. If the differences among the three LD continents are substantial, they are even greater among individual LD countries. For example, in a recent year the average per capita national income was estimated to be only about $70 in Laos and $60 in Ethiopia, while it was $1090 in Puerto Rico, $500 in Panama, and $460 in Jamaica. Similarly, annual population-growth rates vary from lows of about 0.9 percent in Gabon and 1.5 percent in Puerto Rico to highs of 3.5 percent in Mexico, 3.6 percent in Venezuela, and 3.7 percent in El Salvador. Moreover, even where backward countries have similar natural growth rates, those rates may result from very different levels of fertility and mortality. As an example, Dahomey in Africa and Barbados in the Caribbean have similar average annual natural growth rates of about 1.7 percent per year. Yet the Dahomey rate derives from a birth rate of about 50 per thousand and a death rate of around 33. Barbados' 1.7 percent annual increase on the other hand, results from birth and death rates of about 25–26 and 8–9. Hence, while the LD realm has many population characteristics in common that operate to distinguish it from the MD world, it is far from being a homogeneous entity.

NATALITY AND MORTALITY

Only about 36 percent of the earth's total population is covered by a satisfactory registration of births and deaths. But while 99 percent of the population in the MD world is so covered, only 10 percent of the births and 14 percent of the deaths in the LD realm are adequately recorded.[7] Another 50 percent has some degree of death registration. Satisfactory registration of births is highest in Latin America, where 40 percent of the population is so covered; the comparable figures are only 8 percent for Asia and 2 percent for Africa. A somewhat similar distribution prevails for death registrations—42 percent of Latin America's population, 7 percent of Asia's, and 4 percent of Africa's. In the absence of reliable vital statistics, birth rates are commonly estimated from census reports of age structure, or from information contained in sample surveys. This has been done for about 54 percent of the population living in LD countries. But for some 28 countries, containing about 36 percent of the LD realm's population, the United Nations found no satisfactory fertility data, in the form of either registrations or estimates. Any comparative quantitative analysis of the vital rates in the LD countries is obviously based on very incomplete and unreliable data.

Death control is more universally desired than is birth control. Moreover, mortality reduction, unlike that of natality, can precede any significant modernization or economic improvement. Western medicine has thus been unusually effective in slashing death rates in backward societies the world over, and today the LD realm is characterized by almost uni-

[7] United Nations Population Bulletin, No. 6, *World Mortality*, 1962, pp. 12–13. United Nations Population Bulletin, No. 7, *World Fertility*, 1963, pp. 12–13.

versally high birth rates, but with more variable and usually declining (except for temporary reversals) death rates. Such a situation makes for soaring population growth and for an age structure that is heavily weighted in the direction of young dependents. Typically, two to three times as many young people annually reach an age to enter the labor force as there are older people who leave it by death and retirement.[8] Chronically there is a large annual increase in the number of those seeking employment. And since the labor market usually expands only slowly, the result is the hidden unemployment so common in the traditional societies.

Average national birth rates of the earth's countries probably range from a high in the mid-50's (per 1000) to a low of 14 or 15. But these scarcely form a spectrum or continuum, since there is a sharp dichotomy between the natality of the LD and the MD countries. A crude birth rate of about 30–35 per thousand is a useful boundary separating the two groups. No authentic LD country of importance has yet reached a birth rate under 30.[9] No genuine MD country has a birth rate of over 25. There are few countries with crude birth rates between the upper 20's and the upper 30's. Natality is almost universally high in backward societies. In the 1960's the crude birth rate in the LD nations averaged in the lower 40's, and it ranged from the mid-50's to the low 30's. The average for the technologically advanced countries was about 20 per 1000, or roughly half that of the traditional societies. Thus, there is a strong clustering of average national fertilities around a high average in the traditional societies, and a similar clustering around a low average in the economically advanced ones. The pattern is emphatically bimodal.[10] Except for per capita national income, natality is perhaps the best single socioeconomic variable distinguishing the MD from the LD realms.

The wide existing differences in birth-rate levels between LD and MD countries are not the only aspects of the fertility patterns of these two groups that are in contrast. First, in LD countries a larger percentage of women under 25 are married. This feature may account for about a quarter of the total disparity in crude birth rates between the LD

[8] Sadie, "Labor Supply and Employment," p. 126.
[9] Significantly, perhaps, the exceptions are islands—Cyprus, the Ryukyus, Singapore, Hong Kong, Puerto Rico, and a few of the former British West Indies.
[10] Dudley Kirk, "Natality in Developing Countries: Recent Trends and Prospects," in S. J. Behrman, Leslie Corsa, and Ronald Freedman (eds.), *Fertility and Family Planning: A World View*, University of Michigan Press, Ann Arbor, Michigan, 1969, pp. 76–78. See also United Nations Population Bulletin, No. 7, *World Fertility*, 1963, Chapter IX.

and MD groups.[11] Second, wide differences in intramarital fertility in the two age classes of women, 25–29 and 30–34, contribute an additional half of the total differential in crude birth rates between the LD and MD groups. And third, continuation of a fairly high level of female fertility beyond age 35 in the LD group, compared with a rapid decline in the fertility of mature women in the MD countries, may also account for as much as a quarter of the total birth-rate difference.[12]

In any list of economic causes purporting to explain the higher birth rates of LD countries, the following should probably be included: the advantageous use of child labor in agriculture and handicrafts; the reliance on offspring for security in old age; the greater value of children in a traditional than in a market-oriented economy; and the few productive outlets for females in the household.[13] However, their significance can be neither proved nor denied. These economic factors probably exert some influence on birth rates, but others of a social or demographic nature may weigh even more heavily. Very conspicuous among these latter factors is the death rate, which during the period 1960–1964 averaged about 20 per 1000 for the LD group but only 9 per 1000 for the MD countries. If family planning is considered in terms of the *surviving children*, this unlikeness in death rates alone would account for more than half of the observed difference in birth rates between the LD and MD groups. Political and social (tribe, clan, and caste) variables may also affect childbearing.

But if natality appears to be one of the best single socioeconomic variables distinguishing MD and LD countries, among the latter as a group there appears to be a low degree of correlation between natality and degree of socioeconomic development.

What, then, are the causes of the existing national fertility differentials, ranging from the mid 50's to the low 30's, that exist among the LD countries? One valid generalization seems to be that they relate as much, or more, to premodern cultural differences as to the present national ratings in socioeconomic development. Still, this may be due, in part at least, to the fact that the benefits of modernization have not been spread widely throughout the whole population. In other words, the systems of economic and social rewards to the younger generation may not be sufficient to stimulate a desire to limit family size. Or, according

---

[11] Simon Kuznets, "Economic Aspects of Fertility Trends in the Less Developed Countries," in S. J. Behrman, Leslie Corsa, and Ronald Freedman (eds.), *Fertility and Family Planning: A World View*, University of Michigan Press, Ann Arbor, Michigan, 1969, pp. 158–159.

[12] Kuznets, "Economic Aspects," pp. 158–159.

[13] Kuznets, "Economic Aspects," pp. 160–161.

to the "threshold hypothesis," improved economic and social conditions in a LD country may have little or no effect on fertility until a certain economic or social level is reached. Once that level is achieved, fertility is likely to move downward until it is stabilized once more, but at a substantially lower plane.[14]

Among the three LD continents, in the late 1960's, crude birth rates hovered around high levels (estimated: Africa, 46; Asia, 38 [excluding the USSR]; and Latin America, 39), but their per capita national incomes showed far greater differences (Africa, $140; Latin America, $385; and Asia, $184).[15] At this continental scale, any positive correlation between fertility and average per capita income is weak indeed.

If one turns to the individual LD countries, there are even greater discrepancies. Countries with similar high birth rates may be observed to have per capita national incomes that differ as much as eight times. In tropical Latin America there are a number of countries that, over several decades, have shown a combination of constant or rising birth rates, declining death rates, and sustained growth in per capita product.[16] *United Nations Population Bulletin* No. 7[17] analyzes the correlations of 12 different economic, social, and demographic indicators with the gross reproduction rate among countries classified by levels of fertility and belonging to both LD and MD groups. For the LD high-fertility group, 10 of the associations were found to be statistically without significance. Only two show even a slight significance. The evidence is strong, then, that among the LD countries, differences in per capita income and 11 other variables do not appear to account for the national differences in fertility. The causes for the latter remain obscure.

Trends in Fertility and Mortality. Any well-documented trend in fertility within the LD group of countries over the past several decades is hard to discover. Fluctuations caused by war, economic cycles, and major catastrophies in the form of famine and epidemics have been verified, to be sure. But authentic trends are hard to identify. Better registration and estimates of fertility may be involved in what appear to be trends in individual countries.

But while the evidence is not conclusive, it appears very likely that over the last generation fertility has actually risen in some LD regions and countries—certainly in parts of the West Indies, very likely in Middle America, and probably in a number of countries in South America, Af-

[14] United Nations Population Bulletin, No. 7, *World Fertility*, 1963, p. 143.
[15] *World Population Data Sheet—1969*, Population Reference Bureau, Washington, D.C., April, 1969.
[16] Kuznets, "Economic Aspects," pp. 162–163.
[17] Kuznets, "Economic Aspects," pp. 162–163.

rica, and Asia (Pakistan).[18] Jamaica, Trinidad, and British Guiana are clear cases of regions where birth rates have risen in recent years. Among the suggestions as to why increased natality might accompany at least the early stages of modernization are the following: reduction in venereal disease, greater regularization of mating and marriage, reduction of mortality and morbidity, improved nutrition, and slight gains in the level of living.[19]

Yet if there is some evidence of recent fertility increases in parts of the LD group, there are also indications of fertility declines in a limited number of others. Only as late as 1960 had a very limited trend toward a fertility decline been firmly established, and then in only three LD political units: Puerto Rico, Taiwan, and Singapore. Since 1960 the list has slightly expanded to include the former Japanese territories of Ryukyus, Taiwan, and Korea, and the Chinese populations of Hong Kong and Malaysia. In all of these a fall in birth rates is occurring in conjunction with modernization. Significantly, perhaps, most of these declines are in East Asia or where East Asiatics are the dominant group or at least a very numerous element. In addition, there is some tentative evidence of an appreciable fertility decline since 1960 in two *types* of areas: (1) island populations, especially those experiencing the impact of outside influences or a large infusion of immigrants and (2) the populations in areas of mixed culture, including the peoples of Hawaii, Mexicans in the United States, and Moslems in eastern Europe.[20] Most of the islands showing evidence of recent fertility decline are in the West Indies and include, in addition to Puerto Rico, Trinidad, Barbados, Jamaica, St. Kitts-Nevis, Dominica, Grenada, Bermuda, Guadeloupe, Martinique, and the Netherlands Antilles. In a number of the above islands the birth-rate data must be used with caution. Mauritius in the South Indian Ocean and the Indian population of the Fiji Islands have also shown some evidence of fertility decline.

It must be concluded, therefore, that for the vast bulk of the world's LD population, there are no firmly established upward or downward trends in fertility, but instead a continuation of the high birth rates that have prevailed in the past.

Trends in mortality continue generally downward in the traditional societies as a whole, but with regional variations in rates. The current decline is most conspicuous in Africa, the most retarded of the three

---

[18] Kirk, "Natality in Developing Countries," p. 79. See also O. Andrew Collver, *Birth Rates in Latin America*, Institute of International Studies, University of California, Berkeley, 1965.

[19] Kirk, "Natality in Developing Countries," p. 79.

[20] Kirk, "Natality in Developing Countries," p. 81.

LD continents. There death rates continue to be relatively high (an estimated 22 per 1000) because of the later and slower effective application of Western medicine and sanitation. Consequently, the current downward trend in mortality rates is more conspicuous there. But in tropical Latin America, where the successes of Western medicine are farther advanced and the death rate already low (an estimated 10 per 1000), a further decline is expectably slower. Asia, intermediate between Africa and Latin America in current death rates, is similarly intermediate in its rate of mortality decline. In all three continents individual countries show variable rates of mortality change, with the trends, of course, generally downward.

TYPOLOGIES OF POPULATION
CHARACTERISTICS IN LD COUNTRIES

One method for revealing the variety existing among LD countries is to create typologies of some of the principle population characteristics noted earlier and subsequently classify the LD countries according to types and show their distributions on world maps. The most serious obstacle to formulating such typologies is either the lack or the dubious quality of the population data for such a large proportion of the LD countries. This has been pointed out already, specifically for birth and death rates, but it also exists, generally to a larger degree, for other population characteristics.

Fertility. Although satisfactory registration statistics on crude birth rates are available for only about 10 percent of the population in the earth's LD regions, these data can be supplemented by birth rates estimated from census reports on age structure and from information contained in sample surveys. This has been done for about 54 percent of the LD population. But for some 36 percent, the United Nations found no satisfactory natality data.

In the crude birth-rate typology for the earth's LD countries, almost exclusively in Africa, Asia, and Latin America, data for some 83 political units are typed.[21] (Japan and Israel in Asia, and Argentina and Uruguay in Latin America, are excluded because they do not qualify as "less

---

[21] The main data source was *World Population Data Sheet—1968*, published by the Population Reference Bureau, Washington, D.C. Birth and death rates for China (mainland) are from John S. Aird, "Population Growth and Distribution in Mainland China," in *An Economic Profile of Mainland China*, Studies prepared for the Joint Economic Committee, Congress of the United States, Vol. 2, p. 364.

developed.") A birth rate of 35 per 1000 is used as the boundary separating two main fertility types—Type 1, high fertility, 35 and above and Type 2, medium-high fertility, 25 to 35. Some 74 countries fall within the "high" category, and only 9 (Cyprus, Lebanon, Ceylon, Singapore, Hong Kong, Taiwan, Barbados, Puerto Rico and Chile) in the "medium-high" subdivision (Fig. 1.1). But all of these 9 except Chile (which is a borderline LD country) are small in area and population and are relatively unimportant; the sum of their populations is only about 35 million, which is a mere 1 to 2 percent of the total population of the 83 countries typed. On a small-scale world map showing distribution of the two fertility types, Type 1 completely dominates; most of the Type 2 countries are so small as to be scarcely visible. So universal is high fertility within the LD realm that perhaps Type 2 should be designated as only an aberrant subtype. Of the 9 LD countries with birth rates below 35, 6 are in Asia, 3 in Latin America, and none in Africa. Significantly, 7 of the 9 are islands.

A few lines representing the earth's main regional unconformities in fertility may be recognized. The longest one runs from Gibraltar across the Mediterranean and Black Seas and on through Central Asia toward China. Here the fertility gradient separating Europeans of Judeo-Christian culture from Moslems is steep. On one side birth rates of 20 or less per 1000 prevail; on the other they are over 40. A second but shorter fertility boundary lies along the Rio Grande River and passes through the Gulf of Mexico. It separates the United States, with a birth rate of about 17–18, from Mexico and other Latin American countries where fertility is 40 or more. Still a third such boundary separates low-fertility Argentina and Uruguay, with their largely European populations, from high-fertility tropical South America, where racial mixtures predominate.[22]

Mortality. A satisfactory registration of crude death rates is characteristic of only 14 percent of the LD realm's population—42 percent of Latin America's, 7 percent of Asia's, and 4 percent of Africa's.[23] In the typology of death rates, data are used for 83 LD countries.[24] Two main mortality types are recognized: Type 1, high death rate, or 15 or more per 1000; and Type 2, moderate-to-low death rate, or below 15 (Fig. 1.1). As nearly as can be determined from the somewhat imprecise data, some 46 of the 83 LD countries fall within Type 1, with high death rates, and about 37 within Type 2, where death rates are lower. But such a division on the basis of numbers of countries equates

[22] Kirk, "Natality in Developing Countries," pp. 82–83.
[23] United Nations Population Bulletin, No. 7, *World Fertility*, 1963, pp. 12–13.
[24] The main data source is *World Population Data Sheet—1968*.

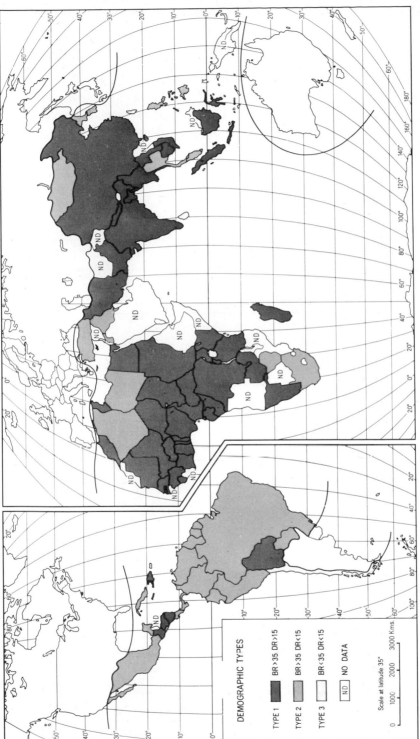

Fig. 1.1. The concept of demographic types combines birth-rate and death-rate values. For the less developed realm three types are recognized. Types 1 and 2 are well represented; Type 3, with annual birth rates under 35 per 1000 and death rates below 15, is meagerly represented, only nine countries qualifying, most of which are relatively small and of minor world importance. (Data source: mainly World Population Data Sheet—1968, Population Reference Bureau, Washington, D.C.) Courtesy of Colloquium Geographicum, Band 12, Carl Troll Festschrift, 1970.

DEMOGRAPHIC TYPES

TYPE 1   BR>35 DR>15
TYPE 2   BR>35 DR<15
TYPE 3   BR<35 DR<15
ND   NO DATA

Scale at latitude 35°

0   1000   2000   3000 Kms.

pygmies and giants. The numerical discrepancy between the two types is far greater if magnitude of population is substituted for countries, since such Asiatic population giants as China,[25] India, Pakistan, and Indonesia are all included within high-mortality Type 1. As a consequence, some 80 percent of the population of the 83 LD countries typed for death rates falls within Type 1. High mortality rates are much more common in Africa and Asia than in Latin America; the latter has advanced farther in the control of death. Of the approximately 37 LD countries described as Type 2, with moderate-to-low death rates, 17 are

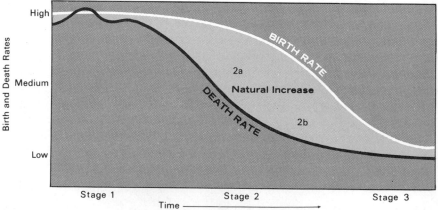

Fig. 1.2. The demographic transition model.

in Latin America and 16 in Asia, but only 4 in Africa. In Africa, Type 2 death rates are concentrated at that continent's northern and southern extremities, where Western influence has been most marked. In Asia they are widely dispersed.

Demographic Types and Demographic Transition Model. A demographic typology of the earth's LD regions has been developed, employing the vital data for the same 83 countries used in the previous birth-rate and death-rate analyses and making use of a demographic-transition-theory model.[26]

The demographic-transition model assumes that a country in the process of its modernization experiences a succession of changes in its birth, death, and natural-increase rates (Fig. 1.2). In Stage 1, preceding modernization, there is a fairly stable balance involving high birth rates, high

[25] China mortality data are from Aird, "Population Growth and Distribution."
[26] See Edward G. Stockwell, "Fertility, Mortality, and Economic Status of Underdeveloped Areas," *Social Forces*, Vol. 4, No. 4, 1963, pp. 390–395.

but variable death rates, and a resulting slow, but variable, natural growth of population. This passes over into a second or intermediate stage characterized by an imbalance between a continuing high fertility and a declining, often rapid, mortality, the consequence of which is a sustained and usually fast growth of population. Early in Stage 2 there is a divergence of the profiles of birth and death rates. Later in this stage births begin to fall off and the decline in deaths slows. Thus convergence of the birth- and death-rate profiles gradually comes to replace divergence, and the gap between births and deaths narrows, resulting in a slowing of natural population increase. Finally in Stage 3, almost a new balance is reached between low-to-moderate birth rates and low death rates. Slow-to-moderate population growth is the result.

In applying the transition-theory model to the earth's LD countries, the same levels of 35 per 1000 for births and 15 per 1000 for deaths are used as the separation points between high and moderate-to-low rates as were used in the two previous typologies. Three broad demographic types may be recognized within the LD realm.

Type 1. Early Transitional.   Included are those countries characterized by crude birth rates of 35 per 1000 or above and crude death rates of 15 per 1000 and over. Such countries are either on the threshold of, or have recently entered the period of declining death rates and accelerated population growth. Of some 83 countries typed, over half fall within this group—30 in Africa and 10 in Asia, but only 6 in Latin America. Their distribution is shown in Fig. 1.1. But if numbers of people are substituted for numbers of countries, it has the effect of greatly enhancing the relative importance of Type 1 (80 percent of the total population of the 3 types), and also the place of Asia within Type 1 (81 percent), since that continent includes populous China, India, Pakistan, and Java.

Type 2. Mid-Transitional.   This more advanced stage includes the LD countries in which fertility still remains high (over 35 per 1000) but in which mortality has dropped below 15 per 1000. Growth rates are unusually high (Fig. 1.3). Twenty-eight countries fall within this type, 14 of them in Latin America and 10 in Asia, but only 4 in Africa. From Fig. 1.1 it becomes clear that Latin America best represents Type 2. It not only corresponds to nearly 60 percent of the type's area, but also accounts for about half the type's total population. Understandably it is in Latin America that natural growth rates of population are the highest, on the average, for the whole earth.

Type 3. Late Transitional.   The countries falling within this type have crude birth and death rates below 35 and 15 per 1000 respectively. In these countries, fertility is beginning to come under control, and de-

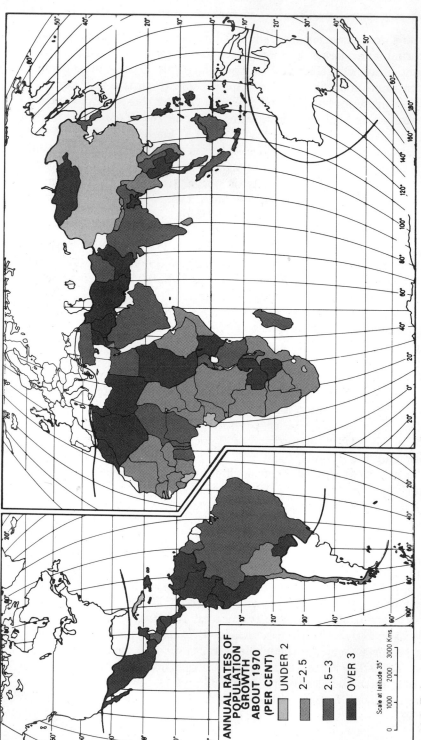

Fig. 1.3. Estimated national annual growth rates of population as of about 1970. In a vast majority of the earth's less-developed countries the annual growth rates represent natural increase, or the excess of births over deaths. In a few countries net migration is also a significant factor. Highest growth rates are characteristic of Latin America; they are lower on the average, and there is more variation between countries, in Africa and Asia. In not a few countries in Africa, unusually high death rates reduce the rate of population increase. (Data source: 1970 World Population Data Sheet, Population Reference Bureau, 1970.)

ANNUAL RATES OF
POPULATION
GROWTH
ABOUT 1970
(PER CENT)

UNDER 2
2–2.5
2.5–3
OVER 3

Scale at latitude 35°

0   1000   2000   3000 Kms.

clining birth rates have started to narrow the "demographic gap" caused by an earlier and sharper decline of mortality. Natural growth rates are slowing (Fig. 1.3). This third type is meagerly represented within the LD realm, with only nine countries qualifying. Six of them are in Asia, three in Latin America, and none in Africa. A majority of the Type 3 countries are relatively small and unimportant ones whose combined inhabitants number less than 2 percent of the total LD population included within this type.

Thus the preceding typology based on demographic characteristics differentiates not only between LD and MD countries but also between subdivisions within the LD group. Natality or mortality alone does not do this. The typology also functions in some measure to differentiate among the LD countries in terms of their social and economic levels (see Table 1.1).

TABLE 1.1   Socioeconomic Characteristics of Less Developed Countries by Demographic Types (Mid-1960's)[a]

Characteristics	Type 1	Type 2	Type 3
Average per capita national income (U.S. dollars)	125 (45)	268 (29)	413 (9)
Per capita energy consumption (kg of coal equivalent per year)	219 (43)	867 (25)	917 (9)
Percent illiterate (over 15 years of age)	66 (45)	49 (28)	25 (9)

SOURCE: Per capita national income and percent illiterate: *World Population Data Sheet—1968*, Population Reference Bureau, Washington, D.C. Per capita energy consumption: *United Nations Statistical Yearbook*, 1966.

[a] Values in parenthesis indicate number of countries on which a given weighted average is based.

Illiteracy (Population Illiterate, 15 Years and Over). Illiteracy is here defined as the inability to read and write. In developing a typology of adult illiteracy in the earth's LD realm, use was made of the information for 89 countries obtained from the Population Reference Bureau's *World Population Data Sheet—1968*. Three types or levels of illiteracy for the traditional societies are recognized: high, 75 percent and over of the adult population; medium, 50–74 percent; and low, under 50 percent (Fig. 1.4). In comparison, an overwhelming proportion of the Western world has an adult illiteracy of only 5 percent and under.

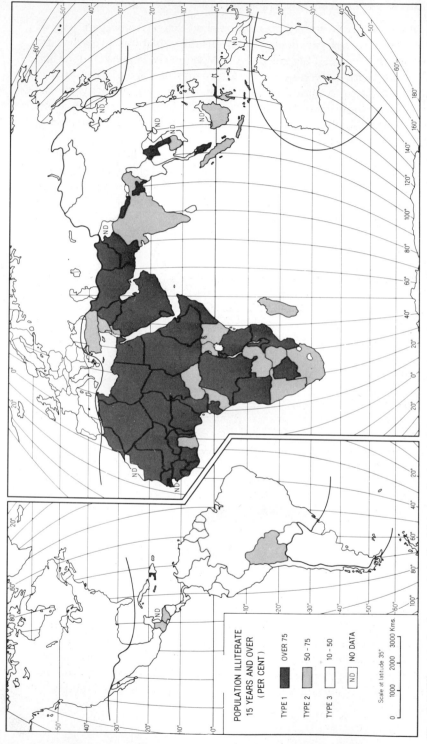

Fig. 1.4. Illiteracy is characteristically high in the less-developed countries; still, the range is relatively large among the individual continents and countries. Africa has the highest average illiteracy and Latin America the lowest. (Data source: World Population Data Sheet–1968, Population Reference Bureau, Washington, D.C.) Courtesy of Colloquium Geographicum, Band 12, Carl Troll Festschrift, 1970.

POPULATION ILLITERATE
15 YEARS AND OVER
(PER CENT)

TYPE 1   OVER 75

TYPE 2   50 - 75

TYPE 3   10 - 50

N.D.   NO DATA

Scale at latitude 35°

0   1000   2000   3000 Kms.

Type 1. High Illiteracy. Some 41 of the 89 LD countries for which illiteracy data are available fall within this class. They represent about 21 percent of the total LD population being typed. Thirty-one of the 41 countries so typed are in Africa and 9 in Asia, but only 1 in Latin America. Of all the continents, Africa represents by far the lowest level of educational accomplishment. In Latin America, only Haiti qualifies for inclusion in the high-illiteracy class. Outside of Africa, the most extensive continuous block of territory with high illiteracy is in Southwest Asia and Pakistan. Within Southwest Asia, illiteracy is lowest in the countries bordering the Mediterranean Sea.

Type 2. Medium Illiteracy. Some 20 LD countries fall within this group, 11 of them in Africa, 6 in Asia, and 3 in Latin America. Most of these are rather widely scattered. But while only about half as many countries are included in Type 2 as in Type 1, because populous India and Indonesia fall within Type 2 this medium-illiteracy group is representative of a much higher total population (33 percent of that being typed) than is Type 1. On the other hand, a smaller total area is involved.

Type 3. Low (Relative) Illiteracy. In all, 28 countries fall within this group, 17 in Latin America and 11 in Asia, but, significantly, none in Africa. But while the number of countries included is fewer than in Type 1, their total population is more than twice as great, amounting to about 46 percent of all the inhabitants in the 89 countries being typed. In area, Type 3 far exceeds Type 2 and is only slightly smaller than Type 1. Of the LD continents, Latin America is by far the most homogeneously Type 3; only 4 of its countries do not fall within this group. Moreover, a large proportion of Latin America's Type 3 countries have illiteracy rates that are distinctly below the upper limit of 50 percent set for that type. In fact, close to a dozen are well below 35 percent. While Asia has fewer countries than Latin America that qualify for this more literate type, because populous mainland China is so classified, the total Asiatic population belonging to Type 3 far exceeds the number of Latin Americans within this same group.

Average Annual Per Capita National Income. This population characteristic is considered by some to be the best single criterion for defining a LD country or region. Polarization of the LD countries at the low end of the income scale and of MD countries at the high end is not quite as complete as it is for some other characteristics. Thus eight LD countries have average per capita national incomes in excess of $500, while six European countries have per capita incomes of less than $500.

Based on average annual per capita national income of some 94 LD countries in the 1960's, three types are recognized, with the separation points set at $150 and $300. The data source is the same as before.

Type 1. Ultralow Incomes; Under $150. This abnormally low-income type, reflecting intense and widespread poverty, is by far the most representative of the LD realm (Fig. 1.5). It includes 49 of the 94 countries being typed, 55 percent of their area, and about 81 percent of their population.[27] Type 1 is especially representative of tropical Africa and Asia (except the southwestern part). Only 2 countries in Latin America are in this class, but there are 32 in Africa and 15 in Asia. But while the *area* characterized by very low incomes is somewhat larger in Africa than in Asia, the *population* within Type 1 is far larger (7 times) in Asia. Within Africa, 32 of the 44 countries have per capita incomes of under $150, and these represent about two thirds of the continent's area and some 77 percent of its population. Four African countries have per capita incomes of less than $50 and 24 of less than $100. The African countries with per capita incomes exceeding $150 are located mainly at the continent's northern and southern extremities (Fig. 1.5).

Type 2. Low Incomes; Between $150 and $300. Type 2 countries, 31 in number, are somewhat better distributed over the 3 LD continents—12 in Asia, 11 in Latin America, and 7 in Africa. Regions falling within this type are most extensive in Latin America, next most in Asia, and least in Africa. Type 2 regions in Asia and Latin America have very similar population numbers; Africa's is far smaller. Tropical South America and Southwest Asia represent the largest contiguous blocks of territory characterized by Type 2 incomes.

Type 3. Modest Incomes; Over $300. Type 3, the highest-income group within the traditional societies, is represented by the fewest countries, the smallest area, and the least numerous population. Of the 15 LD countries falling within this type, 8 are in Latin America, 4 (all of which are very small) in Asia, and only 3 in Africa. The type is somewhat more extensively developed in Latin America than in Africa, but very meagerly indeed in Asia. Eighty-five percent of Type 3's population resides in Latin America. All but one of the Latin American countries with Type 3 incomes are Caribbean oriented. Venezuela, Kuwait, and Libya owe their rank to oil production.

Degree of Urbanization. The term "urbanization" refers to the percentage of a total population that lives in urban places. It is not concerned with absolute numbers. Polarization of LD countries at the low end of the urbanization scale and MD countries at the high end, while strong, is not complete.

United Nation's estimates indicate that as of about 1960 slightly less than one quarter of the LD realm's population was urban (as nationally defined). By 1970 the urban proportion had risen to nearly 27 percent.

[27] See Simon Kuznets, "Population and Economic Growth," pp. 184–185.

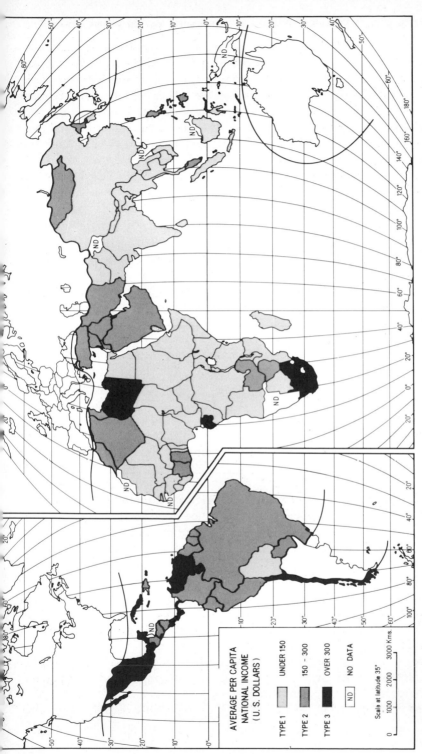

Fig. 1.5. The estimated average per capita national income is prevailingly low in the less-developed realm. Still, there are considerable differences between individual countries. Low incomes are especially characteristic of Africa, and eastern and southern Asia; they are higher on the average in Latin America and Southwest Asia. (Data source: World Population Data Sheet–1968, Population Reference Bureau, Washington D.C.) Courtesy of Colloquium Geographicum, Band 12, Carl Troll Festschrift, 1970.

AVERAGE PER CAPITA
NATIONAL INCOME
(U. S. DOLLARS)

TYPE 1   UNDER 150

TYPE 2   150 – 300

TYPE 3   OVER 300

ND   NO DATA

Scale at latitude 35°

0   1000   2000   3000 Kms.

The expected future acceleration of the urbanization process within the LD regions indicates that more than 40 percent of their inhabitants will be city dwellers by the year 2000. So by the early 1970's city people in the LD realm will nearly equal in numbers those in MD countries, and by 2000 will be about twice as numerous.

The data source used in typing the LD countries according to their level of urbanization is "World Survey of Urban and Rural Population Growth," United Nation's Document E/CN.9/187, 8 March, 1965, Table 5, p. 24. Places with 20,000 or more inhabitants are classed as urban. Reasonably reliable data (for approximately 1960) were found for 59 countries; these represented only 48 percent of the total urban population of the LD realm—62 percent for Africa, 41 percent for Asia, and 80 percent for Latin America. Thus the data gap is very serious. Especially serious is the omission of populous mainland China and most of Southeast Asia.

Four degrees of urbanization are recognized, leading to a classification of the LD countries into four types. The points of separation are 20, 30, and 40 percent.

Type 1. Low Urbanization; Under 20 Percent. Of the 59 LD countries included in this typology, 36 fall within Type 1—25 in Africa, 6 in Latin America, and 5 in Asia (Fig. 1.6). On the basis of population instead of countries, by far the greatest concentration of Type 1 is in South Asia (India and Pakistan). But using area as the criterion, Type 1 is far more extensive in Africa than in Asia. In terms of both area and population, Type 1, or low urbanization, is poorly represented in Latin America. (Four Western MD countries, all in southern Europe, also fall within Type 1.)

Type 2. Medium-Low; 20–29.9 Percent Urban. Sixteen LD countries are included, 7 in Latin America, 5 in Africa, and 4 in Asia. This type is most extensively developed in Latin America and least in Asia. It also represents a larger population in Latin America than in either Asia or Africa. (Four European countries are also classified as Type 2.)

Type 3. Medium-High; 30–39.9 Percent Urban. Only 7 LD countries qualify for Type 3—3 in Latin America, 2 in Africa, and 2 in Asia. Africa and Latin America are about equally well represented in the type, measured by either area or population. It is meagerly represented in Asia. The total population within this type is only about 110 million—less than half that in Type 2, and only one eighth that in Type 1. Twelve European countries also fall within Type 3, among them being the populous U.S.S.R. Clearly, then, Type 3 is a mixture of LD and MD populations, with the latter predominating.

Type 4. High; Over 40 Percent. This type only weakly applies to

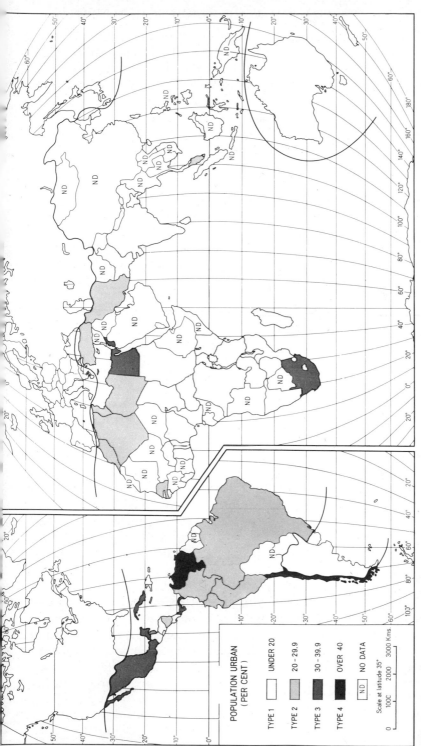

Fig. 1.6. The percent of the total population that lives in urban places having 20,000 or more inhabitants is generally low in the economically less-developed realm. Still, there is a considerable range between the individual countries and continents. The lowest degree of urbanization is most extensively developed in Africa and next most in Asia; it is highest in Latin America. (Data source: World Survey of Urban and Rural Population Growth, United Nations Document E/CN9/187, 8 March 1965, Table 5, p. 24.) Courtesy of Colloquium Geographicum, Band 12, Carl Troll Festschrift, 1970.

the LD realm, since only two traditional countries, Venezuela and Chile, qualify, and even Chile is a marginal case. The combined population of these two countries is only about 19 million.

Scanning Fig. 1.6, which shows distribution of the four urbanization types by countries, Negro Africa is seen to be predominantly Type 1, with a low degree of urbanization. Latin America is a mixture of types, and so is LD Asia. But with population rather than area as a criterion, a different pattern emerges. Latin America is only moderately represented by Types 1 and 4, strongly by Type 2, and moderately by Type 3. Asia's population is classified overwhelmingly as Type 1 and has fair representation in Type 2. Over two thirds of Africa's population is in Type 1, and of the remainder, somewhat more is in Type 3 than in Type 2.

To summarize, the world's population today is clearly divided into economically LD and MD parts. Regrettably, this schism is becoming increasingly more marked. But the LD realm itself is far from being a homogeneous entity. Indeed, the variety that exists there, as indicated by the preceding typologies, just possibly may be a harbinger of a quickening modernization within the foreseeable future.

SOCIOECONOMIC DISHARMONY

Today the LD world is in a somewhat similar stage of demographic transition as European peoples were a century or two earlier. Still, there are important population-related social differences. For one thing, the rate of social change in the traditional societies today is more rapid than it was among European peoples in the previous century. In addition, the contrast between the traditional ways of living and the one replacing it in Africa, Asia, and, to a lesser degree, Latin America today, is ever so much sharper than the one to which Western peoples were exposed. In Europe, also, the modernization process evolved slowly over a period of centuries. But most of the present LD peoples lack this long and gradual period of preparation for, and acquisition of, modernization, although some profited slightly from the tutelage provided by their colonial regimes. Often the most backward traditional societies are the ones most eager for immediate and direct contact with the industrial-scientific culture. Moreover, the modernizing Western peoples of a century or two back were fairly homogeneous, being essentially European in origin and institutions. By contrast, the evolving LD world today represents the greatest heterogeneity of races, languages, religions, and general cultural complexes. And this universal diversity in today's traditional societies has been perpetuated through the persistence of closed subsistence economies and of cultural restrictions that interfere with movement of populations. As a consequence, much of the traditional way of life still prevails among the LD peoples, particularly among the greatly preponderant rural element.

Within the last century or two, a foreign-dominated, market-oriented, industrial-scientific sector has intruded into these already diverse traditional and static societies. It disrupted the feudal coherence of the traditional societies and reoriented what had been an almost wholly self-sufficient economy toward one that produced, at least in part, for the world market. These peoples thus became exposed to the vagaries of that market and the fickleness of international price fluctuations. Their outlook was changed, and aspirations and hopes were aroused that could not be satisfied. Economic instability was fostered. Export-oriented economies in turn have quickened urban development. This is especially true along seaboards where port cities have become the main foci of modernization; regions deeper inland have held faster to the traditional ways.

It should be stressed that modernization is usually accompanied first by changes in the techniques of production. And a backward country will often add a significant veneer of imposed foreign technology without having widespread cultural change in the general population. China can explode a hydrogen bomb and India can erect modern steel mills while at the same time the bulk of their populations continue essentially in their traditional backwardness. But sooner or later the foreign science and technology will rupture the traditional societal structure and bring about comprehensive cultural change. The speed of the modernization process depends on a number of variables, most decisive of which is whether increased production is used to improve the living conditions of the whole population or instead is diverted to support expensive armament or consumed in feeding a burgeoning population at the original substandard level.

One consequence of modernization on LD societies has been a fantastic cultural jump and a phenomenal internal cultural disharmony. Transistor radios are not uncommon in the African bush; aircraft and motor cars exist alongside primitive societies; complex steel plants and oil refineries are operated by native labor; and witch doctors and antibiotics both function in the jungle environment. Thus, the less developed world at present is a confusion of cultures; the base is still traditional, but different parts have experienced varying degrees of modification through injections of Western culture.

This Western-imposed internal disharmony is in no way better exemplified than by the fact that while a native society may well remain backward in most other respects, it can rapidly lower its death rate to a point that may even approach those of the advanced industrial countries. A plummeting death rate in conjunction with a persistently high birth rate can only result in a soaring population growth, which in turn adds its effects as a brake on economic growth. Thus, within the traditional societies there is usually a serious discrepancy between rapid population growth on the one hand and slow economic improvement on the other.

OUTLOOK FOR IMPROVEMENT IN
THE LESS DEVELOPED REALM

Distinctive features of the past 100 to 150 years within the economically advanced nations are the extremely fast growth in both per capita product and population—resulting in rates at least 10 times as high for per capita product and at least 5 times as high for population as in the observable premodern period.[28] Within advanced societies, a continuing capacity has prevailed to supply a rapidly expanding population with an increased per capita volume of goods and services. High growth rates for both population and per capita product stemmed from changes in the production structure associated with industrialization and urbanization. Fundamental to these high rates of growth and the accompanying rapid shifts in the structure of production and ways of living was the application of a greatly expanded stock of technical and social knowledge and inventions to problems of economic production and health. Because the rise in per capita product far outdistanced the growth of population, the standard of living moved upward.

But in the LD realm today it is often implied that the soaring population tends to nullify any modest expansion of the gross national product, thereby hindering a rise in per capita income. However, since people are creators and producers as well as consumers, this suggested stifling effect of a burgeoning population seems to require explanation. Why should not larger numbers achieve a sufficiently larger output to provide for both the current increase in people and a rising per capita output, as it did earlier in Western countries?

One conceivable limiting factor may involve the concept of a fixed supply, and thereby scarcity, of nonrenewable resources, which acts to restrict the productivity of an ever-expanding labor force. Implied in the resource-scarcity idea is the assumption that new discoveries of resource reserves and new techniques for their use will not raise the limits

---

[28] Kuznets, "Population and Economic Growth," p. 170.

of output enough to keep pace with expanding numbers of humanity. This was the fear expressed by Malthus. But in the case of the Western countries, Malthus' gloomy forecast did not materialize, since human knowledge and technology were more than a match for the limitations imposed by any scarcity of natural resources. Will this history be repeated in the case of the present LD world? Admittedly, this is a controversial question to which different experts provide varying answers. It is generally agreed, though, that in some of the earth's regions, such as the polar lands and most deserts, the resource base is absolutely too meager to support many human beings. It may be true also that in some of the already densely populated countries, especially in Asia, a *relative* scarcity of nonrenewable resources is already at hand. Professor J. Spengler[29] has recently reviewed the present thinking of economists on the important question regarding the limits that scarce natural resources are likely to impose on the future per capita productivity in the LD world, given the anticipated increase in population numbers. The consensus of opinion among economists indicates a fairly optimistic attitude, maintaining that scarcity of natural resources is not likely to impose serious constraints on combined economic improvement and population growth in the less developed countries *within the foreseeable future*, perhaps three or four decades. With proper skills, sufficient capita, and effective use of the world's present technology, it should be feasible to multiply food production three or four times within many, or even most, of the retarded countries within the next several decades. The point of view seems to be that "the scarcity of natural resources in the underdeveloped countries is primarily a function of underdevelopment; underdevelopment is not a function of scarce natural resources.' ' Moreover, the spread of international trade to the whole world has caused the individual country to be less dependent on the supply of natural resources within its own border. Japan, Sweden, and Switzerland are illustrations of countries with limited natural resources that have succeeded in reaching high levels of economic development. Hence, what may appear to be a scarcity of resources under a traditional primitive economy may not actually exist if and when modern technology becomes widespread.

A second obstacle to economic improvement in the LD countries is the scarcity of accumulated wealth, or capital, with which to equip their rapidly expanding populations, more particularly the labor-force sector.

---

[29] See Joseph J. Spengler, "The Economist and the Population Question," *American Economic Review*, Vol. 56, No. 1, March, 1966, pp. 1–24; also "Population and Natural Resources," mimeograph, prepared for the United Nations Background Paper, /B.10/6/E/447.

[30] Kuznets, "Population and Economic Growth," p. 174.

This required greater capital can only be secured in two ways: (1) as a gift or loan from outside sources or (2) by increased taxation of the native population in order to nourish the industrializing cities. Where the people are already extremely destitute, the burden of added taxes is difficult to bear, but ultimately self-imposed taxes are probably the only way in which most of the much-needed capital is likely to be accumulated. Of course, the tax is intended to spur the native farmer to produce more, but often it results only in a compulsory further abstention by an already impoverished rural society. Outside sources are wary of investing in, or making loans to, the LD countries, fearing the expropriation of property or a failure to repay the loans. These countries are not considered good risks for foreign capital. Some economists feel that confiscation as a means of financing modernization in LD countries may be justified, even though it is recognized as contrary to Western ethics. As a pragmatic method of capital accumulation it may be argued that it brings results without sacrificing the scale of living of most of the population.[31]

Significantly, economic development in the LD countries is becoming increasingly self-conscious or planned. By contrast, England's, in an earlier day, was unplanned, since it resulted only from the operation of individual entrepreneurs. But there seems to be almost universal agreement that modernization in the world's LD countries requires, or at least will be speeded up by, government direction and planning of economic growth.

The usual assumption that the LD three quarters of the earth's population will go through an industrial and demographic transition similar to that experienced by the advanced countries may be untenable, since the interaction of population and economic growth involves much more than just economic inputs (resources, labor, capital). Also involved are broader aspects of social and political organization, without which modernization is impossible. Within the LD world, stable and efficient governments to plan and manage an economic transition and to attract outside capital are frequently lacking. Moreover, the terms of international trade are adverse to nations based on a peasant-agriculture economy. They have so little to export that an industrialized society needs. If oil is excluded, it is raw products, mainly from agriculture, that greatly predominate in the items which the retarded countries have to sell to world markets, and for these there has been a steady decline in demand. Yet without export earnings the LD countries find it nearly impossible

---

[31] Martin Bronfenbrenner, "The Appeal of Confiscation in Economic Development," in A. N. Agarwala and S. P. Singh (eds.), *The Economics of Underdevelopment*, p. 427.

to improve their standards of living. In addition, the quality of the labor force is low. And finally, the demographic situation, with its wasteful high fertility and, in some countries, large total numbers and high densities; the prevailingly poor health; and an age structure weighted heavily with young dependents, pose conditions that are adverse to modernization and industrialization. Almost certainly any industrial-demographic transition will vary widely among individual LD countries in the rapidity of accomplishment as well as in the amount of distress and dislocation accompanying the modernization process.

The conclusion seems inescapable that the economic backwardness and low productivity of the LD countries is due to their failure to exploit the productivity potential in the stock of knowledge and modern technology now available in the more developed countries.[32] Fundamentally it is not the result of scarcity of natural resources, climatic handicaps, or possible genetic deficiencies of the people. It follows, therefore, that their economic-growth problems cannot be solved with the technology that is now being applied there. A large stock of tested technology is available, but the indigenous social and political organizational structures to make use of it are lacking. The main problems lie in the limited capacity of the present institutions of the LD countries—legal, political, cultural, and economic—to effectively channel the activity.[33]

The possibilities are limited for bringing about a marked modernization in the LD world in the absence of a technological revolution. One such possibility that would expedite modernization involves the imposition of fertility control before overall modernization is accomplished. A decline in fertility would come eventually, of course, as industrialization and urbanization advanced, but in the meantime the population burden could become unbearable. It has scarcely been demonstrated as yet, however, that major fertility reduction can be achieved in the absence of a contemporaneous economic and social advance. Significantly, countries like Puerto Rico, Taiwan, South Korea, and Malaysia, in which there has been a very recent fertility reduction, are the same ones that are experiencing an economic takeoff. Regrettably, the vast majority of LD peoples are not yet in this stage. The real challenge to the national population programs is, then, can fertility reduction be started and continued ahead of the pace it normally takes in conjunction with a nation's socioeconomic development? There are a number of recent favorable developments that permit some degree of optimism as it applies to the not-so-distant future.

For one thing, the present setting in some respects favors a more rapid demographic transition than the one that occurred in Western countries.

[32] Kuznets, "Population and Economic Growth," p. 186.
[33] Kuznets, "Population and Economic Growth," p. 187.

In the backward countries, a previously more restrictive atmosphere on natality limitation is giving way to free discussion and a more permissive attitude, while social and government pressure to adopt birth control has developed. Roman Catholic opposition to limiting fertility is rapidly weakening, a feature that is especially important in Latin America. The rapid decline in infant mortality, resulting in larger numbers of living children in the household, has increased the pressure to control family size. Modernization, as reflected by such indicators of economic and social development as per capita energy consumption and income, urbanization, nonagricultural employment, hospital beds, later marriage, female literacy, newspaper circulation, and life expectancy is spreading. Fertility differentials resembling those of the West suggest a beginning at least of the diffusion of the small-family pattern. For example, lower fertility is almost universal among the better educated, while rural-urban differentials are observable in parts of Latin America and East Asia, but not in others. There have been marked improvements in contraceptive technology, so that a wider choice of methods is now available.

In addition to the favorable setting, future prospects for natality reduction are also related to the impact of national family-planning programs. As of late 1970, the Population Reference Bureau reported that there were 22 LD countries whose central governments had an official population policy; there were 13 others in which the governments were providing assistance to family planning in the absence of any official population policy. Forty-eight had no population policy and provided no assitance to family planning. Several of the family-planning programs have been highly successful in recruiting "acceptors" among the population. However, most of them are very new, having been initiated only within the last few years, so there has not yet been time for them to have an impact on lowering fertility. One demographer suggests that the world is on the threshold of a contraception-adoption program. He believes that the pace of world population began to slacken in about 1965, and that the spread of contraception will proceed with such marked rapidity that from 1965 on, the rate of world population growth may be expected to decline each year, so that the rate of increase will be at or near zero by about the year 2000.[34] Most demographers would probably feel that the empirical evidence scarcely supports this superoptimistic view. To them, the magnitude of the task still seems highly sobering.[35] A more

[34] Donald J. Bogue, "The Prospects for World Population Control," in *Alternatives for Balancing World Food Production Needs*, Iowa State University Press, Ames, Iowa, 1967, pp. 82–83.
[35] Kingsley Davis, "Population Policy: Will Current Programs Succeed?" *Science*, Vol. 158, November 1967, pp. 730–739; Dudley Kirk, "Natality in Developing Countries," pp. 90–93.

temperate optimism is expressed by the United Nations in its population projections to the year 2000, which take into account many of the factors noted earlier. For the LD nations, crude birth rates for 1960–1965 are estimated at about 40 per 1000; by 1980 they are expected to decline to about 35 and by 1995–2000 to 28. This is to be compared with a current birth rate of about 18 in the more developed countries. But while a lowering of birth rates in the LD countries to 28 per 1000 over a period of about three decades would be a remarkable accomplishment, still a birth rate of 28, in conjunction with modern death rates, would by no means accomplish a static rate of growth. It might still represent a mean population growth rate in the LD realm of close to 2 percent per year, or a doubling of the population in about 35 years. And these figures considerably exceed what most of the LD countries, especially the densely populated ones, can tolerate and still be able to appreciably raise their standards of living. According to the United Nations estimates, the best that can be hoped for is a slowing up of the present high rate of population growth in the LD group of countries sufficient to enable their people to have a longer period in which to gain momentum economically. Such an advance will in itself further curb population growth. It is a case of buying time. Probably death decline will also be slower in the future than it has been in the recent past, and this will further reduce the gap between birth rates and death rates. In addition, future methods for slowing human reproduction may involve not only contraception but also such added brakes as later marriage and abortion.

So far, almost the entire effort in national family-planning programs has been focused on the near-sacred doctrine that a family should have only the number of children it desires—no more. The assumption in all such programs is that a woman, or couples, will *choose* to have fewer children, and hence with the widespread dissemination of contraceptives, a spectacular decline in birth rates will follow. This is not necessarily so, and family planning may not achieve the degree of population control desired. In Tunisia, for example, 68 percent of the married couples indicated a willingness to use birth-control methods, but the average number of children considered desirable was 4.3. Similar figures for a village in Java and one in Mysore, India were 4.3 and 4.2. In seven Latin American capitals the average number of children desired was 3.7.[36] Even families in the United States appear to feel that the ideal number of children is 3.2–3.3. Most likely, any family planning in LD countries that is completely voluntary and depends on decisions of individual couples, although it may reduce the present birth rates, will still allow for a too-large increment in population. Voluntary family planning is

[36] Davis, "Population Policy," p. 736.

scarcely adequate. If excessive population growth is to be prevented, it may be necessary to institute a collective determination of a society's birth rate.[37] Because of the near-sacrosanct position of the family, no nation has as yet taken this step. Yet society has within its power the means of deemphasizing the function of the family in population control. These include emphasizing factors that lead people to postpone or avoid marriage and working toward the establishment of conditions that encourage married couples to keep their families small. Even if voluntary birth control in the LD countries were eventually successful enough to lower fertility rates to those of Western nations, this is still not low enough. Societal birth control may have to be resorted to in some already densely populated states.

In the chapters to follow, which deal with individual parts of Asia, Latin America, and Africa, and more particularly with their spatial patterns of population distribution, much of the explanation set forth for the distributions described is mere inference or deduction. Much more detailed research is required before valid interpretations can be offered.

REFERENCES

Agarwala, A. N., and S. P. Singh (eds.). *The Economics of Underdevelopment*, Oxford University Press, 1958.

Arriaga, Eduardo E. "Rural-Urban Mortality in Developing Countries: An Index for Detecting Rural Underregistration," *Demography*, Vol. IV, No. 1, 1967, pp. 98–107.

Beaujeu-Garnier, Jacqueline. "Large Overpopulated Cities in the Underdeveloped World," in *Geography and a Crowding World*, Wilbur Zelinsky et al. (eds.), Oxford University Press, New York, 1970, pp. 269–278.

Biswas, Subir. *Under-developed Areas and India*, Thacker Spink and Co., Calcutta, 1966.

Blanc, Robert. "Population Forecasts: Practical Problems of Making Such Forecasts in the Developing Countries," in United Nations *World Population Conference, Belgrade, 1965*, Vol. II.

Bognár, J. *Economic Policy and Planning in Developing Countries*. Akademiai Kiado, Budapest, 1968.

Boserup, Ester. "Present and Potential Food Production in Developing Countries," in *Geography and a Crowding World*, Wilbur Zelinsky et al. (eds.), Oxford University Press, New York, 1970, pp. 100–113.

Bourgeois-Pichat, Jean. "Social and Biological Determinants of Human Fertility in Nonindustrial Societies," *Population Problems, Proceedings of the American Philosophical Society*, Vol. 111, No. 3, June 1967, pp. 133–193.

---

[37] Davis, "Population Policy," pp. 737–738.

Breese, Gerald. "Urbanization in Newly Developing Countries," in *Modernization of Traditional Societies Series*, Prentice-Hall, Englewood Cliffs, New Jersey, 1966.

Chung, Roy. "Space-Time Diffusion of the Transition Model: The Twentieth Century Patterns," in George J. Demko, Harold M. Rose, and George A. Schnell (eds.), *Population Geography: a Reader*, McGraw-Hill Book Co., New York, 1970, pp. 220–239.

Clarke, John I. *Population Geography and Developing Countries*, Pergamon Press, New York, 1971.

Coale, Ansley, and Edgar M. Hoover. *Population Growth and Economic Development in Low-Income Countries*. Office of Population Research, Princeton University Press, Princeton, New Jersey, 1958.

Concepción, Mercedes B. "The Effect of Current Social and Economic Changes in the Developing Countries on Differential Fertility," in United Nations *World Population Conference, Belgrade, 1965*, Vol. II.

Davis, Kingsley. The Controversial Future of the Underdeveloped Areas. In Paul K. Hatt, ed., *World Population and Future Resources*, American Book Co., Boston, 1952, pp. 14–24.

Davis, Kingsley. "The Population Impact on Children in the World's Agrarian Countries," *Population Review* (Madras), Vol. 9, Nos. 1–2, January–July 1965, pp. 17–31.

Davis, Kingsley. "Population Policy: Will Current Programs Succeed?" *Science*, Vol. 158, November 1967.

Davis, Kingsley. *World Urbanization 1950–1970*. Vol. I, *Basic Data for Cities, Countries, and Regions*. Vol. II, *Analysis of Trends, Relationships, and Developments*. Institute of International Studies, University of California, Berkeley, 1969–1970.

Easterlin, Richard A. "Effects of Population Growth on the Economic Development of Developing Countries," in John D. Durand (ed.), *World Population, The Annals of the American Academy of Political and Social Science*, Vol. 369, January 1967, pp. 98–108.

Errington, Peter S., "Excess Agricultural Labour in Economically Underdeveloped Countries," *Indian Economic Journal* (Bombay), Vol. 10, No. 4, April 1963, pp. 450–453.

Fisher, Joseph L. "The Relationship of Material Resources and Population to Economic and Social Development," in United Nations *World Population Conference, Belgrade, 1965*, Vol. III.

Florence, P. Sargant. "A Note on Recent Age-Pyramids in Underdeveloped Countries," *Eugenic Review*, Vol. 56, No. 3, October 1964, pp. 143–145.

Freedman, Ronald. "The Transition from High to Low Fertility: Challenge to Demographers," *Population Index*, Vol. 31, No. 4, October 1965, pp. 417–429.

Gille, Halvor, "Twentieth Century Levels and Trends of Fertility in Developing Countries," in United Nations *World Population Conference, Belgrade, 1965*, Vol. II.

Ginsburg, Norton S. "Urban Geography and 'Non-Western' Areas," in Philip M. Hauser and Leo Schnore (eds.), *The Study of Urbanization*, John Wiley, New York, 1965, pp. 311–346.

Harroy, Jean-Paul. "The Political, Economic and Social Role of Urban Agglomerations in Countries of the Third World," *Civilisations*, XVII, No. 3 (1967), 166–185.

Kamerschen, David R. "Overpopulation and Under-Development: An Empirical Investigation," *Pakistan Economic Journal* (Lahore), Vol. 15, 1965, pp. 72–91.

Keyfitz, Nathan. Population Trends in Newly Developing Countries. In Ronald Freedman (ed.), *Population: The Vital Revolution*, Anchor Books, Doubleday and Co., Garden City, New York, 1964, pp. 149–165.

Kirk, Dudley. "Natality in Developing Countries: Recent Trends and Prospects." In S. J. Behrman, Leslie Corsa, and Ronald Freedman (eds.), *Fertility and Family Planning: A World View*. University of Michigan Press, Ann Arbor, Michigan, 1969, pp. 75–98.

Kirk, Dudley, and Dorothy Nortman. Population Policies in Developing Countries. *Economic Development and Cultural Change*, Vol. 15, No. 2, Pt. 1, January 1967, pp. 129–142.

Kirk, Dudley. "Prospects for Reducing Natality in the Underdeveloped World," in John D. Durand (ed.), *World Population, The Annals of the American Academy of Political and Social Science*, Vol. 369, January 1967, pp. 48–60.

Kirk, Dudley, "The Accelerating Decline in Natality in the Demographic Transition," author's abstract, *Population Index*, Vol. 36, 1970, pp. 271–272.

Kozlov, V. I. "Some Causes of the High Fertility of the Population of Developing Countries," in United Nations *World Population Conference, Belgrade, 1965*, Vol. II.

Kusukawa, Akira. "Social and Economic Factors on Mortality in Developing Countries," in United Nations *World Population Conference, Belgrade, 1965*, Vol. II.

Kuznets, Simon. Economic Aspects of Fertility Trends in the Less Developed Countries. In S. J. Behrman, Leslie Corsa, and Ronald Freedman (eds.), *Fertility and Family Planning: A World View*. University of Michigan Press, Ann Arbor, Michigan, 1969, pp. 157–179.

Kuznets, Simon. "Population and Economic Growth," in *Population Problems, Proceedings of the American Philosophical Society*, Vol. 111, No. 3, June 22, 1967, pp. 170–193.

Kuznets, Simon. Present Underdeveloped Countries and Past Growth Patterns, in his *Economic Growth and Structure: Selected Essays*, W. W. Norton, New York, 1965, pp. 176–193.

Lacoste, Y. *Géographie du Sous-développement*. Presses Universitaires de France, Collection Magellan, No. 2, Paris, 1965.

Lewis, W. Arthur. "Unemployment in Developing Countries," *The World Today*, XXIII, No. 1, January 1967, pp. 13–22.

Liu, B. Alfred. "Population Growth and Educational Development," in John D. Durand (ed.), *World Population, The Annals of the American Academy of Political and Social Science*, Vol. 369, January 1967, pp. 109–120.

Mountjoy, Alan B. *Industrialization and Under-developed Countries*, Hutchinson University Library, London, 1963.

Notestein, Frank, W. "Some Economic Aspects of Population Change in the Developing Countries," in J. Mayone Stycos and Jorge Arias (eds.), *Population Dilemma in Latin America*, Potomac Books, Washington D.C., 1966, pp. 86–100.

Paddock, William and Paul Paddock. *Hungry Nations*. Little, Brown, Boston, 1964.

Petersen, William. *Population* (2nd ed.), The Macmillan Co., New York, 1969, pp. 560–624.

Ponsioen, J. A. "An Analysis of—and a Policy Regarding—Rural Migration in Developing Countries," in United Nations *World Population Conference, Belgrade, 1965*, Vol. IV.

Ridley, Jeanne C. "Recent Natality Trends in Underdeveloped Countries, in Mindel C. Sheps and Jeanne C. Ridley (eds.), *Public Health and Population Change: Current Research Issues*, University of Pittsburgh Press, 1965, pp. 143–173.

Roberts, G. W. "Reproductive Performance and Reproductive Capacity in Less Industrialized Societies," in John D. Durand (ed.), *World Population, The Annals of the American Academy of Political and Social Science*, Vol. 369, January 1967, pp. 37–47.

Sadie, Jan L. "Labor Supply and Employment in Less Developed Countries," in John D. Durand (ed.), *World Population, The Annals of the American Academy of Political and Social Science*, Vol. 369, January 1967, pp. 121–130.

Shannon, Lyle W. "The Demographic Characteristics of Non-Self-Governing Areas," *Planning Outlook*, Vol. 5, No. 3, 1961, pp. 37–52.

Simpson, David. "The Dimensions of World Poverty," *Scientific American*, Vol. 219, November 1968, pp. 27–35.

Sjoberg, Gideon. "The Rural-Urban Dimension in Preindustrial, Transitional, and Industrial Societies," in Robert E. L. Farris (ed.), *Handbook of Modern Sociology*, 1964, pp. 127–159.

Smith, T. E. "The Control of Mortality," in John D. Durand (ed.), *World Population, The Annals of the American Academy of Political and Social Science*, Vol. 369, January 1967, pp. 16–25.

Spengler, Joseph J. "The Economist and the Population Question," *American Economic Review*, Vol. 56, No. 1, March 1966.

Steel, R. W. "Geography and the Developing World," *The Advancement of Science*, Vol. 23, No. 117, March 1967, pp. 566–582.

Stockwell, Edward G. "Fertility, Mortality, and Economic Status of Underdeveloped Areas," *Social Forces*, Vol. 4, No. 41, 1963, pp. 390–395.

Stockwell, Edward G. "Socio-Economic and Demographic Differences Among Underdeveloped Areas," *Rural Sociology*, Vol. 28, June 1963, pp. 165–175.

Stolnitz, George J. "The Demographic Transition: From High to Low Birth Rates and Death Rates." In Ronald Freedman (ed.), *Population: The Vital Revolution*, Anchor Books, Doubleday and Co., Garden City, New York, 1964, pp. 30–46.

Stolnitz, George J. "Recent Mortality Declines in Latin America, Asia and Africa: Review and Some Perspectives," in United Nations *World Population Conference, Belgrade, 1965*, Vol. II.

Stycos, J. Mayone. "Population and Family-Planning Programs in Newly Developing Countries," in Ronald Freedman (ed.), *Population: The Vital Revolution*, Anchor Books, Doubleday and Co., Garden City, New York, 1964, pp. 166–177.

Taeuber, Conrad. "Population and Food Supply," in John D. Durand (ed.), *World Population, The Annals of the American Academy of Political and Social Science*, Vol. 369, January 1967, pp. 73–83.

Takeshita, John Y. "Birth Control in Some of the Developing Countries of the Far East," in United Nations *World Population Conference, Belgrade, 1965*, Vol. II.

Thein, U Aung. "Some Aspects of Urban Explosions in Developing Countries," in United Nations *World Population Conference, Belgrade, 1965*, Vol. IV.

Trewartha, Glenn T. "Population Typologies Within the Economically Less Developed Realm," in *Colloquium Geographicum*, Geographischen Institut der Universität Bonn, Band 12, 1970, pp. 286–294.

United Nations. *A Concise Summary of the World Population Situation in 1970*. New York, United Nations, 1971.

Vávra, Zdeněk. "Projection of World Population (Distinguishing More Developed and Less Developed Areas at Present)," in United Nations *World Population Conference, Belgrade, 1965*, Vol. II.

Zelinsky, Wilbur. "The Geographer and His Crowding World: Some Cautionary Notes Toward the Study of Population Pressure in 'Developing Lands,' " *Revista Geográfica* (Rio de Janeiro), No. 65, December 1966, pp. 7–28.

Zelinsky, Wilbur. "Rural Population Dynamics as an Index to Social and Economic Development: A Geographic Overview," *Sociological Quarterly*, Spring 1963, pp. 99–121.

Latin America

Latin America, the part of the Western Hemisphere south of the Rio Grande River, is more correctly a culture realm than a continent. While it represents about 15 percent of the total area of the earth's inhabited continents, it supports only 7–8 percent of the earth's population. Accordingly, the average density of population in Latin America is less than half the world average. Its people are fewer in number than its land area might appear to warrant. This paradox of population in Latin America stems mainly from the inability of its culture to effectively organize the region's extensive area and considerable natural resources for the benefit of even a modest population. This inability, which is firmly rooted in Latin America's earlier history, suggests that the region's recent upsurge in population poses serious problems.

In Chapter 1 it was emphasized that while the different continents and countries included within the LD realm have many features in common, there is, nevertheless, considerable diversity. A special feature of Latin America that sets it apart from the other traditional societies is that it is an integral part of Western society; Asia and Africa are not. Its institutional structure is European, and secondarily Latin European, mainly Spanish and Portuguese. Latin America, like Anglo-America and the Antipodes, is the child of Europe, and both North and South America, derive their culture—including their law, their languages, and their religion—from the same primary European source. All the Americas are, to an unusual degree, the product of a gigantic European trans-Atlantic migration during recent centuries, whose southern stream, directed to Latin America, originated chiefly in Mediterranean Europe.

Consequently it is an error to think of the problems of Latin America as foreign in the sense that those of Asia and Africa are foreign. The problems of Latin America are internal problems of Western society. They cannot be understood unless it is recognized that they are problems of our own civilization, modified, to be sure, by strong infusions of native Amerindian and of imported African Negro cultures. Because Latin

America is essentially European in language and culture, transmission of modern Western technology, including medical science and the arts, is easier there than in Asia and Africa. It is doubtless because of its Western culture that Latin America, while still belonging predominantly to the world's LD realm, is one degree more economically and socially advanced than are the other two retarded continents. This is reflected in its higher average per capita national income than that of either Africa or Asia, its lower average death rate, and its higher average literacy rate; and in differentials involving a variety of other population characteristics as well.

INTERNATIONAL MIGRATIONS
AFFECTING LATIN AMERICA

Ethnically and culturally, Latin America is a consequence of population migration and of the miscegenation, culture diffusion, and acculturation that such migrations promote. In each of the 20-odd Latin American countries and dependencies, the ethnic and sociological patterns were already well established by the end of the colonial period or early in the 19th century. The acculturation, then, largely preceded the modern large-scale in-migration of Europeans during the 19th and 20th centuries.

In the pre-Columbian period Latin America was peopled by Asians of Mongoloid stock—the American Indians. They entered the continent from the northwest in the form of successive waves of hunters and food gatherers. By 9000 B.C. they had reached southernmost South America. They advanced to the agricultural stage in Middle America between 5000 and 4000 B.C., and in Peru some 1000 years later.[1]

Over the millenniums these Mongoloid peoples multiplied, until by 1492, on the eve of the colonial period, a recent optimistic conjecture indicates that the Indian population of the Western Hemisphere may have swelled to 90–100 million or even more. Probably 80 million of these lived south of the Rio Grande in Latin America.[2] Population was very unevenly distributed, with numbers and crowding greatest in the two regions of

[1] Artur Hehl Neiva, "International Migrations Affecting Latin America," *The Milbank Memorial Fund Quarterly*, Vol. 43, No. 2, 1965, p. 120.

[2] Henry F. Dobyns, "Estimating Aboriginal American Population: An Appraisal of Techniques with a New Hemispheric Estimate," *Current Anthropology*, Vol. 7, No. 4, 1966, pp. 395–416, esp. p. 415. See also Woodrow Borah, "America as a Model: The Demographic Impact of European Expansion upon the Non-European World," *Actas y Memorias*, XXXV Congreso Internacional de Americanistas, Mexico, 1962, Vol. 3, 1964, pp. 379–387, esp. p. 381.

highest culture—Mexico-Central America (estimated population around 41 million) and the South American Andes (estimated 30 million). In addition, 9 million may have been distributed along the margins of South America and perhaps half a million in the Caribbean Islands.[3]

The immigration of small numbers of Europeans beginning in 1492, which initiated the colonial period, was fraught with great consequences, some good and others disastrous. Foremost among the latter was the phenomenal depopulation suffered by the Indian peoples, which resulted from their contacts with the Europeans. Lacking immunity to the white man's diseases, the Indians were infected in epidemic proportions and died in unbelievable numbers. Warfare and violence, brutal overwork in mines and fields, and alcohol added their effects to that of disease.[4] Still another factor was the breakdown in the native economy, with resulting malnutrition, that originated mainly from the suppression of hunting and fishing, which provided essential proteins. The results were calamitous; hemisphere depopulation ratios of 20 to 1 and 25 to 1 are conjectured. The ratio may even have reached 35 to 1, from contact to nadir, in the tropical lowlands where depopulation was most severe. Thus the nadir aboriginal population in colonial Latin America may not have exceeded four million.[5] The greatest absolute losses were sustained in the regions where the native culture was most advanced and densities originally were highest. Probably actual decline in the native population was halted by around 1675, but the rate of growth rose only slowly thereafter.

Because of the advanced military technology of the European invaders, the period of armed conquest was brief indeed. And subsequently, being motivated by the spirit of adventure, greed, personal advancement, and a fanatical religious zeal, the Spanish conquerors demanded prompt results. Padres closely followed the soldiers; and under coercion the native cultures crumbled and European culture patterns were forcibly imposed, leading to the establishment of extensive Spanish and Portuguese colonial empires. In addition, there were minor French, English, and Dutch enclaves.

Few Spanish and Portuguese settlers came to Latin America between the 16th and 18th centuries. One historian estimates that Europeans comprised only 1.34 percent of the total Latin American population in 1570 and 6.58 percent in 1650, but may have reached 18.85 percent by 1825.[6]

[3] Dobyns, "Estimating Aboriginal American Population," p. 415.
[4] Kingsley Davis, "The Place of Latin America in World Demographic History," *Milbank Memorial Fund Quarterly*, Vol. 42, No. 2, Part 2, 1964, p. 22.
[5] Dobyns, "Estimating Aboriginal American Population," p. 415.
[6] Neiva, "International Migrations Affecting Latin America," p. 122.

As conquistadors and adventurers they did not come to till the fields. Still, food was essential and so agricultural development was required. But because depopulation had made native labor scarce and blacks were probably considered more resistant to disease, African slaves were introduced beginning in the 16th century, thereby further complicating the ethnic and cultural mix. How many Negroes reached Latin America and how they were distributed there is unknown. Neiva accepts the figure of 10 million for the whole region south of the Rio Grande.

These early migrations of Europeans and African Negroes to Latin America were of the utmost importance to the region's subsequent development. The small European minority was composed mainly of young male adults. They were the conquerors; they constituted an exalted and all-powerful elite in the midst of a large passive Indian population whose culture had been forcibly shattered, and a smaller demoralized body of Negro slaves. A situation thereby prevailed that was highly conducive to miscegenation and the practice of polygamy, and such societal features have continued down even to the present.

Extensive miscegenation has had a number of momentous consequences. For one thing, it operated to increase births, and thereby in some measure to offset the catastrophic losses in Indian population. In addition, it gave individual countries and regions distinctive ethnic, demographic, and linguistic characteristics. Most of tropical Latin America is, in varying degrees, composed of racial mixtures in which dark skins greatly predominate. And finally, it permitted the blending of white, Indian, and Negro cultural elements and values, which had the effect of enriching the entire Latin American social fabric and contributing to its regional variations.

The downward trend in Latin American population, which probably continued throughout the first 175 years of the colonial period, was halted and reversed during the fourth quarter of the 17th century. But subsequently growth was slow for some time. The rate accelerated somewhat after 1750, one contributing factor being the increased importation of African Negroes. But if the population estimates for Latin America as of the 19th century are accepted as roughly correct, then the region south of the Rio Grande did not grow in population as rapidly as did Anglo-America. Thus, between 1800 and 1900 the population of Anglo-America increased about 14 times and that of Latin America probably only 3 times. The latter slow rate reflected the economic stagnation and political strife in Latin America, as well as the continuing high mortality rates. Only since about 1920, at which time mortality began to plummet—at least in some areas—has the population growth rate in Latin America exceeded that in Anglo-America. As a consequence, while the two regions were about equal in total numbers by 1950, Latin America surpassed

Anglo-America by 55 million in 1970 and is projected to be 1.8 times as populous by the year 2000.

Expanded recent migration of Europeans to Latin America coincided roughly with the arrival of independence, which in most parts was well after the mid-19th century. Up until World War II the largest streams of European immigrants went to Argentina and Brazil. Ranking next, but with far fewer immigrants, were Cuba, Uruguay, and Mexico. While comparatively few migrants entered other countries, enough did so to significantly affect the country concerned. Among the generalizations relating to recent European emigration to Latin America, the following may be mentioned. (1) It began late and increased from the 1880's to around the turn of the century. There was a second peak just before World War I, and a lower one in the 1920's. It declined after the 1930's. (2) Of the European immigrants who entered Latin America, the number of returnees was large. In Argentina only 52–53 percent remained; in Brazil roughly two thirds did so.[7] (3) A majority of the recent immigrants have been South Europeans—Spaniards, Portuguese, and Italians —followed by Germans.

RECENT POPULATION GROWTH AND VITAL RATES

Of momentous importance is the fact that currently Latin America has the highest average annual rate of population growth among the earth's large continental subdivisions. This soaring rate is a relatively recent phenomenon, dating only from around the third or fourth decades of the present century. General estimates indicate a total of about 63 million inhabitants for all of Latin America as of the turn of the century. The average decade growth rate between 1900 and 1920 was probably under 20 percent. In the 1920–1930 and 1930–1940 decades, it was between 20 and 21 percent; from 1940–1950 it rose to 25.2 percent and in 1950–1960 to 31.1 percent. During the decade 1960–1970 it is expected to be about 30 percent, and in 1970–1980, 32.9 percent.[8] Thus while the population of 1900 took 40 years to double, that of 1950 is expected to double in the short period of only 24 years. In 1900 Latin Americans

[7] Neiva, "International Migrations Affecting Latin America," pp. 124–125.
[8] "World Population Projects Assessed in 1963," United Nations, *Population Studies No. 41*, Table A3.8, pp. 143–144. See also Carmen A. Miró, "The Population of Twentieth Century Latin America," in J. Mayone Stycos and Jorge Arias (eds.), *Population Dilemma in Latin America*, Potomac Books Inc., Washington, D.C., 1966, pp. 1–9; and Carmen A. Miró, "The Population of Latin America," *Demography*, Vol. 1, No. 1, 1964, pp. 15–19.

made up only about 3.5 percent of the earth's population; in 1960 they represented 7.1 percent, and in 1970 an estimated 7.8 percent. Expectably, rates of growth have differed among the several subregions and countries of Latin America.

Three primary factors account for the rate of population growth in any region—fertility, mortality, and net migration. Of the three, migration has been relatively unimportant in accounting for recent population change in Latin America as a whole. For centuries birth rates and death rates must have been very high in all of Latin America, with the former averaging between 40 and 50 per 1000 and the latter between 30 and 40. Modest growth was the result. Sometime after 1900 a remarkable mortality revolution began in temperate South America, and it became general throughout all Latin America during the 1930's and 1940's. This was mainly a consequence of the comprehensive health and sanitation programs initiated by the Rockefeller Foundation and the world health agencies working through the various national governments. As a result, death rates dropped sharply. But the dramatic decline in mortality was not paralleled by a similar fall in fertility. It is the increasing differential between continuing high birth rates and declining death rates, then, that has been responsible for the soaring natural increase. Mainly in temperate South America, but also in a few of the smaller tropical island countries (especially Cuba, Puerto Rico, and Barbados), there has been a well-documented decline in fertility; elsewhere it remains consistently high (Fig. 1.1). There is some inconclusive evidence that a minority of the residents within the burgeoning cities are beginning to limit the size of their families. For all of Latin America, including the temperate south, the current average birth rate is probably around 40 per 1000, and it is between 40 and 45 for the tropical parts. For 11 countries in tropical LD Latin America recording vital statistics since 1930 and together representing two thirds of the region's total population, crude birth rates have continued to inch upward over the three decades 1930–1960, reaching an all-time high of 45–46 per 1000 in the span 1950–1960. The average crude death rate is about 10 per 1000 and probably about 11 or a little more for the LD tropical sections. This suggests a yearly growth rate of about 30 per 1000. In most Latin American countries the death rate can still be lowered considerably.

Two consequences of the demographic revolution in Latin America, in addition to the high and progressively increasing population growth rate, are an age structure heavily weighted in the young age groups and a large migration from rural to urban areas.

Where international migration has not intruded, the age structure of a region or country is mainly determined by the past birth rates. A high birth rate generates a population with a large proportion of children and youths. In 1970, 42 percent of the entire Latin American population was estimated to be under 15 years of age.[9] If temperate South America, where the proportion is distinctly lower, is omitted, then the figure is appreciably higher. The proportion of people 60 years or over is only 6 percent or less. Probably because of the effects of declining mortality, the already high proportion of minors has tended to increase over the last intercensal period.

Although urbanization is a topic for later discussion, it may be noted here that the recent surge of population to the cities is largely a result of the fertility and mortality patterns just described. The low productivity of agriculture in Latin America and the rapidly increasing excess of population measured in terms of effectively exploited natural resources have impelled rural inhabitants to seek employment in the cities.

Other serious indirect and nondemographic consequences of the demographic revolution in Latin America are of a political, social, and economic nature. Thus, rapid population growth creates a scarcity of funds for promoting economic development, both in the countryside and in the cities. Moreover, the large number of young dependents in proportion to the number of active workers produces a situation in which the urgent needs of the minors, particularly in education, reduces the amount of capital available for productive purposes. It also causes difficulties in finding employment for the large and growing number of young adults who annually reach the age when they should enter the labor force. In addition, heavy migration to the cities creates complex economic, political, and social problems in the urban centers.

FEATURES OF POPULATION DISTRIBUTION AND REDISTRIBUTION

A distinctive feature of the spatial arrangement of population in Latin America is its strongly nucleated character; the pattern is one of striking clusters. Most of the population clusters remain distinct and are separated from other clusters by sparsely occupied territory. Such a pattern of isolated nodes of settlement is common in many pioneer regions; indeed, it was characteristic of early settlement in both Europe and eastern North America. In those regions, as population expanded, the scantily occupied areas between individual clusters gradually filled in with settlers, and

[9] *World Population Data Sheet—1970*, Population Reference Bureau, Washington, D.C., April, 1970. See also Carmen A. Miró, "The Population of Twentieth Century Latin America," p. 19.

the nodes merged. But in Latin America such an evolution generally did not occur, and so the nucleated pattern persists. Expectably, the individual population clusters show considerable variations in density.

The origin of the nucleated pattern of settlement is partly to be sought in the gold and missionary fever that imbued the Spanish colonists. Their settlements were characteristically located with some care, since only areas with precious metals for exploitation and large Indian populations to be Christianized and to provide laborers could satisfy their dual hungers. A clustered pattern was also fostered by the isolation and localism that prevailed in the separate territories and settlement areas of Latin America.

Almost invariably each of the distinct population clusters has a conspicuous urban nucleus. To an unusual degree the economic, political, and social life within a regional cluster centers on a single large primate city, which is also the focus of the local lines of transport.

The prevailing nucleated pattern of population distribution also bears a relationship to political boundaries. In some countries (Chile, Uruguay, and El Salvador), a single population cluster represents the core area of the nation. In more instances, however, a population cluster forms the core of a major political subdivision of a nation-state, so that a country may contain more than one cluster. A consequence of this simple population distribution pattern and its relation to administrative subdivisions is that political boundaries ordinarily fall within the sparsely occupied territory separating individual clusters. In Latin America few national or provincial boundaries pass through nodes of relatively dense settlement.[10]

Another feature arising out of the cluster pattern of population arrangement is that the *total national territory* of a country is often very different from the *effective national territory*, since the latter includes only those populated parts that contribute to the nation's economic support.

A further consequence of the nucleated pattern is found in the nature of the transport routes and systems. Overland routes between population clusters are usually poorly developed, while a more efficient network ordinarily exists *within* each cluster, with each such regional network joined by an overland route to the nearest port. Thus, the chief lines of transport connecting individual population clusters are often sea lanes rather than land routes. Gradually, as highways are developed and improved, intercluster overland traffic tends to increase.

Population Redistribution and New Settlement.   The spectacular rates at which population numbers are currently soaring in Latin America

[10] Preston E. James, *Introduction to Latin America*, The Odyssey Press, New York, 1964, pp. 6–11.

are not matched by equivalent changes in their spatial redistributions. Any population map of Latin America reveals extensive areas of unused and underutilized land. Part of such land is highland and plagued by steep slopes, but by far the larger share of it is characterized by a moist tropical climate, either tropical wet or tropical wet and dry. Such a climatic environment, with its associated wild vegetation, soils, and drainage, admittedly presents many discouraging elements to the new settler on virgin lands. But on the other hand, it must be remembered that extensive wet tropical lands in South and Southeast Asia and in parts of sub-Saharan Africa are far more occupied than are the moist tropics of large sectors of Latin America. Thus tropical climate alone is scarcely a sufficient explanation for the abundance of near-empty lands south of the Rio Grande. Cultural factors are involved as much as, if not more than, physical ones. One of the former is the unfortunate land-holding system that has been fastened on the continent, under which vast areas of potentially cultivable land are held out of active use by a small number of absentee landlords, who not only themselves make ineffective use of the land, but at the same time refuse to permit its cultivation by small operators. Because of the land-holding system, peasant proprietors are unable to secure their own lands, a situation that discourages new rural settlement. The bulk of the rural population remains landless and sunk in poverty.

On large latifundia where commercial crops are grown, the paid workers can rarely own land. But in addition to the estates, there are vast areas in Latin America that are used exclusively for the grazing of livestock, with no attempt being made to raise crops for feeding the animals. This extensive pastoral system of land use also tends to exclude the small-farm cultivator. Indeed, throughout much of Latin America a close symbiotic relationship is lacking between crop and livestock enterprises within individual farm units. This age-old conflict between pastoral and agricultural ways of life is without a doubt a major obstacle to rural development and expansion of agricultural settlement throughout Latin America.[11]

The changes now in progress in the spatial distributions accompanying the vast increase in numbers of people do not appear to involve any large-scale push of rural settlement into virgin territory. Only to a rather limited extent is new agricultural settlement taking place. Intercluster regions are not filling rapidly. The overwhelming tendency is for people to continue to pile up in the old centers of settlement, especially in

[11] T. Lynn Smith, "Agricultural-Pastoral Conflict: A Major Obstacle in the Process of Rural Development," *Journal of Inter-American Studies*, Vol. 11, No. 1, 1969, pp. 16-43.

and around their cities, rather than to expand the frontier into new pioneer-settlement areas. To be sure, there are numerous shifting frontiers in Latin America, but for the most part they represent only waves of new but temporary exploitation that move across a region to be followed by partial abandonment of farm lands and a subsequent population decline in back of the advancing outer frontier.[12] Such shifting frontiers do not result in a net gain in population density. Later, and in some places, a degree of reoccupation of the abandoned lands may occur, accompanied by a thickening of rural settlement along this inner frontier.

T. Lynn Smith points out also that in huge Brazil, representing half the area of South America and having fully half its national territory nearly totally unoccupied, only in a few parts were substantial areas of new land brought under cultivation during the decade 1950–1960. These included the northwestern part of the southern state of Paraná, the north central portion of the state of Maranhão in the northeast, certain sections around the new national capital of Brasilia, some northern portions of the state of Minas Gerais, and the extreme northwestern part of the state of São Paulo.[13]

In some Andean countries there is a modest outward movement of population from the densely settled highlands to the interior lowlands at the base of the mountains. Bolivia, Peru, Colombia, and Venezuela are all experiencing such a vertical population shift. In Ecuador the shift is mainly from the highlands to sections of the Pacific Coastal Plain. Likewise, in Central America and in Mexico there are a few scattered areas of new agricultural settlement. But studies dealing quantitatively with population redistribution in Latin America associated with this new agricultural settlement are rare. Hence, the magnitude of the population shift to new agricultural lands in Latin America appears to be unknown. Certain individual cases can be referred to that may offer some indication of relative magnitude. Thus, the 17 new agricultural colonies along the Pacific coastal plain of Guatemala have a combined area of nearly 245,000 acres and the total population exceeds 120,000.[14] This development has occurred over a period of about a decade and a half since 1950, so the number of new settlers added each year could not have been very large.

Considering the costs involved in opening up virgin areas for new

---

[12] James, *Introduction to Latin America*, pp. 9–10.

[13] T. Lynn Smith, "The Population of Latin America," in Ronald Freedman (ed.), *Population: The Vital Revolution*, Anchor Books, Doubleday and Co., Garden City, New York, 1964, p. 184.

[14] Clarence W. Minkel, "Programs of Agricultural Colonization and Settlement in Central America," *Revista Geografica*, No. 66, Junho de 1967, pp. 21–23. See also Ross N. Pearson, "Zones of Agricultural Development in Guatemala: An Experiment in Land Reform," *Journal of Geography*, Vol. 62, January 1963, p. 14.

agricultural colonization, considerable skepticism exists as to whether this type of internal rural migration can by itself provide an important short-term solution to the problems associated with the rapid population growth in Latin America's long-settled areas. Some believe that more and prompter relief can be expected from upgrading the efficiency and productivity of the agricultural workers, so that a larger population can be accommodated in the older regions of rural settlement. Moreover, in parts of these same well-settled regions, there are lands once cultivated but now abandoned that in many instances might more readily be brought into use again than can the virgin frontier lands. Such abandoned areas ordinarily are closer to the lines of transport and to markets than are the more distant frontier lands.

It is certain that at present the stream of rural migrants moving into new agricultural colonies is dwarfed in magnitude by the much larger flow from the rural districts to the cities and their belts of suburban slums. It is estimated that the flood of migrants from rural areas to urban places in Brazil between 1950 and 1960 involved at least one out of every 11, and probably one of every 10, Brazilians alive at the time of the 1960 census.[15] It is the rural-urban migration, then, that constitutes the outstanding feature of recent population redistribution in Latin America.

Urbanization. Although the density of population in relation to agri-cultural land is much lower in Latin America than in East and South Asia, this is offset by the lower average agricultural-worker productivity in the former. Taking this worker inefficiency into consideration, the pressure of population on the presently cultivated land in Latin America is high, and it is becoming increasingly more so with the current rapid rate of population growth, which equals or exceeds the economic growth. It is the increasing pressure of the rural population on the land in the long-settled regions that provides much of the stimulus for the large-scale trek to the cities in search of employment. Still, in a large majority of Latin America's population clusters, omitting those in the West Indies, rural population density is below 100 per sq mi; in many it is under 25.

The Economic Commission for Latin America, on the basis of census returns for 14 countries, estimated the population of all Latin America to have grown at a mean annual rate of about 2.8 percent between 1950 and 1960—only 1.5 percent for the rural population, but 4.5 percent for the urban one.[16] The 1950–1960 intercensal annual growth rates for

[15] Louis J. Ducoff, "The Role of Migration in the Demographic Development of Latin America," *Milbank Memorial Fund Quarterly*, Vol. 43, No. 2, 1965, p. 204.
[16] Ducoff, "The Role of Migration in the Demographic Development of Latin America," p. 198.

rural and urban population varied among individual countries, but invariably the urban rate was higher in all of them (Table 2.1). Since the rural rates of *natural* increase probably are substantially higher than the urban ones, the more rapid urban population growth can be explained only by a large internal migration from the countryside to the cities. Defining *urban* as the population living in localities with 2000 or more inhabitants, the urban population of Latin America, which was estimated

TABLE 2.1   Intercensal Rates of Population Growth by
Residence Category, in Specific Countries

Country	Intercensal Annual Rate of Growth (Around 1950–1960, Percent)		
	Total	Urban	Rural
Brazil	3.1	5.2	1.6
Chile	2.5	3.7	0.5
Costa Rica	3.8	4.0	3.7
Dominican Republic	3.4	5.7	2.5
Ecuador	3.1	4.6	2.3
El Salvador	2.8	3.3	2.4
Mexico	3.0	4.7	1.5
Nicaragua	3.3	4.9	2.2
Panama	2.9	4.1	2.0
Paraguay	2.6	2.8	2.5
Peru	2.4	3.5	1.5
Venezuela	3.9	6.3	0.7

SOURCE: C. A. Miró, "The Population of Latin America," *Demography*, Vol. 1, No. 1, 1964, Tables 6 and 7.

to have been 46.2 percent of the total in 1960, is expected to reach 53.2 percent in 1970 and 59.2 percent in 1980.[17] Including only localities with 20,000 or more inhabitants, the percentage of urban population for all Latin America is estimated to be 32 percent (28 percent if Argentina, Uruguay, and Chile are omitted).[18] Latin America's degree of urbanization is, therefore, considerably above the world average of 24–25 percent and markedly greater than the average for the two other LD

[17] Ducoff, "The Role of Migration in the Demographic Development of Latin America," p. 198.
[18] John D. Durand and Cesar A. Pelaez, "Patterns of Urbanization in Latin America," *Milbank Memorial Fund Quarterly*, Vol. 43, No. 2, 1965, p. 170.

continents of Asia (16–18 percent) and Africa (13 percent). Tropical Latin America is even slightly more urbanized than southern Europe, which belongs to the MD realm.

Throughout the LD world in general, over the last several decades there has been a steady decline in the proportion of the labor force engaged in agriculture. For Latin America the decline was from 59 percent in 1936 to 47 percent in 1960. Nevertheless, the absolute size of the agricultural labor force has continued to increase. There are two causes for this sustained increase. One is the accelerated population growth, and the other is the slow rate of modernization of agriculture accompanied by an associated increase in the per capita output of agricultural labor.

Very little direct information on the magnitude and characteristics of the internal migration of the Latin American population exists. Using indirect methods, the rural-urban movement for the decade 1950–1960 has been estimated at 14 to 15 million persons, or 43 percent of the decade gain in total urban population.[19]

Data are not sufficiently complete to permit generalizations for the whole continent concerning comparative growth rates for cities in different size classes. If only cities of 20,000 or more inhabitants are considered, recent information indicates that growth is proceeding most rapidly in the larger cities of 50,000 inhabitants and over. To the extent that four countries (Mexico, Panama, the Dominican Republic, and Venezuela) can be taken as representative of the continent, it appears that the proportion of people living in places of 20,000 and under has declined during the 1950–1960 decade. In Mexico, Panama, and the Dominican Republic, it is the largest cities, those of 500,000 inhabitants and over, that are growing most rapidly; in Venezuela it is those in the 100,000–500,000 group. Out of seven Latin American countries for whose capital cities annual rates of population growth are available for the decade 1950–1960, all but one (Rio de Janeiro, until recently a capital) showed growth rates in excess of the national urban rate of increase. But in only three capitals was the rate of increase significantly higher than the all-urban national rate.[20]

A characteristic feature of Latin America is the high relative importance of the capital city in terms of both the total and the urban populations of most countries. The capital is also characteristically the metropolis. Ten cities now have more than a million inhabitants and, with the exception of São Paulo, each of these is a capital, although Rio de Janeiro

[19] Ducoff, "The Role of Migration in the Demographic Development of Latin America," p. 202.
[20] Miró, "The Population of Latin America," p. 23.

has recently ceased to be one. Buenos Aires in 1960 accounted for 33.7 percent of the total Argentine population and 47.6 percent of the urban one. For Panama the comparable figures are 25.4 and 61.3; Asunción, 16.8 and 47.5; Quito, 7.8 and 22.6; Santo Domingo, 12.2 and 40.0; Caracas, 17.8 and 28.4; and Mexico City, 13.4 and 26.4.[21] Together the 10 metropolises contain about 25 million people, or 12 percent of the continent's total population.

Still, there is apparently a trend toward a decreasing importance of primate cities in a majority of Latin American countries. Indeed, in 14 of the 17 countries for which data are available for making such comparisons, the percentage of the total urban population found in the largest city was smaller at the time of the latest available census (mostly the early 1960's) than at any earlier census date since 1920.[22]

Other Population Characteristics. One consequence of the large-scale rural-urban migration as it affects population characteristics stems from its sex selectivity. Thus, a significant imbalance in the proportions of males and females has come to prevail in Latin America's rural and urban societies. Data on sex ratios (men per 100 women) are available for 9 countries where censuses were taken in the early 1960's. In all 9 the sex ratio for the *total* population did not depart more than a few points from 100. But on the other hand, there was a consistent and usually strong deficiency of males in the urban populations and in a majority of the countries a strong predominance of males in the rural population.[23] Such a situation reflects a larger out-migration of females than of males from rural to urban localities.[24]

In LD tropical Latin America, the economically active population is to an unusual degree engaged in primary industry, or essentially agriculture. The average for the whole region is over 50 percent. Individual regions where it appears to be under 50 percent include Chile, some of the mainland sections fronting on the Caribbean Sea, and many of the Antilles islands. Still, by comparison with Asia and Africa, the population in tropical Latin America is to a much less degree concentrated in the primary economic sector than in the secondary and tertiary occupations, which are essentially urban-oriented. Moreover, agriculture has gradually continued to lose in relative importance, although there appears to have been no pronounced change over the 1950–1960 census decade. As of 1960 the national percentages of the economically active males

[21] Miró, "The Population of Latin America," pp. 20–21.

[22] Durand and Pelaez, "Patterns of Urbanization in Latin America," pp. 182–183.

[23] Miró, "The Population of Latin America," pp. 24–25.

[24] Juan C. Elizaga, "Internal Migrations in Latin America," *Milbank Memorial Fund Quarterly*, Vol. 43, No. 2, 1965, pp. 148–149.

engaged in agriculture ranges from such high figures as 74.9 percent in Honduras, 71.3 percent in El Salvador, 61.2 percent in Panama, and 59.0 percent in Mexico to lows of 38.1 percent in Venezuela and 34.1 percent in Chile.

Illiteracy is lower in Latin America (estimated at 34 percent of the total population aged 15 and over) than in either Asia (54 percent) or Africa (82 percent). If tropical Latin America alone is considered, the percentage would be appreciably raised. Again, the range of adult illiteracy between the different Latin American countries is large—from highs of 80–90 percent in Haiti and 60–70 percent in Guatemala to lows of 15–20 percent in Jamaica and Puerto Rico (Fig. 1.4).

Per capita national income is also markedly higher in Latin America ($385) than in Asia ($184) or Africa ($140). Of course, the first figure would be lowered somewhat if more economically advanced Argentina and Uruguay were omitted. Expectably, in this feature as well, there is a wide spread between individual Latin American countries—from lows of only $70 in Haiti and $170 in Bolivia to highs of $1210 in Puerto Rico, $880 in Venezuela, and $490 in Mexico (Fig. 1.5).[25]

REFERENCES

Arriaga, Eduardo E. *Mortality Decline and Its Demographic Effects in Latin America.* University of California, Institute of International Studies, Berkeley, 1970.

Arriaga, Eduardo E. "The Nature and Effects of Latin America's Non-Western Trend in Fertility." Demography, Vol. 7, No. 4, Nov., 1970, pp. 483–501.

Beyer, Glenn H. (ed.). *The Urban Explosion in Latin America: a Continent in Process of Modernization.* Ithaca, Cornell University Press, 1967.

Borah, Woodrow, "America as a Model: The Demographic Impact of European Expansion upon the Non-European World," *Actas y Memorias,* XXXV Congreso Internacional de Americanistas, Mexico, 1962, Vol. 3, 1964, pp. 379–387.

Borah, Woodrow. "The Historical Demography of Latin America: Sources, Techniques, Controversies, Yields," in Paul Deprez (ed.), *Population and Economics,* University of Manitoba Press, Winnipeg, 1970, pp. 173–205.

Collver, O. Andrew. *Birth Rates in Latin America: New Estimates of Historical Trends and Fluctuations.* Institute of International Studies, University of California, Berkeley, 1965.

Davis, Kingsley. "The Place of Latin America in World Demographic His-

[25] *World Population Data Sheet—1968,* Population Reference Bureau, Washington, D.C., March, 1968.

tory," *Milbank Memorial Fund Quarterly*, Vol. 42, No. 2, Part 2, 1964, pp. 19–47.

Denevan, William M. "Aboriginal Drained-Field Cultivation in the Americas," *Science*, Vol. 169, August, 1970, pp. 647–654.

Dobyns, Henry F. "Estimating Aboriginal American Population: An Appraisal of Techniques with a New Hemispheric Estimate," *Current Anthropology*, Vol. 7, No. 4, 1966, pp. 395–416.

Ducoff, Louis J. "The Role of Migration in the Demographic Development of Latin America," *Milbank Memorial Fund Quarterly*, Vol. 43, No. 2, 1965, pp. 197–209.

Durand, John D., and Cesar, A. Pelaez. "Patterns of Urbanization in Latin America," *Milbank Memorial Fund Quarterly*, Vol. 43, No. 2, 1965, pp. 166–191.

Elizaga, Juan C. "Internal Migrations in Latin America," *Milbank Memorial Fund Quarterly*, Vol. 43, No. 2, 1965, pp. 144–161.

Hauser, P. M. (Ed.). *Urbanization in Latin America*, UNESCO, Paris, 1961.

James, Preston E. *Latin America*, 4th ed., The Odyssey Press, New York, 1969.

James, Preston E. *Introduction to Latin America*. The Odyssey Press, New York, 1964.

Kiser, Clyde V. (ed.). "Components of Population Change in Latin America," *Milbank Memorial Fund Quarterly*, Vol. 43, No. 4, Part 2, October 1965, pp. 1–384.

Kiser, Clyde V. "Population Trends and Public Health in Latin America," *Milbank Memorial Fund Quarterly*, Vol. 45, No. 1, January 1967, pp. 43–59.

Miró, Carmen A. "The Population of Latin America," *Demography*, Vol. 1, No. 1, 1964, pp. 15–41.

Miró, Carmen A. The Population of Twentieth Century Latin America. In J. Mayone Stycos and Jorge Arias (eds.), *Population Dilemma in Latin America*, Potomac Books Inc., Washington, D.C., 1966, pp. 1–32.

Neiva, Artur Hehl. "International Migrations Affecting Latin America," *Milbank Memorial Fund Quarterly*, Vol. 43, No. 2, 1965, pp. 119–135.

Smith, T. Lynn. "Agricultural-Pastoral Conflict: A Major Obstacle in the Process of Rural Development," *Journal of Inter-American Studies*, Vol. 11, No. 1, 1969, pp. 16–43.

Smith, T. Lynn. "Latin American Population Studies." Gainesville, Florida, University of Florida Press, 1960. 83p. *University of Florida Monographs*, Social Sciences, No. 8.

Smith, T. Lynn. The Population of Latin America. In Ronald Freedman (ed.), *Population: The Vital Revolution*. Anchor Books, Doubleday and Co., Garden City, New York, 1964, pp. 178–190.

Stycos, Mayone J. and Jorge Arias (eds.). *Population Dilemma in Latin America*. Potomac Books Inc., Washington, D.C., 1966.

United Nations. Economic Commission for Latin America. "Geographic Distribution of the Population of Latin America and Regional Development

Priorities." *Economic Commission for Latin America*, Tenth session, Mar del Plata, Argentina, May 1963. E/CN.12/643. (Mar del Plata), Feb. 10, 1963. 42 pp.

World Population Data Sheet. Population Reference Bureau, Washington, D.C. (Annual; latest issue, June, 1971).

Zelinsky, Wilbur. "The historical Geography of the Negro Population of Latin America," *Journal of Negro History*, Vol. 34, 1949, pp. 153–221.

CHAPTER

3

Middle America

Middle America, situated between Anglo-America on the north and South America on the south, has three main subdivisions: (1) Mexico, (2) Central America, and (3) the insular West Indies. The three parts have a number of similarities: they share a common focus on the Caribbean Sea and the Gulf of Mexico; their resources have been inadequately and inefficiently developed in some instances and abusively exploited in others; their populations are highly stratified into a small elite and wealthy minority and a large, poor, and underprivileged majority; and multiple racial elements prevail.

Still, diversity is much more the rule than is similarity. Racial and ethnic variety is ubiquitous. Educational attainment differs from area to area and region to region. Each mainland cluster of population and each island represents a distinctive composite of people, tradition, and culture. Striking contrasts in population density prevail (Fig. 3.1). Standards of living vary remarkably. Isolation has been a particularly potent factor in fostering the diversity so prevalent in Middle America; an intraregional circulation of people, ideas, and commodities has always been small. Most of the trade takes place within the local settlement cluster and between the cluster and overseas markets in Europe and Anglo-America. Consequently the forces making for segregation have been especially strong, and an unusual degree of localism and regional individuality is the result. Almost countless culturally unlike regions prevail.

Before the coming of the Europeans and Africans, Middle America was peopled by various Indian groups representing contrasting cultural and density levels. The degree of Amerindian influence on the present culture and racial composition in different areas varies roughly with the number, density, and level of civilization of the preconquest indigenous population.[1] There are two exceptions, (1) the West Indies, where the

[1] Robert C. West and John P. Augelli, *Middle America, Its Lands and Peoples.* Prentice Hall, Inc., Englewood Cliffs, New Jersey, 1966, p. 9. I wish to acknowledge that throughout the section on Middle America I have made abundant use of materials from this fruitful source.

aborigines were nearly extinguished within a century after the European conquest and (2) certain remote and unattractive areas on the mainland that have remained strongly Indian in spite of the low population densities.

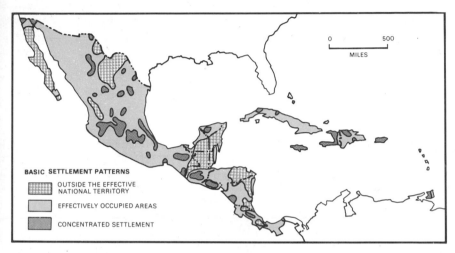

Fig. 3.1. Generalized pattern of population distribution in Middle America. Note that dense settlement is characteristically in the form of isolated clusters, usually separated from each other by territory that is more meagerly settled. Most widespread are regions with sparse or modest settlement density; these nevertheless contribute to the national economy. But fairly extensive also are those regions that are so empty of settlement that they lie outside the effective national territory. After James, Zelinsky, and West and Augelli.

Estimates of the total Indian population in Middle America just prior to the Conquest vary widely. A conservative approximation suggests a total of only about 15 million, of which 14 million or more may have occupied Mexico and Central America and another million the West Indies. A recent and much more liberal conjecture, already noted in an earlier section, places the total inhabitants of all Middle America at about 41–42 million, with perhaps 41 million in Mexico and Central America and somewhat less than half a million in the West Indies.[2] On arrival, the conquering Europeans observed striking contrasts in population densities and culture levels among the aborigines. The high-culture Aztec and Maya areas included the southern part of the central plateau of Mexico, the Yucatan peninsula, and the highlands and Pacific lowlands

[2] Henry F. Dobyns, "Estimating Aboriginal American Population: An Appraisal of Techniques with a New Hemispheric Estimate," *Current Anthropology*, Vol. 7, No. 4, 1966, p. 415.

of Central America (Fig. 3.2). These were the most technologically advanced and populous centers. In them a sophisticated political and social organization directed the economy, with the consequence that agriculture was stable and intensive enough to assure adequate food for a relatively dense population. By contrast, in the West Indies, most of the Caribbean lowland of Central America, and dry northern Mexico, the Indian populations were much smaller, a feature that derived mainly from the inferior food-producing techniques—gathering, hunting. fishing, and slash-and-burn tillage—of their inhabitants.[3] An overwhelming majority of the

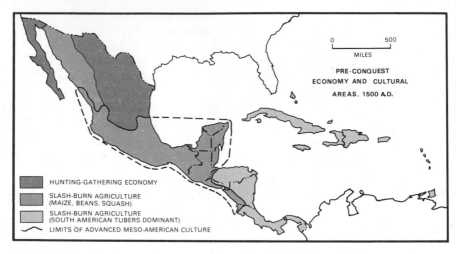

Fig. 3.2. Pre-Conquest economy and culture regions in Middle America (about 1500 A.D.). Modified and simplified from West and Augelli, *Middle America,* Prentice-Hall, 1966.

preconquest inhabitants of Middle America were dependent on agriculture and gathering.

The disastrous effects of the European conquest on the Indian population have been mentioned earlier. In the less populous West Indies, survivors were few and the evidences of their earlier occupance is slight indeed. In the more populous parts of the mainland, in Mexico and Central America, while the reduction in population was severe, quite naturally the total number of survivors was greater. Some were assimilated into the Spanish culture, but many were not. The consequence is that in mainland Middle America, besides a small white minority and a mestizo majority, there is an important unassimilated or partially assimilated Indian element. The fraction that is Indian varies from country to coun-

[3] West and Augelli, *Middle America,* pp. 5–6.

try; in Guatemala it may reach 55 percent, and in Mexico almost 30 percent. But while the racial composition of Mexico and most of Central America is essentially Euro-Indian or mestizo, Indian languages remain locally important and the aboriginal heritage is to be seen in much of the art, diet, house types, and farming practices.

While the imprints of various European countries are to be observed in Middle America, it is the cultural stamp of Spain that greatly preponderates. Hers was the attitude of the aristocratic exploiter. The symbolism of the cross and the sword was paramount; the cultural implant was

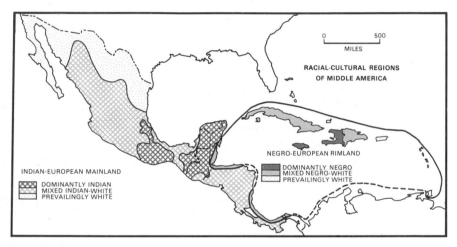

Fig. 3.3. Mainland-rimland subdivisions of Middle America together with racial characteristics. Basic concept from West and Augelli, *Middle America*, Prentice-Hall, 1966, with modifications based on James and other sources.

harshly medieval and feudalistic in tone. England, France, Holland, and Denmark left their stamp on far more restricted territories, located mainly in the West Indies, and to a lesser degree along the Caribbean coast of Central America. Although north European immigrants were relatively few in number, their development of plantation agriculture in the Antilles created a huge demand for labor that could not be met from the depleted Indian pool and so led to a large importation of Negro slaves from Africa. There was a similar influx of blacks to the lowlands along the east coast of Central America.

For diverse Middle America, composed of countless culturally differentiated areas, West and Augelli have proposed a simple but useful culture-area classification (Fig. 3.3). Based on the racial composition of the population, two primary divisions are recognized, a Euro-African Caribbean

Rimland and a Euro-Indian Mainland. The Rimland includes two sectors, the West Indies and the Caribbean coast of Central America. The dominant racial strain of the Rimland is Negro or part Negro. Still, in Cuba, Puerto Rico, and portions of the Caribbean coast of Central America, Negroes represent only a significant minority. On the Mainland, Indian or part Indian (mestizo) blood predominates. Admittedly, the Rimland-Mainland differentiation on the basis of race is genuinely significant only because it represents much more meaningful contrasts stemming from differences in human habitat, inherited cultural patterns, and methods of land use. (See Table 3.1).

TABLE 3.1   Generalized Culture Areas of Middle America

I. The Euro-African (Caribbean) Rimland
   A. Central American Sector
   B. West Indian Sector
      1. Hispanic Zone (Dominican Republic, Cuba, and Puerto Rico)
      2. North European Zone (The Netherlands Antilles, British West Indies, and French Culture Complex)
II. The Euro-Indian Mainland
   A. Mesoamerican Sectors (*marked* Indian influence)
      1. Southern Plateau of Mexico and Yucatan
      2. Guatemala and Chiapas, western Honduras, and western Nicaragua
   B. Mestizo Sector, (*moderate* Indian influence) (Honduras, El Salvador, Nicaragua, Panama, and Central Mexico)
   C. European Sectors (*limited* Indian influence) (Costa Rica, and northern Mexico)

SOURCE: West and Augelli, *Middle America, Its Lands and Peoples*, p. 11. Simplified.

Ninety million people are estimated to live in Middle America in 1970. Probably 49–50 million of these, or 55–56 percent, are in the single political unit of Mexico. Cuba, with 8+ million (9–10 percent), ranks second. The prime spatial groupings of Middle America's inhabitants, which, taken together produce the main features of the region's gross settlement pattern, are as follows:

   1. By far the largest grouping is that of central Mexico, which supports upwards of 25 million people, or over one quarter of all Middle Americans (Fig. 3.1).

   2. A second major grouping is in the highlands and on the western slopes of Central America, where the numbers approach 14 or 15 million.

   3. A third prime concentration, with over 30 million people, is in the Greater Antilles; it is composed of the four main-island clusters.

The first two of the above groupings are overwhelmingly mestizo and Indian. The third is more largely Negro or part Negro. The regions of high rural density of population lie mainly within the three prime groupings. In the very numerous Lesser Antilles, high population densities usually coincide with their restricted coastal lowlands.

Immigration into Middle America from other parts of the world has been negligible for some time now, although it took place on a large scale in earlier periods and continued to do so even as late as the early decades of this century. Of far greater magnitude at present is the out-migration of Middle Americans to foreign parts. Important among these streams of emigration are those from the British West Indies to the United Kingdom; from Puerto Rico, the Virgin Islands, and, recently, Cuba, to the United States; and, on a smaller scale, from Martinique and Guade-loupe to France. Such large outmigration has served to slow somewhat the dangerous rise in population pressure within parts of the Antilles.

Of some importance have been the intraregional movements of people, more especially those of the West Indies. Thus Cuba has attracted a considerable number of Haitians, while many of the islands have contrib-uted laborers to Trinidad and to the Dutch Islands of Aruba and Curaçao. Within Central America there has been an outflow of migrants from crowded El Salvador to newly opened lands in Honduras, and some transfer of Panamanians to adjacent parts of Costa Rica.

MEXICO

Preconquest Period. As of about 1492, on the eve of the Spanish conquest, perhaps about two thirds of the New World's population was concentrated in two regions of advanced culture, one in the area embrac-ing the southern half of Mexico and northern Central America, known as Mesoamerica, and the other in Andean Peru and Bolivia.[4] Together these two populous regions comprised only about 6.2 percent of the hemisphere's land surface. Both of these New World civilizations oc-cupied large territories in which, while the overall population density was light to moderate, there were local areas that were genuinely crowded.

Within Mesoamerica, in the early 16th century, central Mexico alone, according to recent optimistic estimates, may have supported as many as 25 million inhabitants; a more conservative conjecture suggests a figure of not less than 12–15 million. In an area of about 1.25 million sq km,

[4] William T. Sanders and Barbara J. Price, *Mesoamerica: The Evolution of a Civilization*. Random House, New York, 1968, p. 75.

this latter figure would have resulted in an overall density of about 10–12 persons per sq km. At the time of the Spanish invasion, Mesoamerica was occupied by a large number of linguistic and ethnic groups, which in spite of their diversity participated in a single great tradition and unquestionably represented a distinct culture area. The region included a variety of physical environments, the two main ones being the sub-humid and dry highlands and the tropical lowlands. Two distinct agricultural systems correlated with these basic physical divisions. A rudimentary slash-and-burn cultivation, and consequently a relatively low and fairly uniform population density of 5 to 30 persons per sq km, prevailed on the wet lowlands. There large states and true cities did not develop. In the drier highlands, while slash-and-burn agriculture was far from absent, the widely spread intensive techniques, in parts involving irrigation and terracing, supported higher average population densities. There social stratification was more complex, true cities evolved, and craft development of a high level was present. Because of the microgeographic complexity of the highland terrain, which consists of small sediment-filled basins and valleys separated by mountain ranges, the population pattern consisted of numerous small isolated clusters of high density separated by relatively empty lands.

The core region of highland Mesoamerica was an area of some 20,000 sq km located in the central plateau of Mexico. There the Indian civilization reached its maximum development, agriculture was most advanced, and settlement was densest. The core region's Teotihuacán Valley, for example, may have had a total population of about 100,000 and a density of approximately 200 persons per sq km (500 per sq mi.) at the time of the conquest.[5] In both the Virú and Teotihuacán valleys urbanization was present, a feature that was characteristic of the drier Mesoamerican highlands and everywhere correlated with high population densities. On the northwestern margins of Mesoamerica, in the Sierra Madre Occidental and on the Pacific coastal plain, the farming methods were more primitive and population was less dense. But still more sparsely settled was the whole northeastern and northcentral parts of Mexico and the peninsula of Baja California, where a primitive hunting and gathering economy prevailed.

The impact of the Spanish conquest on Mesoamerica involved not only a drastic reduction in the number of Indians and the mixing of Indian and white bloods to produce the dominant mestizo element but also changes in the spatial distribution of the people. As a rule, the hot tropical lowlands, where mortality due to disease was greater than in the cooler highlands, were almost depopulated. The highlands thereby acquired a

[5] Sanders and Price, *Mesoamerica*, p. 77.

relatively greater significance. An estimated 250,000 Negro slaves were imported during the colonial period, but the number in Mexico at any one time was small. Most blacks were concentrated on the tropical lowlands, where the losses in Indian population had been most severe.

Modern Mexico. The racial composition of modern Mexico is estimated to be about 60 percent mestizo, 30 percent Indian, and 10 percent white. The Indian blood has been largely absorbed into the mestizo majority. Only about 2.5 million, or 7 percent of the population, speak Indian languages. But more significant than race or language is the large number

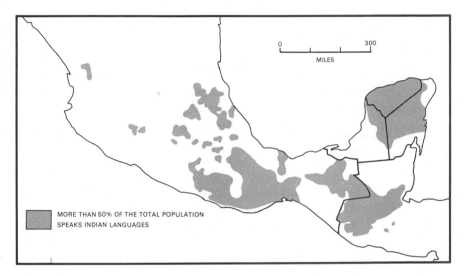

Fig. 3.4. Areas of strong Indian speech concentration. There are three extensive regions in Mexico and adjacent parts of Central America where over half the population speaks Indian languages. One of these is in the rugged Mexican states of Oaxaca, Guerrero, and Puebla in the extreme southeast; another is in the northern part of Mexico's Yucatan peninsula, and a third is mainly in central Guatemala and adjacent parts of Chiapas in Mexico. Modified from West and Augelli, *Middle America*, Prentice-Hall, 1966.

of Indian customs—relating to food crops, food habits, native dwellings, and farming practices—still retained in Mexican life. While Indians continue to dominate the population only in certain isolated sections of the country, Indian customs and habits pervade almost all aspects and parts of rural Mexico. As a rule, the Indian population is at the bottom of the economic scale and has the lowest living standards. Most of the pureblood Mexican Indians occupy isolated highland areas where the agricultural potential is low and modern transportation facilities meager or lacking (Fig. 3.4). The white minority in Mexico lives mainly in the cities, where it forms the core of the professional group.

When independence was attained in 1821, Mexico's population may have numbered not more than 6.5 million, or far fewer than the population three centuries earlier at the time of the Spanish conquest. Until 1880 the annual rate of population increase was only about 0.5 percent per year. Subsequently the rate quickened to about 1 percent during the more stable Diaz regime of the late 1800's and early 1900's, but there was an actual decline in population during the turbulent decade

TABLE 3.2   Demographic Indicators of the Mexican
Population, 1930–1969

Year	Population (Thousands)	Birth Rate (Per 1000)	Death Rate (Per 1000)	Rate of Natural Increase (Per 1000)	Annual Rate of Growth (Percent)	Life Expectancy at Birth (Years)
1930	16,553	43.8	26.6	17.2		33.26
1940	19,653	44.3	23.2	21.1	1.73	38.40
1950	25,791	45.5	16.2	29.3	2.75	49.71
1960	34,923	46.0	11.5	34.5	3.08	58.96
1969[a]	49,000	43.0	9.0		3.4	58–64[b]

SOURCE: Raúl Benítez Zenteno and Gustavo Cabera Acevedo, The Future Population of Mexico: Total, Urban and Rural. World Population Conference, Belgrade, 1965, Vol. II, United Nations, New York, 1967, p. 54. 1969 estimates from, World Population Reference Sheet, 1969, Population Reference Bureau, Washington, D.C., 1969.
[a] Estimates.
[b] 1968.

1910–1920, which witnessed the Agrarian Revolution. Since 1920 the average annual rate of population increase has been relentlessly upward—about 0.7 percent in the 1920's, nearly 2.0 percent in the 1930's, approximately 2.5 percent in the 1940's, and 3.2 percent in the 1950's. Currently the rate is an estimated 3.4 percent annually, which is one of the highest national growth rates anywhere on the earth. At this rate, population will double in 21 years, and Mexico's population will approach 98 million by 1990. The recent spectacular acceleration in population growth rates has not been caused by a significant increase in fertility; rather, it is related to a drastic reduction in mortality through the introduction of public sanitation, preventive medicine, and the widespread use of DDT sprays to eradicate yellow fever and malaria (see Table 3.2).[6]

[6] "Mexico: The Problem of People," Population Bulletin, Vol. 20, November 1964, pp. 174–178.

The current birth rate is estimated to be about 43 to 46 per 1000 and the death rate between 9 and 11.5. While mortality is as low as or lower than those in the United States and in many European countries, this is only because 46 percent of Mexico's population is under 15 years of age. In such a young population death rates are expectably low.

Since it is not anticipated that the birth rate will decline much within the near future, while death rates may even fall a little more, the outlook is good for a continued burgeoning of population numbers over the next decade or two. The question posed, then, is whether the improving Mexican economy can go on expanding at a more rapid rate than will the population. During most years in the last two decades, economic expansion has outdistanced population growth. The consequence has been a significant gain in both per capita income and per capita gross national product. But ominously, both are still very low, and both also appear to be increasing at a decreasing rate.[7] This could spell trouble unless population increase is slowed. Significantly, the proportion of the population that was economically inactive rose sharply over the period 1930–1960.

Regional variations in Mexico's vital rates are significant. Thus, in crude birth rates, where the national average was 44.2 in 1965, the figures ranged among the individual states from a high of 54.2 in Aguascalientes to lows of 37.4 in Quintana Roo Territory in Yucatan and 38.0 in the Federal District, or a differential of 16–17 points. Seven states had unusually high birth rates of over 48 and so exceeded by 4 points or more the country average of about 44. These high-birth-rate states are of a variety of sizes, are widely scattered in location, and are to be found in greatly contrasting environments, so that generalizations concerning causation are difficult to make. Relatively low birth rates of more than 4 points below the national average were characteristic of only the 2 states mentioned above. Below-average birth rates in the Federal District reflect its strong degree of urbanization, associated with the metropolitan area of the primate and capital city.

Provincial crude death rates in 1965 varied from a high of 14.1 in the strongly Indian state of Oaxaca to a low of 4.8 in Quintana Roo territory in Yucatan. Of the states with death rates that were more than two points higher or lower than the national average of 9.5, 6 had mortality rates below 7.5 while 5 were above 11.5. Five of the states with low death rates are in the drier north, where the American influence is relatively stronger. Distinctly above-average death rates were charac-

[7] Paul Cross Morrison, "Population Changes in Mexico, 1950-1960," *Papers of the Michigan Academy of Science, Arts and Letters*, Vol. 49, 1964, pp. 352-354. See also "Mexico: The Problem of People," pp. 180-185.

teristic of three states in the overcrowded and impoverished southeastern rural parts of the central plateau and therefore not far from the Federal District. In addition, there were the two mountainous Indian states of Oaxaca and Chiapas.

Natural increase for the whole country in 1965 averaged 34.8 per 1000, while the extremes for the individual states were 28.3 and 46.0. Only two political subdivisions, Oaxaca and the Federal District, had low rates that were more than five points below the national average. Seven widely scattered states, mainly in the drier north, had high rates that were more than five points above the national average.

The national average infant mortality rate was 60.7 per thousand live births (1965), but it rose to above 80 in four states in the overcrowded southern part of the central plateau. It dropped below 50 in Yucatan, the two Gulf states of Vera Cruz and Tabasco, and in 6 dry northern and western states.

To say that Mexico's average population density in 1969 was about 64 per square mile is not very revealing because of the unequal spatial distribution of the people. More significant is the fact that since only a meager 10 percent of Mexico's territory is crop land, the country has a density of about 640 per sq mi of arable land. But since in any given year only 5 percent of the land area is actually cultivated and only a trifle more than 3 percent yields harvested crops, the realistic nutritional density is far higher than 640. Since slightly less than 50 percent of Mexico's people are rural, rural density per square mile of cultivated land is about 315, a relatively high figure.

Nearly one half of Mexico's people are concentrated in the central parts of the country, a situation that has prevailed for centuries (Fig. 3.5). Most of them are crowded together within the more humid southern half of the Mexican plateau, or what is designated as the Mesa Central. Its surface is characterized by low mountains separated by detritus-filled basins, with the latter comprising about two fifths of the region's total area. The basins are the favored agricultural areas, and in them the population is strongly concentrated, so that their rural densities commonly exceed 500, or even 1000, per sq mi. The present crowding of people onto the basin rimlands of the Mesa Central repeats an ancient pattern, one that was already conspicuous in the colonial and even preconquest eras. Overcrowding and rural poverty in this traditional core region of the country pose a grievous national problem.

By comparison with the teeming Mesa Central, the average population density of the south and east is only moderate. Settlement thickens in some of the mountain valleys. An overall sparse population is characteristic of dry northern and northwestern Mexico. It is especially thin in arid Baja California. The main exceptions within the dry north are certain irrigated spots, as well as a few centers of recent industrialization and mineral exploitation. The Yucatan peninsula, with its karst terrain and thin droughty soils, is also a region of sparse settlement, except in its northern parts. There impoverished Maya Indian farmers comprise nearly half the population.

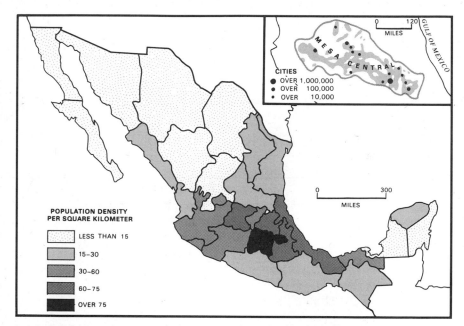

Fig. 3.5. Mexico: density of population by states, 1970 census. Density is highest in central Mexico, especially in the Mesa Central (inset map). There high densities, shown in gray, exhibit a fragmented pattern, with crowding greatest in topographic basins and on their surrounding slopes. Inset map modified from James, and West and Augelli.

Population Movements. The increasing mobility of Mexico's population has taken the form of three kinds of migrant movements of rural people. The main source of all three migrant streams is the overcrowded Mesa Central; yet the losses due to out-migration have not significantly decreased the population pressure in this core area of the country.

One significant group of out-migration streams has as its destination the northern irrigated districts, the tropical lowlands, and the newly exploited oil, gas, and coal fields. A second stream has been attracted to the United States. At present almost a million Mexicans reside permanently on the American side of the border. In addition there has been until very recently a seasonal labor migration to the United States amounting to 200,000 to 450,000 persons. Since 1960 a marked decline in the number of these migrant seasonal farm hands has occurred.[8]

But as in other parts of Latin America, by all odds the greatest migrant movement is that from the population-saturated rural areas to the cities.[9] The markedly increased mobility of the Mexican population dates from the national revolution of 1910. While direct quantitative data on cityward migration in Mexico are lacking, something of its magnitude can be appreciated by noting the differential rates of urban and rural growth over recent decades. As far back as 1930–1940, urban population increased at the annual rate of 2.22 percent and rural population at only 1.49 percent. But in the two subsequent decades the differentials were much

TABLE 3.3   Average Annual Rates of Population Growth
(Percentages), 1930–1960

Period	Total Population	Urban Population	Rural Population
1930–1940	1.73	2.22	1.49
1940–1950	2.73	4.77	1.50
1950–1960	3.08	4.89	1.51

SOURCE: Zenteno and Acevedo, "The Future Population of Mexico," p. 55.

greater, with urban percentage increases more than three times those of rural ones (See Table 3.3). From 1950 to 1960 the urban population increased 61 percent and the rural population only 16 percent. Or, stated another way, during this same decade, 73.6 percent of the total increase in Mexico's population in 1960 was in the cities.[10] Since immigration from outside the country is inconsequential, and because birth rates in the cities, at least in those having a population of 50,000 and over, are lower than those in the rural countryside,[11] the differential rates in urban

[8] Nathan L. Whetten, "Population Trends in Mexico," *Population Bulletin*, November 1963, pp. 181–182.
[9] Little is known in detail from actual studies about the causes or processes of migrations in Latin America, including Mexico. On this topic see Harley L. Browning, "Recent Trends in Latin American Urbanization," *Annals of the American Academy of Political and Social Science*, Vol. 316, March, 1958, pp. 118–119.
[10] Morrison, "Population Changes in Mexico, 1950–1960," p. 360.
[11] Whetten, "Population Trends in Mexico," p. 183.

and rural growth can only point to a high rate of net immigration from farm to city. The process appears to be irreversible and will continue into the foreseeable future.[12]

Within Mexico there are significant regional differences in the degree of urbanization (1960), and also in the relative gain in urban population from 1950–1960. For statistical purposes the country is commonly divided into five regions, each embracing several states. The highest degree of urbanization (58 percent) in 1960 was in the Central region, the heart of Mexico, which contained about one half of its population (Table 3.4). The dry, sparsely populated North Pacific region and the semiarid

TABLE 3.4 Degree of Urbanization in Mexico, 1960, and Rate of Urban Increase, 1950–1960, by Regions

Regions	Percent Urban, 1960	Percent Urban of Population Increase, 1950–1960	Relative Increase of Urban Population, 1950–1960
North Pacific	52.5	78.4	103.3
North	51.3	79.1	61.0
Central	58.4	81.1	60.6
Gulf Coast	41.9	58.6	51.6
South Pacific	26.2	38.1	46.0
Total Mexico	50.7	73.6	61.2

SOURCE: Morrison, "Population Changes in Mexico, 1950–1960," p. 360.

North also had slightly more than half their populations in urban places. The mountainous South Pacific subdivision was least urbanized, with only a little more than a quarter of its people classed as urban.

Of the total population increase 1950–1960, the percent that was urban was high, and above the country average, in the Central, North, and North Pacific regions. It was lowest in the South Pacific (Table 3.4).

The relative 1950–1960 increase in urban population (the 1950–1960 gain as a percent of the 1950 number) was unusually high in the North Pacific region. It was low in both the South Pacific and Gulf Coast regions (Table 3.4).

Many stubborn problems have arisen as a consequence of the rapid acceleration of urban concentration in Mexico, because a mere massing

[12] Luis Leñero Otero, "The Mexican Urbanization Process and Its Implications," *Demography*, Vol. 5, No. 2, Special Issue, 1968, pp. 866–867.

of population in an urban area is not equivalent to creating an organic urban structure.[13] Such a condition of incomplete urbanization greatly affects the millions of people who, although physically within an urban cluster, are functionally not integrated into it. It also presents difficult problems for the city organization, involving such sectors as employment, education, public services, and social organization.

While cities of all size classes have felt the effects of the nation's vast rural-urban migration, it is probably the larger ones, and especially the capital city, that have been affected most. In 1900 the Federal District, which embraces most of the capital's metropolitan area, contained only 4 percent of the country's population. In 1960 its almost 5 million people accounted for nearly 15 percent. The next largest Mexican cities ranked in order of size are Guadalajara, 734,000 people; Monterrey, 600,000; Ciudad Juárez, 294,000; and Puebla, 285,000. The size gap between these and the capital is striking but scarcely unusual, because as indicated in an earlier section, the disproportionately large concentration of a country's inhabitants in one primate political and economic center is a characteristic feature of Latin America's urban structure.

The ever-increasing proportion of Mexico's total population that is urban is revealed in Table 3.5. From it we gather that by 1960, for the first time, the urban population was equal to or even greater than half the total. A significant threshold appears to have been passed, with all that this seems to signify in terms of increasing emphasis on secondary and tertiary industry. It must be cautioned, however, that the Mexican census defines urban as including places with 2500 or more inhabitants. Yet for Mexico this is a somewhat unrealistic definition, since so many of the farm villages have populations of well over 2500. Perhaps a more suitable rural-urban boundary would be 5000 or even 10,000. Probably only about 35 percent of Mexico's inhabitants live in cities and towns with over 5000 population.[14]

Other Population Characteristics.   Mexico is not only the largest and most populous of the Middle American countries; it is also one of the most progressive and advanced. Still, in a number of population characteristics usually thought of as indicators of progress, Mexico does not make an appreciably better showing than the regional average. To a considerable degree this can be accounted for by the country's unusually large Indian population, amounting to nearly 30 percent of the total. It is the primitive and backward Indian group that pulls down the national averages of several population characteristics. Employing two indirect

[13] Otero, "The Mexican Urbanization Process and Its Implications," p. 866.
[14] West and Augelli, *Middle America*, p. 313.

indicators of general health conditions in a population, it is found that Mexico's infant mortality rate of 61–63 per 1000 is only slightly lower than the estimated Latin American average (66), while its life expectancy at birth (58–64 years) just about duplicates the estimated regional average of 60. With approximately 30–35 percent of its population aged 15 years and over illiterate, Mexico corresponds with the Latin American conjec-

TABLE 3.5 Proportion of Mexico's Population Classed as Urban and Rural, 1930 to 1960, and Projections to 1980.[a]

Year	Urban (Percent)	Rural (Percent)
1930	33	67
1940	35	65
1950	42.6	57.4
1960	50.7	49.3
1970	59.7	40.3
1980	66.6	33.4

SOURCE: Todd Fisher and Helen A. Barth, "Mexico: the Problem of People," *Population Bulletin*, Vol. 20, November, 1964; John M. Ball, "The Migration of People in Mexico," *Professional Geographer*, Vol. 19, January, 1967, p. 5; and Luis L. Otero, "The Mexican Urbanization Process and its Implications," p. 867.

[a] Urban defined in terms of localities with 2500 or more inhabitants.

tured average of 34. Mexico's unusually high birth rate is reflected in the youthfulness of its age structure, in which 46 percent of the population is under 15 years of age (1970) compared with an estimated 42 for the whole of Latin America. In general economic well-being, however, as measured by per capita gross national income, Mexico's $470 stands considerably above the estimated Latin American average of $385. Of the tropical Latin American countries of significant size, only Panama, Puerto Rico, and oil-rich Venezuela have higher per capita incomes.

CENTRAL AMERICA

This isthmian region, situated between Mexico and South America and consisting of six small states plus the two foreign jurisdictions of British Honduras and the Panama Canal Zone, had an estimated total population somewhat in excess of 16 million in 1970. Its average population density, representing a composite of wide regional variations, exceeds 70 per sq mi or 181 per sq km. A salient feature of the gross pattern of distribution is that the region's 16 million people are strongly skewed toward the drier Pacific side of the isthmus, where they occupy both cooler highland and hotter lowland locations; with minor exceptions, the hot, wet and forested Caribbean lowlands and slopes are thinly settled (Fig. 3.6). Indeed, this entire eastern versant of Central America falls largely outside the realm of Euro-Indian Mainland Hispanic culture and belongs instead to the Euro-African Caribbean Rimland.

But even within the better-populated Pacific zone, densities vary greatly. In many mountainous parts, densities as low as 5 to 15 per sq mi prevail. By contrast, the overall density for tiny El Salvador is about 400 per sq mi, while rural densities of over 1000 per sq mi are reached in the Meseta Central of Costa Rica.

A refinement of the above-described gross pattern of settlement distribution derives from the political fragmentation of the isthmus, which prevailed even in colonial times. During Spanish rule all six of the present Central American countries were provinces within more extensive political jurisdictions. Within each of the six there developed a single core of population grouped around a provincial capital. Examples of such national clusters are the Meseta Central of Costa Rica, the silver-mining area of Honduras, and the lake lowlands on the Pacific side of Nicaragua.[15] Each of the provinces and its population cluster were relatively isolated from the others and so tended to develop local loyalties and characteristics. With the breakup of the Spanish Empire in Latin America, the provinces became separate countries, and the earlier provincial nuclei of settlement persisted as the populous cores of the new states. Even today, most Central American states are dominated by a single population cluster whose nucleus is the capital city and metropolis. In one or more states secondary clusters of later origin have emerged.

Birth rates are consistently high, averaging about 43–45 per 1000. Overall death rates have declined dramatically in recent decades, but a considerable range still persists—from a low of 6–7 in Costa Rica to a high

---

[15] West and Augelli, *Middle America*, pp. 378–379.

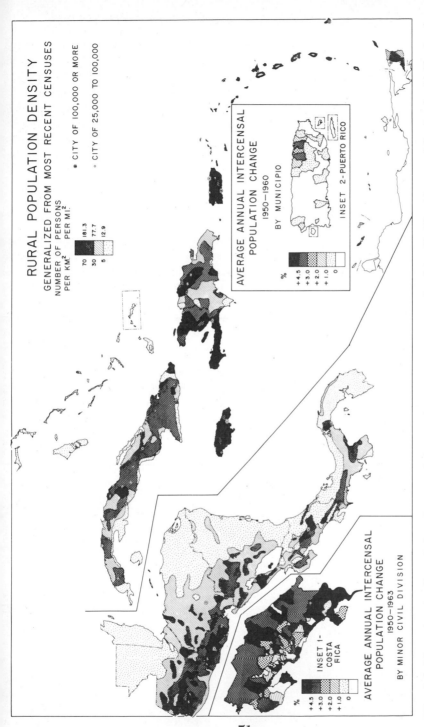

RURAL POPULATION DENSITY

GENERALIZED FROM MOST RECENT CENSUSES

NUMBER OF PERSONS
PER KM²   PER MI.²

70	181.3
30	77.7
5	12.9

● CITY OF 100,000 OR MORE

○ CITY OF 25,000 TO 100,000

AVERAGE ANNUAL INTERCENSAL
POPULATION CHANGE

1950—1960

BY MUNICIPIO

%
+4.5
+3.0
+2.0
+1.0
0

INSET 2- PUERTO RICO

AVERAGE ANNUAL INTERCENSAL
POPULATION CHANGE

1950—1963

BY MINOR CIVIL DIVISION

INSET 1-
COSTA
RICA

%
+4.5
+3.0
+2.0
+1.0
0

71

Fig. 3.6. Note that in Central America, population tends to concentrate on the drier Pacific side, especially in the highlands; the wetter, densely forested Caribbean lowlands are usually sparsely settled. In the West Indies, Cuba shows a conspicuously lower rural population density than most of the other islands. Courtesy of Wilbur Zelinsky and of the publication, *Mineral Industries*, Pennsylvania State University.

of 17 in Honduras. Such vital rates can only result in abnormally high rates of natural increase, ranging from a high of about 3.8 per 1000 in Costa Rica to a low of 2.8 in Guatemala. At the present average rate of growth, population in Central America will double in about 22 years. A consequence of such a rapid multiplication of people in a region where the original and long-standing population clusters are already over-crowded is a large-scale trek from the burdened countryside to the cities and a modest colonization of relatively empty lands on both the eastern and western versants of the isthmus.

Immigration into Central America from other parts of the world has been inconsequential for some time. In contrast, out-migration is of larger magnitude, particularly that to the United States. In 1950 over 22,000 persons born in Central America were living in the United States; in 1960 this figure had risen to over 46,000. The principal intra-Central American population shifts between countries have been the out-migration from crowded El Salvador to newly developed lands in Honduras and the transfer of some Panamanians to Costa Rica.

By all odds the population movement of greatest magnitude is that from rural parts to city and from smaller urban units to larger ones. During the intercensal interval (1950–1963), the proportion of Central America's total population living in urban places rose from 30.3 to 32.9 percent.[16] Growth rates were markedly higher in the larger cities of over 250,000 than in those of the 25,000–50,000 class. Smaller places barely matched the rural increase, while the smallest ones, in the 1000–5000 class, grew at a rate even less than that of the open country. Most of the urban growth took place within the older settlement areas.

Despite the rural-urban migration and the emigration abroad, rural numbers at home continue to soar. Overcrowding has reached such an intensity in several of the old, densely settled areas that in them population gains are modest and in a few, absolute losses have even been sustained. Yet except for a few congested areas such as Costa Rica's Meseta Central and western Guatemala's upland basins, no significant intensification and improvement in agricultural land use are apparent.

Pioneer colonization of new lands in Central America has accelerated somewhat since World War II. It began earlier, and has proceeded farther, in Costa Rica than elsewhere. There a migration from the congested highlands to the more desirable parts of the Caribbean and Pacific low-

[16] Wilbur Zelinsky, "Population Growth in Central America and the West Indies," *Mineral Industries*, Vol. 35, March, 1966, p. 5.

lands, which has been in progress for some time,[17] may even exceed in magnitude the population transfer from countryside to cities. Similar movements have occurred in Honduras, Guatemala, and Nicaragua. There is still an abundance of unused land in Central America; however, much of it is of questionable value for tillage. But the obstacles to new pioneer settlement, and with it an associated redistribution of population, are serious. Not the least of these is the resistance that conservative farm people show to moving into unfamiliar environments.

Racially, Central America is exceedingly complex. In Guatemala more than half the population is pure Indian. Elsewhere the aboriginal remnants are relatively fewer. Costa Rica claims a strong predominance of Caucasian blood. In other parts the population is largely a mixture of Indian and white strains. The relatively small Negroid element is located mainly on the Caribbean coastal plain, where most blacks are descendants of English-speaking West Indians who came to work on the banana plantations or on the Panama Canal.

Other population characteristics can be mentioned only briefly. The fact that general health conditions have been improved is indicated by the decline in the death rate, which at present is as low as 7 or 8 per 1000 in two countries, but averages about 15 in the 4 others. Life expectancy at birth has risen sharply and the average at present is probably 55–60+. This is to be compared with about 71 in the United States and 74 in Sweden. Infant mortality, another health indicator, is still distressingly high, varying from a low of 40–60 per 1000 live births in Panama to a high of 91–92 in Guatemala. The average is slightly over 70. By comparison, the figure for Anglo-America is only 23 and for Europe 31.

Considering the prevailingly high birth rates, an age structure that emphasizes the preponderance of children and youths is to be expected. For the whole isthmus, 45 percent of the population is under 15 years of age. For the United States the comparable figure is 30 and for Europe 24. The extraordinarily large percentage of young dependents is a serious drag on the Central American economy.

Expectably, the average per capita income in Central America is small—probably as low as $350. The range is significant, however; from a low of $220–240 in Honduras to about $550 in Panama. Educational

[17] Gerhard Sander, "Agrarkolonisation in Costa Rica," *Schriften des Geographischen Instituts der Universität Kiel,* Vol. XIX, Heft 3, Kiel, 1961. See also Minkel, Clarence W., "Programs of Agricultural Colonization" and Settlement in Central America, *Revista Geográfica,* No. 66. June 1967, pp. 19–50, and West and Augelli, *Middle America,* pp. 378–380.

attainments are relatively low and the percentage of illiterates in the population high, probably around 40–50. Still, the percent classed as illiterate varies greatly among the 6 individual countries—from lows of 10–20 percent in predominantly Caucasian Costa Rica and 20–30 in Panama to a high of 60–70 in strongly Indian Guatemala.

Guatemala has some distinction among the six Central American countries: it is the most populous (population estimated at 5.1 million in 1970), has the largest proportion of Indians (55 percent), and boasts the largest city. Probably it also has the highest infant mortality rate, a feature that signifies a low state of health and general physical well-being. This fact is reflected in the relatively high death rate of about 16 per 1000.

Guatemala's overall population density of nearly 120 per sq mi is exceeded only by that of El Salvador. As in pre-Columbian times, a large majority of the people live in the southern highlands, which form the heartland of the country. The wetter northern highlands, containing fewer basins, have far lower average densities. Nearly one third of the country's total population is concentrated in the basins and on the lower mountain slopes of the volcanic highlands that form the western part of the general southern highlands, a section appropriately called *Los Altos*. There the intensive cultivation of steep mountain slopes, often carried up to a great height by means of terracing, testifies to the superabundance of tillers and the scarcity of tillable land. Lowlands in general are less well peopled than the highlands, but both lowlands and slopes on the wetter Caribbean side are more sparsely occupied than those facing the Pacific. It is the introduction of coffee as a cash crop on the higher Pacific slopes that stimulated an increase in population there. The average lowest population density (about one person per sq mi) is to be found in the extensive northern forested lowland of the Petén that makes up one third of the national area, a region that more than a millennium back was the domain of the highly cultured Maya Indians.

Guatemalans are classified into two main ethnic groups: Indian and *Ladino* (chiefly persons of mixed Indian and Caucasian blood). Pureblood Indians make up about 54–55 percent of the total population; it is they who have not adopted the characteristic features of Western culture. By contrast, Ladinos speak only Spanish and their customs are of Spanish origin. While they are usually either mixed-bloods or Caucasians, even a pureblooded Indian would become a Ladino if he adopted European ways of living.

The spatial distribution of Indians and Ladinos within Guatemala is complex and highly variable. Indians strongly predominate in two of the country's regions, the West (78 percent) and the North Central (84 percent), which are the most rugged parts. There the greater inaccessibility may have helped the Indians to resist acculturation, but cultural and historical factors are also involved.[18] Ladino concentration is greatest in the East (70.5 percent), Central (80.4 percent), and North (77.9 percent) regions. The concentration of the Ladino population in the eastern part of the country reflects the early Spanish settlement in the lower, drier parts that provided natural forage for livestock. Some 15 percent of the country's total population lives in plantation communities; nearly half of these people are concentrated along the Pacific Piedmont, where coffee, sugar cane, and bananas are important commercial crops.

A rural population greatly predominates; only 15–25 percent dwell in urban places. Guatemala City, with a population of over 400,000 in 1963, is the largest urban community in all Central America. This figure is several times larger than that of the combined populations of all the lesser cities, a feature typical of Latin American countries in general.

El Salvador has the distinction of being the smallest and most densely populated state in all of mainland Latin America. Its estimated 3.4 million people (1970) provides an overall national density of about 400 per sq mi. While population distribution is widespread, there are still heavy concentrations in the central upland basins and on nearby volcanic slopes where soils are most fertile. The Pacific coastal plains, with their large cattle haciendas, are less densely settled. Most sparsely occupied are the northern rugged volcanic lands along the Honduras border.

Three quarters to four fifths of El Salvador's people are Ladinos of mixed Indian and white ancestry. Perhaps nearly 20 percent are of pure Indian blood, but less than 3 percent follow the aboriginal way of life.[19]

A large-scale rural in-migration has more than doubled the population of San Salvador, the national capital and primate city, between 1940 (105,000) and 1960 (230,000). Sixty to 65 percent of the total population are farmers.

Honduras has the dubious distinction of being the most backward, culturally and economically, of the six Central American countries. Its estimated birth rate of 49 per 1000 and death rate of 16, (current growth rate 3.4), are probably the highest for any of the six states. Hondurans number scarcely 2.5 million, so the overall density of population is only about 60 per sq mi, or one seventh to one sixth that of crowded El Salvador. More than two thirds live in the country's western and southern highlands, which are the traditional colonial heartland and contain the capital city. Some one quarter inhabit the wet, forested Caribbean

[18] Nathan L. Whetten, *Guatemala: the Land and the People*, Yale University Press, Caribbean Series, 4, New Haven 1961, pp. 48–49; see also map, p. 52.
[19] West and Augelli, *Middle America*, p. 409.

lowlands where commercial banana development during the present century has stimulated rapid settlement.

Racially only about 7 percent are estimated to be pure Indian; 2 percent may be Negro and perhaps 1 percent white. The remaining 90 percent are mixed bloods of Indian and white parentage. Culturally the population is Ladino. The small Negro element is confined mainly to the Caribbean lowlands. That the aboriginal group is modest in numbers reflects the fact that all but the western part of the present Honduras territory lay outside the cultural hearth of classical aboriginal Middle America.

Nicaragua's two million people, unlike those of most of Central America, are mainly lowlanders. Thus, three fourths of the population live on the less-rainy Pacific side within the Nicaraguan Rift Valley, which forms an important natural passageway across the isthmus. Within this natural region the fertile volcanic soils have been one factor attracting rural settlement, with the result that population density there averages 150–200 per sq mi. In this same depression, too, are located most of the cities, including the capital, Managua, with its 230,000 inhabitants, or about 15 percent of the national population in 1960. A second and lesser population concentration, developed in response to coffee planting, is located in the northwestern part of the central highlands. There population densities are only one third to one half as great as in the Rift. The relatively empty, rain-drenched Caribbean lowland, where the meager population is strongly concentrated in the river valleys, has an average density of only about 4–5 persons per sq mi. Most of it remains outside the effective national territory.

Three quarters of the population is mestizo. The Negro element, almost exclusively confined to the Caribbean lowlands, comprises about 10 percent of the total inhabitants. A similar percentage is classed as white. Indians are relatively few.

Costa Rica is unique among tropical American countries because 80 percent or more of its population asserts that it is of pure Spanish ancestry. Since almost all of the present Costa Rica territory lies outside Mesoamerica, the preconquest aboriginal cultural hearth of ancient Mexico and western Central America, it lacks the strong Indian heritage so typical of Guatemala and El Salvador. The relatively small Indian population that originally inhabited the Costa Rican highlands was culturally allied to South America rather than to Mesoamerica. A drastic reduction in Indian numbers during and following the conquest left the Spanish invaders with such a meager labor force that instead of developing their characteristic estate-type of agriculture, they turned to small-scale subsistence farming. And although large farms and commercial agriculture have increased during the present century, small farms and a peasant societal structure still prevail. A great majority of the population (65 percent) continues to be rural, and in all social strata a strong urge for land ownership exists. Mestizos are estimated to make up about 17 percent of the nation's population, Negroes 2 percent and Indians less than 1 percent.

Between 55 and 60 percent of the total population of 1.8 million is concentrated in the *Meseta Central*, a high intermont basin about 40 miles long by 15 miles wide within the central highlands (Fig. 3.7).

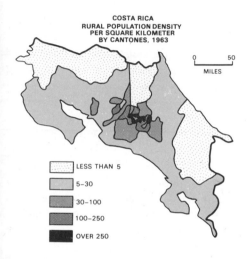

COSTA RICA
RURAL POPULATION DENSITY
PER SQUARE KILOMETER
BY CANTONES, 1963

0   50

MILES

LESS THAN 5
5–30
30–100
100–250
OVER 250

Fig. 3.7. The salient feature of rural population distribution in Costa Rica is the strong concentration of settlement in the central highland, in conjunction with thinly populated marginal regions. After map by Gerhard Sandner, in *Geography and a Crowding World*, Wilbur Zelinsky et al., Eds., Oxford University Press.

This is the core region—economically, politically, and socially—of contemporary Costa Rica, as well as its ancient cultural hearth. In a striking fashion, therefore, Costa Rica exemplifies the single-cluster type of national population distribution. The Meseta Central's San José Basin, containing the national capital with close to 275,000 inhabitants, is one of the most densely populated areas in all Central America. Outside the Meseta Central the remaining minority of the population is distributed very unevenly, with the drier Pacific versant having considerably more inhabitants than the wetter Caribbean side (Figs. 3.6, 3.7). On the generally low-density Caribbean lowlands, by all odds the greatest concentration is along the coast and rivers near Puerto Limón and along the railroads extending inland from that port city toward the Meseta Central. There small-scale farmers, a goodly number of them squatters on abandoned banana plantations, cultivate food crops as well as cacao, rubber, manila hemp, and coconuts. The Pacific lowlands and slopes show a much more continuous settlement pattern; still, there are a number of recognizable population clusters.[20]

Perhaps a third or a little more of the Costa Ricans are classed as urban; one-sixth to one-fifth are concentrated in the capital city. But in no other Central American country is the ratio of the population of the primate capital city to that of the one next in rank as large as in Costa Rica (100:9 in 1963).

In spite of a largely Caucasian population, the birth rate is typically Central American and therefore high (estimated 45 per 1000), but the death rate of 8 is by far the lowest in Central America. The result is a phenomenally high annual national growth rate of 3.8 percent.

In no other country in Central America is population mobility as great as in Costa Rica. The volume of international migration is relatively unimportant; of far greater significance is migration within the country. In 1963 only 66 percent of the population lived within their native districts, and this was typical both of city areas and the peripheral parts of the country.[21] Emigration is mainly characteristic of the central highlands, especially the crowded rural portions of the Meseta Central.

Panama's mixed-bloods, including both mestizo and mulatto, make up some 65 percent of the country's 1.4 million people. While Indians may represent only about 6 percent of the total population, they nevertheless thinly occupy a large area of the country, chiefly the less accessible parts. Perhaps 15 percent may be classed as Negro. While some blacks are to be found in the older banana-plantation zone along the Caribbean side, they are numerous as well in the Canal Zone and in the newer banana-plantation areas along the Pacific side.

About three fifths of Panama's total population and three quarters of its rural people are located along the Pacific versant west of the Panama Canal. This largely farm population is one of mixed-bloods—Indian, white, and Negro. On the Pacific lowland, population density considerably exceeds the country average of about 48 per sq mi. A second concentration of settlement coincides with the transit belt, which includes the Panama Canal Zone and the nearby terminal cities of Colón and Panama City. Here the people are mainly urban, and a number of races and nationalities are represented. Least populous is the Caribbean lowland,

[20] For details concerning the spatial distribution of population in Costa Rica see Robert E. Nunley, "The Distribution of Population in Costa Rica," *Office of Naval Research, Report No. 8*, National Academy of Sciences National Research Council, Publication 743, Washington, D.C., 1960. Note map on back of front cover.

[21] Gerhard Sander, 'Population Pressure upon Resources in Costa Rica,' in *Geography and a Crowding World*, Wilbur Zelinsky et al (eds), Oxford University Press, New York, 1970, pp. 535–555.

where densities of the largely black inhabitants are usually under 10 per sq mi.

The estimated Panama birth rate of 41 per 1000 (1969) is the lowest of any of the Central American countries. But the relatively low death rate of about 8 still assures a high rate of natural increase.

THE WEST INDIES

The Indian cultures that prevailed in the Antilles prior to the Spanish conquest, being greatly inferior to those of Mesoamerica on the mainland, were unable to support a large native population. Densities were consequently low. Estimates of the original total Indian population in the archipelago vary widely, but perhaps one million is a reasonable conjecture, with the main aboriginal settlement clusters in Cuba, Hispaniola, and Puerto Rico.

Discovery and conquest by Spain led to exclusive Spanish control and exploitation of the Antilles down to the latter part of the 16th century. Gold was the most influential lodestone determining locations of Spanish settlements within the region, and so it was Hispaniola that was exploited earliest and most intensively and therefore became the primary base for the conquest and settlement of other islands. Where gold was lacking, as it was in Jamaica, western Hispaniola (Haiti), the Bahamas, and the Lesser Antilles, Spanish settlement was either absent or meager. After about 1530, as gold was exhausted and the Indian labor force all but destroyed, Spanish activity shifted from the West Indies to more profitable parts on the mainland. New migration from Spain ceased, and many of the earlier settlers moved out, with the result that the Antilles were reduced to a stagnant and limited subsistence economy based on agriculture and grazing.

Beginning in the latter part of the 16th century and continuing to the end of the 18th, the Caribbean realm became the scene of intense international rivalry as England, France, and Holland challenged Spain's exclusive control. Active early colonization by the north Europeans focused on the unoccupied Lesser Antilles, western Hispaniola (Haiti), the Bahamas, and certain other parts of the Rimland. By about the mid-17th century, on the eve of the sugar revolution, the Windward Islands were still largely unoccupied; North Europeans controlled the Leewards; Spain remained in possession of Cuba, Puerto Rico, eastern Hispaniola and Trinidad; and the French controlled western Hispaniola and the English, Jamaica. Each European group left its imprint on its own colonies. As of about 1650 the total population of the Rimland was probably not over 100,000.[22] This figure included not only the more numerous white settlers but also remnants of the original Indian population and some Negro slaves.

A new era for the West Indies was ushered in by the colonial plantation, a system of land use, devised for the exploitation of a low-latitude environment, that was able to provide cane sugar and a few other tropical products for the European market. The system was already well established by the late 1600's, reached its peak development in the 18th century, and declined in the 19th as it was replaced by the more modern plantation system that is in vogue today. The original plantation system had a variety of effects on the Rimland, not the least of which were those associated with numbers and characteristics of the population. Faced with the need for an abundance of sturdy, cheap labor on the sugar plantations and in view of the earlier catastrophic reduction in the numbers of Indians, the Europeans resorted to the importation of Negro slaves from Africa. The result was not only an increase in population numbers but also a radical change in the racial composition. In Barbados, where the sugar revolution came earliest, the total number of inhabitants may have reached 43,000 in 1640, of whom 37,000, including indentured laborers, were white and only 6000 Negro. By 1678, the number of whites had declined to 20,000 and the blacks had risen to 40,000. By 1809 Negroes outnumbered whites 5 to 1.[23] The Rimlands, as a consequence of sugar culture, were destined to be predominantly black or a mixture of black and white (mulatto). A plural or multiracial society is characteristic of the West Indies even today, and emancipation of the slaves only operated to intensify the color distinctions. Most West Indian territories are dominated by a small white or light-colored elite group. Throughout the Antilles, status is strongly correlated with color.[24] Moreover, since sugar cane was very much a lowland crop, population was similarly concentrated. Thus, the Middle American Rimlands came to represent striking contrasts in population with the mainland in race, culture traits, and altitudinal concentration. Along with the African slaves came new food plants, new agricultural tools and practices, new ways of food preparation, and new forms of hut construction.

The most recent period in Caribbean development—from the late 19th century to the present—has witnessed at least two important man-land happenings: (1) the emergence of the modern plantation and (2) such a marked acceleration of population growth as to tax the economic re-

[22] West and Augelli, *Middle America*, p. 80.

[23] West and Augelli, *Middle America*, p. 94.

[24] David Lowenthal, "Race and Color in the West Indies," *Daedalus*, Vol. 96, 1967, p. 584.

sources of many of the territories. The first of these two events has indirectly operated to intensify class and racial frictions. Especially on the larger islands, there is, in addition to the wage labor on plantations, a significant rural population composed of peasant farmers engaged in small-scale agriculture.

Vital Rates and Natural Increase. The West Indies, representing a variety of cultural backgrounds, also exhibit variations in vital rates and their trends. For about 1970 the Caribbean population of nearly 26 million had estimated average birth and death rates of about 35 and 11. The former figure is well below that for Central America or Mexico. But within the individual Caribbean islands, estimated birth rates range from 25 to 48 and deaths from 6 to 20. And while mortality still remains somewhat higher in a number of the Caribbean islands than in the advanced industrial countries of Europe and North America, most of the differential is a result of a relatively high infant mortality, which still prevails in many of the West Indies. But, on the other hand, the mean life expectancy after the age of one year is not greatly lower in the Caribbean region than in the more advanced industrial societies.

In the English-speaking, or Commonwealth, Caribbean, for which reliable statistics are available, general death rates fell from between 20 and 30 per thousand at the beginning of the century to under 10 by 1960.[25] Infant mortality, which was well over 100 per 1000 in all territories in the five-year period 1921–1925, fell to 40–60 per 1000 by 1960–1964.

For the non-Commonwealth Caribbean countries, mortality data are more meager and less reliable, but in the French and Dutch islands it is likely that death-rate declines paralleled those of the Commonwealth territories. For the three states, Cuba, Dominican Republic, and Haiti, where the data are still less satisfactory, one authority concludes that Cuba may be at a mortality level close to that of the most favored British territories; in Dominican Republic the level may be somewhat lower, while Haiti has a level that resembles that of the British colonies in the early 20th century.[26]

In the Commonwealth Caribbean countries, fertility rates moved up-

[25] Jack Harewood, "Recent Population Trends and Family Planning Activity in the Caribbean," *Demography*, 1968, Vol. 5, No. 2, p. 874. See also G. W. Roberts, "Populations of the Non-Spanish-Speaking Caribbean," in J. Mayone Stycos and Jorge Arias (eds.), *Population Dilemma in Latin America*, Potomac Books, Washington, D.C., 1966, pp. 79–80.

[26] G. W. Roberts, "The Demographic Position of the Caribbean," in *The Study of Population and Immigration Problems*, Committee on the Judiciary, Subcommittee No. 1, House of Representatives, Washington: U.S. Government Printing Office, 1963.

ward in the period immediately following World War II, as they did in the United States. Why this occurred is not known for sure.[27] Because of the meager and unreliable fertility data for most of the non-Commonwealth Caribbean, fertility trends there in the postwar decade remain in doubt.

The most recent trends in fertility (since 1960) show an almost universal and significant decline in birth rates for the whole Caribbean in the territories for which reliable and up-to-date information are available. To what factors this most recent downward trend in fertility is related is still not known. It is just possible that the increased activity in family planning in the region has begun to show results. Improvement in education, especially of women, may also be a factor.

Cuba and Puerto Rico were among the first colonies established by Spain in the Caribbean. But following the conquest of richer Mexico and Peru on the mainland, both islands were neglected and as a consequence growth of their populations and their economies lagged. This situation was corrected in the 1800's, however, as the plantation system became well established and blacks were introduced in large numbers. Spanish control was maintained until the war with the United States in 1898.

Cuba's first census in 1774 revealed a population of nearly 172,000, of which 56 percent were whites and 44 percent Negroes. Throughout the 19th and 20th centuries there was a strong positive correlation between sugar production and population growth. During the first seven decades of the 1800's population increase even outdistanced that of plantation output. Natural increase made a modest contribution to the island's population growth, but in addition there was a continuous stream of Spanish immigrants, and more than a million African slaves were brought in. During the last three decades of the 19th century the wars of independence caused sugar production to slump and population growth to slow or temporarily decline as immigration fell off sharply.

The beginning of the recent upsurge in population growth occurred at the turn of the century, which coincides with the rapid expansion of sugar output and the emergence of the modern plantation. As of about 1900, the Cuban population only slightly exceeded 1.5 million. By 1930 it approached 4 million and in 1970 the estimate was 8.4 million. Large-scale immigration of laborers played a leading role in the 20th-century population growth, although an accelerated natural increase due to greater political stability and the successes attained in combating such diseases as yellow fever and malaria also made important contributions.

[27] Harewood, *Recent Population Trends*, p. 879.

Immigration has been a main determinant not only of population growth in Cuba but also of its racial composition. Because the Indian population early suffered almost complete obliteration, the present population is chiefly one of Spanish whites, African Negroes, and a mixture of the two in various proportions. A large-scale immigration of Spaniards occurred in the first half of the 20th century; immigrants from other European countries have been far fewer. Cuban blacks are of two groups. Most numerous are those who are descendants of slaves arriving before the abolition of slavery in 1887. Already by 1817 blacks outnumbered whites, and they continued to form the majority until after the mid-19th century. After independence the proportion of Negroes declined, in part because of an increase in Spanish immigrants but also because of widespread miscegenation. The second and smaller Negro group includes those who came to Cuba as free laborers after 1900, mainly from Haiti and Jamaica, as the modern plantation began to flourish. The inflow of black West Indians was sharply reduced after the collapse of the sugar market in the early 1920's.

With an estimated population of 8.4 million in 1970, Cuba's average population density is only about 185 persons per square mile making the ratio of people to arable land the lowest in the West Indies. Based on arable land alone, Cuba would require 150 million people to give it a density equivalent to that of Puerto Rico. Only about one fifth of the island is under tillage, although two thirds are considered physically arable. Some two fifths are in pasture. Seemingly, Cuba is not suffering from any serious population problem associated with a dearth of productive land in comparison with its present population.

Until the end of the 18th century, Havana and its environs formed the single conspicuous population cluster in Cuba, since early sugar production was focused in the western part of the island in closest proximity to the capital city and main port. As late as the middle of the 19th century, nearly two thirds of the population were still concentrated in the three western provinces, which included only one fourth of the island's area. Settlement began to push eastward especially after about 1900 as modern sugar plantations developed and new sugar lands were sought. By 1943 the center of population approximately coincided with the east-west geographical center of the island. The eastward shift of population continues, although slowly, since it is offset in part by the rapid growth of Havana in the west.

Rural settlement is by no means evenly spread, however. Low densities are usually coincident with regions of infertile soils, poor drainage, steep slopes, or a deficiency of rainfall such as characterizes the southeastern coastal strip. High densities are especially characteristic of the urbanized localities but also of the famed tobacco region of the Pinar del Rio in the extreme west where small farms prevail, and of certain sugar lands with soils of high fertility, most of them in the longer-settled western half of the island.

The trend toward increased urbanization has been strong in Cuba, and it shows no signs of abatement. Perhaps over half the island's population is authentically urban. Defining "urban" to mean those living in places of 1000 or more inhabitants, the census of 1953 counted 51 percent of the population as belonging in that category. Cuba, like most Latin American countries, has a single primate city, since the urban agglomeration of Havana, with over 1.6 million people, is more than five times the size of the next largest city. Increasing ubanization reflects not only the legitimate growth of industrial, commercial, and governmental functions but also the glamour and lure of the city as compared with the drab way of life in the countryside.

Recent census data on population are not available for Cuba, so that estimates must be resorted to. The United Nations estimated the average 1960–1965 crude birth rate to have been 34–36 per 1000; the Population Reference Bureau's estimate in 1970 was 28. The latter figure, one of the lowest for any Caribbean territory, nearly matches that of Puerto Rico. Average death rate is probably only 8 or 9 per 1000, which also is low for the Caribbean area. The current growth rate is judged to be about 2 percent per year, a figure that anticipates a population of slightly over 10 million by 1980. While Cuba's population is younger than that of most industrialized Western countries, its estimated 37 percent under 15 years of age is intermediate between the European average of 25 and the Latin American average of 43. Per capita national income has slumped in recent years with the takeover by the Castro regime and now stands at about $330. This is less than one third of Puerto Rico's income and well below Mexico's or Jamaica's. It is also considerably below the Latin American average.

Puerto Rico, with less than 8 percent of Cuba's area but one third as many people (an estimated 2.8 million inhabitants), is by far the more crowded of the two Spanish islands. Moreover, its agricultural potential is markedly lower than Cuba's as a consequence of three fourths of its surface consisting of worn-down mountains and hills with low crop productivity. Puerto Rico is one of the earth's most densely peopled countries, roughly equaling Belgium in this respect. The simple ratio of people to area in 1970 was roughly 815 per sq mi and about 2000 per sq mi of cultivated land. A large-scale exodus of Puerto Ricans to the United States has distinctly slowed population growth, so the actual growth rate has been well below what the natural increase would indicate. Consequently, population pressure has been kept within tolerable limits. Highest densities are relatively coincident with the narrow belt of coastal plain that encircles the highland core (Fig. 3.8). Crowding is especially high on the humid northern or windward side, which is the richest agricultural area. This same coastal section contains the principal cities, including San Juan, the capital and chief regional focus, with a population of 754,000 (1966) within its standard metropolitan area. The dry southwestern margins have fewer people, except where irrigation is possible. The eastern interior, consisting of valleys and highlands, and with the city of Caguas as its regional focus, is another area of relatively high density.

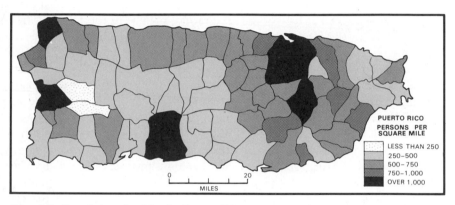

Fig. 3.8. Population densities in Puerto Rico are among the highest in the world. A zone of especially high density coincides with the humid northern coastal plain. After a map by D. L. Niddrie, *Journal of Tropical Geography,* June 1965.

About 80 percent of Puerto Rico's population are usually classed as white, the highest proportion for any territory within the West Indies. Pure Negroes or mixed Negro-whites make up nearly all the remainder. The black element, which has been steadily decreasing during this centruy, is mainly concentrated in the sugar lands of the coastal lowlands.

Once classed among the poorer islands of the Antilles, Puerto Rico since World War II has emerged as a shining example within the LD realm of what an energetic and determined people can accomplish in spite of limited natural resources; it is currently one of the most rapidly developing and most advanced of all the Latin American territories. While much credit for this accomplishment goes to the Puerto Rican people and their leaders, the island's ties with the United States have been a great boon as well. Yet in spite of a strong Yankee influence, Puerto Rico has proudly retained much of its Spanish cultural heritage.

Evidences of Puerto Rico's enviable position are to be seen in a variety of its population characteristics. Not only has its crude death rate (6 per 1000) been reduced to what is probably the lowest in the Western Hemisphere, but, still more unusual, the birth rate (estimated 25 per 1000) has been lowered to a remarkably modest level as well. In vital rates it stands as a rarity among the world's LD territories. The recent decline in both fertility and mortality have been spectacular; birth rates fell from nearly 45 per 1000 in 1940 to an estimated 25 in 1970, and death rates from 35 in 1900 to only 6 in 1970. In the same 70-year period, life expectancy rose from 33 years to about 70.[28] Its low current rate of population growth (1.1 percent annually) resembles that of Anglo-America, reflecting both a relatively low rate of natural increase (2 percent) as well as a large out-migration, mainly to the United States. Emigration to the United States has dwindled during the present decade, so that recently the return migration to Puerto Rico cancels out the departures.[29] Infant mortality (33 per 1000 live births) is the lowest in all Latin America, while the life expectancy at birth (68–73 years) is the highest. Puerto Rico's illiteracy rate is among the very lowest for LD countries; its per capita national income of over $1200 has no equal in Latin America. Puerto Rico is one of the most urbanized of the Antilles, with over 40 percent of its people living in cities and towns. A strong rural-urban migration has been in progress, especially since World War II.

Hispaniola, a rugged island of 9–10 million people, is divided between two states—Negro Haiti, with a faint French background, on the west, and the mulatto Hispanic Dominican Republic on the east. The boundary separating the two states represents a remarkably sharp cultural divide.

Compared with Cuba, Puerto Rico, and the other Hispanic Caribbean islands that are predominantly white, and the plantation colonies of the North European countries that are prevailingly black, Dominican Republic's largely mulatto population is unique in the region. Some 25 percent of the people are classed as essentially white, about 12 percent are Negroes, and the remainder represents a wide range of white and Negro mixtures. This prevalence of a mixture of white-Negro blood in an area that for three centuries was Hispanic and white in its colonial culture must be attributed to the invasions during the 19th century of

---

[28] José L. Vazquez, "Fertility Decline in Puerto Rico: Extent and Causes," *Demography*, 1968, Vol. 5, No. 2, pp. 856, 862.

[29] José Herández-Alvarez, *Return Migration to Puerto Rico*, Institute of International Studies, University of California, Berkeley, 1967, p. 6. See also D. L. Niddrie, "The Problems of Population Growth in Puerto Rico," *Journal of Tropical Geography*, Vol. 20, pp. 30–32.

Haitian soldiers who mated with the captured white women. During the Spanish period the absence of plantations led to only a small import of African slaves.

The more than four million Dominicans, nearly three quarters of whom are classed as rural, tend to crowd onto the restricted lowlands. Thus there is a strong correlation between population density and intensity of agricultural land use. Over one half the total population is situated on the limited northern lowlands of the Cibao and adjacent coastal strips where early colonial settlements were focused. Another one third dwell on the southern or Caribbean coastal lowlands, where the metropolitan center of Santo Domingo is located. No serious man-land problem has as yet developed, but with an estimated high birth rate of 49 and a still relatively high, but declining, death rate of about 15, the current annual growth rate of 3.4 percent is ominous.

Haiti's over five million inhabitants represent the most hopelessly impoverished and retarded national group in all Latin America. Its death rate is probably the highest, and its annual per capita gross national product of only about $70 is by all odds the lowest. The pressure of population on the limited and debased resources is one of supersaturation, and the outlook is grim indeed.

Under French control during the 17th and 18th centuries, large numbers of Negro slaves were imported from Africa, since Haiti represented the richest plantation colony of the whole Caribbean. With over 500,000 inhabitants in the 18th century, Haiti was then the most populous unit of the West Indies. But the turmoil and instability that began with the slave revolts toward the end of the 18th century and have continued down to the present have so crippled the economy that abject human poverty is the result.

The estimated overall density approaches 500 per square mile, but it is several times this figure if population is related to arable land only. Small-scale peasant farming predominates. Densities vary widely, depending on terrain, soil quality, and rainfall. The most meager human occupance coincides with the higher slope lands on the dry leeward side. Most crowded are the lowlands, either humid or irrigated, and the well-watered windward lower and middle slopes (Fig. 3.9). Two relatively large regions of high rural density stand out. The first includes the humid northern lowlands and slopes facing the trade winds from the Atlantic Ocean. During the colonial period this was a focus of plantation agriculture and its black slave population. A second zone of strong peasant concentration is in the south, also mostly well watered, and includes the southwest peninsula and the adjacent part of the Cul-de-Sac Depression around Port-au-Prince. A third and much smaller concentration of

rural settlement lies intermediate between north and south in the Arti-
bonite Valley and the adjacent slope lands.

Haiti's population is about 95 percent black. The other 5 percent are
mulattoes, descendants of offspring resulting from the mating of French
fathers with black mothers in the 18th century. Mulattoes represent the
elite; they are urban dwellers who are employed in business, government,
the professions, trade, and industry, and hold themselves rigidly aloof

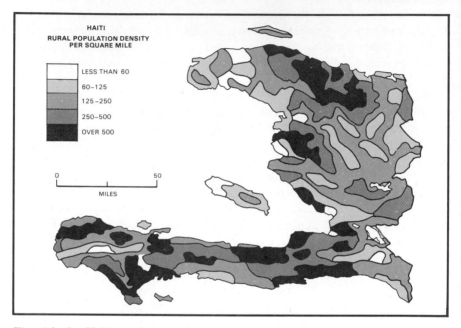

Fig. 3.9. In Haiti rural population density is relatively high over much of the
country, but the pattern of distribution is complex. Highest densities are on the
well-watered lowlands and lower slopes; drier leeward areas and high mountains
show the least concentration. From West and Augelli, *Middle America*, Prentice-
Hall, 1966.

from the largely rural Negro majority. Negroes and mulattoes are sharply
separated from each other by other characteristics as well, including
language, religion, education, and cultural background. French, the official language, is spoken only by the mulatto elite. The Negro peasants
speak a patois that is a blend of French, Spanish and English, with some
African and Indian elements thrown in. The mulattoes are nominally
Roman Catholics; the Negroes practice voodoo as well. Mulattoes display
a veneer of European culture; the Negro peasants exhibit many primitive
African elements derived from the colonial slave era.

Reliable data on Haiti's population characteristics are notoriously scarce. An estimated high crude birth rate of about 45 per 1000 is matched by a high death rate of nearly 20, which allows for an annual natural increase rate of close to 2.5 percent. Infant mortality is excessively high, perhaps as much as 110–130 per 1000 live births. Life expectancy at birth is only 35–45 years, figures that resemble those of many African countries. Of the population aged 15 years and over, 80–90 percent may be illiterate.

Jamaica, a small, rugged island of only 4.4 thousand square miles, contains some 1.8 million people. The overall resource base is meager, but

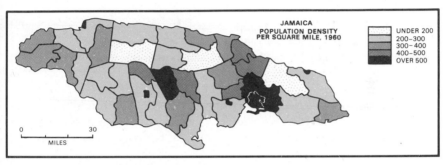

Fig. 3.10. Average population density is high in Jamaica and the pattern of distribution is unusually complex. Heaviest concentration of rural settlement is characteristically on well-watered lowlands, and on the lower and middle slopes of windward uplands. Low densities are associated with dry leeward slopes. Reprinted by permission of *Focus* and the American Geographical Society.

in spite of that fact the general population density has grown to over 400 per sq mi, a high figure indeed for a Western-Hemisphere country. But since only about 15 percent of the area is under crops (another 21 percent is in pasture) the density per unit area of the occupied and cultivated lands is several times higher than 400. In Jamaica a serious population problem already exists.

In such a region of complex hilly terrain, population distribution is almost bound to show complicated patterns and strong regional variations in density. The single greatest concentration is in the irrigated southeastern lowlands, which are also the location of the Kingston metropolitan area (Fig. 3.10). Densities are high as well on the other coastal lowlands, in the larger solution basins of the interior limestone upland, and along the major river valleys. They are lowest along the driest part of the southwest coast, in rough honeycombed limestone regions, and in the highest mountain lands of the island's central and eastern parts.

While Jamaica's population is multiracial, over three quarters are of African origin, descendants of the colonial plantation slaves. Another 15 percent are an Afro-European mixture. In addition there are sizable groups of East Indians, Chinese, and whites.

The recent birth rate is estimated to be about 40 per 1000 and the death rate a low 8–9, resulting in a natural increase slightly in excess of 3 percent per year. Probably the actual annual increase is closer to 2.1 percent, for there has been an important out-migration. In 1961, 38,000 people, or 73 percent of the natural population increase, emigrated. Destinations were mainly Britain and very recently the United States. The flow to Britain is now greatly restricted. Compared with the Caribbean average, infant mortality (35.0) is relatively low, life expectancy (63–68) is high, adult illiteracy (15–20 percent of the population 15 years and over) is low, and per capita national income ($460) is high.

The Lesser Antilles, a multitude of small islands, contains so much variety in population numbers, characteristics, densities, and distribution patterns as to discourage treatment of individual islands. While they are multiracial, the Negroid element greatly predominates almost everywhere, reflecting the islands' colonial plantation past. Because sugar, a lowland crop, has been preeminent, population tends to crowd the plains, which are mainly coastal in location.

REFERENCES

Middle America

Ball, John M. "The Migration of People in Mexico," *The Professional Geographer*, Vol. XIX, January 1967, pp. 5–8.

Beaujeu-Garnier, J. "La Population de Mexico," *Bull. Asso. Géog. Français*, 1967.

Benítez Zenteno, Raul, and Gustavo Cabrera Acevedo. "The Future Population of Mexico: Total, Rural and Urban," World Population Conference, Belgrade, 1965, Vol. II, United Nations, New York, 1967, pp. 54–57.

Borah, Woodrow and Sherburne F. Cook. "Conquest and Population: a Demographic Approach to Mexican History," *Proceedings of the American Philosophical Society*, Vol. 113, No. 2, April, 1969, pp. 177–183.

Browning, Harley L. "Recent Trends in Latin American Urbanization," *Annals of the American Academy of Political and Social Science*, Vol. 316, March 1958.

Cook, S. F. and L. B. Simpson. "The Population of Central Mexico in the Sixteenth Century," *Ibero-Americana*, Vol. 31, Berkeley, California, 1948.

Dale, E. H. "The Demographic Problem of the British West Indies," *Scottish Geog. Mag.*, Vol. 79, 1963, pp. 23–31.

Dyer, D. R. "Distribution of Population on Hispaniola," *Economic Geography*, Vol. 30, 1964, pp. 337–346.

Dyer, D. R. "Urbanism in Cuba," *Geographical Review*, Vol. 47, 1957, pp. 224–233.

Fertility and Educational Attainment—Puerto Rico—1962. U.S. Department of Health, Education and Welfare, Washington, D.C., September, 1967.

Geisert, H. L. *The Caribbean: Population and Resources*, George Washington University, Population Research Project, Washington, D.C., 1960.

Harewood, Jack. "Recent Population Trends and Family Planning Activity in the Caribbean," *Demography*, Vol. 5, No. 2, 1968, pp. 874–893.

Hernández-Alvarez, José. *Return Migration to Puerto Rico*. Publication No. 1, Population Monograph Series, Institute of International Studies, Berkeley, California, 1967.

Lowenthal, David. "The Range and Variation of Caribbean Societies," *Annals of the New York Academy of Science*, Vol. 83, 1960, pp. 786–795.

Lowenthal, David. "Race and Color in the West Indies," *Daedalus*, Vol. 96, No. 2, 1967, pp. 580-626.

"Mexico: The Problem of People," *Population Bulletin*, Vol. 20, November 1964, pp. 173–203.

Minkel, Clarence W. "Programs of Agricultural Colonization and Settlement in Central America," *Revista Geográfica*, No. 66, June 1967, pp. 19–50.

Morrison, Paul C. "Population Changes in Mexico, 1950–1960," *Papers of the Michigan Academy of Science, Arts and Letters*, Vol. 49, 1964, pp. 351–365.

Niddrie, D. L. "The Problems of Population Growth in Puerto Rico," *Journal of Tropical Geography*, Vol. 20, June 1965, pp. 26–33.

Nunley, Robert E. *The Distribution of Population in Costa Rica*, National Academy of Sciences—National Research Council, Publication 743, Washington, D.C., 1960.

Otero, Luis Leñero. "The Mexican Urbanization Process and Its Implications," *Demography*, Vol. 5, No. 2, 1968, pp. 866–873.

Peach, C. *West Indian Migration to Britain: A Social Geography*, Institute of Race Relations, Oxford University Press, London, 1968.

Perez de la Rivaj. "La population de Cuba et ses problèmes," *Population*, Vol. 22, 1967, pp. 99–110.

Roberts, G. W. *The Population of Jamaica*. Cambridge University Press, 1957.

Roberts, G. W. "Populations of the Non-Spanish-Speaking Caribbean," in J. Mayone Stycos and Jorge Arias (eds.), *Population Dilemma in Latin America*, Potomac Books, Inc., Washington, D.C., 1966, pp. 61–85.

Sanders, William T. and Barbara J. Price, *Mesoamerica: The Evolution of a Civilization*. Random House, New York, 1968.

Snyder, David E. "Urbanization and Population Growth in Mexico," *Revista Geográfica* (Rio de Janeiro), No. 64, June 1966, pp. 73–84.

Tekse, Kalaran. "Internal Migration in Jamaica." Jamaica Department of Statistics, *Demography and Vital Statistics Section,* April 1967, Kingston, Jamaica.

United Nations. Economic Commission for Latin America. "Human Resources of Central America, Panama and Mexico, 1950–1980," in *Relation to Some Aspects of Economic Development,* prepared by Louis J. Ducoff. Catalogue No.: 60.XIII.1. N.p., 1960.

Vazquez, José L. "Fertility Decline in Puerto Rico: Extent and Causes," *Demography,* Vol. 5, No. 2, 1968, pp. 855–865.

Welch, Barbara. "Population Density and Emigration in Dominica," *Geographical Journal,* Vol. 134, 1968, pp. 227–235.

West, Robert C. and John P. Augelli. *Middle America, Its Lands and Peoples.* Prentice-Hall, Inc., Englewood Cliffs, New Jersey, 1966.

Whetten, Nathan L. *Guatemala: The Land and the People,* Yale University Press, Caribbean Series No. 4, New Haven, 1961, pp. 19–63.

Whetten, Nathan L. "Population Trends in Mexico," *Population Bulletin,* November, 1963, pp. 180–184.

Zelinsky, Wilbur. "Population Growth in Central America and the West Indies," *Mineral Industries* (Pennsylvania State University), Vol. 35, No. 6, March, 1966, pp. 1–2, 4–7.

CHAPTER

4

South America

In the earlier overview of all Latin America in Chapter 2, it was pointed out that the preconquest Indian population of that grand cultural sub-division was strongly concentrated in four regions of more elaborate civilization involving sedentary agriculture, two of which, the domains of the Incas and Chibchas, were located in Andean South America. If Dobyn's recent and perhaps optimistic estimate of a preconquest aboriginal population of about 39 million in all South America is used, then his conjecture that 30 million of these were of the Andean civilization, mainly the Inca Empire, which embraced the highlands of Peru, Ecuador, Bolivia, and northern Chile, may not seem so unusual. An earlier and much more conservative estimate for the population of the whole Inca Empire at the time of the conquest was only 6 million. By still another writer some 3.5 million inhabitants were estimated for the Central Andes alone, a region considerably smaller than that embraced by the entire Inca Empire and its highland culture. Even in the Central Andes the overall density may have been only about 4 persons per sq km (10 per sq mi), since certainly less than 2 percent of the land (a figure considered to be the arable maximum) was under cultivation. Accordingly, the pattern of population distribution in the highland Inca realm was one of high local densities involving isolated settlement clusters of several tens of thousands of people separated by extensive unoccupied mountain land.[1] The other 9 million in Dobyn's estimate are thought to have inhabited chiefly the marginal lowlands of the continent, mainly in its tropical parts. In the Inca and Chibcha highland culture areas it was the sedentary agricultural economy, intensive in numerous parts, that made it possible to support many more people per unit area than did the much more extensive lowland economy based on shifting agriculture, gathering, hunting, and fishing. The densest lowland populations were probably along

[1] William T. Sanders and Barbara J. Price, *Mesoamerica: The Evolution of a Civilization*, Random House, New York, 1968, p. 76.

93

coasts and large rivers where fish, which provided the necessary protein in the diet, were plentiful.

Very recently, concepts of pre-Columbian agriculture and population in tropical lowland South America have been somewhat altered by the discovery of relic systems of preconquest fields in open savannas and newly cleared forests.[2] The fields consist of man-made earth ridges or platforms alternating with ditches, the latter furnishing the materials for the former. These ridgings are all found on level land subject to seasonal flooding, and so probably served to provide dry sites for cultivation. The existence of the ridged fields is indicative of locally dense aboriginal populations in certain lowlands.

GROSS DISTRIBUTION PATTERNS OF POPULATION

The present South American population is a grand melange of different races, nationalities, and cultures. Although completely of Asiatic origin, the aboriginal population, at the time that the Europeans arrived, represented wide differences in physical characteristics and culture. Especially noteworthy were the differences between the elaborate cultures of the Andean Indians and those of the more primitive and thinly-spread natives in other parts. Culturally more advanced Andean Indians still predominate in much of the western highlands, while more primitive Indian cultures, are the rule in the greater share of interior tropical South America (Fig. 4.1). European peoples prevail mainly in southeastern Brazil and in Argentina and Uruguay. A large infusion of African blood in a generally mixed population is typical of a few areas, mainly coastal Northeast Brazil, the Rio de Janeiro region, and extensive lowland areas in Colombia. Elsewhere on the continent a mixed Euro-Indian population prevails.

A population map of South America reveals great inequalities in spatial distribution (Fig. 4.2). Thus, 2.6 percent of the continent's total area supports about 26 percent of its population, while 52 percent of the total area has slightly less than 5 percent of the population. What is most striking is the vast, relatively empty core of the wide tropical part of the continent, in which the density is less than 3 persons per sq km (nearly 8 per sq mi). This is mainly the Amazon Basin, with its humid tropical climate (both wet and wet-and-dry types), large parts of which are forested, but other parts of which are mantled with coarse grasses with scattered low trees (wooded savanna). Smaller but still extensive

[2] J. J. Parsons and W. M. Denevan, "Pre-Columbian Ridged Fields," *Scientific American*, Vol. 217, No. 1, 1967, pp. 92–100.

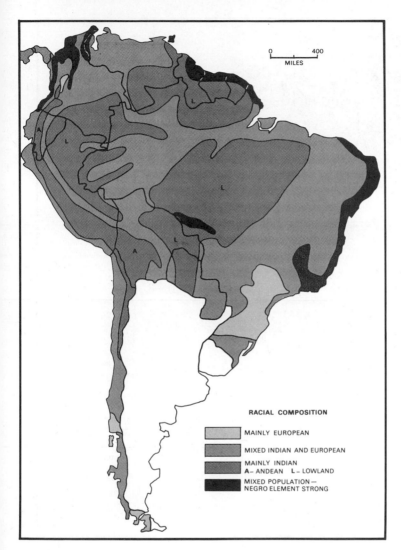

Fig. 4.1. Three main racial elements make up South America's population. People of European ancestry predominate in the more temperate parts of the continent and in the uplands of southeast Brazil. Pure Indian blood prevails both in the Andes and over large parts of the Amazon Basin. Negroes are most numerous in parts of the Atlantic margins of Brazil, in the Guianas, and in Colombia. Mestizos, a blend of white and Indian blood, who probably comprise over half the total population, are widespread throughout the tropical parts. Modified and simplified from Preston E. James, *Introduction to Latin America,* The Odyssey Press, by permission of Bobbs-Merrill.

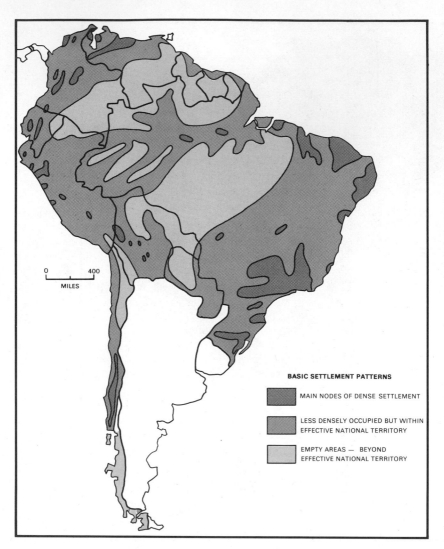

Fig. 4.2. Densest settlement in South America exists in the form of isolated clusters. But most such clusters do not have average rural population densities over 125 per square mile. Far more extensive are those regions with only a moderate density, but which still make a significant contribution to the national economy. In addition, there are large regions, mainly interior in location, whose inhabitants are so few and so primitive that little or no contribution is made by them to the support of the nation. Such regions lie outside the effective national territory. Adapted from Preston E. James, *Introduction to Latin America*, The Odyssey Press, by permission of the Bobbs-Merrill Co.

96

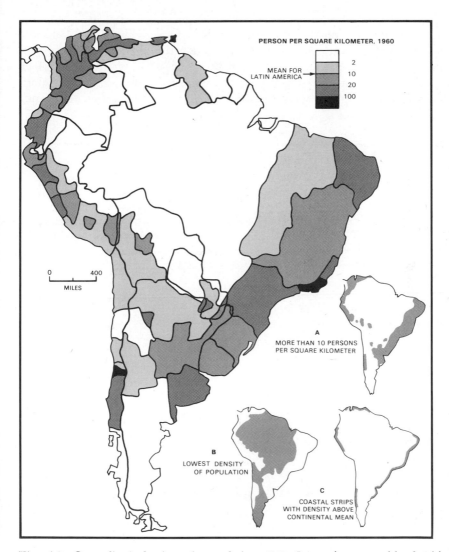

Fig. 4.3. Generalized density of population 1960. Inset *A*, areas with densities above the continental average of about 10 persons per sq km. Inset *B*, areas with lowest densities, or under 3 per sq km. Inset *C*, coastal strips in which density of population is above the continental mean. Modified from maps in John P. Cole, *Latin America*, Butterworths, London.

regions, also with low densities, are dry Patagonia, subtropical dry interior Argentina farther north, and dry northern Chile (Fig. 4.3). Thus the concentration of settlement throughout much the larger part of the continent is strongly peripheral, although not necessarily coastal (Fig. 4.4). It is highly noteworthy, also, that the marginal belts of above-average population density characteristically are composed of a series of separate

Fig. 4.4. Cities in South America with more than 50,000 inhabitants, 1960.

population clusters of various sizes (Fig. 4.5). The peripheral concentration of population is denoted by the fact that the most interior 25 percent of the continent has only 3.9 percent of the total population; the next most interior 25 percent contains 9.6 percent of the people, while the remaining 50 percent has 86.5 percent. But while the inhabitants of South America are distinctly oriented toward its seaward margins, it is not strictly true that it is coastal in its concentration. For if one takes a coastal belt 50–100 mi wide around the continent, about equal proportions of the littoral strip have population densities above and below the continental average (Fig. 4.3c). The longest stretch of meagerly or modestly populated seaward margin extends both northwestward and southeastward from the mouth of the Amazon River, or from about the Venezuela border southeast to São Luis in northeast Brazil. Focal points of population along this wet tropical strip are a few cities of only modest size. A second gap in the peripheral population belt is along the super-wet west side of Colombia, where mountains approach close to the sea. A third is in intensely arid northern Chile. The entire southern tip of South America south of about 38° or 39°, dry on the east and super-wet and mountainous on the west, is also very sparsely occupied. Thus, the effectively occupied territory of the several countries of South America resembles a belt of settlement clusters bordered on one side by the ocean and on the other by the great interior wilderness. Such an arrangement poses serious problems, since it is easier and cheaper for these cluster of settlement to trade with Europe and Anglo-America than with one another. A sense of national and continental unity is lacking. If in the United States a wilderness existed between the Pacific Coast states and the Atlantic margins, there would be no political union and no economic base for political stability. The vast undeveloped core of South America and the population fragmentation characteristic of its peripheral nations may be the paramount deficiency of that continent, and one difficult to overcome.

Marginal rather than interior concentration of South America's population has resulted from both push and pull factors. The immense drainage basin of the Amazon River has never been, for a variety of reasons (especially physical and locational ones) an attractive region for settlement. Much of it still lies outside the effective national territory of any country. Low-grade soils, a difficult climate, tropical diseases, and relative inaccessibility all play a part. But in addition to the repellent nature of the interior, there were a number of features that positively attracted Spanish and Portuguese colonists to the continent's periphery. First of all, since they came by sea, it was there that the new settlers made their landings. Moreover, it was along the margins of the continent that the aboriginal

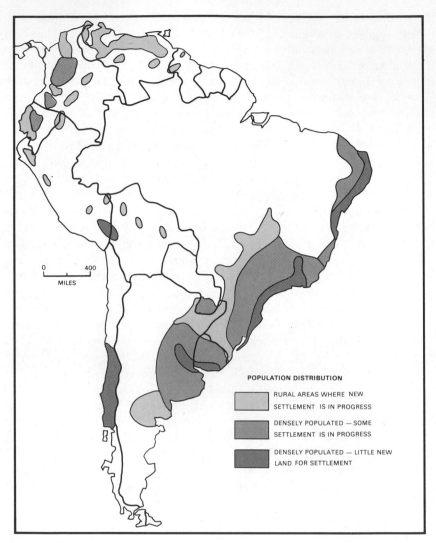

POPULATION DISTRIBUTION

RURAL AREAS WHERE NEW
SETTLEMENT IS IN PROGRESS

DENSELY POPULATED — SOME
SETTLEMENT IS IN PROGRESS

DENSELY POPULATED — LITTLE NEW
LAND FOR SETTLEMENT

0   400
MILES

Fig. 4.5. Intensity of rural settlement with emphasis on those rural areas where new settlement is in progress. Greatly supplemented and modified from map in John P. Cole, *Latin America*, Butterworths, London.

inhabitants were concentrated, and where as a result there existed a potential labor supply for any ventures in plantation agriculture, numerous souls to save, and, in parts, important accumulations of native wealth. It was especially in the marginal highlands in Peru and Bolivia that the rich and populous Inca Empire provided such a lodestone for the Spanish conquerors. In addition, a near-tidewater location was highly advantageous for plantation enterprises producing sugar and cotton, since the market for these tropical products was overseas, mainly in Iberia. The marginal highlands were also a source of greatly coveted mineral wealth in the form of gold, silver, and precious stones, while at the same time they provided some relief from the heat and tropical diseases of the lowlands.

NORTHERN SOUTH AMERICA

This northern subdivision includes the two independent states of Colombia and Venezuela, both fronting on the Caribbean, as well as what were until recently the three Guianas (British, Dutch, and French) farther east, which face the Atlantic.[3] The Guiana population is located almost exclusively along the littoral. In the other two, the major concentrations of settlement are in the highlands, but with secondary groupings on the coastal lowlands. The deep interior of the entire region is largely wilderness.

Colombia. Colombia, with an estimated population of 21–22 million in 1970, ranks next to Brazil within tropical South America in numbers of people. The western two fifths are composed of lowlands of variable width along both the Caribbean Sea and the Pacific Ocean, backed by a broad belt of Andean highland consisting of three north-south ranges separated by deep river valleys. Colombia's effective national territory consists of these two subdivisions. The eastern three fifths are wet tropical lowlands drained by the Amazon and Orinoco rivers, a region that has been very ineffectively organized by the state and that probably supports only 1–2 percent of the total population. Of the two occupied regions, the highland subdivision probably supports more than 80 percent of the population; on the coastal lowlands dwell less than 20 percent (Fig. 4.6).

From preconquest times down to the present, the highland sector has remained the focus of human settlement and of economic and political power. It is the country's core region. Even before the coming of the Europeans, the highlands had emerged as the main concentration of

[3] British Guiana has recently become independent Guyana.

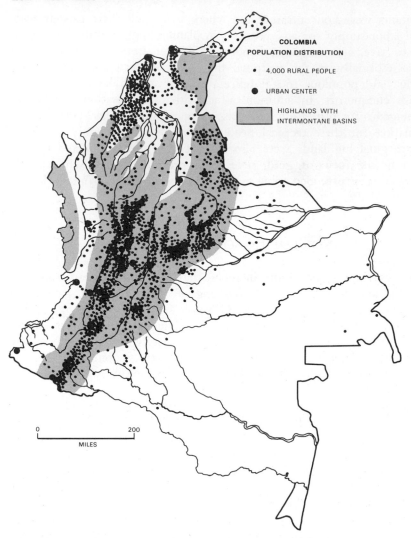

Fig. 4.6. The inhabitants of Colombia are mainly in the highlands, where they are concentrated in basins and valleys.

aboriginal settlement and the focus of an advanced Indian culture, that of the Chibcha tribes. These were a sedentary agricultural people who dwelled in the remote high basins of the Andes. Maize and potatoes were their staple foods. While somewhat less advanced than the Incas of Peru and the Aztecs of Mexico, they had progressed farther than the other tribes dwelling within the present Colombian territory. The

Chibchas were skilled craftsmen in gold and in alloys of gold with copper and silver.

When the Spanish conquerors arrived during the first half of the 16th century, their earliest colonies were along the coast at Santa Marta and Cartagena. But shortly, as they penetrated the highlands to the rear in search of gold and other mineral wealth, they discovered in its eastern parts relatively dense populations of sedentary Indians, which for a variety of reasons stimulated settlement. Large estates were established in the highland basins, on which Indian serfs cultivated European cereals and cared for European domesticated animals. Bogotá, near the site of an earlier Chibcha capital, became the center of economic and political life during the colonial period, and continues, as the capital city, to be the political center of modern Colombia.

In the parts of the country where the more primitive Indian cultures prevailed, the indigenous labor supply was much less abundant and also of a lower quality. In addition, the native peoples, especially those on the tropical lowlands, were soon nearly wiped out by imported diseases and the rigors of their forced labor. Thus the conquerors were obliged to bring in large numbers of African slaves to work on their lowland plantations, which were largely given over to growing sugar cane and indigo.

In such a region as Colombia, with its complex terrain and climatic patterns and its variety of peoples, it is most difficult to do justice to the details of population distribution in a brief description. One geographic specialist on Latin America has distinguished six main regions of concentrated settlement.[4] Five of these are in the highland zone; the sixth is on the Caribbean coastal lowlands (Fig. 4.6). Significantly, most of the main political subdivisions (called departments) into which the western two fifths of the country are divided have a single nuclear area of concentrated settlement. The department boundaries, by contrast, usually lie in thinly peopled zones between the population clusters. In all, there are some 14 such population clusters. Each of the six main regions of denser settlement warrants brief comment.

1. *The High Basins of the Eastern Range.* These high intermontane basins, the original home of the Chibcha Indians, are among the country's most densely peopled areas. In the largest of the basins is located Bogotá, a metropolis of 1.7 million people and the nation's political and cultural capital. Spanish-owned large estates, for which the Indian communities provided the required labor, were the characteristic form of economic

---

[4] Preston E. James, *Latin America*, 4th ed., Odyssey Press, New York, 1969, pp. 401–422. The following description is chiefly from this source.

organization during the colonial period. Food production is still the economic activity of most of the people. Rural poverty among the predominantly Indian and mestizo population is rife.

2. *The Upland Valleys of the Eastern Range.* Here at intermediate altitudes, usually below about 7000 feet, the pre-Spanish population was one of primitive Indians, relatively few in numbers. It was less attractive to the Spanish conquerors, therefore, than were the more populous high basins, even though the valleys were more comfortable climatically. Consequently the settling of these valleys was delayed and the main movements of Europeans into them did not occur until the 19th century. Concentrations of small-farm settlements developed in several different localities, one of these being the flanks of deep Magdalena Valley.

3. *The Antioquia Region of the Central Range.* In this rugged section there are no high intermontane basins, but in places along a number of streams, at an elevation of several thousand feet, the valleys widen, providing significant isolated areas of flattish land. The Antioquia part of the central range is characterized by volcanic soils of exceptional fertility. Spanish settlement here was retarded both by isolation and by the scarcity of Indian labor, so it was not until the late colonial period that new agricultural colonies were established and population grew, with the main concentration of activity developing in the vicinity of the town of Medellin which soon became the economic hub of the region. But it was not until the 19th century that new colonies began budding off from the original Medellin nucleus. Growth of population was remarkable; in the first decade of the 19th century, the Antioquia region counted only 110,000 people; in the ninth decade, the figure was up to 500,000 and over; it was 1.2 million by 1918 and 2.8 million by 1954. This increase was accomplished mainly as a consequence of an abnormally high birth rate, unsupported by any significant in-migration. It may also reflect a higher survival rate stemming from the beneficial effects of European influence. The economic base for the transformation that occurred in Antioquia began with the introduction of coffee and continued with the development of manufacturing. By the 1930's Medellin had become the country's foremost manufacturing city. But underpinning all of these extraordinary features of growth and development is the praiseworthy qualities of the Antioquian people. They represent a distinctive and cohesive group whose reputation throughout Colombia is one of aggressive, hardworking individuals known for their energy, efficiency, and ability to successfully colonize new lands.

4. *The Cauca Valley Between the Cities of Popayán and Cartago.* Chief sites for settlement in this area are the floodplain and the depositional terraces that line the valley. The early Spanish settlers grew

sugarcane on their estates, using African slaves as laborers. Supporting the modern population cluster is an economy that includes both large wealthy landowners who pasture cattle and grow sugarcane, cacao, and tobacco as commercial crops; and more numerous poor, small-scale subsistence farmers. Cali, the metropolis of the valley, which boasts over 800,000 people, is Colombia's second largest city. Its recent industrial growth has been one factor causing the city's population to soar. Large numbers of poor peasants have been attracted to Cali, where many eke out a miserable existence in shabby shantytowns on the city's margins.

5. *The Pasto Region in Southernmost Colombia.* Last of the highland sector's areas of concentrated settlement, it lies in the southern continuation of the great rift depression that separates the central and western ranges. Much of the settlement has taken place on fragments of high volcanic-ash terraces and the small bits of floodplain near the rivers. The largely Indian population is engaged in subsistence agriculture supplemented by the grazing of cattle on the high alpine pastures. The focus of this southernmost population cluster is the town of Pasto.

6. *The Caribbean Coastal Lowlands.* Some 17 percent of the Colombian people dwell on this plain, a majority of them Negroes. Most of the Caribbean plain is a product of the alluvium brought down by the Magdalena, Cauca, and other rivers originating in the highlands to the rear. It is an amphibious lowland with some parts permanently covered by shallow water and others submerged mainly in the rainy season. Its vegetation cover is largely wet savanna and scrub woodland. By far the most universal form of land use is the grazing of cattle on the poor natural pasture. Three subclusters of population, largely urban, focus on the three seaports of Cartagena (200,000), Barranquilla (500,000), and Santa Marta, all of which compete for the trade into and out of the interior. Over the alluvial lowland in back of the coast, rural settlement is scarcely dense. Still, there is a striking difference between the parts to the east and to the west of the Magdalena River. The wetter east, where inundation is more universal and permanent, is relatively empty except within a north-south strip along the base of the highlands back of Santa Marta. The somewhat less swampy western part, inland from Barranquilla and Cartagena, is far better occupied. The rain-drenched narrow lowland on the Pacific side of Colombia is without any significant concentrated cluster of settlement.

Population Characteristics. Colombia is fairly typical of the LD realm in many of its population characteristics. Its birth rate of 45 is very high; the death rate has been lowered to about 11, with the result that its natural increase of 3.4 is among the world's highest. Such a rate, if continued, will result in a doubling of the present population in about

21 years. It is estimated that the present population of 21–22 million will swell to 31–32 million by 1980. Infant mortality is high. Forty-five to 50 percent of the total population is composed of young dependents under 15 years of age. Probably 30 to 40 percent of the population aged 15 years and over are illiterate. Poverty abounds and the average per capita national income is only about $300.

Indian, white, and Negro strains have contributed to the composition of Colombia's present predominantly mixed population, both mestizos and mulattoes. The former are mainly highland dwellers, while the mulattoes and pure Negroes are most numerous on the tropical lowlands. The proportion of mulattoes is also high in the northern highland departments of Antioquia and Santander. What the absolute and relative proportions of Indians, whites, Negroes, and their blends are, and what their regional distributions may be, can only be inferred. Estimates by different writers vary widely. One recent estimate by an American sociologist widely known for his Latin American studies is as follows: white, 25 percent; Indian, 5 percent; Negro, 8 percent; mestizo, 42 percent, and mulatto, 20 percent.[5] Of course, these proportions are far from uniform throughout the country.

Some 31 percent of the total population are estimated by the United Nations to live in urban places with 20,000 or more inhabitants, a figure distinctly lower than that for Venezuela. Still, as is true in most Latin American countries, Colombia in the three decades from 1930 to 1960 has witnessed a remarkable surge of poor rural dwellers into the cities, especially the larger ones. Between 1930 and 1940 urban population increased by over 85 percent, and during each of the two subsequent decades by 90–95 percent. Rural-urban migration has been motivated largely by a search for employment in the booming cities, but also by an attempt to escape from the violence and terrorism stemming from the peasant revolts in the countryside.

Venezuela. Venezuela has only about half the population (10.8 million) of Colombia. Birth rates (estimated 43–44) and death rates (estimated 10) are only slightly lower, but the resulting high natural increase (3.4 percent) is similar, as is the high percentage of the dependent young (46 percent) and the proportion of illiterate adults (30–35 percent). The racial ingredients comprising the Venezuelan population are much the same as those found in most of tropical Latin America, including neighboring Colombia, but the proportions of Indians, whites, Negroes, and their mixtures may vary. In the absence of reliable census data, these

[5] T. Lynn Smith, "The Racial Composition of the Population of Colombia," *Journal of Inter-American Studies*, Vol. 8, No. 2, 1966, pp. 213–235.

proportions can only be inferred. A United Nations estimate indicates that those of unmixed European ancestry may amount to as much as 20 percent, pure Indian 2 percent, and pure African 8 percent. Some 70 percent are judged to be of mixed blood, mostly mestizos. A large in-migration of over 800,000 Europeans since World War II has significantly altered the racial composition of Venezuela. Pure Indians linger only in the more remote parts; whites are most numerous in the larger urban places. Blacks and mulattoes are at a maximum along the Caribbean coast.

In at least two population characteristics Venezuela appears to depart from the norm for less developed countries—its higher average per capita national income ($880) and its larger percentage of urban dwellers (45 percent).[6] The former reflects the wealth derived from oil. Regrettably this wealth is not widely dispersed throughout the population, and poverty is still widespread.

As far as the somewhat unreliable statistics permit of a judgement, Venezuela appears to be the most highly urbanized country in all Latin America.[7] During the three decades 1930–1960, there has been a remarkable acceleration of the urbanization process as the percentage of the total population living in places of 20,000 or more inhabitants has soared from 13 percent in 1930 to 19 percent in 1940, 33 percent in 1950, and 45 percent in 1960.[8] Between 1930 and 1940 the urban population increased by 75 percent, between 1940 and 1950 by 143 percent, and in the subsequent decade by 94 percent.[9] These decade growth rates for the urban population far exceed those of the total population, and of course the rural population as well.[10] The phenomenal rate of urbanization can only be explained by a large-scale migration from the impoverished rural areas to the cities. Over extensive rural areas there has been an actual net loss of population, a feature suggested by the fact that while 51 percent of the nation's labor force was employed in agriculture in 1955, by 1961 this had been reduced to about 33 percent.

Prior to the Spanish conquest in the early 1500's, the present Venezuela region was sparsely occupied by backward tribes of Carib and Arawak

---

[6] "Urban" is defined as the population in localities with 20,000 or more inhabitants.

[7] "Urban and Rural Population Growth, 1920–1960, with Projections," United Nations, Population Division, *Working Paper No. 15*, September, 1967, p. 123.

[8] According to a less restrictive definition for "urban," the country's population living in urban places amounts to 67.5 percent; that in rural environments totals only 32.5 percent.

[9] "Urban and Rural Population Growth," p. 109.

[10] The growth rate for total population between 1950 and 1960 was about 48 percent or just about half that of the urban rate.

Indians. They were for the most part food gatherers and migratory cultivators. Because the local Indian population provided only a meager and
inefficient labor supply, and also because an Indian accumulation of treasure was lacking, the Spanish invaders did not find the region as attractive
as were Mexico, Peru, or highland Colombia. Settlement consequently
was slow, although some colonies were eventually established both on
the Caribbean coast and in the highlands. But even by the early 19th
century the total population was estimated to be only 1 million, while
by 1920, or more than a century later, it had grown to only about 2.4
million. The genuinely rapid acceleration of population growth occurred
after World War II, when death rates fell rapidly as a result of public
health programs and the better control of insect-borne diseases. This
recent rapid growth was also assisted by a large in-migration from
Europe. Venezuela's present growth rate of 3.4 percent per year is one
of the highest in all Latin America.

Four main physical divisions of the country are usually recognized.
From north to south these are the Caribbean Lowlands, the Northern
Highlands, the Orinoco Llanos Lowlands, and the Guiana Highlands. Perhaps some 70 percent of the total population is in the Northern Highlands;
somewhat more than 10 percent may inhabit the Caribbean Lowlands;
and less than 20 percent are in the Orinoco Lowlands (Fig. 4.7). The

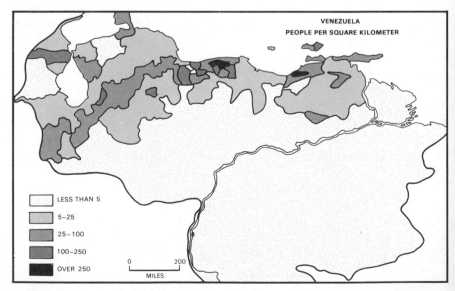

Fig. 4.7. Venezuela—density of population by districts, 1961 census. After Marchand.

Guiana Highlands, which lie outside the effective national territory, have an unknown number of inhabitants but it must be a small figure.

The Northern Highlands. The populous Northern Highlands are not only the present core region of the country but its historical heartland as well. Initially, it was the lure of gold that drew the Spanish conquerors into the highlands. But shortly the farming land of the pleasantly situated intermontane basins emerged as the focal centers of Spanish settlement, where large estates with enslaved Indian laborers became the rule. Much of the original highland settlement took place in the 16th century.

The country's main population axis coincides with the highland belt in the north and west, where it is composed of several ranges and groups, including the high Sierra Nevada de Merida in the northwest, the Segovia Highlands, the lower ranges along the Caribbean coast, and the massif of Sucre east of the Gulf of Barcelona. Over the past several decades a degree of modification of the population axis has occurred as a result of the strong attraction on immigrants exerted by certain areas, mainly basins and lowlands. Of first importance as a magnet for settlers is the city of Caracas and its environs, where new industry has moved in and thrived. To a lesser degree the following regions have also served to attract in-migrants: the oil regions of the Maracaibo Basin and of the eastern Orinoco Plain; the industrial region of Valencia and Maracay in the Valencia Basin west of Caracas; the southern piedmont of the Andes, which has experienced extensive new agricultural settlement; and very recently the Ciudad Bolivar region on the northern margins of the Guiana Highlands, where heavy industry has begun to develop.[11]

As a generalization, then, it can be said that the past few decades have witnessed a draining away of inhabitants from the highland population axis (except for the urbanized coastal central highlands) toward peripheral regions. From a recent census it can be determined which states in Venezuela, and hence roughly which regions, experienced net out-migration and which net in-migration, and what the magnitude of the movement was. All states in the northern highland zone were net losers in terms of migrants with the exception of those in the coastal central highlands where the main cities are located, including the Federal District (Fig. 4.8). Also modest losers were the central and western parts of the Orinoco Llanos. Net gainers in the migrant transfer were the following: the central highlands core region, including the Federal District, with much the highest rate of gain, and the industrial upland basins containing Valencia and Maracay; the southwestern piedmont of

[11] Bernard Marchand, "Étude géographique de la population du Vénézuéla," *Annales de Géographie*, 72 année, No. 394, November–December 1963, pp. 734–737.

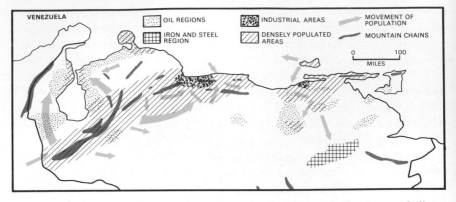

Fig. 4.8. Venezuela—zones attracting new settlement; arrows indicate general direction of population movement. After Marchand.

the Sierra Nevada de Merida; the petroleum regions of the Maracaibo Basin and those of the eastern Orinoco Llanos.[12]

The part of the Northern-Highlands population axis that fronts on the Caribbean for about 150 miles between Puerto Cabello and Cape Codera is to a striking degree the more restricted heartland of Venezuela. Designated the coastal central highlands, it not only represents the political focus of the country, containing the national capital city of Caracas with a population approaching 1.7 million (or nearly one fifth of the total), but it also supports most of the light industry, has probably half of the purchasing power of the national market, is characterized by the densest rural populations, and is the focus of the nation's transportation system. If the present relative rate of growth continues, the coastal central highlands may account for 40–50 percent of the nation's total population by the end of the century.

Other parts of the Northern Highlands are less populous. The high southwestern limb extending from San Cristóbal to the coast at Tucacas, known as the Merida Range, is rugged and forbidding. Until the introduction of coffee as the prime commercial crop it was relatively isolated. Three distinct clusters of population within the Merida Range coincide with the intermontane basins and valleys in which the cities of San Cristobal, Merida, and Valera are situated. Mestizos greatly predominate. Lying northwest of Barquisimeto are the Segovia Highlands, a dry and relatively poor region where overall density of population is under 10 per sq mi. There are only a few small clusters of population, including

[12] Bernard Marchand, "Étude géographique," pp. 736–737.

those in the vicinity of Barquisimeto, Coro, and the oil refineries on the Paraguaná Peninsula. In the northeastern highlands of Sucre, eastward from the Gulf of Barcelona, is another retarded region of very modest population.

The Caribbean Lowlands. Until 1918 the Lake Maracaibo Lowland was a poor and neglected region. Since then it has developed into one of the world's richest oil fields, with an associated rise in population. As one example, the town and port of Maracaibo had a population of only 18,000 in 1918; very recently it exceeded 530,000. Outside the oil-producing and refining areas, the Maracaibo lowland is mainly the home of backward tribal Indians.

Eastward from Lake Maracaibo the coastal lowlands are few and relatively small in area, since in most parts the highlands reach down to tidewater. The two most expansive lowland areas are the one in the vicinity of Puerto Cabello and the second in the broad coastal indentation westward from Barcelona. Both regions are handicapped by drought, but intensive cultivation and dense populations are present in restricted areas where water can be provided.

The Orinoco Llanos Plains. This vast, almost featureless plain situated between the Andes and the Guiana Highlands is covered by a vegetation mantle of savanna grasses and scrub woodland. Although the tall, coarse native grasses provide poor natural pasture, still it is this resource that has largely supported a sparse settlement based on extensive cattle ranching. The Indians avoided the Orinoco country with its (to them) uninviting environment. It remained for Europeans to introduce cattle and initiate settlement in the area. Recently the exploitation of the oil and gas resources has added a new factor in population distribution, a development that may have added half a million people to the eastern end of the valley. For the most part the population is grouped in small riverine settlements around the ranch headquarters, or in the vicinity of recent mining developments.

The Guiana Highlands. These comprise nearly half of Venezuela's area, but on the whole they lie outside the effective national territory. On the northern margin of the Guiana Highlands a major concentration of heavy industries is being developed which will result in a distinctly new node of population. Grouped around Ciudad Bolivar, located at the junction of the Orinoco and Caroni rivers, are a steel plant using the abundant local iron ores, a large hydroelectric plant, an aluminum refinery, an oil refinery, and the beginnings of an integrated petrochemical establishment.

The three Guianas, British (Guyana), Dutch (Surinam), and French together have a population of only around a million people, two thirds of whom are in the western, or formerly British, subdivision, now the new state of Guyana. They are exceedingly varied in racial composition, with Europeans representing less than 5 percent of the total. The overwhelming majority live in a narrow coastal strip of swampy alluvium, usually under eight miles in width, where agriculture, both small-scale and estate, is the dominant economy. Close to a quarter of the people in Guyana, and nearly 40 percent and 50 percent respectively of those in the Dutch (Surinam) and French subdivisions, live in the capital and main port city of each of the three small political units.

THE CENTRAL ANDEAN COUNTRIES

Since the pre-conquest era, this central Andean group of countries, including Ecuador, Peru, and Bolivia, has been distinguished by a predominantly highland culture. And even today, although to a somewhat less degree than before, the population continues to be concentrated in the mountain subdivision. Doubtless this modern partiality for the higher altitudes has its roots in the fact that these Pacific mountains were the site of the empire of the ancient Incas, whose descendants are the modern Indian inhabitants. Together these three Andean states have an estimated population of 24–25 million (1970).

Ecuador. Among Latin America's two dozen LD political units, Ecuador, with its six million people, clearly falls within the lower range of countries in terms of degree of economic advancement. Most of its population characteristics illustrate this retarded development: estimated birth rate 47; death rate 13; rate of annual increase 3.4 percent, which will permit a doubling of the present population in about 21 years; high infant mortality; a young population with 48 percent under 15 years of age; a per capita national income of only $210; and illiterates comprising an estimated 30–35 percent of the population 15 years of age and over. The urbanization process is considerably less advanced in Ecuador than in most Latin American countries; in 1960 only 15 percent of the total population lived in communities with 20,000 or more inhabitants. Still, the percentage that is urban has been expanding rapidly in recent decades.

Estimates of the proportions of the total national population belonging to the several ethnic groups vary widely. Officially the proportion of Indians in the total population is estimated at 39 percent; people of unmixed European (mainly Spanish) ancestry, 10 percent; Africans and mulattoes, also 10 percent; and mestizos, 41 percent. But it is the conjecture of one anthropologist that Indians may represent as much as 60 percent of the inhabitants.

Ecuador's population divides into two large unlike groups, each with a different outlook and each concentrated in a different part of the country, a situation that poses a serious problem for national cohesiveness. There is slight communication between the two. Thus the large Indian group lives almost exclusively in the high Andean basins, where they function as small-scale subsistence farmers dwelling in small rural communities. They are little concerned with production for a national or international market and have small interest in the nation and its well-being. The second group, composed mainly of Spanish whites and mestizos, are concentrated on the coastal lowlands in back of the metropolis and port of Guayaquil, or in highland cities. They are especially concerned with producing items for sale, either for export or for the national market. They also have pride and interest in the nation and its programs for economic development. For the sake of national unity, and in the face of such population polarity, it is unfortunate that the country's political and economic centers are so far removed from each other. Thus the national capital (Quito, over 400,000) is situated in the midst of the Indian environment in the high Andes and is therefore remote from foreign political and economic contacts. By contrast, the country's metropolis, main port, and economic focus (Guayaquil, over 600,000) is located on the Pacific coastal lowland.

The Inca Indian population in the highland sector of Ecuador was already fairly numerous before the European conquest in the early 16th century. But the Spaniards discovered little gold or hoarded wealth there to attract settlement, so in spite of the relatively large labor supply available, the Ecuador highlands remained relatively isolated and under-developed.

The Highland Population. The predominantly sedentary Indian population of highland Ecuador exists in the form of a series of distinct clusters, each coincident with one of the ten linearly arranged basins situated between the two parallel cordilleras (Fig. 4.9). Basin elevations are between 7000 and 10,000 feet, so their climates are distinctly cool. Violating a general rule for Latin America that important political boundaries rarely cut across dense population clusters but instead traverse the meagerly occupied territory between them, the international boundary separating Ecuador and Colombia does bisect the settlement cluster coincident with the intermontane Basin of Tulcán. This was done inadvertently, however, because of a lack of knowledge concerning the Tulcán basin and its settlement node.

The Indian population, predominantly rural, is engaged mainly in producing foods for local consumption, either as tenant farmers on large estates or as members of Indian land-owning communities where they

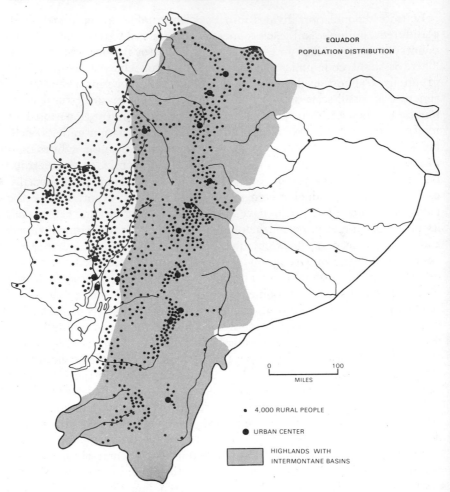

Fig. 4.9. Ecuador—population distribution. The population is about equally divided between the highlands and the Pacific lowlands. In the former a cluster pattern is conspicuous.

practice a communal form of tenure. Cattle are the main commodity marketed outside the locality.

Over the last century the rate of population increase in Ecuador's highland subdivision has lagged behind that of the coastal lowland. In the Andean basins rural population density is too great to be supported by what is nearly exclusively an agricultural economy. Consequently there has developed a downslope migration from the overburdened highland basins to the Pacific lowland, where employment opportunities are greater and the attraction of urban Guayaquil is strong. In 1870 it is believed that more than 90 percent of Ecuador's population lived in the highlands; the proportion had dropped to about 60 percent in 1941, 58 in 1950, and 56.7 in 1955, and in the late 1960's the population was about equally divided between the highlands and the Pacific lowlands.[13]

The Lowland Population. On the Pacific lowland the mestizo element dominates in numbers. The people of Spanish ancestry are concentrated in cities, both in the highlands as well as on the coastal lowland. Blacks are fairly numerous in the northern part of the lowland, and Indians along the coast north of Guayaquil. Unlike the highland inhabitants, those on the coastal lowland are mainly supported by producing items for sale, including bananas, coffee, and cacao.

Overall population density is not unusually high on the coastal lowland, but it varies considerably from one part to another. As a general rule the southern end of the lowland is the most closely settled part, and density dwindles toward the north as the alluvial plain becomes more constricted, the tropical climate wetter, the tropical forest denser, and distance from Guayaquil, the metropolis and the main port, greater (Fig. 4.9). More specifically, two regions of concentration stand out, (1) a more important one on that part of the Guayas Lowland just north of Guayaquil and (2) a southward extension of the above along the eastern shore of the Gulf of Guayaquil. In the first of these it is more especially on the better drained eastern and western parts of the lowland that rural settlement is most closely spaced. But the flat and lowest central part of the Guayas Lowland is poorly drained, so that there agriculture is mainly limited to dry sites such as natural levees and the rural population is strikingly reduced.

The isolated Ecuadorian Oriente, which includes the rainy forested eastern slopes and piedmont of the Andes, is a relatively empty region whose population growth rate is far below that of the national average.

Peru. Peru, with its 13–14 million inhabitants, ranks third in population among tropical South American countries. Even from preconquest days it has ranked as one of the main population and cultural centers in the New World, since it was chiefly in the Peruvian highland sector that the Incas had created one of the great pre-Columbian civilizations in the Americas. Thus, at an early date, Peru, like Mexico, came to be a main focus of Spanish conquest, and Lima, like Mexico City, became a primary settlement center in Spanish America. Appropriately, Peru

[13] James, pp. 440–441. See also John van Dyke Saunders, *The People of Ecuador: A Demographic Analysis.* Latin American Monographs, No. 14, Gainesville, University of Florida Press, 1961, pp. 6–7.

has been called "the Egypt of the New World," since well-developed aboriginal cultures had arisen in these Central Andes long before the rise of the Inca Empire, which prevailed from the 12th to the 16th centuries.

It has been pointed out in an earlier section that estimates of the Inca Empire's population on the eve of the Spanish conquest vary so widely as to make them dubiously valuable. Within the Inca Empire the overall population density was very low indeed, since much the larger part of the Andean domain was unoccupied because of aridity, high altitude and associated low temperatures, and rugged terrain with steep slopes. It is estimated that only 2 percent is under cultivation today, and this must be close to the arable maximum. The Inca distribution was one of local clusters of dense population separated by vast unoccupied territories—obviously a very difficult population arrangement out of which to weld an effective political empire. It is difficult to see how 30 million people could have been supported in this inhospitable land.

The Spanish were attracted to the Inca region of the central Andes for many of the same reasons that they were to the central highland of Mexico. Precious minerals were available; there was a large supply of native labor relatively advanced in culture, which provided a fertile field for Christian missions; and accumulated treasure was present in abundance. As Indian labor was drafted to work on Spanish estates and in mines, the food supply consequently decreased, and this, together with the exhausting labor in the mines and the white man's diseases, led to a drastic decline in the Indian population. By the late 1500's the Inca Empire's population may have been reduced by one third.

Indians and Spaniards met and mixed in Peru, but there was no wholesale blending of the two cultures into a unique society. The present population is estimated to be about 46 percent pure Indian, a figure unusually high for Latin America. Mestizos add another 38 percent, while perhaps 15 percent are of unmixed European blood, predominantly Spanish. The remaining 1 percent is largely Asiatic; Negroes are scarce. Spanish is the official language. An estimated 46 percent of the people speak only Spanish; perhaps about one third speak only Indian languages.

The Peruvian population divides into a number of broad social classes. At the top is a small aristocratic, elite group of pure-blooded Spaniards, who for a long time have formed the governing class. They were originally the large landowners but recently have branched out into a variety of occupations. Then there is a large and vigorous middle class, mainly mestizos, that is engaged in a variety of occupations, both urban and rural. The urban mestizos are in the professions and work as laborers in factories and in a variety of small-scale enterprises. In addition there are the mestizo peasant farmers whose standard of living is usually lower than that of those employed in cities. A third group, the largest, is composed of Indians—dour, taciturn, and seemingly lacking in spirit. For the most part they are a self-sufficient lot, engaged chiefly in subsistence farming and herding, although a small minority is engaged in mining.

Peru is composed of three natural regions—the arid coastal strip, the Andean highlands, and the eastern slopes and lowlands. A majority (some 61 percent) of the people live in the highland subdivision; about 29 percent are in the coastal desert; and close to 10 percent live in the forested eastern slopes and lowlands, known as the montaña (Fig. 4. 10). The approximate proportions of the Peruvian population residing within the several altitude zones are as follows:[14]

Above 11,500 feet	16 percent
7500 to 11,500 feet	44 percent
1000 to 7500 feet	8 percent
Under 1000 feet	32 percent

The Andean Highlands. Indians, predominantly rural, make up 70–75 percent of this subdivision's total population. They are the agriculturists and herders. The remainder are whites and mestizos, mainly urban, who earn a living in a variety of ways, including income from land ownership, military and government employment, shopkeeping, and services of various kinds. Indian occupance of the Andean Sierra goes back a millenium and more in time. A strongly clustered pattern of population distribution was prevalent in Inca times and it persists even today, with the densely populated settlement clusters composed mainly of Indian peasant farmers characteristically coincident with high-altitude basins or river valleys (Fig. 4.10). One important cluster of rural Indians is located on the marginal plains of Lake Titicaca in the extreme south. Also in southern Peru are population clusters coincident with the high basins of Cuzco, Anta, and Urubamba, situated at elevations of 11,000 to 13,000 feet above sea level. In the Cuzco Basin, one of the most densely populated, is the old Inca capital of Cuzco, a city of nearly 100,000 inhabitants.

Within the central section of the Peruvian Andes are a number of population clusters whose prime economic base is mining. Largest, oldest, and best known of these is Cerro de Pasco at an elevation of over 14,000 feet. The laboring population in mines and smelters is chiefly Indian.

Parts of the high country between the clusters of concentrated agricultural and mining settlement are occupied by a thin scattering of Indian

[14] Dyer, Donald R. "Population and Elevation in Peru," Festschrift: Clarence F. Jones. *Northwestern University Studies in Geography*, No. 6, 1962, p. 15.

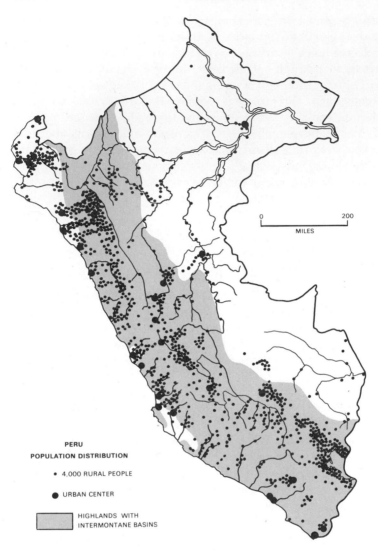

PERU
POPULATION DISTRIBUTION

• 4,000 RURAL PEOPLE

● URBAN CENTER

⬛ HIGHLANDS WITH
    INTERMONTANE BASINS

Fig. 4.10. Peru—population distribution. About 61 percent of the inhabitants are located in the highland subdivision; close to 29 percent reside in the coastal desert, while only 10 percent live on the forested eastern slopes and lowlands.

118

shepherds living in small isolated communities. Many of them are tenants of large landowners.

The fact that the sierra region contained about 71 percent of the nation's population in 1876, but only 61–62 percent at present, signifies an out-migration of the highlanders, chiefly to the coastal valleys. Regional differential rates of population growth indicate that the highlands have experienced a *relative* loss of approximately one million persons since 1826.[15] The descent of the highland peoples reflects both push and pull factors. The limited opportunities for earning a living in the overcrowded highlands and the poor living conditions there urge out-migration. At the same time, the multiple attractions of the cities, including their better economic and social opportunities, lure the migrants, particularly to Lima but also to the other coastal cities. There has likewise been some migration from the highlands toward the eastern slopes and lowlands, or the montaña.

The Pacific Coastal Strip. This natural subdivision of Peru is a region of intense aridity. Yet it contains about 29 percent of the total national population and is the economic heartland of the country. In this coastal desert strip, life is dependent on water. Hence population and settlement are rigidly confined within the narrow riverine oases of some 52 small parallel streams of Andean origin, most of which fail to reach the sea. Only about 10 of the desert streams have water in their channels throughout the entire year.

A number of small- or modest-sized port cities dot the coast, each characteristically serving an individual riverine oasis hinterland, although some serve a tributary highland region as well. A number are also fishing ports of importance, since Peru at present boasts the world's largest fishing industry, while fish products are the country's most important export. Talara in the far northern part is an oil port and an oil-refinery center.

The giant among Peruvian cities is Lima, the capital, whose 1.7 million inhabitants represent about 13 percent of the total national population. It is a classical example of the importance of the single primate city as a feature of the urban structure of Latin American countries. Lima is multifunctional in character, since it is the political, social, and economic focus for all the separate population clusters of Peru.

The Eastern Slopes and Lowlands. Fully half of Peru's total national territory lies east of its spine of highland, yet it supports only an estimated 10 percent of the total population (Fig. 4.10). The montaña, as it is called, is a land of heavy rainfall and dense tropical forests. The total number of its inhabitants roughly approximates that of the single city

[15] Dyer, "Population," p. 71.

of Lima. Because of the great difficulty in penetrating this inland empire from the west, important settlement groups have been established in only three sections. Some of the settlements originated as early as the 16th century, but it is only with the recent development of surfaced highways over the highlands, thereby providing access to market by motor truck, that they have expanded and modestly prospered.

Population Characteristics. Among Latin America's LD countries, Peru holds a middle position in terms of the degree of social and economic advancement of its population. Its vital rates (estimated fertility 44 per 1000, mortality 12, annual rate of growth 3.1 percent) are neither the highest nor the lowest. The estimated infant mortality (63 per 1000) resembles that of Mexico and is neither as high as Ecuador's and Brazil's nor as low as Venezuela's or Cuba's. The percentage of adult illiterates (34–40) is fairly close to the average for Latin America. Its per capita national income of about $350 is somewhat below the continental average but is well above those of Ecuador and Bolivia or even Brazil, although below those of Mexico and Jamaica.

Of the gainfully employed population in Peru, some 56 percent are in agriculture and nearly 53 percent are classified as having rural residence. About 47 percent are urban according to the national definition, although only 26 percent live in localities with 20,000 or more population.[16] But in Peru, as in almost all Latin American countries, the process of urbanization is relentlessly upward. In 1920 only 6 percent of Peru's population lived in places with 20,000 or more inhabitants. In four succeeding decades it rose to 10, 13, 18, and 26 percent. Using the local definitions of rural and urban population, between 1940 and 1961 Peru's rural population increased only 42.4 percent; the total population increased 67 percent, but the urban population increased 96.7 percent.[17] The increasing concentration of people in urban places is chiefly a consequence of a rural-urban migration, spurred at least in part by the disparity in economic opportunities as between cities and countryside and by the differentials in the earnings of rural and urban workers. Expectably, the metropolis of Lima outdistances all other cities in drawing power for immigrants.

Bolivia. Among Latin American countries, Bolivia vies with Haiti for the bottom position in the scale of economic and social advancement. Its estimated 4.6 million people are desperately poor, and the rate of improvement is slow indeed. By all the criteria ordinarily used to charac-

[16] Urban and Rural Population Growth, 1920–1960, with Projections. United Nations, Population Division, *Working Paper No. 15*, September 1967, p. 123.
[17] David A. Robinson, *Peru in Four Dimensions.* American Studies Press, Lima, 1964, p. 107.

terize LD countries, Bolivia consistently qualifies for inclusion in that group. Actually, in a number of characteristics it resembles more the African level of advancement than that of Latin America.

Its high estimated crude birth rate of 43–45 per 1000 is not unusual for tropical Latin America, but its remarkably high death rate of 20–24 is. Only Haiti comes close to matching it in Latin America. As a result of the high mortality, the current rate of annual population growth (2.4 percent) is well below the average for Latin America. Infant mortality is extraordinarily high; 55–65 percent of the population aged 15 years and over are judged to be illiterate; the annual per capita national income may be as low as $170. Only Haiti's is lower. Some 68 percent of the national labor force is engaged in primary industry—mainly agriculture, of course. The degree of urbanization is unknown, but it must be small. La Paz, the capital, with about 370,000 people, is the only city of important size.

An official estimate of the ethnic composition of the Bolivian people classifies 54 percent as pure Indian, 34 percent as mestizo, and 12 percent as of European ancestry, predominantly Spanish. The Indians, descendants of those who formed the backbone of the Inca Empire, are a hardy, dour group, conservative in outlook, suspicious of change, and fanatically attached to the niggardly environment of the highland country where most of them live. Mestizos, representing a middle class between Indians and Spanish, show more initiative and are more enterprising than the Indians. The whites, together with the more ambitious and better educated mestizos, control the economic and political life of the country.

The environment in which the Bolivian people operate is a difficult one. The highland western third of the country includes a cool, dry, wind-swept plateau called the Altiplano, lying at an average elevation of 12,000 feet, and the higher cordillera which flank it on both east and west. Strangely enough, it is in this forbidding highland section that a great majority of the people live (Fig. 4.11). The eastern nearly two thirds of the country, consisting of vast interior lowlands drained by the Amazon and Paraná Rivers whose drainage is eastward into the Atlantic, lies outside the effective national territory.

More so than elsewhere in most of Latin America, the people of Bolivia are distributed in small clusters and ribbons of settlement situated in restricted irrigated basins and valleys, in the vicinity of mining centers, and in the main cities. These scattered spots of concentrated settlement are isolated from each other by extensive barren areas nearly void of population. Over half of the Bolivian people dwell on the Altiplano, mainly on its least dry northern part just south from Lake Titicaca, where annual rainfall is usually sufficient for the cultivation of crops without irrigation (Fig. 4.11). Greatest crowding within this cluster exists on the marginal plains of Lake Titicaca, where in places the density exceeds 125 per sq mi. Not too far removed from the lake is La Paz, the nation's capital and metropolis. Southward for some distance from the lake, Indian settlements continue to be relatively numerous

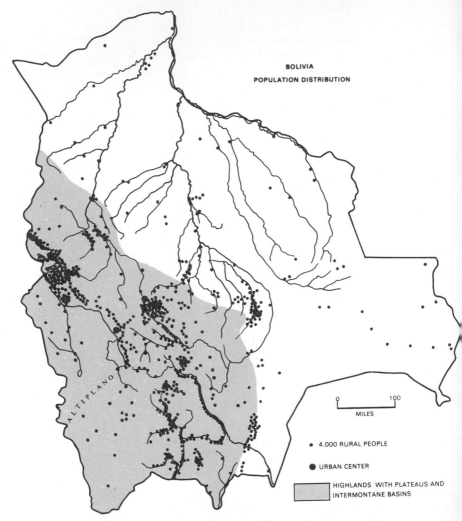

BOLIVIA

POPULATION DISTRIBUTION

ALTIPLANO

0   100

MILES

• 4,000 RURAL PEOPLE

● URBAN CENTER

HIGHLANDS WITH PLATEAUS AND INTERMONTANE BASINS

Fig. 4.11. Bolivia—population distribution. A majority of the people are concentrated on the cool dry intermontane plateau, known as the Altiplano. Over one third dwell within the Eastern Cordillera, mainly in basins along its eastern slopes.

along the valley of the Desaguadero River, until they are finally terminated by increasing aridity. As drought intensifies southward, spacing of the riverine settlements becomes farther and farther apart. A fairly continuous band of Indian settlements also continues southward from the lake, following the alluvial piedmont zone at the western base of the Eastern Cordillera where supplementary water from mountain streams is available for irrigation. Much of the central and southern Altiplano is so arid and desolate that it is largely uninhabited except for a sprinkling of seminomadic Indian shepherds. The large lacustrine cluster of settlement is not of recent origin; from the earliest times for which any records are available, the lake area has supported a relatively dense population. It matters little to the Indian farmers of this Titicaca population node, who make up some three quarters of its population, that the international boundary separating Bolivia and Peru nearly bisects it.

In addition to the groupings of mainly agricultural settlements on the Altiplano, there are two other population clusters within the plateau region that have developed as a result of mineral exploitation. One of these is the copper-mining center at Corocoro, south and slightly west of La Paz. The other is related to the tin-mining operations around Oruro, a city of nearly 80,000 inhabitants.

While the high and dry Western Cordillera is meagerly inhabited, the same is less true of the better watered and more mineralized eastern range. Here is located the ancient silver-mining center of Potosi, now better known for its tin production. The focus of this population cluster is the city of Potosi, with some 43,000 inhabitants. There are a number of other mining communities, some more important than Potosi, based on the extraction and processing not only of tin, but a variety of other ores as well.

In addition to the Eastern Cordillera's population clusters based on mineral wealth, there are others whose foundation is agriculture. These latter occupy the intermontane basins and valleys at lower elevations than the mining centers, where the climate is warmer and more pleasant. Most of the important ones are located within the rugged eastern slopelands of the Eastern Cordillera, a region called the *Yungas*. Although the Yungas region embraces only about 14 percent of the national territory, it contains more than one third of the population. Without doubt it is Bolivia's richest and most productive agricultural area. The inhabitants of the Yungas are mostly peoples of European ancestry or strongly Europeanized mestizos. Their agriculture is of a commercial type, which contrasts with the subsistence farming of the Indians on the Altiplano. Recently constructed motor highways have opened up more extensive markets for the products grown in the Yungas basins, largest and most populous of which are Cochabamba, Sucre, and Tarjita. These, together with the many smaller valley communities, represent the heart or core of Bolivia, since it is the people of the Yungas who have a well-developed sense of nationality. The Cochabamba Basin, with dimensions of about 15 by 6 miles, has a population density exceeding 325 people per sq mi. Its metropolis has a population of about 100,000.

Bolivia's extensive interior lowlands, representing nearly 70 percent of the national area, have only a thin sprinkling of inhabitants, mostly Indians (Fig. 4.11). According to the 1950 census their total numbers were only about half a million. Since then improved transportation, combined with government colonizing efforts, has resulted in a modest inflow of new settlers from the overcrowded lands of the Titicaca and Cochabamba Basins. Santa Cruz has become a main center for this pioneer settlement.

Chile. It is debatable whether Chile is more appropriately classed as a LD or a MD country; it has attributes of both groups. As noted earlier, it is tropical Latin America that consistently fits the LD category. But Chile lies mainly outside the real tropics, and certainly its most populous parts are either subtropical or temperate in climate, as are those of Argentina and Uruguay, which countries are logically excluded from the LD realm. Chile's birth rate of about 34 per 1000 is intermediate between the norms for the LD and MD realms, since, while it is almost double Northwest Europe's rate and half again as high as Uruguay's and Argentina's, it is, on the other hand, some 7 or 8 points below that of tropical Latin America. Chile's death rate of 11 is about the same as the average for both Europe and Latin America and so is not very distinctive. The current annual rate of population growth (2.3 percent) is almost 3 times Europe's and twice that of Anglo-America, but it is distinctly less than Latin America's. Strangely, Chile's infant mortality rate of about 100 (deaths under one year per 1000 live births) is among the highest anywhere in the whole Western Hemisphere. Children represent a high percentage of the total population. Some 32 percent of the economically active inhabitants are engaged in primary industry, mainly agriculture, a figure distinctly low for bona fide LD countries, but still high for the economically advanced ones. Urbanization is far advanced in Chile, the percentage of the population living in localities with more than 20,000 inhabitants (53 percent) probably being the highest in all LD Latin America; indeed, it matches similarly defined urbanization figures for Canada and West Germany, and is well above those for the U.S.S.R., Japan, and most countries of Western and Central Europe. Using the local definition of urban (places that have an "urban character"), Chile's urban fraction in 1960 was 66.5. What is more, nearly 70 percent of the total population increase in Chile's cities is currently due to natural growth and only 30 percent to migration. A per capita national income of $470 gives it fifth rank in this measure of well-being among the sovereign countries of tropical Latin America.

Although slender, rod-shaped Chile is 2630 miles long, over 90 percent of its 9.8 million people dwell within the middle part, or roughly between latitudes 30° and 41° or 42°S. Middle Chile is thus the nation's core region—its single, compact area of concentrated settlement, a feature that gave the elongated country a remarkable advantage in developing a unified state. Niggard environments plague the country's two extremities—unbelievably intense aridity in the northern third or so and rain-drenched, rugged mountain land in the southern part poleward of about 42°. In between is the beautiful country, the California of South America.

When the Spanish succeeded in penetrating to middle Chile they promptly came into conflict with the Arucanian Indians who originally occupied the region. These Chilean aborigines, while they were sedentary farmers who practiced simple irrigation, were unlike the Indians farther north in Peru and Bolivia over which Inca rule had been established. The Arucanians were more warlike, independent, and seemingly possessed of more initiative. The result is the Chilean mestizo, who is an unusually energetic and vigorous individual. Chile is predominantly a mestizo country; only some 5 percent are pure Indian, and perhaps 30 percent are of unmixed Spanish ancestry.

The Desert North. The Atacama desert of northern Chile has the distinction of probably being the world's driest region. Its vague southern boundary is at about the 30° parallel, near where Coquimbo is located. Within such a discouraging environment, and nearly lacking in irrigation water, population is almost bound to be small—actually there are only 500,000 to 600,000 inhabitants, or 7–8 percent of the nation's total, but even this number seems large for such an arid region. Three kinds of settlements exist—those based on mining, a series of port cities along the coast, and a very limited number of Indian farmers in the vicinity of a few small oases.

The main oasis settlements consist of one at Arica, just south of the Peruvian border, and two others in narrow riverine belts bordering the Loa and Copiapo rivers, the only two streams to reach the sea within the dry north. In addition to these three, there is a belt of tiny piedmont oases supporting a series of small Indian villages near the western base of the Western Cordillera.

The mining settlements are based chiefly on the extraction of nitrate and copper, but also to a smaller degree, iron ore, sulfur, and borax.

Those population nodes based on nitrate are scattered within the bolsons lying east of the coastal plateau; those associated with the mining of copper are in three or four separate locations within the Western Cordillera.

The string of small ports along the coast of northern Chile serve as outlets for Chile's mineral products and also for the more general trade of Bolivia, a country that lacks sea frontage.

The Far South. The part of Chile southward from about 42°S supports less than 1.5 percent of the nation's population, and of these a large majority live on Chiloe Island in the extreme northern part, where the environment is somewhat less harsh, and in the Tierra del Fuego section at the southern extremity of South America. This whole southern archipelagic section of Chile is an inhospitable region of rugged terrain with steep slopes, cool temperatures, heavy rainfall, and high winds. Land sufficiently level for agriculture is scarce indeed, and a more unpleasant climate would be difficult to find. The Tierra del Fuego region has recently had something in the nature of a boom based on the discovery of oil and gas, as well as on the expansion and improvement of the sheep industry, which in turn is related to the substitution of planted grasses for the inferior wild grasses. Punta Arenas, the regional metropolis, with more than 50,000 inhabitants, has responded with a new burst of activity. Very primitive tribal Indians continue to sparsely populate the poorest parts of southern Chile.

Middle Chile. While a great preponderance of Chileans live in middle Chile (about 30° to 42°S), population distribution within this subdivision is by no means evenly spread. Thus, northern middle Chile, or roughly that part between 30° and 33°, where the climate is semiarid and lowland is largely absent, is only modestly peopled. Mediterranean middle Chile, between about 33° and 38°, or that part between Valparaiso and Concepcion, is the real core of the country. Here, on the most productive and most urbanized 18 percent of the national area, are located some three quarters of the total population. It is here that the Central Valley, a fertile structural depression lying between the Andes and the coastal plateaus, is most continuous and best developed. The combination of a mild sunny Mediterranean climate with a winter maximum of rainfall, a favorable lowland terrain, fertile alluvial soils, and abundant supplies of irrigation water, make this region physically attractive for settlement. Contrasts in population density in an east-west direction are discernable, even within Mediterranean middle Chile and its Central Valley. Expectably, the Andes are sparsely settled. Moreover, the coastal ranges and plateaus, where a mixture of woodland, wild pasture, and nonirrigated agriculture prevail, are only moderately peopled. The greatest congestion is in the Central Valley itself. But even there population is densest along the eastern side where, in the alluvial piedmont belt, availability of irrigation water from the Andes is greatest and irrigated crop farming most widespread.

Within Mediterranean middle Chile there has been such a remarkable growth of multifunctional cities as to result in the country becoming the most urbanized one in all LD Latin America; over half its people live in communities with 20,000 or more population. The capital and chief metropolis is Santiago, with more than 2.4 million inhabitants in the metropolitan area. The port city for the highly productive Central Valley is Valparaiso, whose conurbation includes 400,000–450,000 inhabitants. Greater Concepción, third in rank and also a port, has a population of 270,000–300,000. Population pressure within middle Chile has been obvious for more than a century, a condition that has led to an out-migration of rural people to mining areas, to the Argentine oases on the east side of the Andes, and to the frontier settlements in the woodlands of southern middle Chile. But it is mainly the burgeoning industrial cities of middle Chile that have absorbed its excess of rural population.

Southern middle Chile, south of Concepción, or between about 38° and 42°S, is less congested than the Mediterranean section. The climate is cooler and the greater rainfall is distributed throughout the year, isolated alluvial basins take the place of a central valley, and forest becomes the predominant wild vegetation. This part is mainly peopled by immigrants from Western and Central Europe, especially Germans. Particularly notable is the smaller urban element in southern middle Chile, Valdivia (under 100,000) and Puerto Montt (60,000) being the only noteworthy cities.

Brazil and Paraguay. Brazil is the giant of South America; its estimated population of 93 million in 1970 is very close to one half that of the entire continent and about one third the number in all Latin America. Considering its enormous area of nearly 3.3 million square miles—larger than the conterminous United States—and its early settlement by Europeans, expectably its present population might be even larger. But it must be recalled that a great proportion of interior Brazil lies within the tropical wilderness core of the continent mentioned previously, and so lies outside the effective national territory.

To an unusual degree Brazil typifies the gross continental pattern of spatial population distribution already described, since its people are strongly concentrated along the country's seaward margins southward from about 5°S, in a belt several hundred kilometers wide. Some 92 percent of the Brazilian people live within the seaward belt just defined, and not quite 8 percent within the vast wilderness interior (Figs. 4.12,

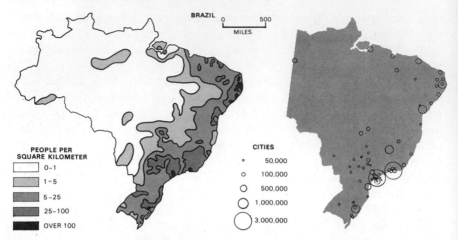

Fig. 4.12. (Left) Brazil—density of population, 1960. After a map by Artur Heil Neiva in *Population Dilemma in Latin America,* Columbia Books, Inc. (Right) Brazil—distribution of cities with over 50,000 population. After a map by Dyer.

4.13). Within this populous marginal belt, the settlement pattern is in the form of a number of large clusters.

Data on vital rates in Brazil (see Table 4.1) are scattered and unreliable, so when precise figures are given they must be taken with some reservations. During the present century it is believed that the crude decennial birth rate has oscillated between 45 and 42, very high figures indeed.

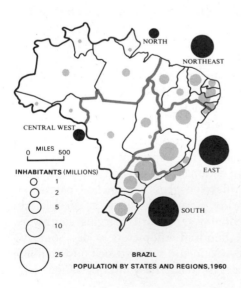

Fig. 4.13. Brazil—population numbers by individual states, and by regions made up of groups of states, 1960. Gray circles refer to states; black circles to regions. After Dyer.

TABLE 4.1   Estimated Vital Rates in Brazil, 1872–1960

Period	Birth Rate[a]	Death Rate[a]	Annual Natural Increase (Percent)
1872–1890	47	30	1.7
1890–1900	46	28	1.8
1900–1920	45	26	1.9
1920–1940	44	25	1.9
1940–1950	44	20	2.4
1950–1960	42	12	3.0
1970	39	11	2.8

SOURCE: (IBGE) Instituto Brasileiro de Geografia e Estatistica. For 1970, World Population Data Sheet, Population Reference Bureau.
[a] Per 1000 inhabitants per year.

By 1970 it is thought to have receded to about 39. Death rates have fallen far more rapidly—from an estimated 26 per 1000 in the period 1900–1920 to around 12 in 1950–1960, and perhaps as low as 10–11 in 1970. Thus, the natural increase, which had been below 2 percent until about 1940, has risen rapidly in the following two decades and reached 3 percent or slightly more in the decade 1950–1960. It is believed to have declined slightly to about 2.8 in 1970. This is still a high rate, which, if continued, would result in a doubling of the nation's population in 25 years. Infant mortality continues to be high, the 1969 estimate being 79 deaths under 1 year of age per 1000 live births.

Brazil's people are predominantly a mixture of different races and nationalities. The three basic original elements were Indians, Portuguese, and Africans. As of about 1500 the territory of present Brazil was occupied by a few million primitive Indians, non-Andean in culture, who were hunters, fishers, collectors, and shifting cultivators. Their basic food crop was manioc, not maize. Large numbers died during the early years of the conquest, but the remaining males, unaccustomed to hard agricultural labor, proved of little use as workers on the Portuguese plantations. Intermarriage between Indian women and Portuguese men caused many Indian physical and cultural traits to be introduced into the subsequent Brazilian population.

It is from the Portuguese conquerors, however, that the fundamental characteristics of the present Brazilians are mainly derived. But even the colonists arriving from Portugal originated from a population pool that itself represented a remarkable mixture of racial and cultural elements, including an infusion of Moorish blood. Like the Spanish, the Portuguese retained many of the traditions of feudalism, including a craving for large private land holdings, and they came in search of quick riches associated with the exploitation of the New World's natural wealth. Hard individual labor in mines or on farms was unattractive. In contrast to the Spanish, however, they exhibited much less zeal in converting the natives to the Christian faith. They had long been accustomed to carrying on trading operations in the far corners of the world, an experience that had made them more cosmopolitan and tolerant. The African element in the Brazilian population derives from Negro slaves who were brought in, beginning in 1538, to work on the sugar plantations of the coastal northeast and later in the mines. In the early 19th century, Alexander von Humboldt, a renowned German geographer, estimated that out of a total Brazilian population of about 4 million, only some 920,000 were people of European origin, about 1.96 million were of African origin, and some 1.12 million were Indians and mixed bloods.

After about 1850 a period of new immigration began, resulting not only in a rapid increase in Brazil's total population, but in major changes in its racial and nationality composition as well. Between 1822, when Brazil became independent, and World War II, some five million immigrants arrived in the country, most of them after 1900. Over half went to São Paulo state, where expanding coffee-growing offered a new labor market. While most of these later immigrants were Europeans, they were of various nationalities. An estimated 34 percent were Italian, 30 percent Portuguese, 12 percent Spanish, and 3 percent German. The remaining 21 percent represented a variety of nationalities, including Japanese and eastern Europeans. This new immigration is reflected in the figures for Brazil's racial composition as given by the 1950 census: whites, 62 percent; blacks, 11 percent; mixed, 26 percent; and yellow, under 1 percent. Of the 429,000 Japanese immigrants and descendants in Brazil in 1958, 76 percent resided in São Paulo state and another 18 percent were in adjacent Parana.[18] Doubtless, Brazil's population has become progressively paler with time. But the present predominantly white element represents a veritable melting pot of different nationalities.

Regional Population Clusters and Economic History. The modern cluster pattern of settlement, which dominates eastern Brazil, can scarcely be understood without reference to certain features of the country's economic history. From the beginning of the 16th century, Brazil's

[18] Teiiti Suzuki, "Japanese Immigrants in Brazil," *Population Index*, 31, April, 1965, p. 120.

economic development has been controlled by a succession of single-commodity cultures. Three main products—sugar, gold, and coffee—have in turn dominated a particular period of the country's evolution. Each period has seen the rise of a commodity that for a period was in the ascendancy in the world market, only to decline subsequently as outside competition became severe. Each of the successive dominant products fostered the development of a particular region and simultaneously generated there a distinct cluster of concentrated settlement around a city nucleus. In the cycle, as each of the products passed its peak and then declined, some of its dependent population moved on to a new commodity frontier, and a degree of stagnation overspread the original settlement cluster. Besides the three main economic cycles, there have been a number of lesser ones, such as those associated with cotton and rubber. Settlement of Brazil was dominated by the bonanza tradition, in which the end sought was great and quick riches.

Sugarcane, the earliest of the commercial crops, was introduced into Brazil in about 1532. The sugar plantations, employing African labor, were strongly concentrated on the humid coastal lowlands of the northeast around Recife and Bahía. Throughout the 17th century, northeastern Brazil's sugar dominated the world market, and the sugar region's population grew accordingly. Thus, the first of Brazil's main population clusters, located on the northeastern coastal lowlands, was one whose support was a profitable plantation economy based on sugarcane and African slaves. By the end of the 17th century, competition for the European sugar market by other tropical countries led to a decline of sugar cultivation in Brazil. But this early period of sugarcane dominance in Brazil's northeast has left its mark on the country's present spatial distribution and regional composition of population. Northeastern Brazil, and especially the coastal sections from Cape São Roque southward to southern Bahía, continues to be one of the country's main population concentrations. It is also a region where blacks comprise an important element of the total population. What is customarily designated The Northeast (excluding Bahía) contained, in 1960, 15–16 million inhabitants, or about 22–23 percent of the nation's people (Fig. 4.12). But the northeastern belt of high population density extends deeply into Bahía state, and if that state is included, then the region's total population in 1960 was over 22 million, or 31–32 percent of the country's total (Table 4.2). To be sure, these figures include what is really an extended northeastern region, including both the dry coastal strip northwest of Cape São Roque and the dry back country (sertão), farther inland, as well as the core region of dense population that focuses on the humid coastal belt south of Cape São Roque. In recent times this large concentration of people has been supported by a more varied agriculture than was true in the colonial period, in which sugarcane, cacao, and cotton are the main commercial crops; citrus fruits and tobacco are of lesser importance.

The gold-and-gems economic cycle began in the late 17th century at a time when sugar planting in the northeast had passed its zenith. It reached its peak during the third quarter of the 18th century, and between 1700 and 1800 Brazil was the world's largest gold producer. Thus the gold fever lasted for somewhat less than a century. During this period the mineralized region in eastern Brazil, including central and southern Minas Gerais (meaning "mines everywhere") and the three adjacent small coastal states of Espirito Santo, Rio de Janeiro, and Guanabara, was transformed from what in most parts had been a thinly settled wilderness into a well-populated mining, pastoral, and agricultural region. Thus was born the second (chronologically speaking) of Brazil's great population concentrations. The trek to this region involved new immigrants from overseas, mainly Portuguese, but also many from nearby São Paulo, and sugarcane planters and their African slaves from the ebbing northeast. Rio de Janeiro was developed as the prime urban nucleus and port for the burgeoning region, and the capital of the nation as well.

The well-defined population cluster around and inland from Rio de Janeiro contained about 18 million people in 1960 and spread over parts of four states, although these figures include some living within the dry interior sertão as well (Fig. 4.12, Table 4.2). Obviously this large modern concentration, which began with the gold rush of more than two centuries ago, cannot be explained in terms of present mineral exploitation. As the gold cycle waned and a period of decadence set in, the people were forced to find other economic bases or to move on to other regions. Actually they did both. There was a large outmigration during the first third of the 19th century, but the main relief was sought in other types of economic development, as repeated attempts were made to discover other bases for speculative profit. This led to a succession of economic endeavors in different locations, most of which were successful only for limited periods. The first of these speculative cycles to develop within the region was the growing of sugarcane. This was followed by coffee. Still others were based on rice and oranges. But through several centuries the grazing of cattle has remained the most stable and permanent support of the rural people. The modern population cluster has not only an agricultural and pastoral economic base, but in addition leans on mineral exploitation, especially iron ore, and manufacturing, construction, and the service industries of the urban centers.

The third chief product that punctuated Brazil's history and changed its map of population was coffee. Although coffee planting had begun along the east coast during the 18th century, by the first quarter of the 19th century there was a definite concentration of that crop in the Paraíba Valley inland from Rio de Janeiro. But it was only after the mid-19th century that coffee planting spread rapidly westward into São Paulo state, so that by the latter part of the 19th century this, Brazil's third major staple, began to dominate the economy and raised Brazil to first rank in world coffee production. It was the coffee cycle that led to the development of São Paulo state and to the growth of the great, modern São Paulo population cluster, the country's third chronologically. The state's population figures point up the story of growth. In 1872 São Paulo had only 837,000 inhabitants, and most of these were in the lowlands and hills not so far removed from the coast. By 1890 there were 1,384,000 people and this had nearly doubled by 1900, when the population reached 2,280,000. During the half century 1886–1936, the new immigrants to São Paulo numbered 2,848,000, and in several years the number exceeded 100,000. Many nationalities were represented. Listed in order of their numbers were Italians, Portuguese, Spaniards, Japanese, Germans, Russians, Poles, and Austrians. There was also a large in-migration from other states of Brazil. As the wave of coffee planting spread inland to the north and west and so on to the plateau surface, São Paulo, between 1885 and 1900, was transformed from what had been only an adjunct to the Rio de Janeiro population cluster into a distinctly new and independent settlement focusing on the city of São Paulo and its port of Santos. By 1960 São Paulo state had a population of 13 million (Fig. 4.12, Table 4.2).

But overplanting and overproduction led to financial disaster and finally to the revolution of 1930 and the termination of the coffee boom and cycle. São Paulo state still produces over a third of Brazil's coffee, but this is done on a greatly reduced acreage of land. Many of the large coffee estates are being broken up and occupied by small-farm settlers who plant a variety of crops, both commercial and subsistence.

The city of São Paulo, with a population of well over five million within its metropolitan area, is the metropolis of Brazil's richest state, the commercial center for the country's most productive region, and the leading manufacturing city in all Latin America.

Brazil's seaward peripheral band of relatively dense population continues southward from São Paulo into the southern most states of parana, Santa Catarina, and Rio Grande do Sul. Together they contain nearly 12 million people, or close to 17 percent of the country's total. But this southern region differs in a number of respects from the remainder of effectively occupied Brazil. In some ways it is quite un-Brazilian. The climate is more subtropical than tropical. Settlement dates from only about 1822, so it is relatively recent. Portuguese occupation of this part has never been substantial; Germans, Italians, and Poles represented the most numerous early settlers. More recently the immigrant stream has included Dutch, Czechs, Ukrainians, and Japanese. In a large measure, the various nationalities tend to form distinctive groups and endeavor to preserve their national characteristics in terms of language, religion, house types, and agricultural pursuits. There have been no speculative cycles here based on a single main commercial product, as was true elsewhere; this is a region of diversified farming and of small-scale farmers engaged in commercial agriculture but doing their own hard labor on their own farms. There is no single well-defined main cluster of concentrated settlement whose focus is a great metropolis. Instead, there are several smaller clusters and in addition, extensive areas with a widely and rather evenly dispersed rural population. Each of the three states has a distinct core or cores of concentrated settlement and population, and each core was in the beginning a colony of small-scale immigrant farmers from Europe.

In Parana, as in São Paulo, the main clusters of settlement are on the upland, as is the chief urban center. In the two more southern states the uplands are sparsely settled and the population clusters are situated in the lowlands and valleys. Parana actually has two population clusters. One of these is focused on the city of Londrina in the north-western part of the country. It is essentially a later-developed part of the older São Paulo cluster, and is like the latter in its thorough specialization in coffee. The source of its settlers has been mainly São Paulo. The second Parana settlement cluster is in the eastern part of the state in the vicinity of the city of Curitiba, where the colonization, some of it conceived and carried out by the government mainly in the latter part of the 19th century, involved large numbers of Polish, Italian, Russian, German, and Dutch immigrants. All nationalities engage in small-scale commercial farming.

The single population cluster within eastern Santa Catarina, focused on the towns of Blumenau, Joinville, and Florianopolis, had its origins about the mid-19th century, when it was settled chiefly by immigrants from Germany. Austrians, Swiss, Italians, and Portuguese were added later. Within this stabilized agricultural region, general small-scale commercial farming prevails.

The population cluster of Rio Grande do Sul, whose urban focus is Pôrto Alegre, is the largest within the three southern states. Much the larger part of the zone of concentrated settlement lies within the basin of the Rio Jacui, at whose sea end is Pôrto Alegre. A second smaller concentration exists in the form of a linear zone of settlement, representing a southward extension from the original Rio Jacui cluster, along the inner margins of the large lakes, dos Patos and Mirim. It is a region of irrigated rice culture. Within the main settlement region of the Rio Jacui Basin, on the floodplain, Brazilians of Portuguese origin grow irrigated rice on large estates worked by tenants. On higher land within the basin, German and Italian settlers are engaged in small-scale farming involving both crops and livestock. Cattle ranching and wheat farming are the main supports of the more widely disseminated population in the other less populous parts of Rio Grande do Sul.

The Less Populous Brazilian Interior: Central-West and North. Over 90 percent of Brazil's population is marginally concentrated within those parts of the country already described—in the states on or near the Atlantic coast south of about Cape São Roque. The remaining 64 percent of the country, belonging to the interior North and Central-West, supports only 8 percent of the inhabitants. While the near-empty North is mainly the wet and forested Amazon Basin, the sparsely occupied Central-West is the tropical wet-and-dry interior part of the Brazilian plateau, where the vegetation cover is a mixture of savanna grassland and scrub woodland.

In each of the settlement regions bordering the Atlantic, previously described, there was seen to be a thinly peopled interior part, beyond the area of concentrated settlement, or the sertão. But the heartland of the sertão lies still farther inland, in the states of Goiás and Mato Grosso, which comprise most of the Central-West. In 1960 only three million people were counted in the states of Mato Grosso, Goiás, and the new Federal District, where the average density is under 1 per sq mi.

Commercial grazing is the dominant occupation of the interior Central-West. Its animal industry is almost completely dependent on the natural pastures, and very little supplementary feed is provided. What little planting is done consists of growing food crops for local human needs. Thus the economy is such that few people can be supported. There is a perceptible thickening of settlement on the high plains of southern Goiás and central Mato Grosso, where the elevations are higher and climatic conditions somewhat more favorable. Such is particularly the case in southern Goiás, which is less remote than Mato Grosso from the seaboard belt of concentrated settlement. Settlement in southeastern Goiás has also felt the stimulating effects of the recent establishment there of the new Federal District and its capital city, Brasilia, and of a rail connection with the coast as well. There is undoubtedly something of a thrust toward the vast, sparsely settled Brazilian interior, but as yet the successes within this pioneer zone have not been remarkable.

The future of population growth in the Central-West sertão is uncertain. At present it seems to be dubiously a region destined for small-scale farming and a large population increment. There would appear to be more hope for a type of agricultural settlement that involves an extensive form of land utilization, including as it does huge acreages, the use of modern technology, and a minimum of human labor.

The North is essentially an immense, thinly populated region of tropical rainforest situated within the Amazon Basin. In this vast area, which constitutes some 40 percent of the national territory, the 1960 census counted only 2.6 million people, or 3 percent of the nation's total.

Two quite unlike population communities sparsely occupy the Amazon Basin, the aboriginal Indians and descendants of immigrant settlers. The former, living in tribal groups and widely scattered throughout the immense forest domain, are estimated to number only 30,000 to 50,000. Missionaries and a few immigrant settlers entered the region as early as the 16th century, but it was not until the 19th century, as wild rubber became important, that these outlanders penetrated in significant numbers. The present immigrant population is largely a mixture of white and Indian blood. Some 65 percent of the Basin's population are located within its eastern third, where the settlers concentrated around the mouth of the river. There the port of Belém, a metropolis of half a million people, thrives on a commerce based on the products of its forested hinterland. Within the basin proper the immigrant settlers are congregated along the main river and its chief tributaries, so that the pattern of distribution is riverine and dendritic. Almost all economic activity focuses on the rivers, and all trade is waterborne. Manaus, a city of over 175,000 and the metropolis of the basin's interior, is strategically situated at the confluence of the Amazon and its main tributary, the Rio Negro. There it is able to control the trade, mainly of forest products, of the whole interior basin.

Regional Population Growth Rates. Brazil's population is not only growing rapidly but it is also growing at an ever increasing rate. During the 1940–1950 decade, population rose by some 11 million, or 27 percent; in the 1950–1960 decade the increment was more than 19 million, a 37 percent national increase. These decade changes are affected by two factors, the natural increase, or the difference between births and deaths, and the net external migration. The former is believed to be by far the more important in accounting for the nation's burgeoning population. To be sure, the data on births and deaths in Brazil are scattered and unreliable, so the precise rate of natural increase is impossible to establish. Moreover, Brazil does not collect official emigration statistics, so that net migration figures are not available. During the decade 1950–1960, some

TABLE 4.2   Population Changes in Brazil by Regions, 1950–1960

Region	Population (1960)	Population Increase (Absolute)	Population Increases (Percent)
North (Amazonia)	2,601,519	756,864	41.03
Northeast (including Bahia)	22,428,873	4,455,460	24.78
East	18,081,733	4,667,662	34.79
São Paulo	12,974,699	3,840,276	42.04
South	11,873,495	4,032,625	52.71
Central-West	3,006,866	1,269,901	73.11
Brazil	70,967,185	19,022,788	36.62

SOURCE: Roland E. Chardon, "Changes in the Geographic Distribution of Population in Brazil, 1950–1960," in *New Perspectives of Brazil*, Eric N. Baklanoff (ed.). Vanderbilt University Press, Nashville, 1966, p. 155.

600,000 persons were officially listed as entering Brazil, and there was an additional "hidden" immigration of unknown size from surrounding countries. It seems to be a reasonable assumption that as many as two thirds of the immigrants remained. Hence, probably considerably less than 5 percent of the total national population increase between 1950 and 1960 was due to net external migration.

There are significant regional differences in population growth within Brazil (See Table 4.2). Two of the country's six main regional subdivisions, over the decade 1950–1960, grew at rates that were below the national average—the drought-ridden Northeast (including Bahía) was well below the mean, while the East (Minas Gerais and four small coastal states) was only slightly below the national average. The lag in the latter was due largely to the slow population increase rate (26.96 percent) of the large state of Minas Gerais, since the three small coastal states were all above the national average, but especially Rio de Janeiro, which contains the former Federal District and the metropolis of Rio de Janeiro. It was the attractions of the latter, and the associated industrial development in the small state of the same name, that lured immigrants. The slow growth in the Northeast reflects an important out-migration from that chronically drought-plagued region to other more prosperous sections, especially the cities of the southeastern and southern parts, including São Paulo and Rio de Janeiro.

While population in the four other main subdivisions grew at a rate exceeding the national average, growth was especially rapid in the frontier region of the Central-West and in the South. To be sure, while in the former the *rate* of increase is far and away the highest for the country, the absolute numbers involved are small, since the total population in 1960 was only about three million. Doubtless the rapid percentage growth was due to new agricultural colonization as well as to the stimulus associated with the transfer of the national capital to Brasilia, which is situated within this interior wilderness.[19]

The next-fastest-growing region was the South, where, if only the three states of Parana, Santa Catarina, and Rio Grande do Sul are included, population growth amounted to 52–53 percent for the decade. If slower-growing São Paulo state is included, as it is in some schemes of regionalization, then the overall regional average is reduced to 46.38 percent. In reality, this grouping of the three (or four) southernmost states into a single region tends to mask where the real expansion occurred, for the growth rate in Rio Grande do Sul was only 30.83 percent, or well below the national average, while that of Santa Catarina was only slightly above. Hence the high regional growth rate must be attributed to Parana, the fastest-growing state in Brazil, which more than doubled its population during the decade. This can only be explained by a large net in-migration, mainly from São Paulo state, of newcomers whose destination was chiefly a zone of pioneer settlement in the uplands of northern interior Parana, which, economically speaking, is essentially a part of São Paulo state. A major recent development in this region is the establishment of new coffee plantations, which in 1966 produced 30 percent of the nation's crop.

São Paulo state, most populous of all the Brazilian states with nearly 13 million inhabitants, added 3.84 million to its total over the 1950–1960 decade, resulting in a state growth rate (42.04 percent) that, if not spectacular, was at least substantially above the national average. This indicates an important net in-migration. Much of this immigrant stream probably gravitated toward the metropolitan area of São Paulo, which is the leading industrial city of all Latin America and capital of São Paulo state. The state accounts for 53 percent of the total industrial production of Brazil. The part of the nation included within a rough triangle whose apexes are São Paulo, Rio de Janeiro, and Belo Horizonte is the core region or heartland of Brazil. As such, it provides the best social and

[19] Donald R. Dyer, "Population," p. 420.

economic opportunities, pays the highest wages, has the best educational facilities, represents the highest intensity of urbanization and industrialization, and until recently contained the nation's capital. Consequently the triangle is very attractive to those living in other parts of Brazil, as well as to migrants arriving from other countries. It is not surprising, then, that this heartland region, with its great metropolises, should show a high growth rate.[20]

Population Characteristics. Two contrasting types of population movement are currently in evidence in Brazil; in fact, they exist in nearly all the countries of Latin America. One of these is the trek from countryside to city. The other involves a relatively weak but widespread tendency for an outward movement to new settlements around the margins of the established population clusters, creating pioneer zones. In Brazil this is popularly known as *Marcha para o Oeste*, into the undeveloped lands of the interior. Within the country three main areas of pioneer settlement stand out, but local colonization of moderate significance is proceeding in a few other sections as well. While all of the pioneer settlement is of an unplanned or spontaneous type, federal, state, and private assistance has been forthcoming in some instances. The creation of Brasilia, a new Federal capital in the deep interior, is one instance in which Federal funds have functioned indirectly to stimulate pioneer colonization.

The most important of the pioneer zones is the one that forms a great outer arc with the city of São Paulo as its hub. It includes western Minas Gerais, southern Goiás, southern Mato Grosso, western São Paulo, and northwestern Parana. Official figures are lacking concerning how many people settled in this pioneer zone between 1950 and 1960, but Chardon estimates about two million. Here new settlement is associated in part with the further westward expansion of coffee, especially into northwestern Parana. The creation of Brasilia, which already has 350,000–400,000 inhabitants, has been an important stimulus to new settlement in southeastern Goiás, a process already begun before the advent of the new capital city. A number of frontier boom towns have also sprung up.

A second but far less important pioneer zone includes southwestern Parana and smaller areas of Santa Catarina and Rio Grande do Sul. It is estimated that between half a million and a million settlers moved into this frontier region during the decade 1950–1960, where they are

---

[20] Roland E. Chardon, "Changes in the Geographic Distribution of Population in Brazil, 1950–1960," in Eric N. Baklanoff (ed.), *New Perspectives of Brazil*, Vanderbilt University Press, Nashville, 1966, p. 161.

engaged in small-scale diversified farming.[21] By this new settlement most of the previously unoccupied good land has been filled in up to the borders of Argentina.

Brazil's third important area of pioneer settlement is in central Maranhão in the Northeast, where close to 600,000 persons have been involved in new colonization. What could have instigated this pioneer movement is not so clear; one suggestion is that it represents a flight from the drought areas farther east. Pioneer expansion here, unlike that in the south, involves largely subsistence farming; the commercial crops grown are planted mainly to supply food for travelers on the Belém-Brasilia highway.

In summary, within the four pioneer states of Parana, Matto Grosso, Gioás (including the new Federal District), and Maranhão, which embrace the three main pioneer zones mentioned above, the population increased by about 4.3 million between 1950 and 1960, or nearly one fourth (23 percent) of Brazil's total national increase. This remarkable increase of 78 percent is to be compared to only 37 percent for the nation as a whole. Such a differential is largely a consequence of rural expansion into pioneer belts, since less than 18 percent of the population growth was a consequence of urbanization.[22]

But of greater magnitude than the trek to pioneer regions is that from settled rural areas to the cities, especially the larger ones. The census of 1960 indicates that Brazil's population as of that year was about 55 percent rural and 45 percent urban. Because the term "urban" as used in the Brazilian census operates to include many small places that are dubiously cities, the above proportions tend to exaggerate the urban sector and understate the rural. In reality, Brazil is still a strongly rural country, and the rural environment remains a powerful determinant of Brazilian culture and personality. According to the United Nations estimates, only 20.3 million of the inhabitants, or 29 percent, were living in localities with 20,000 or more inhabitants in 1960; 71 percent were either genuinely rural or else living in small rural-urban communities.

But if the truly urban sector is still relatively small, it has, nevertheless, been increasing rapidly and at an accelerating rate over the past few decades. Using the census definition of "urban," the proportion of the whole population so classified was only 31.2 percent in 1940, but it rose to 36.2 percent in 1950 and 45.1 percent in 1960. This was an intercensal annual geometric growth rate of 3.9 percent in 1940–1950 and 5.4 percent in 1950–1960. By the more restrictive United Nations definition, the pro-

[21] Chardon, "Changes in Geographic Distribution of Population," p. 170.
[22] Chardon, "Changes in Geographic Distribution of Population," p. 172.

portion that was urban rose from 16 percent to 21 percent to 29 percent over the same period.

Moreover, if one considers the increases in population numbers, somewhat over 19 million people were added to Brazil's total population between 1950 and 1960, 13.2 million of whom were urban and only 5.8 million rural (census definition). This was a 70 percent decade increase in the urban population but only a 17–18 percent increase in the rural one, and a 36.6 percent increase in the total population.

The individual states of Brazil show great differentials in the proportion of the population increase during the 1950–1960 decade that is accounted for by urban places. Rio de Janeiro-Guanabara exhibited the largest relative increases in urban population. At the opposite extreme are the pioneer states of Maranhão, Parana, Goiás, and Mato Grosso, in which the urban increase was small indeed compared with the total population growth. The intensity of urbanization is above the country average of 45.1 percent (census definition) in two regions, the South and the East; in the other three subdivisions, the Northeast, Central-West and North, the degree of urbanization is below the national average.

If we take the top ten cities of Brazil, all over 100,000 in population and with a combined population of 12,875,000 or nearly 70 percent of the urban total (census definition), their combined rate of growth, 1950–1960, was close to 70 percent, or about the same as that for the entire urban population. It has been estimated that of the total population increase in these ten cities, about 70 percent could be attributed to net migration.[23] The large cities, therefore, are attracting an important stream of migrants from other parts of Brazil. The two urban giants, São Paulo and Rio de Janeiro, each with over three million inhabitants and with an additional million or two within their urban metropolitan regions, add even greater numbers from outside the country.

As in those other parts of the world where birth rates are high and death rates relatively so, Brazil's population is strongly concentrated in the younger age groups. The proportion of the aged is low indeed. In 1950, there were 80 dependents (persons under 15 and over 65) for every 100 of those between 15 and 65, who may be thought of as the economic producers. As a general rule the young are relatively more numerous in rural parts; those in the reproductive ages are proportionably higher in urban places. Also, because of the prominence of internal migration in Brazil, which tends to select persons between 16 and 30, it is

[23] Chardon, "Changes in Geographic Distribution of Population," p. 166. For a relatively comprehensive treatment of internal migration in Brazil, see T. Lynn Smith, *Brazil: People and Institutions*, 1963 ed., pp. 144–198.

to be expected that age structure in the several states will vary. Thus, Sergipe in the northeast, which has furnished many out-migrants, has a marked deficiency of young adults and excessive proportions of the aged.

Illiteracy, which characterized 65 percent of the population age 15 and over in 1920, had been reduced to 57 percent by 1940 and an estimated 30–35 percent in 1968. But in spite of this good showing, because of the rapid population growth the number of adult illiterates rose from 1.4 million in 1920 to 15.8 million in 1960. Illiteracy is three times as high among rural people as among those in urban places. It is also far higher among blacks than among whites and Orientals.

In spite of the recent strides in urbanization and industrialization, Brazil is still basically agrarian, with slightly over half of its labor force engaged in primary industry in 1960, compared with 64.1 percent in 1940. In the same period the percentage engaged in the secondary and tertiary economic sectors rose from 27.7 to 36.2 percent. Between 1940 and 1960 real per capita output plus real per capita income rose steadily, but during the decade of the 1960's both output and income fell behind population increase, resulting in a lowering of the per capita figures.[24]

Paraguay. If Brazil is the population giant of South America, landlocked Paraguay is the pygmy, since its estimated population in 1969 was only 2.3 million. Although overwhelmingly mestizo in composition, the predominant racial strain in the Paraguayans is that of the Guarani Indians, whose contribution includes language and habits of living as well as blood. Less than 5 percent of the people are pure Indian, and the number with exclusive European ancestry is smaller. There are almost no Africans.

The core of the Paraguayan state is the single cluster of population located in the country's southern extremity, in a hilly portion of the Parana Plateau with Asunción, the national capital, forming its nucleus. The extensive Chaco region lying west of the Paraguay River is relatively empty of settlement. One of the least modernized of the Latin American countries, Paraguay's population characteristics are typical of the LD realm.

REFERENCES

"Brazil: a Prodigy of Growth," *Population Bulletin*, Vol. XXV, No. 4, 1969, pp. 89–115.

[24] "Brazil: A Prodigy of Growth," *Population Bulletin*, Vol. XXV, No. 4, September 1969, pp. 111–113.

Butland, G. J. "Frontiers of Settlement in South America," *Revista Geográfica*, Vol. 65, 1966, pp. 93–108.

Chardon, Roland E. "Changes in the Geographic Distribution of Population in Brazil, 1950–1960," in Eric N. Baklanoff (ed.), *New Perspectives of Brazil*. Vanderbilt University Press, Nashville, 1966, pp. 155–178.

Cole, J. P. *Latin America: An Economic and Social Geography*. Plenum Press, New York, 1966, pp. 12–21, 48–49.

Costa, Manoel A. "Distribuição espacial da população do Brasil" (Spatial distribution of the population of Brazil). Instituto Brasileiro de Estatística. *Estudos e Análises*, 2. Rio de Janeiro, 1969. 44 pp.

Crist, Raymond E. "Bolivians Trek Eastward," *Americas*, Vol. 15, No. 4, 1963, pp. 33–38.

Diégues, Manuel. "Internal Migration in Brazil," *United Nations World Population Conference*, Belgrade, 1965, Vol. 4.

Dyer, Donald R. "Growth of Brazil's Population," *Journal of Geography*, Vol. 65, 1966, pp. 417–428.

Dyer, Donald R. "Population and Elevation in Peru." Festscrift: Clarence F. Jones, *Northwestern University Studies in Geography*, No. 6, 1962.

Fifer, J. V. "Bolivia's Pioneer Fringe," *Geographical Review*, Vol. 57, No. 1, 1967, pp. 1–23.

Gendell, Murray. "Fertility and Development in Brazil," *Demography*, Vol. 4, pp. 143–157.

Heer, David M. "Fertility Differences Between Indian and Spanish-Speaking Parts of Andean Countries," *Population Studies*, Vol. 18, pp. 71–84, July 1964.

James, Preston E. *Latin America*, 4th ed. The Odyssey Press, New York, 1969, pp. 708–720 and passim.

Lowenthal, David. "Population Contrasts in the Guianas," *Geographical Review*, Vol. 50, No. 1, 1960, pp. 41–58.

Marchand, Bernard. "Étude géographique de la population du Vénézuéla," *Annales de Géographie*, 72 année, No. 394, November–December 1963, pp. 734–745.

Neiva, Artur Hehl. "The Population of Brazil," in *Population Dilemma in Latin America*. J. Mayone Stycos and Jorge Arias (eds.), Potomac Books, Inc., Washington, D.C., 1966.

Parsons, J. J. and W. M. Denevan. "Pre-Columbian Ridged Fields," *Scientific American*, Vol. 17, No. 1, 1967, pp. 92–100.

Robinson, David A. *Peru in Four Dimensions*. American Studies Press, Lima, 1964, pp. 67–152.

Robinson, Harry. *Latin America: A Geographical Survey*. Frederic A. Praeger, New York, 1967, pp. 326–329.

Saunders, John van Dyke. "The People of Ecuador: A Demographic Analysis," *Latin American Monographs*, No. 14, University of Florida Press, Gainesville, 1961, pp. 6–7.

Smith, T. Lynn. *Brazil: People and Institutions*, 1963 ed. Louisiana State University Press, Baton Rouge, 1963, especially pp. 39–198.

Smith, T. Lynn. *Colombia: Social Structure and the Process of Development,* University of Florida Press, Gainesville, 1967.

Smith, T. Lynn. "The Racial Composition of the Population of Colombia," *Journal of Inter-American Studies,* Vol. 8, 1966, pp. 210–235.

Stycos, J. Mayone. "Culture and Differential Fertility in Peru," *Population Studies,* Vol. 16, March 1963, pp. 257–270.

Suzuki, Teiiti. "Japanese Immigrants in Brazil," *Population Index,* Vol. 31, April 1965, pp. 117–138.

Weeks, John R. "Urban and Rural Natural Increase in Chile," *Milbank Memorial Fund Quarterly,* Vol. XLVIII, January 1970, pp. 71–89.

Whitehead, L. "Altitude, Fertility and Mortality in Andean Countries," *Population Studies,* Vol. 22, 1968, pp. 335–346.

CHAPTER 5

Africa

While all three of the LD continents are seriously deficient in reliable population statistics, such data are most scanty for Africa, the least developed of the triad. As of 1962, only about one half of Africa had been covered by census counts, and a number of these were dated pre-1959. Sample surveys were available for a dozen or so additional countries. Only partial counts or conjectural estimates were available for eight.[1] Since 1962, 16 countries have had population censuses or some other type of population tabulation. While the mere existence of population data is no assurance that they are reliable, still, there is an almost irresistible temptation to regard any population figures as better than none. It must be evident, however, that conclusions based on faulty data can be seriously in error. But makeshift tools are often the only kind available to the student of African population. It is mainly since World War II that a majority of the African countries have compiled sufficient population data to allow at least the primary, and even some of the tertiary, spatial distribution patterns of the continent's inhabitants to become discernable. Some kind of useful statistical data on population are now available for almost all parts of tropical Africa except Ethiopia, Somalia, and French Somaliland.

Racial and Ethnic Features. Africa's racial-ethnic-cultural complexity is so great as to almost defy making a brief but meaningful statement concerning it. Two grand subdivisions, Caucasoids and Negroids, are usually recognized, with the zone of separation lying for the most part between the 20° and 30° N parallels, although toward the east side of the continent the boundary's trend becomes more north-south (Fig. 5.1). Unquestionably this zone of demarcation in northern Africa is one of the

---

[1] For discussions of African population data and population enumeration since World War II, see Gordon Wolstenholme and Maeve O'Connor (eds.), *Man and Africa*, Little Brown and Co., Boston, 1965, pp. 65–67, and William Brass et al., *The Demography of Tropical Africa*. Princeton University Press, Princeton, N.J., 1968.

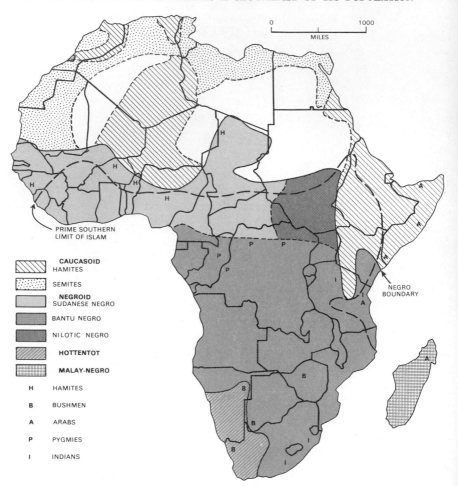

Fig. 5.1. Africa—main racial-ethnic groups. After Grove, Harrison Church, and others.

world's great cultural boundaries; it has important validity as an ethnic divider as well. The zone is scarcely a sharp one, since there are overlaps and transitions. Significantly, it is not too far removed from the southern margins of desert climate. To the north of the dividing zone, Caucasoid peoples, mainly tillers and nomadic herders, predominate. To the south, where the climate is more humid and tropical, black Africa prevails. There the Negroid people are primarily sedentary and may be either pastoralists or cultivators. Among the latter, some supplement their cropping with animal raising, while others do not.

The Caucasoid peoples of northern Africa belong to the Afro-Asian language group. They are usually divided into the Semites, whose language is mainly Arabic, and the Hamites, who speak Berber, Ethiopian, Cushitic, and other tongues. It is believed that the Hamites penetrated Africa from Southwest Asia. They are mainly nomads whose forebears were proud and warlike peoples who early established their superiority and founded some of the more important states in northern Africa. They exhibit a wide range of physical characteristics, but in general they are reasonably tall and have lightly pigmented skins, dark wavy hair, and thin faces with straight noses. On either side of the great cultural dividing zone there has been a large-scale mixing of Hamitic and Negro blood.

The Semites, or Arabs, forced their way into northern Africa from Southwest Asia as conquerors between the 7th and 14th centuries. They brought with them the Arabic language and the Moslem religion. Mixing has gone on to such a degree that it is nearly impossible to distinguish Arabs from Berbers on the basis of physical characteristics alone. Although the original Arab conquerors were overwhelmingly nomads, their more versatile progeny are cultivators, traders, and town dwellers as well. Dry northern Africa is the western limb of the much more extensive Moslem cultural world, which spreads across southern and central Asia as far as India and into China. The great cultural dividing line, therefore, fairly represents the southward-advancing front of Islam in Africa.

Black Africa, south of the cultural divider zone, includes nearly three fourths of Africa's total population and about the same fraction of all the world's Negroids. Here the more humid climate creates an environment characterized by tropical forest and savanna. It is mainly the Horn region of East Africa and the southwestern part of the continent that are genuinely dry. Black Africa is inhabited by a wide variety of Negroid peoples, many of whom have a Hamitic strain and also have incorporated a degree of Hamitic culture. Characteristically the black Africans are organized into a vast array of groups and tribes that possess in different degrees a common culture.

Among the large language groupings within black Africa the two largest (in terms of numbers of adherents), which are of about the same size, are a West African-sudan group speaking West African languages and another in equatorial and southern Africa speaking mainly Bantu. In the north, eastward from about Lake Chad, is a smaller group that speaks a variety of Central African languages.

The purest Negro strains appear to be located in West Africa along the Atlantic coast from Guinea to Cameroon. They are characterized by black skins, moderate height, kinky hair, flat noses, and thick lips. It was these peoples who developed such powerful kingdoms as those of the Ashanti and Yoruba. Farther north in the savanna zone of western and central Africa are the sudan blacks who are darker, taller, and show a greater protrusion of the jaw. The Hamitic influence is strong. In the past the powerful Fulani and Hausa states dominated large parts of the savanna zone.

Within the Central-African language group, especially in its eastern parts, which include the headwaters of the Nile, is a great variety of peoples representing varying mixtures of Negro and Hamitic blood. These are known as the Nilotes and Nilo-Hamites. They are tall, slender, and dark, and their facial structure is more Hamitic than Negro. The cattle-herding Masai of the East African plateau, east of Lake Victoria, are included in this subgroup.

The populous Bantu-language group occupies mainly central and southern Africa. Among the Bantu considerable physical variety prevails, resulting from different degrees of infusion of Hamitic blood, with Hamitic features being most conspicuous in the eastern and southern parts of the Bantu realm. This may account for the greater emphasis on cattle-herding among such tribes, since the Bantu of the Congo Basin are primarily agriculturists. The same is true of the blacks in West Africa.

Three almost insignificantly small African groups can only be mentioned. Two of these, the Pygmies and the Bushmen, are remnants of ancient aboriginal groups. The former are largely confined to the equatorial forests of the Congo Basin. The Bushmen, mainly hunters and gatherers, are found in the remote and dry parts of southwestern Africa. A third minor group, the Hottentots, are the result of the mixing of Bushmen and the early Hamitic invaders. They too are confined to the southwestern part of South Africa, where the pure strain is engaged in pastoral nomadism. Others have mixed with Europeans and Asiatics.

People of European descent living in Africa numbered about six million in the mid-1950's. Probably five sixths of these were in two large concentrations, one at the northern and the other at the southern extremity of the continent, where the climate is mostly subtropical and temperate. At present over three million, mainly descendants of Dutch and English settlers, comprise a dominant white minority in the Republic of South Africa. In Mediterranean Africa the large pre-1956 white minority of about two million has been drastically reduced to approximately 430,000 as a consequence of the hasty exodus following the wave of independence that swept the region in the period after World War II. Here there has been only minor mixing of whites with the native peoples. The over three quarters of a million whites in tropical Africa are widely and irregularly dispersed.

Excluding the early Arabs, peoples of Asian descent in Africa probably

number nearly one million. The single greatest concentration of Asiatics
is the large Indian community of nearly half a million in South Africa.
A second primary concentration is the 400,000 Asians, chiefly from India
and the Levant, who are located in equatorial East Africa, mainly Kenya,
Uganda, and Tanzania.

Population Numbers and Vital Rates.   Africa's estimated population
in 1970 is about 344 million; it may be assumed that this figure is probably
within 15 percent of the truth. So while Africa represents some 22 percent of the earth's land area, it has somewhat less than 10 percent of
its population. Consequently its overall population density is only two
fifths to one half that for the earth as a whole. By this crude yardstick,
therefore, Africa can be said to be sparsely populated, and so it is also
by comparison with Asia and Europe. But on the other hand, Africa's
average population density is very similar to that of the Americas and
is five to six times that of Australia and New Zealand.

If estimates of Africa's current population are of dubious reliability,
then those for the past several centuries should be regarded with even
more suspicion. Walter F. Willcox surmises that the population of the
whole continent was stationary at the level of about 100 million for
two centuries after 1650 (Table 5.1).[2] Since this was a period of accelerated population growth for the world as a whole, it is obvious that

[2] Walter F. Willcox, "Increase in the Population of the Earth and of the Continents
Since 1650," in Imre Ferenzi (ed.), *International Migrations, Vol. II, Interpretations.*
New York, National Bureau of Economic Research, 1969, pp. 33–82.

TABLE 5.1   Population Estimates for Africa (Millions)

Year	Willcox	Carr-Saunders	Durand[a]	United Nations
1650	100	100		
1750	100	95	106	
1800	100	90	107	
1850	100	95	111	
1900	141	120	133	
1920				136
1930				164
1940				191
1950			222	222
1960				277
2000			768	

[a] "Medium" estimates.

over those two centuries Africa must have slipped appreciably in the proportion of the world's people that it contained. This situation reflected the extremely backward conditions in Africa, which did not participate in the modernization processes that were influencing population growth in the rest of the world and particularly the peoples of European origin. Since 1920 or 1930, however, as mortality declined, Africa's population growth rate is believed to have markedly accelerated, and over the past few decades it has probably exceeded the world average. The annual rate of growth in 1970 is estimated to be a high 2.6 percent.

Africa has the dubious distinction of currently having the highest fertility and mortality rates among the three LD continents. Thus, her estimated average crude birth rate of 47 per 1000 is to be compared with the distinctly lower figure of about 38 for each of the other two retarded continents. Similarly, Africa's inferred average crude death rate of 20 per 1000 strikingly exceeds Asia's estimated 15, and is more than double Latin America's conjectured 9. Clearly, Africa's vital rates most closely resemble those of the pre-modern world; western medicine and sanitation have been less effective in lowering the death rate there than elsewhere in the LD realm. Indeed, the period immediately following the European occupation of Africa in the late nineteenth century may have witnessed a temporary increase in the continent's mortality rate, resulting in an arrested population growth, or even a decline, although this feature cannot be substantiated. Africa's present estimated annual population growth rate of 2.6 percent is intermediate between those of Latin America (2.9) and Asia (2.3), and is well above the estimate for the whole earth (2.0). Birth, death, and natural increase rates show considerable regional variation (Fig. 5.2; see also Figs. 1.1 and 1.3).

Spatial Distribution. It is only recently, since World War II, that sufficient data have become available to make possible the construction of useful maps showing the continent's spatial distribution of people (Figs. 5.3, 5.4).

Compared with tropical South America, tropical Africa does not exhibit such a strong peripheral concentration of population. This reflects both Africa's less-empty interior and a less-striking occupancy of its continental perimeter. Africa's most empty region is its vast Saharan drought area spanning the entire continent, and not its humid tropical interior. To a degree this contrast in gross population pattern may be attributed to a later and more modest exploitation of African resources by European peoples, whose paramount commercial interest was in overseas markets. Primitive subsistence farming, much of it of the slash-and-burn type, is more characteristic of humid tropical Africa than of its South American counterpart, and hence overseas markets are of less importance. Also

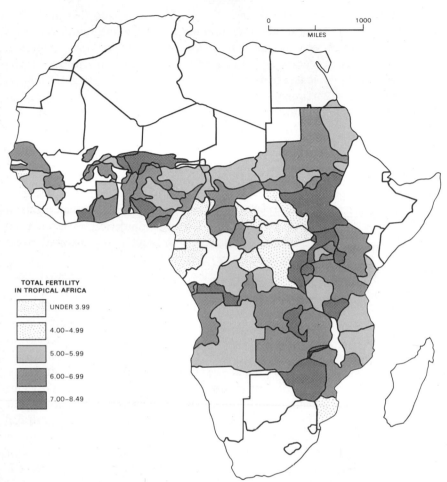

Fig. 5.2. Total fertility rates (the number of children that would be born during the lifetime of each woman experiencing the given fertility rates) of black Africa. After map by Ansley J. Coale in *Population Index*, April 1966, supplemented from a map by Etìenne van de Walle and Hilary Page in *Population Index*, January–March 1969.

unlike Latin America, a cluster or a node of relatively dense population (whose nucleus is a major city) less characteristically forms the core area of African political units (either nations or their provinces), with political boundaries typically located within the intervals of sparse population between the centers of population concentration. Indeed, it is not uncommon in Africa for political boundaries to bisect nodes of population, or even to cut across tribal areas. This reflects the fact that relatively stable political units with durable boundaries were not, until recently, a feature of much of tropical Africa as they were in Latin America. In the centuries preceding the penetration by Europeans, most of the tribal peoples in tropical Africa had been in a very fluid state locationally, with constantly changing positions. The Negroid peoples had long been engaged in a variety of complex migrations, variously stimulated, that resulted in a succession of somewhat fortuitous population distributions determined, often irrationally, by accidents of warfare, hunger, tribal leadership, and the like. During the 19th century, with the partition of Africa by the European nations, this migratory character of the Negroid tribal peoples was terminated abruptly, resulting in a freezing of those populations in the relatively arbitrary positions they had attained at that particular time. As we view the present population patterns, they often seem highly irrational. Thus, many relatively uninhabited areas owe their condition to historical accidents rather than to any environmental disability, while numerous dense clusters cannot be attributed to environmental generosity.

Certainly within Negro Africa the present patterns of population-density inequalities do not consistently reflect the qualities and potentialities of the physical resource base. Of course the term "quality" as applied to natural resources is as much a function of varying tribal cultures as of the physical earth itself. Expectably, such physical attributes as aridity, widespread deficient drainage, and high and rugged terrain do impose settlement limitations on all native cultures. But within that range of environmental conditions which is permissive for agricultural settlement, there are striking localisms in the population pattern that more often are rooted in culture, tradition, political stability, or even accident than in environmental quality. And since tribal culture traits are exceedingly slow in their transfer or diffusion from one group to another, it is common to find contrasting densities of native settlement even within what appear to be relatively similar environments. For example, tribal tradition expressed through attachment to a particular area, even when that area is miserly in physical productivity, appears to explain some of the apparent inconsistencies of spatial population distribution, which reveal seemingly inferior lands to be crowded, while nearby areas with far better agricultural environments are only thinly occupied.

The broadest pattern of spatial population distribution in Africa is set by certain types of non-ecumene, or lands physically hostile to man. Of these the arid lands create by far the most extensive unpopulated or meagerly populated domain. This is in contrast to tropical South America, where the empty lands are largely regions with wet tropical climate. By far the most extensive arid non-ecumene is the Sahara, which stretches clear across the widest part of Africa, the Nile oasis being the single interruption (Fig. 5.3). Smaller areas of relatively empty dry ecumene are to be observed in Somali and eastern Ethiopia, and likewise in the Kalahari Desert of southwestern Africa. The Saharan waste provides a relatively effective barrier separating the Caucasoid realm of Berber and Arab to the north from Negroid Africa to the south. Still another, but much more restricted, form of non-ecumene is the swampy

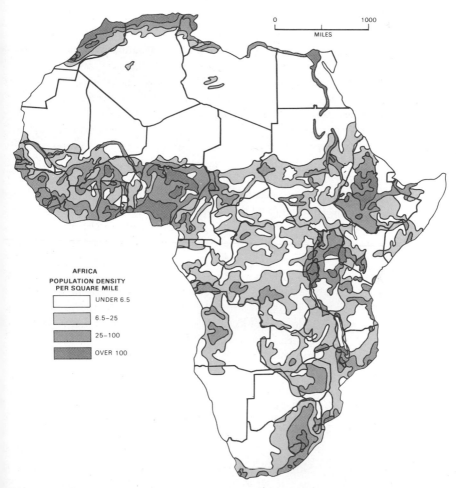

Fig. 5.3. Population density in Africa about 1960. Greatly simplified from density map by Else Schmidt and Paul Mattingly. Scale 1:10,000,000, published by *Geographische Rundschau*, 1966, Heft 12.

plains, so widespread in northern Botswana, Zambia, Mali, and the central Congo Basin. The evidence of a strong correlation between tsetse fly-induced sleeping sickness or other tropical diseases on the one hand and the gross continental patterns of population distribution on the other have scarcely been proven. But local and regional dislocations of human settlement doubtless have been induced by trypanosomiasis.

On the positive side, population densities well above the continental average are characteristic of both the subtropical northern and south-eastern extremities of the continent, especially the former. In both regions there is an important minority of European peoples, who in a variety of ways, including an efficient exploitation of resources, the development of overseas commerce, and the introduction of Western medicine and sanitation, have influenced the growth of the nonwhite population. The conspicuous Nile riverine settlement strip that is Egypt is doubtless the most densely settled locality in all Africa. Northern Africa (Morocco, Algeria, Tunisia, Libya, and Egypt), fronting on the Mediterranean Sea, has a total population (1970 estimate) of about 71 million, nearly half of which (47–48 percent) is in Egypt. Southern Africa (South Africa, Southwest Africa, Lesotho, Botswana, and Swaziland) is less than one third as populous (23 million).

Within tropical Africa, containing some 251 million, mostly blacks, or about 70 percent of the continent's total inhabitants, three population regions may be distinguished: (1) a West Africa-sudan region of moderate density; (2) a larger East (including the northeast) Africa region also of moderate density but somewhat lower than that of the West; and (3) a Central Africa region that is distinctly more sparsely peopled than either of the other two subdivisions.

The West Africa-sudan region contains some 28 percent of the land area of tropical Africa and probably 40–41 percent of its population, or about 101 million (1970).[3] The East Africa region as here defined includes nearly 41 percent of tropical Africa's area and probably 45 percent of its population (114 million). Its overall density is therefore somewhat more than three fourths that of West Africa. Central Africa is just slightly larger than West Africa, but it supports only 35 million people, so that its average density is only about one third that of West Africa and nearly three fifths that of East Africa. Internal population patterns of these three main subdivisions will be dealt with in a later section.

Urban Population. Almost certainly Africa is the least urban of all

---

[3] *1970 World Population Data Sheet*, Population Reference Bureau, Washington D.C., April 1970.

the continents, but any precise figures are of dubious reliability. In tropical Africa less than 10 percent of the population are believed to live in communities with more than 5000 inhabitants, and even many of the small places exceeding 5000 are more rural than urban in function. Down to the beginning of the present century nearly all the black Africans were gatherers, subsistence cultivators, or herdsmen. United Nations sources indicate that of 26 countries in tropical Africa for which estimates are available, all but one have less than 20 percent of their total populations living in places of 20,000 or more inhabitants.[4] Using the same definition of urban, the estimated average for all of tropical Africa in 1960 was only 7 percent.[5] A mere 1 percent lived in large cities with more than 500,000 inhabitants. In the northern and southern extremities of the continent, where there are important white minorities, the proportion of the people living in places of 20,000 or more inhabitants is distinctly higher—26 percent in northern Africa and 32 percent in southern Africa.[6]

But if the estimated proportion of tropical Africa's population that is urban is at present low, the recent rates of increase are dramatically high. It seems to be a case of making up for a slow start. In fact, the tempo of urbanization in black Africa outdistances that of any of the United Nation's 21 world regions, excepting only the LD parts of insular Oceania. Thus, the 1950–1960 decennial urban increase for tropical Africa was 112 percent; this is to be compared with 88 percent for tropical South America, 65 percent for mainland East Asia, 59 percent for Southeast Asia, and 97 percent for mainland Middle America.[7] The rate is also far higher than those for northern Africa (53 percent) and southern Africa (47 percent). To be sure, tropical Africa's extraordinarily high *percentage* increase in urban population represents only a relatively small absolute increase.

In the technically advanced Western countries, urbanization has proceeded in step with industrialization and the increase in employment opportunities. In tropical Africa, however, the urban growth rate is proceeding at a pace that is much faster than the economic development in urban centers and the possibilities they offer for employment. The high 1950–1960 decennial growth rate of urban population in tropical Africa (112 percent) is out of all proportion to the total population

[4] "World Survey of Urban and Rural Population Growth," United Nations, *Document E/CN.9/187*, March 8, 1965, p. 24, Table 10.
[5] "Urban and Rural Population Growth, 1920–1960, with Projections," United Nations, *Working Paper No. 15*, September 1967, p. 143.
[6] "Urban and Rural Population Growth," p. 143.
[7] "Urban and Rural Population Growth," p. 141.

growth (24 percent) or to economic growth over the same period. Such a phenomenal rate of increase in urban people can only be explained by a mass migration from the rural areas to the cities. If most urban centers were isolated from rural in-migration for a few generations, they would suffer a loss in number of inhabitants, since the *natural* growth rates of urban communities are generally lower than those of rural areas. This feature stems from the debased health conditions in the congested and squalid cities and also their imbalance in the male-female ratio.[8] African towns and cities are centers of poverty, disease, and malnutrition. The large-scale trek from country to city of the economically most active population may be one reason why agricultural production in many African countries has lagged increasingly behind population growth. In much of tropical Africa the problems associated with urbanization are especially aggravated because there is little or no urban tradition and hence no experience with urban living that could help in solving the city problems.[9]

Large parts of Africa had practically no urban places until modern times. This is not true of Mediterranean Africa, since in Egypt and the Maghrib the origins of towns and cities go back millenniums in time. But over most of Negro Africa south of the Sahara, urban places were few or absent until the arrival of the Europeans. The earlier paucity of urban places is related to a variety of causes, among them lack of industry, the tribal nature of the social organization, the prevalence of nomadism and slash-and-burn agriculture, and the policy of creating a new capital with the establishment of each new ruler.[10]

The old towns of tropical Africa, antedating the arrival of Europeans, are of a variety of ages and origins. A number of them stood at the southern terminals of trans-Saharan caravan routes. Kano, Kayes, and Timbuktu are of this type. In addition, a number of ancient but small Arab towns, which functioned as ports and as craft, market, and religious centers dotted the east coast. A few interior cities such as Kumasi, Addis Ababa, and Kampala functioned as the capitals of military states. But probably the outstanding example of long-established towns in tropical Africa founded by native peoples are those of the Yoruba groups in southwestern Nigeria. There Ibadan, Ife, Oyo, and a number of other towns had populations that numbered in the tens of thousands. And while some Yoruba towns were important craft and trading centers, they were

---

[8] P. Smit, "Recent Trends and Development in Africa: Urbanization in Africa," *Journal of Geography* (South Africa), Vol. II, 1967, pp. 73, 75.

[9] Smit, "Recent Trends," pp. 75–77.

[10] R. J. Harrison Church et al., *Africa and the Islands*. Longman's, London, 1964, p. 98.

mostly agro-towns and lacked buildings of conspicuous size. According to the 1952 census, 47 percent of the population in the western, or Yoruba, region of Nigeria were living in communities of 5000 or more inhabitants.[11]

But during the colonial period in Africa a considerable number of new towns were created chiefly because of European developments, since urbanization in Africa is usually farthest advanced where European influence is strongest. The colonial towns were mainly administrative and commercial centers and were joined by railroads and roads; a few were mining centers and industrial complexes. Growth was more rapid in the ports, either coastal or riverine, and especially those located at the terminals of railroads. A distinctive feature of the new towns was the segregation of the European, African, and sometimes Asian populations in distinct quarters.

Throughout tropical Africa the non-black minorities are preponderantly urban dwellers. Even so, blacks form the majorities in the cities, although as a group they are overwhelmingly rural.

In terms of the absolute numbers of urban people, four main regions of concentration occur (Fig. 5.4). Two of these are along the northern or Mediterranean margins of the continent—one in the Maghrib and the other in Egypt. A third is at the opposite or southern extremity of the continent, which is also a region of strong European influence. The fourth main concentration of urban population, and the only one in tropical Africa, is in West Africa, within the part reaching from the Ivory Coast to Nigeria. There a considerable proportion of the urban population is in cities whose origins antedate the colonial period.

Trading operations appear to have been a prime agent stimulating the origin and growth of modern African towns. Accordingly, a large proportion of the continent's urban population lives close to the sea in port cities. Of some 239 cities with over 30,000 inhabitants (about 1960), 72 were ocean ports whose combined populations amounted to 39–40 percent of the continent's urban total. For tropical Africa (omitting Nigeria), the comparable figure was 41 percent. In three fourths of the African countries that have sea frontage, the largest city had a tidewater location.[12] Such a focusing of urban population at tidewater reflects the fact that for many decades European contacts with Africans were centered at coastal points where trade in slaves, ivory, and gold was carried on. Subsequently, many of these coastal centers became the focal

[11] K. M. Barbour and R. M. Prothero (eds.), *Essays on African Population.* Routledge and Kegan Paul, London, 1961, pp. 253, 279–301.
[12] William A. Hance, *The Geography of Modern Africa.* Columbia University Press, New York, 1964, p. 54.

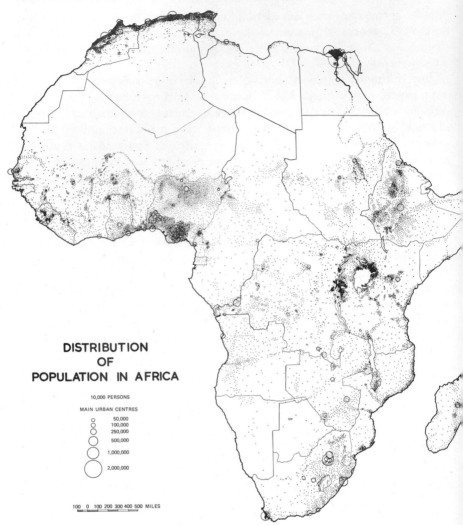

Fig. 5.4. Population distribution in Africa, about 1960. Courtesy University of Stellenbosch.

points of roads, and later the terminals of rail lines that connected the ports with the interior. It was common, also, for the port cities to become colonial capitals. Other cities, which, like the coastal ports, owe their growth and importance mainly to commercial functions, are the river and lake ports and the communities situated at the crossroads of land routes. Leopoldville on the Congo River, Khartum-Omdurman on the

Nile, and Fort Lamy on the Chari are illustrations of river ports. Salisbury, Lusaka, and Kano are examples of market towns situated at important nodes of land routes. In addition, there are a fair number of African cities that owe their importance to mining activities. The best known of the latter is the South African metropolis of Johannesburg.

Migration. The complexity and heterogeneity of modern migration patterns in Africa discourage important consideration of the topic in this volume.

In premodern times, among the more important migrations were the following: people from Southeast Asia entering Madagascar; Arab movements across northern Africa into the sudan belt and subsequently beyond into tropical West Africa; and a southward shift of Nilotic and Hamitic groups into East Africa and of Bantu peoples into eastern and southern Africa.

Within the modern period, but precolonial in time, unusually noteworthy migrations were those associated with (1) slave raiding and (2) tribal movements. The forced out-migration of an estimated 15 million African slaves over the three centuries preceding 1850 not only nearly depopulated certain African areas but also served to markedly change the racial composition of large sections of the New World. As noted in an earlier section, the precolonial period was one in which the African tribal population was unusually fluid. With the coming of the Europeans and the founding of states with central governments and recognized territories and boundaries, widespread tribal movements have been greatly curbed and tribal lands have taken on fixed locations and boundaries.

During the colonial period migration came to be more economically motivated, while at the same time group migrations waned in importance and those of individuals increased. Of unusual consequence was the inflow of large numbers of Europeans into Africa, especially at its northern and southern extremities where as a consequence the racial mix has been greatly modified. Since World War II there has occurred a large-scale exodus of European settlers from North Africa, Senegal, Congo, Kenya, and Tanzania.

Especially in recent decades a major form of population movement has been the large-scale internal labor migration from rural areas to cities and mines. Stimulating this movement of laborers are both push and pull factors. Among the former are the poverty and the meager economic opportunities prevailing in rural areas. In some localities of high population density, there exists a genuine shortage of land for cultivation and grazing. A main pull factor stimulating rural-urban migration is the growing number of opportunities for employment as wage laborers in the expanding industrial, mining, and commercial-agricultural enterprises, since Africans have learned to appreciate the value of cash wages and the goods that money can buy. Initially the labor migration was of a temporary kind, in which the male migrant left his village with the intention of earning enough money to satisfy the needs of his family for a short time and then returning home. He did not take his family with him. Indeed, many governments actively urged young male laborers to return to their native villages, since it was they who represented the most progressive and vigorous part of the labor force on which food production and the general well-being of the tribe depended. Moreover,

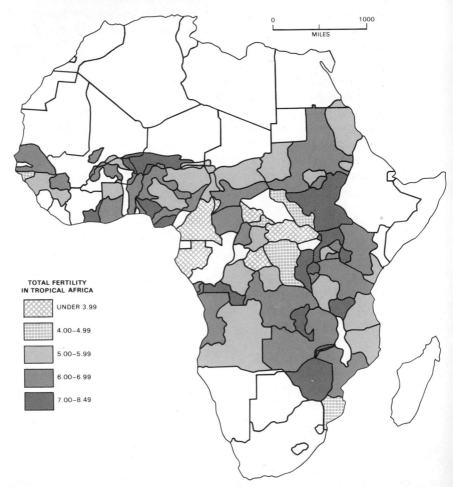

Fig. 5.5. Main migratory movements of population in Africa. Modified from maps by Grove, Prothero, and Dresch.

the governments of the countries and cities experiencing in-migration and the companies employing migrant labor discouraged permanent family migration, because they did not relish the expense involved in creating immigrant communities.

But gradually the attitudes of governments and employers toward migrant labor have been changing. Temporary labor migration is now recognized as wasteful in time and resources. Besides, it is increasingly the more experienced, and even semiskilled, labor that is in demand, and the temporary migrant is unable to qualify for positions requiring such labor. Consequently, more and more migrant Negro families are settling permanently in the swollen cities, where they live in squalid shanty towns that mushroom in the suburbs. Some of the more important migratory movements are shown in Fig. 5.5.

Of a very different nature is the migration of Moslem pilgrims that occurs between the western sudan belt and the holy city of Mecca. The poorer ones still make most of the trip on foot; others ride, at least part of the way, on trains, trucks and buses; a few fly. Some 10,000 religious pilgrims use the land routes each year, many taking several years to complete the journey, since they stop en route to earn money for the next stage of the trip.

REFERENCES

"Africa: Maps and Statistics," *Population*, No. 1, July, 1962, Africa Institute, Johannesburg, South Africa.

Balandier, Georges. *Ambiguous Africa: Cultures in Collision.* Translated by Helen Weaver. Pantheon Books, New York, 1966.

Barbour, K. M. "Rural-Urban Migrations in Africa—a Geographical Introduction," *Cahiers de l'ISEA*, Vol. 47, 1965.

Barbour, K. M. *Population in Africa: A Geographer's Approach.* Ibadan University Press, Ibadan, Nigeria, 1963.

Barbour, K. M., and R. M. Prothero (eds.), *Essays on African Population,* Praeger, New York, 1962.

Beaujeu-Garnier, J. *Géographie de la Population,* Tome 2, Editions M. Th. Génin, Paris, 1958.

Bourgeois-Pichat, Jean. "Problems of Population Size, Growth and Distribution in Africa." In Gordon Wolstenholme and Maeve O'Connor (eds.), *Man and Africa.* Little, Brown, Boston, 1965, pp. 65–97.

Brass, William, et al., *The Demography of Tropical Africa.* Princeton University Press, Princeton, N.J., 1968.

Caldwell, John C., and Chukuka Okonjo (eds.), *The Population of Tropical Africa,* Longmans, Green, London, 1968, pp. 28–49, 152–154, 179–198, 214–224, and 250–263.

Carlson, Lucile. *Africa's Lands and Nations*. McGraw-Hill, New York, 1967, pp. 25–43.

Church, R. J. Harrison, et al. *Africa and the Islands*, 2nd ed., 1967. Longmans, London, pp. 55–73.

Coale, Ansley J. "Estimates of Fertility and Mortality in Tropical Africa," *Population Index*, Volume 32, No. 2, 1966, pp. 173–181.

Colson, Elizabeth. "Migration in Africa: Trends and Possibilities," in Frank Lorimer and Mark Karp (eds.), *Population in Africa*. Boston University Press, Boston, 1960, pp. 60–67.

Commission for Technical Cooperation in Africa South of the Sahara. *Migrant Labour in Africa South of the Sahara*. Abidjan, 1961.

Dumanowski, Bolesaw. "The Influence of Geographical Environments on Distribution and Density of Population in Africa." *Africana Bulletin* (Warsaw) Vol. 9, 1968, pp. 9–33.

Economic Commission for Africa, *Report of the Seminar on Population Problems in Africa*, E/CN/14/186.

Elkan, Walter. "Migrant Labor in Africa: An Economist's Approach," *The American Economic Review*, Vol. XLIX, No. 2 (May 1959), pp. 188–97.

Frazier, E. Franklin. "Urbanization and Its Effects Upon the Task of Nation-Building in Africa South of the Sahara," *The Journal of Negro Education*, Vol. XXX, No. 3, Summer 1961, pp. 214–222.

Gabel, Creighton. "Prehistoric Populations of Africa," in J. Butler (ed.), *Boston University Papers on Africa*, Vol. 2. Boston, 1966, pp. 1–37.

Gann, L. H., and Peter Duignan. *White Settlers in Tropical Africa*. F. A. Praeger, New York, 1967.

Gleave, Michael B. "Hill Settlements and Their Abandonment in Tropical Africa," *Institute of British Geographers, Transactions*, No. 40, December 1966, pp. 39–49.

Greenberg, Joseph H. *The Languages of Africa*. University of Indiana Press, Bloomington, Indiana, 1963.

Grove, A. T. *Africa South of the Sahara*. Oxford University Press, 1967, pp. 40–51.

Gutkind, Peter C. W. "The African Urban Milieu: A Force in Rapid Change," *Civilisations*, Vol. XII, No. 2, 1962, pp. 167–195.

———. "Urban Conditions in Africa," *The Town Planning Review*, Vol. XXXII, No. 1, April 1961, pp. 20–32.

Hamdan, G. "Capitals of the New Africa," *Economic Geography*, Vol. XL, No. 3, July 1964, pp. 239–53.

Hance, William A. *Population, Migration, and Urbanization in Africa*. Columbia University Press, New York, 1970, pp. 128–208.

Hodder, B. W., and D. R. Harris (eds.). *Africa in Transition: Geographical Essays*. Methuen and Co., London, 1967.

Kimble, George H. T. *Tropical Africa*, Vol. 1. The Twentieth Century Fund. New York, 1960, pp. 81–123.

Lee, R. H. "Urbanization and Race Relations in Africa," *Journal of Human Relations*, Vol. VIII, Nos. 3–4 Spring-Summer 1960, pp. 518–33.

Little, Kenneth L. "Some Contemporary Trends in African Urbanization." *Melville J. Herskovits Memorial Lecture*, 2. Evanston, Northwestern University Press, 1966. 15 pp.

Lorimer, Frank, and Mark Karp (eds.). *Population in Africa*. Boston University Press, Boston, 1960.

Lorimer, Frank. *Demographic Information on Tropical Africa*. Boston University Press, Boston, 1961.

Lorimer, F., W. Brass, and E. van de Walle. "Demography," in Robert A. Lystad (ed.), *The African World; a Survey of Social Research*. Praeger, New York, 1965, pp. 271–303.

Mason, P. "Inter-Territorial Migrations of Africans South of the Sahara," *International Labour Review*, Vol. LXXVI, No. 3, September 1957, pp. 292–310.

McCall, Daniel F. "Dynamics of Urbanization in Africa," *The Annals of the American Academy of Political and Social Science*, No. 298, March 1955, pp. 151–60.

Miner, Horace (ed.). *The City in Modern Africa*. Praeger, New York, 1967.

Mountjoy, Alan B., and Clifford Embleton. *Africa: A New Geographical Survey*. Praeger, New York, 1967.

Murdock, George P. *Africa: Its Peoples and Their Culture History*, McGraw-Hill, New York, 1959.

Prest, A. R. "Population as a Factor in African Development." United Africa Company Limited, *Statistical and Economic Review*, No. 30, September 1965, pp. 1–16.

Problems in African Demography, International Union for the Scientific Study of Population, Paris, 1960.

Prothero, R. Mansell. "Continuity and Change in African Population Mobility," in Robert W. Steel and R. Mansell Prothero (eds.), *Geographers and the Tropics: Liverpool Essays*, Longmans, London, 1964.

Prothero, R. Mansell. *Migrants and Malaria in Africa*. Pittsburgh University Press, Pittsburgh, 1965.

Prothero, Robert M. "Population Mobility and Trypanosomiasis in Africa," *Bulletin of the World Health Organization*, Vol. 28, No. 5–6, 1963, p. 615.

Read, Margaret. "Migrant Labour in Africa and Its Effects on Tribal Life," *International Labour Review*, Vol. XLV, No. 6, June 1942, pp. 605–31.

Sadie, J. L. "Manpower Resources of Africa." *South African Journal of Economics*, Vol. 31 (4), December 1963, pp. 264–284.

Schmidt, Elsa. *Die Bevölkerungskarte von Afrika*. H. u. E. Steinbauer, München, 1959. (Folded population density map, scale 1:10,000,000.)

Schmidt, Else A., and Paul Mattingly. "Das Bevölkerungsbild Afrikas um das Johr, 1960." *Geographische Rundschau*, Vol. 18, 1966, pp. 447–458. (Map, in color, scale, 1:10,000,000.)

Seligman, C. G. *Races of Africa*, 4th ed. Oxford University Press, 1966.

Smit, P. "Recent Trends and Developments in Africa: Urbanization in Africa," *Tydskrif vir Aardrykskunde*, II, No. 10, April 1967, pp. 69–77.

Spengler, J. J. "Population Movements and Problems in Sub-Saharan Africa," Chapter 10 in E. A. G. Robinson (ed.), *Economic Development for Africa South of the Sahara*. St. Martin's Press, New York, 1964, pp. 281–311.

Steel, Robert W. "The Towns of Tropical Africa," in K. M. Barbour and R. M. Prothero (eds.), *Essays on African Population*. Routledge and Kegan Paul, London, 1961, pp. 249–278.

————, and R. Mansell Prothero (eds.). *Geographers and the Tropics: Liverpool Essays*. Longmans, Green and Co., London, 1964.

Stephens, Richard W. *Population Pressures in Africa South of the Sahara*. Population Research Project, George Washington University, Washington, 1959.

Stevenson, R. F. *Population and Political Systems in Tropical Africa*, Columbia University Press, New York, 1968.

Trewartha, Glenn T., and Wilbur Zelinsky, "Population Patterns in Tropical Africa," *Annals of the Association of American Geographers*, Vol. XLIV, No. 2, 1954, pp. 135–162.

United Nations Economic Commission for Africa. "Recent Demographic Levels and Trends in Africa." *Economic Bulletin for Africa* (*Addis Ababa*), Vol. 5, January 1965, pp. 30–79.

Verhaegen, P. "L'Urbanisation de l'Afrique Noire," Centre de Documentation Économique et Sociale Africaine, Brussels, 1962.

Wood, Eric W. "The Implications of Migrant Labour for Urban Social Systems in Africa," *Cahiers d'Études Africaines*, Vol. VIII, No. 29, 1968, pp. 5–31.

CHAPTER

6

Northern Africa

Northern Africa, including the Mediterranean borderlands and the Sahara, is to be distinguished from the part of the continent south of the Sahara, or Negroid tropical Africa. The Caucasoid north, dominated by Arabs and Berbers, has a degree of unity because of the common bond of its Islamic-Arabic social, religious, and language structure. Indeed, this is the western extension of the Moslem world, whose 60–70 million believers about equal in number those in Southwest Asia, which is usually thought of as the root area of the Mohammedan realm.

The true natives of the north are the Berbers, a Hamitic group whose origin is unknown. They were already firmly established in Mediterranean Africa when the Phoenicians first began to colonize along the coast in the 12th century B.C. Everywhere there has been a considerable admixture with the Arabs and practically a complete adoption of the Islamic faith, but in some regions Berbers speaking the Berber tongue remain dominant. This is especially true in certain relatively inaccessible highland strongholds, as well as in a large area of the Tuareg Sahara. Probably about one quarter of northern Africa's population has Berber as its mother tongue, and three quarters has Arabic. Heirs of the first Phoenician colonizers along the north African coast founded, in 814 B.C., the maritime city and the state of Carthage in what is now northern Tunis and later came to control nearly the whole western Mediterranean Basin.

Rome defeated Carthage in 146 B.C. and from then on dominated the north African region for over six centuries. But in spite of such long tenure, the effects of Phoenician and Roman control are minor. Even the Roman-induced Christianity, which had become rather widely spread among the Berbers, died out completely in the later competition with Islam.

The Moslem Arabs, invading from the east, reached Libya as early as the mid-7th century. And although it required nearly another century to conquer the Berbers militarily, the resulting spiritual and cultural conquest was complete, since Arabic culture and the Moslem faith were accepted nearly in total. In certain periods Mediterranean Africa was ruled as a unit from an Asiatic base; at other times there were multiple local centers of political control within North Africa. And while much of the splendor and many of the accomplishments of Arab civilization derived from Asiatic sources, North Africa also had its own focal centers and periods of cultural diffusion involving Islamic religion, law, and learning. Today that Arabic splendor has become dimmed throughout the whole Moslem world. Still, active religious proselyting goes on along the zone of contact between Caucasoids and Negroids in the sudan region.

Within northern Africa with its over 70 million inhabitants, the vast bulk of the population is concentrated in two distinct assemblages, one in the Atlas region in the northwest and the other in the Nilotic lands of Egypt in the northeast. Elsewhere Saharan aridity makes human settlement meager indeed. The two population groupings have about the same number of inhabitants, but they are spread over a much wider area in the Atlas concentration, where the overall population densities are as a consequence greatly lower.

THE MAGHRIB

The name Maghrib (or Maghreb) is applied to the part of northern Africa dominated by the Atlas highlands. It is essentially the three independent states of Morocco, Algeria, and Tunisia, although it is convenient to exclude the very extensive Saharan part of Algeria.

The Maghrib is bounded on the north by the Mediterranean Sea, on the west by the Atlantic, and on the south by the Sahara. To the east is mostly barren desert, but with a slightly more humid and populous coastal corridor connecting the Atlas lands with Southwest Asia. It is understandable, therefore, why the Maghrib has been greatly influenced by the civilizations, ancient and modern, that circumscribed the Mediterranean Sea and by the Arab nomads of western Asia.

The European (mainly French) occupation of the Maghrib, begun in 1830 and continued down to the 1950's and 1960's, introduced Western technology and culture, which in turn revolutionized the ways of living and powerfully affected population numbers and characteristics. An overlay of French culture was added to that of the Arab-Moslem base; many Moslems adopted European dress, spoke French or south European languages, and became less intensely religious. Partial Europeanization and modernization of the several economies and means of transportation gradually took place. In addition there was improvement in public sanitation, food supply, health, and education, all of which left their marks on the native peoples. Death rates fell, population growth was speeded up, education and literacy became more widespread, and the process of urbanization accelerated.

The number of Europeans in northwestern Africa peaked in the mid-1950's, at which time there were close to two million outlanders, many of them, second and third generation residents. About 54 percent, or over a million, lived in Algeria; 31 percent were in Morocco and the adjacent territory, and over 13 percent were in Tunisia. Still, the European element represented only about 8–9 percent of the total population of some 22 million in 1956. Four fifths of the Europeans lived in towns. By 1963 the total population had risen to 27 million, but the European element had been reduced by more than 1.5 million as a consequence of a large-scale exodus following independence. Besides the large French minority, there were smaller ones of Italians in Tunisia, and Spaniards in Morocco and northwestern Algeria, and still lesser ones of Maltese, Greeks, and Jews.

The generalized pattern of the population's spatial distribution within the Maghrib is fairly simple: a narrow and fragmented belt of high densities (100–200 per sq mi, 40–75 per sq km), occupying both coastal

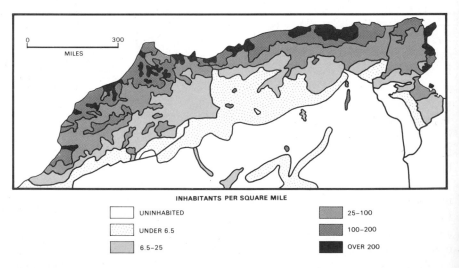

INHABITANTS PER SQUARE MILE

UNINHABITED	25–100
UNDER 6.5	100–200
6.5–25	OVER 200

Fig. 6.1. Population density in the Maghrib of northern Africa. Simplified from density map by Else Schmidt and Paul Mattingly, in *Geographische Rundschau,* 1966, Heft 12.

plain and adjacent Atlas slopes, borders the Mediterranean Sea and the Atlantic (Fig. 6.1). Understandably, proximity to the sea has continued to provide a great attraction for settlement throughout millenniums of time. There cities are numerous; agriculture, some of it involving irrigation and high-value commercial crops, dominates the rural parts. With significant exceptions, population density declines inland as altitude increases, terrain roughens, rainfall drops off (except at higher elevations), and land use is pastoral as well as agricultural. Density is lowest on the Saharan margins.

The details of spatial distribution of the Maghrib's inhabitants are exceedingly complex. Many of these are directly related to the quality of the physical environment, others to cultural and historical factors. For example, in the forbidding Tell Atlas Mountains of Kabylia in eastern Algeria, between Algiers and Bougie, is located one of the high-density areas of the region. Almost every fragment of usable land is utilized. Rugged Kabylia embraces only about 4 percent of Algeria's area, but is estimated to have about 15 percent of its population. Such a concentration in an inhospitable physical environment can only be explained by the fact that this region has served as a refuge, first nearly a millennium back when the sedentary Berbers fled before the invading Arab nomads, and then again much later during the last century and more, as the Europeans took over the towns and the lowlands.

Morocco. In the western, or Moroccan, section of the Maghrib, the population in 1970 was estimated to be about 15–16 million, giving the country an average density of 87 or 88 persons per sq mi. This is the lowest for any of the three Maghrib states, and reflects Morocco's greater deficiency of lowland rainfall, her higher and more rugged mountains, her greater isolation behind the mountain barriers of Rif and High Atlas, and her later introduction to European influence. In 1963, when the population of Morocco was around 12–13 million, there were still some 140,000 Europeans (even after an exodus of 240,000) and 105,000 Jews in the country; the remaining population was almost entirely Arab or Berber. Between 2 and 3 million Moslems probably still speak Berber, but even these are more or less Arabized.

In 1920 only 7 percent of the total population was estimated to live in communities with more than 20,000 population; the comparable figure for 1960 was 24 percent, a differential that indicates a recent strong acceleration of the urbanization process. But the country still remains overwhelmingly rural.

Morocco has the advantage of possessing two maritime frontages. Significantly, it is the coastal administrative subdivisions, including those along both Atlantic and Mediterranean, that support some 35 percent of the total national population, even though they represent only 11–12 percent of the total area. The Mediterranean littoral is short, and in addition it is almost continuously backed by the rugged Rif Atlas, so that lowland is largely absent. But in spite of the difficult terrain, some sections are so densely populated that the region is chronically threatened by crop failure and famine. Along the coast are a scattering of modest-sized port cities.

The plains of Atlantic Morocco are more extensive and also more closely settled than those facing the Mediterranean. Still, these Atlantic lowlands are handicapped by a general rainfall deficiency, with the dryness increasing in intensity toward the south. Fortunately, a number of streams descending from the High and Middle Atlas in places provide water for irrigation. Highest densities on the Atlantic lowlands lie within a coastal strip that on the average is 20–30 miles wide, but the width increases in the vicinity of river valleys. Except for a dune belt bordering the sea, the black-soiled coastal plain is highly suitable for cereal farming. In the cool waters of the Canaries Current, fish are relatively abundant, exploitation of which resource supports a considerable coastal population. Along this coast are located the leading ports of Morocco. The zone of relatively dense rural settlement within the coastal strip extends inland in the form of a riverine belt along the Tensift Valley, in which the city of Marrakech is located. The populous strip then bends northward until it merges with a well-occupied piedmont zone situated in front of the High Atlas, where streams are numerous and irrigation water is available. Deficient rainfall is the main handicap throughout, so that supplementary irrigation must be relied on in many districts. Inland from the coastal belt is the 60- to 80-mile-wide Meseta, a low tableland where seminomadic pastoralists predominate and settlement is sparser.

North of the Meseta and the Middle Atlas the Atlantic coastal lowland extends well inland along the Sebou River to form the richest and most populous part of the country, where the cities of Fez and Meknes are situated.

The Atlas ranges of Morocco, and the high plateaus that they enclose, are regions of essentially self-sufficient populations, mainly engaged in tillage and seminomadism. Quite naturally the highland region as a unit lies outside the peripheral belt of the country's highest densities. But in spite of the difficult terrain, certain parts of the highlands support relatively dense settlement. A number of valleys within the western parts of both the High Atlas and Anti-Atlas are well peopled by sedentary Berber cultivators who live in perched stronghold villages. By contrast, the drier eastern Atlas is more sparsely populated by seminomadic peoples.

Algeria. Departmental Algeria, which excludes the southern 90 percent of the country that is Saharan, is estimated to have about 14 million inhabitants in 1970, with an overall density of around 120 per sq mi. The country stretches for over 600 mi along the Mediterranean Sea and extends for 120 to 200 mi inland to beyond the Saharan Atlas. Like Morocco, it is a land of east-west mountain ranges separated by an intermontane plateau, and a narrow coastal plain that is in the nature of a series of somewhat isolated patches of lowland separated by northward-thrusting prongs of the Tell Atlas. From west to east the main lowlands are those inland from Oran and their eastward extension in the Chelif Valley, that of the Mitidja inland from Algiers, and the ones near Bejaia and Annaba. Each lowland is coincident with a cluster of dense population (Fig. 6.1). Together these Tell lowlands, which are one of the continent's quality regions, represent only 2–3 percent of the national area, but they contain over half of its people and most of its irrigated acreage. Over 2 million urban people reside in the Tell's cities.

The Algerian highlands consist essentially of a northern and a southern range with high plateaus between. The better-watered northern, or Tell, Atlas, although representing a harsh environment, is in places well populated by sedentary tillers. The steppelike intermontane plateau, about 3300 feet in elevation, has an overall density of only about 11 per sq mi, since nomadic and seminomadic herding is the dominant form of land use, and it becomes increasingly more prevalent toward the drier southern side. But along the plateau's more humid northern margins there is a fairly numerous sedentary farm population engaged chiefly in raising cereals.

Tunisia. Tunisia, the smallest (48,000 sq mi) and least populous (5.1 million, 1970 estimate) of the three Maghrib states, has an average density of about 100 persons per sq mi. It has much in common with the other two Maghrib countries, but at the same time there are noteworthy contrasts: it is drier; plains cover a larger proportion of the national area; it is culturally and economically more advanced; it has a stronger central government; and it is less zealously Islamic. Tunisia has also been more completely Arabized, since the relatively isolated Berber-speaking inhabitants represent only about 1 percent of the population. The large exodus of Europeans (mainly French and Italians) and Jews after independence has left only about 42,000 Europeans and less than 5000 Jews in the country as of about 1968, or less than one tenth of the total in 1956.[1] Nearly a third of the population is urban; metropolitan Tunis alone has

---

[1] John I. Clarke, "Population Policies and Dynamics in Tunisia," *The Journal of Developing Areas*, Vol. 4, No. 1, October 1969, pp. 46–49.

about one fifth of the country's total inhabitants. Nearly two thirds of the Tunisians derive their living from the land.

Tunisia, broadly speaking, may be divided into two parts, a fairly well-watered and hillier northern one third, which contains about 70 percent of the inhabitants; and a drier, more level, semiarid-to-arid southern two thirds, which support the remaining 30 percent (Fig. 6.1). Characteristically, there is a relatively large out-migration from the drier south to the more-favored north, where there is more land under cultivation and where European colonization has been more widespread. The largest cities and a disproportionately large share of all the urban people are located in the more prosperous north. The most densely populated and intensively used section is the Medjerda Valley and the other small lowlands around Tunis and Cape Bon. In addition to the usual cereal monoculture, the country's high-value Mediterranean tree crops are also concentrated in this locality.

South and east of the Dorsal Atlas, whose easternmost projection forms Cape Bon, is by far the most extensive plain of the country, called the Sahel. But in spite of its size it supports only a modest population, since it is semiarid and steppelike in character. Extensive unirrigated cereal agriculture and livestock herding are the most characteristic forms of land use in the Sahel, although its eastern parts do contain extensive olive orchards. South of about Gafsa, even grazing becomes sporadic and population is truly sparse.

The Sahara. Sahara is the world's largest desert and also one of its driest. Expectably, also, it is one of the most extensive uninhabited regions on the earth. Indeed, this near-void rather effectively separates Africa into two unlike population subdivisions, the Caucasoid north and the Negroid center and south. The essential physical unity of the Sahara is the reason for its separate and unified treatment, even though it is fractured into a number of political units. No sharp boundary separates the Sahara from the Mediterranean Maghrib to the north and the sudan grasslands to the south. The 4- or 5-in. annual rainfall line is sometimes considered to mark its approximate limits, but the location of such a line itself is vague and uncertain.

If for the moment the population of the Mediterranean fringes of Libya and that of the Nile Oasis, which is Egypt, are excluded, then the vast remaining Sahara may have no more than two to three million inhabitants. The concept of an average density of less than one person per sq mi obviously has little value, because immense areas are completely without human settlement, while by contrast, a few highly restricted oasis spots teem with people. An estimated four fifths of the Saharan inhabitants are concentrated along the northern margins of the desert, where the modest winter rains account for somewhat better grazing and where oases are more numerous because there the ground-water table is higher.

Two main economic groups may be recognized: (1) the pastoral nomads engaged in herding sheep, goats, and camels and (2) the sedentary cultivators. The latter are believed to be increasing in numbers more rapidly than the former and may at present comprise two thirds of the Saharan people, in spite of the migration currently taking place from the northern oases to cities along the Maghrib's Atlantic and Mediterranean margins. Several forms of nomadism prevail. There are, for example, the semi-nomads who combine herding and tilling and periodically sow cereals in stream beds and other moist spots. Most of these are located on the desert's less-arid margins. In addition there are the nomads who spend the whole year within the Sahara and others who seasonally move outside the desert in search of pasture. Other than the northern Sahara, where underground water is more abundant and the ground-water table closer to the surface, the remaining parts of the Sahara where comparable settlement densities prevail are chiefly the Ahaggar and Tibesti highlands, whose altitude fosters increased rainfall.

A considerable ethnic variety characterizes the Sahara's peoples, but it is difficult to distinguish the different groups by their physical appearance, since mixing has been so widespread. Language differences are somewhat clearer. The core area of Berber speakers includes the Taureg tribes of Saharan Algeria, eastern Mali, and western Niger. This Berber core is flanked by Arabic-speaking tribes on the west, north and east.

Libya. Libya is almost entirely Saharan in climate and associated desert landscapes. The only exceptions are places where the country thrusts farthest north into a Mediterranean-steppe environment—in Tripolitania in the northwest, and in Cyrenaica in the northeast. There, in a very restricted coastal area, annual rainfall exceeds eight inches. Only 0.5 percent of the whole country is under cultivation. Libya's population in 1970 was estimated to be only 1.9 million, with over two thirds of this in northernmost Tripolitania and less than one third in northernmost Cyrenaica (Fig. 6.2). The gross population pattern, then, consists of two main coastal nuclei separated by some 500 miles of desert. Rivalry prevails between the two main settlement clusters, since the larger and more progressive western node is mostly Berber and the eastern one mostly conservative Arab Bedouins. Some 40 percent are believed to be sedentary rural dwellers and over 50 percent nomads and semi-nomads. The native peoples are all Moslems and speak Arabic.

Italian control during the period 1912–1943 led to an influx of colonists from that country, who by 1941 numbered around 100,000; there were in addition some 30,000 Jews. Both foreign groups contributed im-

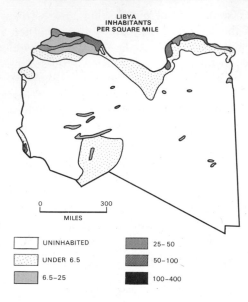

LIBYA
INHABITANTS
PER SQUARE MILE

0   300
MILES

UNINHABITED

UNDER 6.5

6.5–25

25–50

50–100

100–400

Fig. 6.2. Libya—population density. Population is almost exclusively confined to the slightly more humid Mediterranean margins. The main exception is where a narrow spur of denser population follows the Jebel escarpment inland from about Homs in a southwesterly direction. Simplified from a density map by Else Schmidt and Paul Mattingly in *Geographische Rundschau*, 1966, Heft 12.

portantly to the country's economic development. Recently, their numbers have declined sharply—Italians to an estimated 29,000 in 1962 and Jews to 3200 in 1961.

Within Tripolitania the strongest concentration of settlement coincides with a series of discontinuous oases that occupy the seaward parts of a coastal plain less than six miles wide. Dunes and salt marshes separate the individual oases. Inland from the coastal oases is a broader upland belt where precarious dry-farming of cereals, tree crops chiefly of olives and almonds, and herding are the main forms of land use. A second inhabited zone thrusts diagonally inland from about Homs following the more humid spine of the Jebel plateau, which rises to an elevation of 2000–3000 feet. Cyrenaica, unlike Tripolitania, lacks an appreciable belt of coastal plain, since there a low plateau descends abruptly to the sea and the water table is deep. Livestock herding and dry farming form the dominant economy. The main settlement area is the Barce Plain, a low limestone plateau that lies just inland from the coast.

Egypt. This country which comprises the northeastern sector of the Sahara, is quite non-Saharan in the size of its population, which in 1970 was estimated at nearly 34 million. Next to Nigeria it is the most populous country in Africa. Although the state of Egypt includes a total area of 386,000 sq mi (nearly a million sq km), the real Egypt, which is essentially the floodplain and delta of the Nile plus minor strips along the Suez and Sweetwater canals and a few scattered oases, represents in total only about 13,000–14,000 sq mi, or 3.5 percent of the political area. An additional 1.5 percent includes the semiarid coast and certain regions of the Sinai Peninsula, where population is sparse but scarcely absent. The remaining 95 percent is characteristically uninhabited desert. Several tens of thousands of people live in a few scattered oases in the Libyan Desert west of the Nile. A few hundred thousand destitute Arabs, mostly refugees, are inhabitants of the Asian sector east of the Suez Canal. The remainder of the nearly 34 million Egyptians, or almost 99 percent, are largely dependent on the Nile River. Of the 99 percent, 35 percent live in Upper Egypt or the narrow riverine floodplain section and the remaining 64 percent in the delta, which includes the capital city of Cairo (Fig. 6.3).[2]

Not only do Nile waters provide the essential irrigation for the intensive cropping; over millenniums of· time Nile silts also have fructified the basically fertile alluvial soils. Overall population density on the Nile alluvial lands is over 2000 per sq mi; in parts the rural densities reach

[2] M. A. El-Badry. "Trends in the Components of Population Growth in the Arab Countries of the Middle East: A Survey of Present Information," *Demography*, 1965, Vol. 2, p. 142.

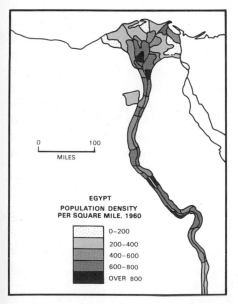

0   100
MILES

EGYPT
POPULATION DENSITY
PER SQUARE MILE, 1960

0–200
200–400
400–600
600–800
OVER 800

Fig. 6.3. Population density in riverine Egypt. After a map in *Focus* (American Geographical Society), March 1969.

2500, while the ratio of men to tilled land is over 3100 per sq mi.[3] Such densities are scarcely equaled in any other country; most certainly they have closer resemblance to parts of eastern and southern Asia than to Africa. So great a degree of crowding is made possible only by a labor-intensive agriculture that makes use of a highly fruitful physical environment.

The Nile oasis as a region of population concentration is as old as human civilization, since it and the Tigris-Euphrates region were among the earliest to experience the beginnings of agriculture and with that event the stimulation of population growth. By about the beginning of the Christian era, Beloch estimates that Egypt was one of the most populous parts of the Roman Empire, with some 5 million inhabitants and a density of 465 per sq mi, which was by far the highest for any of the Empire's subdivisions.[4] But over the next millennium and a half there is reason to believe that Egypt's population suffered a decline, so that by about 1500 it may have numbered no more than 2.5 million. Possibly it had not increased perceptibly by even as late as 1800. Growth accelerated during the 19th and 20th centuries, and there was more than a 10-fold increase in population over the 16 decades from 1800 to 1960. During the period 1960–1965 the annual rate of natural increase has varied between about 2.6 and 3.0 percent. Accelerated growth has resulted almost entirely from a decline in mortality. This in turn reflects changes in the Egyptian economy whereby the food supply was expanded, but it involves also the introduction of Western medicine and sanitation. Within the period 1800 to 1965 there was likewise a threefold increase in the cultivated area.[5] In addition, the introduction of perennial irrigation has had the effect of greatly augmenting the crop area by making possible two harvests from the same field. Crop yields have been increased as well, and land reform has distributed land ownership more widely. Without a doubt, remarkable progress has been achieved; this is witnessed by the accomplishments chalked up during the period of the last five-year plan, when the average annual growth in national income was 6.5 percent and the average annual per capita income growth was 3.5 percent. These are to be compared with an average annual population increase of 2.7

---

[4] But sir.ce about 75 percent of the agricultural land bears two crops, the density per unit of crop area is less, or a little over 1800 per sq mi of crop area. See Marcin Rosciszewski, "Population Growth and Economic Development in Egypt," in Wilbur Zelinsky, Leszek A. Kosinski, and R. Mansell Prothero (eds.), Geography and a Crowding World, Oxford University Press, New York, 1970, pp. 332–347.

[4] J. Beloch, Die Bevolkerung der griechisch-romanischen Welt, Dunncker and Humbolt, Leipzig, 1886, p. 507.

[5] Rosciszewski, "Population Growth," p. 340.

percent.[6] At least between 1962 and 1965, the index of agricultural production growth has exceeded that of population increase. But this situation is unlikely to endure, because population continues to soar and the unemployed segment remains large. In towns and cities only 40 percent of the people able to work actually have employment. In the countryside great differences exist in the incomes of different social groups. Thus it appears that nearly four fifths of the rural people receive only 15–20 percent of the total rural income. The redundant rural population is estimated to be as great as 10 million.[7]

Although the Egyptians were originally a pure Hamitic type, over the centuries the Hamitic culture has been forced to yield before the spread of Arabic in Mediterranean Africa. All Egyptians speak Arabic and they are all Moslems except for about 2 million Coptic Christians and perhaps 100,000 or more Jews. Most of these non-Moslems reside in urban places within Middle and Lower Egypt, where they engage in commercial and craft enterprises.

Egypt's vital rates are relatively typical of LD countries and fairly resemble those of the Maghrib states. The estimated birth rate (1970) was about 43 per 1000 and the death rate is close to 15, so that the current rate of population growth is slightly below 3 percent per year, a rate that would double the present population in 24 or 25 years. For 1980 the projected population is 46.7 million. Currently the birth rate is slightly below the conjectured African average (46) and the death rate distinctly below that average (22), so the rate of increase is above the African mean. This is a feature of great concern considering the already supercrowded conditions within the country and the widespread abject poverty. The specter of hunger is ever present, while the prospect for the future is dismal or even alarming. There appears to be no possible cure for the dilemma other than limitation of population growth, hopefully through reducing the births, but otherwise through a rise in mortality.

Expectably, Egypt's is a young population, 43 percent of the total being 15 years of age and under. Such a large unproductive sector is a huge drain on the country's economic resources and acts to aggravate the current poverty. Infant mortality is excessively high. Seventy-five to 80 percent of the population 15 years of age and over are illiterate. Per capita average national income is only about $160.

Egypt's population is preponderantly rural, and an estimated three fifths are tillers of the rich alluvial soils. But while Egypt is thoroughly

[6] Rosciszewski, "Population Growth," p. 344.
[7] Rosciszewski, "Population Growth," p. 334.

rural and agricultural, still, urbanization has advanced further there than in most LD countries and farther than anywhere else in Africa except South Africa. In 1960 the percentage of the total population living in localities with 20,000 or more inhabitants was estimated at 36 percent. The comparable figure was 18 percent in 1920, 21 percent in 1930, 24 percent in 1940, and 31 percent in 1950. Moreover, in the two decades 1940–1960 the rate of urban increase has been much more rapid than in the period 1920–1940. This reflects, in part, expanded employment opportunities in the cities, but perhaps even more it signifies the serious condition of overpopulation in the countryside and an apparent preference for urban over rural poverty.

Much the greater share of the urban population is concentrated in the delta and particularly within its apex, which is sometimes designated the metropolitan triangle. At the head of the delta is Cairo, a city of nearly 3.5 million, the largest in Africa as well as in the whole Arab world. Along the delta coast is Alexandria, the main port, which boasts a population of over 1.5 million. Of 11 other cities with populations in excess of 100,000, 8 are in or on the margins of the delta.

Migration. Two different population migrations can be distinguished in Egypt: (1) that from the Nile Valley toward the delta region and (2) that from the countryside toward the towns and cities.

The reason for the migration toward the delta (both seasonal and permanent) is the more serious overpopulation in the valley section. In the delta there are still certain possibilities for reclaiming new agricultural lands and for extending the irrigated area. This is less true up-river. As a consequence, rural living conditions are somewhat less difficult in the delta. This is suggested by the fact that the per capita amount of arable land in the valley is only 0.176 hectare as against 0.248 hectare in the delta, not counting the populations of Cairo and Alexandria.[8] In the valley the gross per capita income derived from agriculture amounts to only two thirds that of the delta. An additional attraction in the delta is the concentration there of the country's larger cities and the modern industries that they contain.

The drive of population toward towns and cities has been mentioned earlier in connection with the urbanization process. Between 1947 and 1963 the proportion of the population in rural places dropped from nearly 75 percent to about 62 percent. Between 1897 and 1960 the urban population grew almost 2.5 times more rapidly than the total population. Urban growth was most rapid in the vicinity of the Suez Canal, but in Cairo

---

[8] Rosciszewski, "Population Growth," pp. 332–333; see also El-Badry, "Population Growth in the Arab Countries," pp. 159–161.

also it was well above the urban national average. About 40 percent of the whole urban population now lives in Cairo and 56 percent in Cairo and Alexandria together. In 1897 these two cities contained only 9.5 percent of the total Egyptian population; in 1960 they included 20.1 percent.[9] Over the same period the share in all towns and cities, excluding Cairo and Alexandria, dropped. It would appear that an overconcentration of urban dwellers in a very few of the largest cities has developed.

Factors stimulating the drift of population to urban places are numerous and complex; social and cultural factors as well as economic ones are involved. In 1958 the average per capita income was 4.3 times as great in urban places as in the rural areas. Further aggravating the economic situation throughout the countryside is the fact that over the period 1960–1965 some 80 percent of the rural inhabitants received only 17–18 percent of the rural income. These were the landless people and those owning farms smaller than about 1 acre, and it is this group that makes up a great majority of those migrating to urban places.[10]

Spatial Distribution. Within the crowded Nile oasis, significant variations in population density exist, of both general and local character (Fig. 6.3). Of the former type it may be pointed out that densities are highest near the head of the delta, in what is called the metropolitan triangle, and from there they decline both upriver and downriver. In rural areas it is said that population density fairly follows the importance of maize, the main food crop.

Localisms in density are even more striking. Overall, the rural delta does not represent one of the most densely inhabited parts of the oasis. There landholdings are larger and cash crops more widespread then is true for the whole oasis. Density variations also exist within the delta. Along the coastal margins where sand and marsh intermingle, the widespread dry farming and herding are not conducive to high population densities. In the northern and eastern parts of the delta, inland from the coastal dune belt, extensive swamp and marsh lands have long existed, some of which still await reclamation. The northeastern parts in particular, which are designated a development zone, continue to have densities that are well below the delta average.

Nearly everywhere along the riverine oasis strip south of the delta, high cliffs on both sides separate—with razor sharpness—the land of green (which varies in width from almost nothing up to 10 mi) from the bordering desert. But about 60 mi south of Cairo the bordering cliffs

---

[9] Rosciszewski, "Population Growth," pp. 334–335; El-Badry, "Population Growth in the Arab Countries," pp. 161–163.

[10] Rosciszewski, "Population Growth," pp. 333–334.

on the west break down; only a narrow gravel ridge separates the Nile Valley from the nearby Faiyum structural depression and its population cluster, and canals are able to bring fresh water from the Nile to irrigate and fructify 700 square miles of land within the depression. The Faiyum node of population, including more than 900,000 people, appears as a conspicuous western excrescence on the main Nilotic ribbon of population. The new High Dam near Aswan, at present under construction, will, it is claimed, permit the cultivation of an additional 1.3 million acres, convert another 700,000 acres from basin irrigation to a more efficient year-round type, make Egypt secure from floods, and provide an important hydroelectric power resource. Some redistribution of population will doubtlessly follow upon the completion of the High Dam project.

REFERENCES

Abu-Lughod, J. I. "Urbanization in Egypt," *Economic Development and Cultural Change*, No. 3, 1965.

Awad, Hassan, "Morocco's Expanding Towns," *The Geographical Journal*, Vol. CXXX, March 1964, pp. 49–64.

Barbour, K. M. "The Nile Basin: Social and Economic Revolution," in R. Mansell Prothero (ed.), *A Geography of Africa*, Frederick A. Praeger, New York, 1969, pp. 126–135.

Bardinet, Claude. "Densités de population en Algérie au recensement de 1966." *Annales Algériennes de Géographie* Vol. 2(4), July-December 1967, pp. 1–18.

Beaujeu-Garnier, V. *Géographie de la Population*, Tome 2. Editions M. Th. Génin, Paris, 1958, pp. 48–84.

Carlson, Lucile. *Africa's Lands and Nations*. McGraw-Hill Book Co., New York, 1967, pp. 44–128; scattered references to population.

Carlson, Lucile. "The Lower Nile Valley," in Paul F. Griffin (ed.), *Geography of Population: a Teacher's Guide*, The 1970 Yearbook of the National Council for Geographic Education. Feardon Publishers, Palo Alto, California, 1969, pp. 193–208.

Church, R. J. Harrison et al. *Africa and the Islands*. Longmans, London, 1964, pp. 104–173; scattered references to population.

Clarke, John I. "Northwest Africa Since Mid Century," in R. Mansell Prothero (ed.), *A Geography of Africa*, Routledge and Kegan Paul, London, 1969, pp. 21–77 (32–44).

Clarke, J. I. and Fisher (eds.), *Population of the Middle East and North Africa*, 1971.

Clarke, John I. "Summer Nomadism in Tunisia," *Economic Geography*, Vol. XXXI, No. 2, April, 1955, pp. 157–67.

El-Badry, M. A. "Trends in the Components of Population Growth in the Arab Countries of the Middle East: A Survey of Present Information," *Demography*, 1965, Vol. 2, pp. 140–186 (Egypt, pp. 141–167).

El Daly, S. "The Problem of Population in the U.A.R.," *Arab Journal*, Vol. 3(2), 1966, pp. 42–45.

Geography of Population: A Teacher's Guide, Paul F. Griffin ed., The 1970 Yearbook of the National Council for Geographic Education, Feardon Publishers, Palo Alto, California, 1969. See especially pages 117–134, 163–176, 191–268.

Glauert, Günter. "Veränderungen in der Bevölkerungsstruktur Nordafrikas in den letzten Jahrzehnten," *Die Erde*, Vol. 88, 1957, pp. 298–319.

Good, Dorothy. "Notes on the Demography of Algeria," *Population Index*, Vol. 27, No. 1, 1961, pp. 3–32.

Hance, William A. *The Geography of Modern Africa*. Columbia University Press, New York, 1964, pp. 77–141; scattered references to population.

Houston, James M. *The Western Mediterranean World: An Introduction to Its Regional Landscape*. Praeger, New York, 1967.

Institut Scientifique Chérifien. *Atlas du Maroc*. Rabat, 1960.

Isnard, Hildebert. *Le Maghreb*. Presses universitaires de France, Paris, 1966.

Mattingly, Paul F. and Else Schmidt. The Mahgreb: Population Density; map scale, 32 miles to the inch. Map Supplement Number 15, Annals of the Association of American Geographers, Vol. 61, No. 3, September, 1971.

McDonald, J. R. "The Repatriation of French Algerians, 1962–1963." *International Migration*, Vol. 3, No. 3, 1965, pp. 146–156. Maps.

Noin, D. *Atlas du Maroc, Notices Explicatives: Population (1960)*. Comité National de Géographie du Maroc, Rabat, 1963.

Noin, D. "La Population du Maroc." *Information Géographique* (Paris), Vol. 26(1), January-February 1962, pp. 1–12.

Rosciszewski, Marcia. "Egypt: Population Growth and Economic Development in Egypt," in, *Geography and a Crowding World*, Wilbur Zelinksy et al. (eds.), Oxford University Press, New York 1970, pp. 332–347.

Schmidt, Elsa *Die Bevölkerungskarte von Afrika*. H. and E. Steinbauer, Munich, 1959, pp. 42–53.

Stamp, L. Dudley. *Africa: a Study in Tropical Development*. Sec Ed., John Wiley and Sons, New York, 1964, pp. 201–269.

Stechman, Stanislaw. "Map of Population Distribution in Libya." *Africana Bulletin* (Warsaw), No. 3, 1965. pp. 49–56.

Stevens, R. W. *Population Factors in the Development of North Africa*. George Washington University, Washington, D.C., 1960.

Suter, Karl. "Die Bevölkerung Algeriens," *Erdkunde*. Vol. 15, 1961, pp. 192–201.

United Nations Educational, Scientific, and Cultural Organization (UNESCO). *Nomades et nomadisme au Sahara*. Paris, 1963. 195 p. Maps. (Recherches sur la zone aride, 19.) Contributions by various authors.

CHAPTER 7

Tropical Africa:
West and Central Africa

Africa south of the Sahara is a region composed, for the most part, of states that have emerged over the last decade or two as a consequence of the breakup of the African colonial empires of several European nations. Some of them lack historical roots and hence are artificial creations; most are weak economically and politically, have somewhat ambiguous and perhaps temporary boundaries, contain relatively few inhabitants, and are of small world importance. A goodly number of them remain almost nonentities to foreigners, even to knowledgeable ones. With this situation in mind, in the discussion on black Africa attention is focused on large regions as well as on individual countries.

WEST AFRICA

West Africa, by long usage, is considered to be the part of the continent lying south of the Sahara and west of the highlands separating Nigeria from Cameroon. Its dimensions are roughly 600–700 mi in a north-south direction and about 2000 mi east-west. More than 100 million people live there. All or parts of some 15 main political units are involved, including the southernmost sections of the three Saharan states of Mauritania, Mali, and Niger. Much the larger part of the region was formerly included in what was French and British West Africa.

It is impossible at present to provide a reasonable explanation for the population-density pattern of West Africa in all its nuances and shadings. Neither the general nor the detailed patterns can usually be correlated with any other single distribution map, either physical or cultural. Indeed, much of the distribution does not appear to be particularly rational. It is scarcely a pattern that has matured following a trial-and-error period lasting over centuries or even millenniums of time by sophisticated civilizations operating in a variety of environments. Tradition, which is unusually strong among the tribal peoples of Negro Africa, plays a more than ordinary role. The mix of factors making for the present patchwork of empty and crowded regions varies from place to place; among them should be included the following: water availability, soil quality, the incidence of tsetse fly infestation, defense considerations, intensity of slave raiding, the scourge of warfare, and the varying abilities of different peoples in ordering their political and economic affairs. The literature is full of instances in which a single specific causal factor has glibly been given credit for a particular density pattern, when in fact the explanation is much more obscure and complex and often is deeply rooted in the past. Unfortunately the historical record in West Africa is discouragingly incomplete. Because a great preponderance of African blacks draw their livelihood directly from the soil, one might expect a close correlation between population density and the environmental factors affecting agricultural productivity, but such is by no means always the case. A recently proposed thesis strongly relates population densities in tropical Africa with political systems, and purports to find a general correlation between broad density patterns there and state development. Accordingly, where African societies have been organized into strong and durable national units, population density was, and still is, likely to be high. Stateless societies are commonly associated with low densities.[1]

West Africa, extending southward from the northern limits of the wooded steppe or the sahel savanna (thereby excluding large areas of the three desert-steppe states of Niger, Mali and Mauritania), with few exceptions, has a minimum density of three persons per sq mi (1.2 per sq km); its average is about 60 per sq mi (23 per sq km).[2] The latter figure is higher than for either Central or East Africa, a feature that some writers attribute to the higher agricultural productivity of West Africa.

One noteworthy feature of gross spatial distribution of population in West Africa is the fact that some two thirds of the inhabitants are concentrated in its eastern half (including Nigeria, Dahomey, Togo, Ghana, and Upper Volta), compared with only about one third in the remaining western part. The north-south dividing zone between the eastern and western subdivisions is roughly the boundary between Ivory Coast and

---

[1] R. F. Stevenson, *Population and Political Systems in Tropical Africa*. Columbia University Press, New York, 1968.
[2] W. B. Morgan and J. C. Pugh, *West Africa*, Methuen and Co., London, 1969, p. 9.

Ghana. This asymmetry in population density between east and west does not seem to have a physical basis; rather, the dividing zone appears to separate contrasting cultures. In the south, at least, the suggested dividing zone separates western peoples with a culture dependent largely on the growing of rice (both upland and swamp varieties) from those in the east who are supported mainly by the cultivation of yams and other root crops that are able to support the higher population densities. In West Africa's drier north the Hausa group, located east of the dividing zone and culturally linked with Nilotic peoples, has exploited not only the narrow floodplains but even to a much greater extent the spacious unirrigable uplands, where crops are dependent on the modest seasonal rainfall. Their counterparts west of the zone of separation, the Songhay and Malinke peoples, have, on the other hand, usually confined their population concentrations to the restricted floodplains.[3] Some writers have pointed out that the generally more closely settled eastern half of West Africa may have profited from being under British control, which usually meant more active resource exploitation than was true in the predominantly French colonies in the west.

A second frequently noted feature of settlement distribution in West Africa is the real or presumed zonal pattern of its population densities, a feature that in turn is thought by some to relate to the far more striking zonation of physical features, especially rainfall and wild vegetation (Fig. 7.1; also Figs. 5.3, 5.4). A zonal pattern of soil belts has scarcely been proven. The well-defined climatic and vegetation zones, it can be argued, should affect the choice of farming systems and crops, and so in turn influence the population density in a society whose economy is so thoroughly based on agriculture. Still, to the degree that a belted disposition of population densities exists, perhaps it relates as much or even more to the spatial arrangements of trading relationships with outside areas, a feature to be described later. Quite naturally there is an expected abrupt falling off of population densities along the southern margins of the Sahara, or northward of about 15°.

The so-called "triple-belt" concept of population-density arrangement was first applied specifically to Nigeria and subsequently extended to all of West Africa. It involves the existence of a rather well-defined, populous seaward belt, which approximately coincides with a zone of heavy rainfall and dense tropical rainforest, and a second interior northern belt of relatively high density located in the subhumid sudan savanna (Fig. 5.4). In between these two is the well known "Middle Belt" of presumed lower average population density, which approximately coin-

---

[3] Morgan and Pugh, *West Africa*, p. 12.

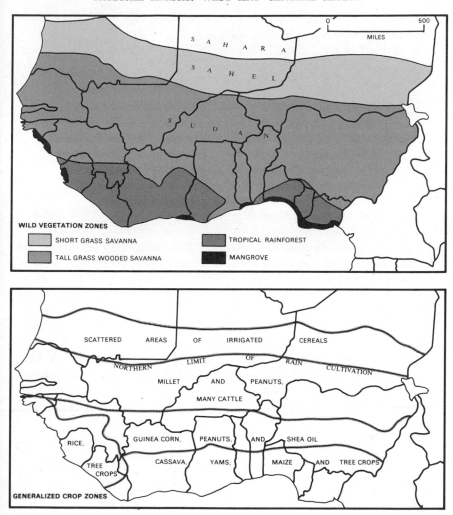

Fig. 7.1. Belted arrangement of wild vegetation and agriculture in West Africa. Crop zones after R. J. Harrison Church.

cides with the wooded guinea savanna where rainfall amounts are intermediate between those of the rainforest to the south and the sudan savanna to the north. Admittedly the triple-belt concept as it applies to population densities over the whole of West Africa requires a certain amount of imagination, since one or more of the belts becomes dim over considerable reaches of longitude. Without a doubt, a belted alignment of population densities is more conspicuous in the eastern half of West

Africa than it is in the west. And even in the east the belts are likely to exist in interrupted, or nodular, form.[4]

Best defined is the seaward forested belt of concentrated settlement, a feature that is variable in width but in Nigeria reaches inland for 200 mi or more. It is scarcely a continuous belt, and a wide break exists in the vicinity of the Ivory Coast and Liberia where the zone of rain-forest is particularly dense and broad, the coast is a difficult one for sea trade, and there is an absence of gold; all of these features operated to delay European development. The humid, seaward environment has at-tracted native settlement partly because it permitted the production of, and overseas trade in, a number of products derived from commercial tree crops, particularly oil palm and cacao. There cities, many of them ports, are concentrated. In addition, the relatively favorable physical conditions, especially a heavier and more year-round rainfall, have allowed for a greater production of subsistence crops than elsewhere. For the latter reason the seaward belt of denser population was present, apparently in less intensive form, even in the precolonial period.

The interior sudan-savanna belt of above-average population density, located along the Sahara's southern margins between about the 10° and 14° parallels, is most apparent in that part of West Africa east of about the 5°W meridian, particularly in Nigeria and Ghana. Farther west it tends to weaken and becomes more diffuse. Moreover, beyond West Africa, in the states of Sudan and Chad farther east, the savanna popula-tion belt continues to be perceptible. Still, even in the Nigeria-Ghana sector of densest settlement, the population belt is scarcely continuous; rather, it has a nodular appearance, a feature that may be attributable to the functional interrelation between trans-Saharan trade routes and state formation. The sudan savanna belt is associated with an impressive list of states that have arisen and fallen there over a millennium and a half of history. In this marchland traditional markets flourished as a result of the exchange with Mediterranean Africa via the trans-Saharan caravan routes. The trading centers in time became the nuclei of extensive nodes of population whose base was a form of land use in which pastoralists and tillers were symbiotically integrated. An important feature was that animal manure was thereby made available for fertilizing the arable soils.[5] Very significantly, however, the two most densely populated general regions within the sudan savanna belt correspond reasonably well

---

[4] On this topic of a belted arrangement of population densities in West Africa see M. B. Gleave and H. P. White, "The West African Middle Belt: Environmental Fact or Geographer's Fiction?" *The Geographical Review*, LIX, January 1969, pp. 123–139.

[5] Morgan and Pugh, *West Africa*, p. 10.

with the two most durable savanna cultures and the associated political and economic stability that they brought. One of these centers is in northern Nigeria, where the Hausa states had a long history. The other is in Upper Volta and northern Ghana, which was the territory of the Mossi states for over half a millennium.[6]

Between the humid forested seaward belt and the sahel-sudan savanna zone, both of relatively high density, is an intermediate belt of lower density, situated roughly between the 7° or 8° and the 11°N meridians. This belt can be traced from the upper Niger in the west eastward to eastern Nigeria. But because the feature of a belted arrangement of population densities is most conspicuous eastward from about the Ivory Coast, it is there that the less populous Middle Belt becomes most obvious. Numerous writers have offered general explanations for the overall sparser population of this intermediate belt, the ones most frequently emphasized include the following: (1) a low-grade physical environment for agriculture, (2) widespread tsetse-fly infestation, and (3) slave raiding from both north and south. No doubt one or more of these features has some validity locally, but as explanations for the overall sparse settlement of the Middle Belt they are not so convincing. The forces making for sparse settlement are highly complex and their operation is usually local or regional rather than applicable to the entire belt. It is true that the Middle Belt has less annual rainfall, a longer dry season,[7] and a lower rainfall dependability than the forested seaward belt. But still it is not as handicapped climatically as the drier sahel-sudan savanna belt farther north where settlement is denser. Inferior soils do exist and may be widespread within the Middle Belt, but it has scarcely been proven that on the average they are greatly inferior to those in the flanking belts, both to the north and south. The tsetse fly, which spreads sleeping sickness, is more widespread in the Middle Belt, to be sure, than in the sudan savanna, and therefore restricts the raising of cattle in the former, but this handicap is no worse than in some densely populated regions farther south. Moreover, the current relatively dense settlement in parts of the Middle Belt, such as around Kaduna and in southern Ilorin (both in Nigeria), indicate that the tsetse fly is not an insuperable barrier to higher overall population densities than now prevail. Slave raiding within the Middle Belt from both north and south did exist, but it was nowhere

[6] Stevenson, *Population*, p. 170.
[7] Pullan defines the Middle Belt in Nigeria as the area where over a period of years, 50 percent or more of all years have a dry season of 4 or 5 months' duration. See R. A. Pullan, "The Concept of the Middle Belt in Nigeria: An Attempt at a Climatic Definition," *The Nigerian Geographical Journal*, Vol. 5, No. 1, 1962, pp. 39–52.

nearly as severe as in the more populous seaward forested belt. And while the region's agriculture is avowedly less commercially oriented than it is in the bordering zones, the Middle Belt still provides a substantial proportions of the yams consumed in the more populous northern and southern belts. Actually, the present densities within the Middle Belt of eastern West Africa (east of 5°W) are not significantly lower than those found in the seaward forested belt and the sudan savanna zone in the western half of West Africa. It seems likely, therefore, that the Middle Belt's lower densities derive more from a weakness or absence of the stimuli, both political and economic, that operated most strongly in the northern and southern belts but were weaker in the zone between.

A further feature of the spatial distribution of inhabitants as seen on a density map is the conspicuous nodal pattern of the main concentrations of settlement, with the clusters separated by extensive areas of much lower density. At a lower level in the hierarchy of density clusters, there are local variations, or lesser nodes, within the several density groups, which are apparent only on a detailed dot or point map, a type capable of revealing distribution patterns not evident on a choropleth density map, which must be based on administrative subdivisions of greatly varying sizes and shapes. Thus, the population map of West Africa is really a patchwork of small density cells, with the denser nuclei existing in the most favored part or parts of each of the areas occupied by a distinct native community. West Africa's population is divided into a bewildering number of social groups or communities, each of which has some common social bond. Communities may be further subdivided into *states* and *tribes*. The states are groups of people having a common government, which normally rules through native chiefs. Tribes are groups of people who feel they have a common bond—cultural, linguistic, political, and economic.[8] With such a hierarchy of sociopolitical subdivisions, it is not difficult to appreciate the complex nature of the population nodes, large and small, and their distribution in West Africa.

The nucleated or cellular pattern of population has evolved through the interaction of both cultural and physical factors. Of unusual significance was the prevailing practice, until recently, of leaving a kind of no-man's-land of sparse population between individual African communities or even their subdivisions. Such a practice fostered a cellular pattern of spatial distribution, representing nodes of different sizes and densities. The pattern was somewhat fluid, since some communities tended to expand as a result of overcrowding in the original center; others contracted and developed greater density because of attack. Some increased their own high densities by enslavement of neighboring communities.

[8] Morgan and Pugh, *West Africa*, pp. 13–17.

Existence of durable and militarily strong states was responsible for creating some of the largest and most lasting population nodes. Local variations in water, soil, and terrain also functioned, in the past as in the present, to produce a nucleated density pattern. Particularly conspicuous on a dot map, as well as on a dasymetric map, of population distribution are the linear concentrations of people on the floodplains of the main rivers, especially those of the Niger and the Senegal.

Population Changes Associated with European Control. A reconstruction of the spatial distribution of population as it existed in West Africa in the precolonial period is scarcely possible. It appears likely, however, that in its broadest features it resembled the pattern that prevails at present. Both the sudan savanna belt and the humid forested seaward belt early stood out because of their higher densities. In both of these two environments population density was higher in the east than in the west. In addition to these two large populous belts, three less extensive environments of close settlement may be mentioned: (1) the major floodplains in the drier north, especially those of the middle Niger Inland Delta and the Senegal; (2) good defensive sites of high relief in the Middle Zone; and (3) the estuarine lands of the wet southwest where swamp rice could be grown.[9]

During the period of European colonization several significant changes in the pre-European population pattern occurred. One such change was increased occupance of the humid, seaward, rainforest belt (the Guinean environment), particularly in what is now southwestern Nigeria and the southern parts of Dahomey, Togo, and Ghana, even on the heavy soils. Another was the emergence of a narrow high-density coastal strip studded with numerous port cities. A third was the birth of a population node in coastal Senegal in the extreme west. The Europeans, oriented toward overseas commerce, established their main trading stations on the coast, thereby destroying much of the earlier trans-Saharan caravan traffic. The volume of the trade at the coastal ports gradually came to exceed that from across the Sahara, while European influence along the coast surpassed that of the Saharan traders in the sudan zone. And as the latter had brought Islam to the north, so the Europeans introduced Christianity along the coastal zone and also Western science, technology and medicine. In addition, they stimulated the development of new export crops in the lands not too distant from the sea, including cacao, oil palm, rubber, and coffee in the guinea savanna, and peanuts in Senegal and the sudan savanna of northern Nigeria. The introduction of stable government (and with it law and order) and the increase in trade may also have spurred population growth. Interior market towns, oriented toward

[9] Morgan and Pugh, *West Africa*, p. 421.

coastal trade, developed along transport routes, first roads and later rail lines, within the guinea zone. The effect of all these developments was to cause population to shift seaward, toward the south and west, to the hinterlands of the ports, and into the less densely settled parts of the guinean zone, except for southwestern Ghana and the southwestern Ivory Coast. Since the seaward margins grew more populous at the expense of the northern and middle belts, it is to be expected that these later regions suffered varying degrees of depopulation.

Another effect, one of the first and most direct, of European contacts on the African population, resulted from slave raids and overseas trading in slaves. Depopulation by slave raiding was no doubt most drastic in the populous seaward belt, but it was also widespread deeper in the interior. The well-populated Ibo region in southern Nigeria east of the Niger especially suffered. What the magnitude of the slave raids and associated depopulation were can never be known, but most of the intelligent guesses for the Atlantic slave trade lie within a range of 8 to 20 million persons with much the largest share coming from Atlantic parts of Africa.[10] In view of the great loss of native lives associated with both the raiding operations and the subsequent shipment of the human cargo to the coast and thence overseas, it is believed the actual depopulation suffered may have been several times as great as the numbers arriving at their foreign destinations. Over a period of three centuries West Africa may have lost between 20 and 40 million of its inhabitants, even though that region probably had fewer than 20 million people at any one time.

It is often suggested that the slave trade is responsible for the low population densities of certain areas in West Africa today. But somewhat negating this argument is the fact that it is the seaward belt between Ghana and eastern Nigeria that has at present the highest population densities, and yet it was this same region that supplied by far the greatest number of slaves.

Nigeria. Nigeria is not only the most extensive country in tropical Africa; it is also by far the most populous in all of Africa. The official government estimate of 64.8 million based on the 1963 census is now considered too high; the Population Reference Bureau's 1970 estimate is 55.1 million. Since Nigeria contains about 55–60 percent of West Africa's total population, it appears to be more worthy of extended individual treatment than are the region's other countries.

To accommodate the human variety within Nigeria, the country, prior to June 1967, had been politically organized into a federation of five regions. (See Table 7.1 for population numbers and densities in each

[10] Philip Curtin, *The Atlantic Slave Trade: A Census.* University of Wisconsin Press, Madison, 1969, pp. 3–13.

TABLE 7.1   Area and Population of Nigeria's Regions

Pre-1967 Regions[a]	Area (Sq Mi)	Population 1952–53 Census (Millions)	Population 1962 Estimate (Millions)	Population Density 1952	Population Density 1962
Northern Nigeria	281,782	16,840	22,027	60	78
Western Nigeria	30,454	4,595	8,158	151	268
Midwestern Nigeria	14,922	1,492	2,365	93	158
Eastern Nigeria	29,484	7,218	12,332	245	418
Lagos Federal Territory	27	272	450	10,070	16,681
Total Nigeria	356,669	30,417	45,332	85	127

SOURCES: R. J. Harrison Church et al., Africa and the Islands, p. 265; Chukua Okonjo, A Preliminary Medium Estimate of the 1962 Mid-Year Population of Nigeria," in J. C. Caldwell and C. Okonjo (eds.), The Population of Tropical Africa, p. 96.

[a] Since 1967 there has been a reorganization of Nigeria's administrative subdivisions into 11 states.

of the regions.) Significantly, this regionalization reflects the dominance of particular tribal groups within the population. The Northern Region, by far the largest, had a population of nearly 17 million (estimated 22 million in 1962), according to the 1952–53 census.[11] Here, especially in the central and western parts, the dominant tribal groups are the crop-growing Islamic Hausa (six million) and the pastoral and more warlike Fulani (three million), who early in the last century extended their rule over the Hausa states (Fig. 7.2). In the northeast the people are mainly Fulani and Kanuri. The southern two thirds of the Northern Region, one segment of West Africa's Middle Belt, has a relatively sparse overall population composed of diverse ethnic groups. The average density of the whole Northern Region is the lowest for any of the subdivisions (Fig. 7.3).

The Western Region, comprising the southwestern part of the country, has the most homogeneous population of any of the regions, with Yoruba peoples greatly predominating. Average density is two to three times that of the North. The Eastern Region has the highest population density. There Ibo people numbering about six million greatly prevail. Between

[11] The results of the 1963 census are considered in error and have been annulled.

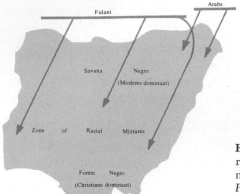

Fig. 7.2. Nigeria—some features of the racial composition. Modified from a map by Buchanan and Pugh, *Land and People in Nigeria*, University of London Press.

the East and West is the relatively small and least populous Midwestern Region, with only about 1.5 million inhabitants and an overall density that is the lowest for any of the subdivisions except for the North. The Midwestern subdivision coincides with a transition zone between Ibo and Yoruba concentrations; its tribal composition is diverse. The immediate coastal strip is well populated mainly at its eastern and western extremities; in between, the Niger Delta creates an inhospitable environment that acts to repel settlement (Fig. 7.3).

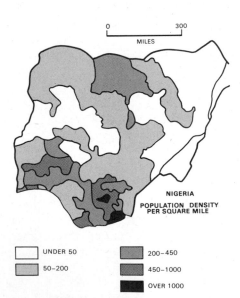

Fig. 7.3. Population estimates by provinces and divisions for 1962 are from the Ibadan Center of Population Studies as given in Caldwell and Okonjo, *The Population of Tropical Africa*.

It is in the Nigerian section of West Africa that a belted arrangement of population distribution is best exemplified. The populous northern sudan savanna and seaward forest belts are separated by a central zone in which settlement is much sparser. Still, even the more densely populated northern and southern belts exist in the form of a series of nodes rather than as continuous bands of high densities. For example, abnormally low densities are to be found in both the extreme northeast (Bornu Province), eastward from Kano, and in the southeast, eastward of Iboland. Neither is the Middle Belt a zone of continuous low density, even though its overall degree of occupance is well below that of both the northern and the southern belts.

Within its two' populous belts of settlement Nigeria displays three striking nodes of dense population: those of the Ibo in the southeast, the Yoruba in the southwest, and the Hausa and Fulani in the north around Kano (Fig. 7.3). Together the three centers contain over two fifths of the national population, but they represent only one seventh of the country's area. Each of the population nodes coincides with a key area in the nation's economic geography.

The single greatest high-density cluster of population is that of Iboland situated in the south, east of the Niger River. Because of its serious overcrowding, the Ibo population cluster presents one of the most critical economic situations in all of West Africa. Out-migration is chronic, as a consequence of which Ibo workers are to be found widely scattered throughout the country. For the whole Eastern Region, population density in 1963 was 420 per sq mi, but this high average is composed of local variables ranging from a low of 103 per sq mi in the Ogoja Division, to a high of 1632 in the Orlu Division of Owerri Province, even though the latter is overwhelmingly rural in character. Moreover, Iboland's general high density has been attained in spite of environmental handicaps associated with dissected terrain, soils of indifferent or even poor quality, and seasonal deficiencies of water.

The most striking feature of population distribution within the Ibo country is the northwest-by-southeast axis of unusually high densities, extending from near Onitsha on the Niger to the Cross River estuary—a distance of about 120 mi, with an average width of 25 to 30 mi. Within this belt of crowded settlement the average density is close to 890 per sq mi or over twice the regional average.[12] On the flanks of the high-density axis, the demographic gradient is relatively steep in most directions.

[12] Barry Floyd, *Eastern Nigeria; A Geographical Review.* Frederick A. Praeger, New York, 1969, p. 41.

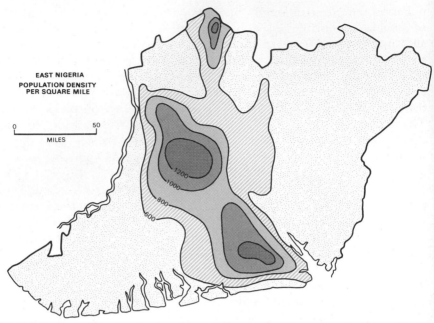

Fig. 7.4. Iboland, Nigeria—density of population, 1963. After a map by Barry Floyd, *Eastern Nigeria: a Geographical Review*, Frederick A. Praeger, New York.

Actually the belt of concentrated settlement in Iboland consists of a northwestern and a southeastern core area separated by a saddle of lower density (Fig. 7.4). In the northwestern core, or Ibo heartland, the average density is over 1300 per sq mi; in the one to the southeast it is 1078. Within the saddle between them, which coincides with the former no-man's-land between Igbo- and Ibibio-speaking ethnic groups, density drops to about half the above figures. Fifty to 75 mi north of the Ibo heartland and connected with it by a narrow belt of only medium density is the much smaller Enugu-Ezike population node, at whose center density rises to over 1000 per sq mi. The lowest densities (under 200) within the Eastern Nigeria Region are to be found over extensive areas in the extreme east toward Cameroon, and also in the swampy Niger Delta.

Factors shaping the pattern of population in the Eastern Nigeria Region are manifold, and they have operated conjointly through time to create the existing arrangement. One factor of unusual significance was the slave trade, whose center for recruiting and assembling its raw materials was at Arochuku in the Cross River Basin in the southeast, from which point the unfortunate captives were transported downstream to the port of Calabar, one of the main slave markets and ports of embarkation in all Nigeria. An alternate route involved an overland march via Bende, an interior slave market, to the port of Bonny. In this Bende-Bonny slave route lies an additional probable explanation for the perseverence, even down to the present, of the saddle of lighter settlement separating the two core areas within the Ibo population axis previously described.[13] The consequence of the extensive and long-time man-drain throughout the middle and upper Cross River Basin was a massive depopulation of southeasternmost Nigeria, from which the region has not as yet recovered. And although the termination of slave trading and pacification of southern Nigeria under British control led to a freezing of preexisting population patterns, the struggle between Britain and Germany during World War I for political control along the Nigeria-Cameroon border led to a further depopulation of this marchland region.

In earlier periods a fundamental consideration in the selection of areas for settlement, other than that they provide land of sufficient size and quality to support the group, was that they offer defensive sites for villages. So it remains even today that hilltop locations for settlements, in the midst of a generally protective environment of dissected plateau country or high plains, are to be found in most parts of Eastern Nigeria where medium and high densities prevail. The low-lying, poorly drained river valleys were shunned, not only because of their difficult clay soils, dense forests, and serious infestation with tsetse fly and sleeping sickness, but also because rivers were the routes by which slave raiders traveled inland from the coast.

For the most part soils have not played an important role in localizing the degree of population concentration. It is mainly in the easternmost 15 percent of the region, underlain by igneous and metamorphic rocks, where the soils are heavy and difficult to work with the crude implements available, that the soil factor has acted to inhibit settlement.

On first thought, densely populated Iboland seems to refute the hypothesis that there is a correlation between high population densities and the presence of states powerful and durable enough to guarantee the security of their people, which in turn permits a substantial economic development capable of supporting a dense population. But while the Ibos had no powerful central government, their Aro Chuku trading organization and their strong cultural cohesiveness may have served as substitute stabilizing forces.[14] Despite an unusually dense population, Iboland

---

[13] Floyd, *Eastern Nigeria*, pp. 43–44. See also R. K. Udo, "Patterns of Population Distribution and Settlement in Eastern Nigeria," *The Nigerian Geographical Journal*, Vol. VI, No. 2, 1963, p. 83.

had scarcely any genuine urban settlements until after the coming of the Europeans. Even now only about 14 percent of the Eastern Region's people live in towns with more than 5000 population.

A second main nodal area of population lies within the Southwest Region, where it forms the heartland of the Yoruba country and the core of the highly developed cacao belt of the western dry-forest zone (Fig. 7.3). Yorubaland shows important contrasts with Iboland—rainfall is less and more seasonal; fallow periods are longer; soils, derived from Pre-Cambrian rocks, are distinctly better; water is widely available; and cacao, rather than oil palm, is the main commercial crop. Also remarkable is the degree of urbanization in Western Nigeria, where the urban sector represents nearly half of the whole population (Fig. 7.5). Yorubaland is a region characterized by a complex political organization and many urban settlements. Moreover, in contrast to Iboland, urbanization in the Yoruba country is indigenous and antedates the coming of Europeans. Unlike the early cities in northern Nigeria, which owed their origins mainly to trans-Saharan trade, the medieval Yoruba towns represented, in the main, a feature of that people's settlement organization, contrived for the purpose of dealing with the more backward, and perhaps hostile, tribes into whose territory they had intruded.[15] The towns

[14] J. G. N. Adams and R. J. Harrison Church, "The Population of West Africa," in Paul F. Griffin (ed.), *Geography of Population, A Teacher's Guide*. Feardon Publishers, Palo Alto, Cal., 1969, pp. 215–216. See also Stevenson, *Population*, pp. 188–227.

[15] Akin L. Mabogunje, *Urbanization in Nigeria*. London, University of London Press, 1968, p. 76. See also N. C. Mitchel, "Yoruba Towns," in Barbour and Prothero, *Essays on African Population*, pp. 282–284.

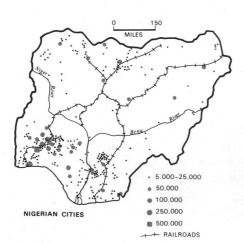

NIGERIAN CITIES

- 5.000–25,000
- 50,000
- 100,000
- 250,000
- 500,000
- ╂ RAILROADS

Fig. 7.5. Nigeria—distribution of urban places by size classes, 1952 census. After a map by Mabogunje in *Urbanization in Nigeria*, University of London Press.

were a means of colonial domination. But if they originated primarily as administrative centers, their continued survival depended on trade, which involved an exchange of agricultural surpluses of the countryside for craft products and personal services of the urban centers. As of about the middle of the 19th century, 6 Yoruba towns are estimated to have had populations exceeding 40,000 (3 of the 6 had close to 100,000 inhabitants); 10, of 20,000 to 40,000; 6, of 10,000 to 20,000; and 10, under 10,000.[16] A distinctive feature of most present Yoruba towns is the large percentage of their working males who are engaged, at least part time, in agriculture; even in Ibadan, the metropolis, the figure is as high as 35 percent, and in some other cities of over 100,000 inhabitants it rises to between 60 and 70 percent.[17]

A third major cluster of population concentration within Nigeria, and one of the greatest in all Africa, is the one grouped around the primary nucleus which is Kano city in the Northern Region. The Kano concentration is even more unusual considering the semiarid nature of the region's climate. While this northern cluster is mainly contained within Kano Province, still it spreads, significantly, northwestward into the vicinity of the city of Katsina (53,000 inhabitants, 1952 census) and toward the southwest into Zaria Province, where a secondary nucleus is centered on the city of Zaria (54,000 inhabitants, 1952 census).

Several hundred miles from the main Kano cluster is a much smaller one located in the Sokoto valley in northwestern Nigeria, whose focus is the city of Sokoto (52,000 inhabitants, 1952 census). Population distribution within the Sokoto secondary cluster is uneven, and the density pattern is similarly fickle. Most important of the environmental factors influencing this distribution pattern is the availability of adequate potable water during the long dry season. Consequently, settlement is concentrated in the main river valleys and in the areas of sedimentary rocks in the northern and western parts where groundwater is most readily available.[18] Both the Kano-Katsina and the Sokoto population clusters spill across the international boundary into the southern part of the Republic of Niger. Separating the Kano and Sokoto clusters is a relatively empty region in which limited water supplies are a prime deterrent to widespread occupance. The same is true of sparsely settled northeastern Nigeria, east of the Kano population cluster. Two filaments of relatively

---

[16] Mabogunje, *Urbanization in Nigeria*, p. 91.

[17] Mitchel, in Barbour and Prothero, *Essays on African Population*, p. 281.

[18] Mansell Prothero, "Population Patterns and Migrations in Sokoto Province, Northern Nigeria," in L. Dudley Stamp (ed.), *Natural Resources, Food and Population in Inter-Tropical Africa*. Geographical Publications Ltd., London, 1956, p. 49.

dense settlement connect the main Kano cluster with the secondary Sokoto cluster; these linear concentrations follow river valleys, which are also the routes of highways and a railroad.

Early settlement in northern Nigeria was facilitated by the light, easily tilled soils derived from wind- and water-laid deposits and by the relative freedom from the tsetse fly and associated sleeping sickness. Still another fundamental and positive element of the explanation for the growth of these northern population clusters, located on the semiarid margins of the Sahara, was the efficiency as tillers of the Hausa peoples, whose intensive cropping was made possible by their use of fertilizers in the form of sheep, goat, and donkey excrement, household refuse, straw, and ash. A limiting factor in this semiarid region was water, but where that essential was available, it was certain specific circumstances that favored the growth of particular settlement concentrations. Thus, Sokoto is renowned as an old cultural center, while Kano, Katsina, Zaria, and Sokoto profited by trade, since they were on trans-Saharan caravan routes. They were also political centers of emirates and were able to survive because of their more efficient political and military organization.[19] In more recent times the development of a commercial agriculture based on peanuts, cotton, certain food crops, and the cattle of Fulani herdsmen has broadened the economic base for population support, while rail and highway development has facilitated the marketing of the agricultural surplus.

More than seven million people are probably included within the extended Kano population cluster, including the satellite Zaria and Katsina nodes. Kano city and township are estimated to have had a population of 249,000 in 1962. Population densities are highest in close proximity to the city of Kano and decline outward with increasing distance from that center (Fig. 7.6). The average density for Kano Province, containing 4.3 million people in 1962, was 260 per sq mi. In the innermost zone

[19] R. J. Harrison Church, *West Africa*, Longmans, Green and Co., London, 1957, p. 447.

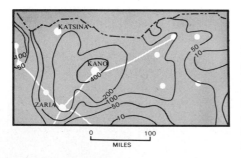

Fig. 7.6. Population densities per sq mi in the Kano region of northern Nigeria. Modified from a map by Grove in *Essays on African Population*, Barbour and Prothero, eds., Routledge and Kegan Paul. (The Grove and Mortimore maps show some disharmonies).

it is over 500 per sq mi, and the figure drops to 150 at distances of 50–100 mi from the primate city. Outwards from Kano there is a noticeable steepening of the density gradient at a density of about 360 per sq mi; this figure may be adopted as a minimum density in defining what Mortimore calls the closely settled zone.[20] It forms an irregular area, oriented in a northwest-to-southeast direction, with the dimensions of the longer axis somewhat over 100 mi and that of the shorter one about 60 miles.

The outer limits of the Kano population node may be set by population densities of about 50–100 per sq mi. On the north this corresponds approximately with the 20-in. annual rainfall line; it is also close to the Nigeria-Niger boundary and to the earlier frontier of the Fulani Empire of Sokoto. On the west the sparsely populated country that roughly corresponds with the boundary between Katsina and Sokoto Provinces was for long a marchland between the warring kingdoms of Katsina and Gobir and a routeway for raiders.[21] A part of it is an unpopulated forest reserve. On the south an environment heavily infested with the tsetse fly and afflicted with inferior laterized soils derived from crystalline rocks discourages close settlement. This same region also suffered seriously from slave raiding originating in states farther north. The eastern frontier of the Kano population cluster coincides with a variety of handicaps—a drier climate, more meager water supplies and these reached only at greater depths, more wet-season swampland, and a political no-man's-land between warring and slave-raiding states.[22] Fulani pastoralists moved into this unsettled Bornu region during the 19th century; that immigration functioned to perpetuate the already sparse settlement. But during the last few decades Hausa and Kanuri slash-and-burn farmers have settled in the region, with a consequent increase in population.

It is a valid generalization that the Middle Belt, forming the southern two thirds of the Northern Nigeria administrative subdivision, has an overall density (about 40 per sq mi, 1962) that is markedly lower than that of either the northern savanna or the southern forested zone (Fig. 7.3). But the low average density figure is scarcely typical of the region; instead, the average is a composite of striking local variations. Virtually empty areas are numerous and widespread, but there are also several localities of moderately close settlement. The explanation of the overall

[20] M. J. Mortimore, "Population Distribution, Settlement and Soils in Kano Province, Northern Nigeria 1931–1962," in J. C. Caldwell and C. Okonjo (eds.), *The Population of Tropical Africa*. Longmans, Green and Co., 1968, pp. 298–300.
[21] A. T. Grove, "Population Densities and Agriculture in Northern Nigeria," in Barbour and Prothero (eds.), *Essays on African Population*, pp. 118–119.
[22] Grove, "Population Densities," p. 119.

low density of the Middle Belt can be derived only from an interpretation of the patchwork of local densities, and in the present stage of our knowledge concerning Nigeria this is all but impossible. Of the variety of explanations offered for the Middle Belt's overall sparse settlement, one or more apply to certain localities but are not relevant to others. Since the Middle Belt as it relates to West Africa in general has been touched on earlier in this chapter, at this point emphasis will be upon its Nigerian sector only.

Two approaches to an understanding of the overall low, but still highly variable, density pattern of Nigeria's Middle Belt are recognized—the historical and the environmental.[23] Agboola has noted that some of the virtually empty regions tend to coincide with the boundaries separating different tribal groups. This suggests an earlier devastation associated with tribal warfare and slave-raiding, resulting in the depopulation of certain intertribal areas. Other regions became foci of political stability and military power, and so escaped a similar fate. Such a one was the Ilorin emirate south and west of the Niger River, which is at present a settlement cluster of moderate density.

Doubtless the physical environment has discouraged settlement in some parts. Insufficient information concerning soils in the Middle Belt is available to be able to judge how important this factor is. Accessible evidence seems to indicate a widespread but interrupted occurrence of infertile iron-pan subsoils with a normally thin overlying topsoil layer. Such a condition may be a deterrent even to subsistence food-crop agriculture. It is a more serious obstacle to commercial farming, especially that of a mechanized character. The more lush wild vegetation—both grass and trees—in the Middle Belt compared with the sudan belt farther north is thought to be responsible for the widespread prevalence of tsetse and trypanosomaisis and the resulting adverse effect on cattle raising. On the other hand, the luxuriant and coarse grasses do not provide suitable cattle forage. A failure to grow export crops on a considerable scale is doubtless an important factor inhibiting economic development and population increase within the Middle Zone. Some would attribute this neglect to adverse climatic and other environmental conditions. But the specific interrelationships are not well established.

Two of the most striking concentrations of population within Nigeria's Middle Belt lie along its southern border, one south of the Benue River and east of the Niger and the other centered on Ilorin, south and west

[23] S. A. Agboola, "Some Factors of Population Distribution in the Middle Belt of Nigeria: the Examples of northern Ilorin and Kabba Provinces," in J. C. Caldwell and C. Okonjo (eds.), *The Population of Tropical Africa*. Longmans, Green and Co., London, 1968, pp. 291–296.

of the Niger. A third is situated near the center of the Middle Belt and is fairly coincident with the Jos Plateau. Earlier this plateau became a refuge for non-Moslem peoples during the invasions of the Fulani from the north. It still remains an island of retarded non-Moslems, almost surrounded by Islamic peoples. Along the northeastern margins of the Nigerian Middle Belt, bordering Cameroon, is another section where settlement thickens appreciably. A similar situation prevails on the Cameroon side of the boundary as well.

Other Political Units in West Africa. Westward from Nigeria, the seaward forested belt of relatively dense population continues, with minor interruptions, through Dahomey, Togo, and Ghana, but in reduced intensity and with generally reduced width. The northern savanna population belt, so prominent in Nigeria, fades farther west in northern Dahomey and Togo, and in adjacent southwestern Niger and eastern Upper Volta, but reappears again in northern Ghana and in central Upper Volta. The thinly populated Middle Belt of Nigeria continues westward through Dahomey, Togo, and Ghana, but with even sparser settlement.

Ghana (estimated nine million inhabitants, 1970) has a seaward belt of relatively dense population, variable in width and density, that is terminated abruptly inland by a zone of hills and highland separating it from the interior Volta Basin, a region underlain by sandstone from which is derived highly infertile and droughty soils (Fig. 7.7). A steep population gradient marks the transition zone between the relatively empty Volta Basin inland and the populous seaward belt, which includes both coastal plain and hill-and-valley country. The well-inhabited seaward belt itself varies greatly both in width and in population densities. It narrows to 50 miles or so at about the longitude of Accra, where highlands bounding the Volta Basin thrust closest to the sea. From that waist it broadens abruptly both to the east and the west, and in the latter direction attains a breadth of 200 miles or so close to the western boundary. But within this broad western part of the Ghana seaward belt, overall densities are not so high. The large, relatively empty regions close to the Ivory Coast boundary are attributed to the earlier depopulating effects of tribal wars and to a continuing difficult access to the coast.[24] The most prominent feature in the western section is a very narrow zone of high density along the port-studded coast, in which there is a conspicuous density node in the vicinity of the rail terminus and port of Sekondi-Takoradi. Farther eastward in the seaward forested belt, the details of population distribution correspond closely with cacao pro-

[24] Kwamina B. Dickson, *A Historical Geography of Ghana*. Cambridge University Press, London, 1969, p. 271.

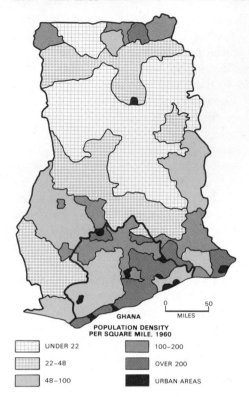

GHANA
POPULATION DENSITY
PER SQUARE MILE, 1960

UNDER 22

22–48

48–100

100–200

OVER 200

URBAN AREAS

Fig. 7.7. Ghana—population density by "local authority" subdivisions, 1960. Data from *Atlas of Population Characteristics*, Ghana, 1964.

duction and with the lines of transport that facilitate the movement of that commodity to tidewater. The highest densities are in a coastal strip served by numerous short lengths of good road leading inland, where there exist a flourishing fishing industry and port cities, including Accra the capital and metropolis.

Within the general seaward belt, but located 100 mi or more inland and therefore somewhat separated from the populous littoral strip, is the striking population cluster that has the city of Kumasi as its nucleus (Fig. 7.7). Kumasi, strategically located on one of the secondary routes of trans-Saharan caravans, was founded in the early 1700's when it became the capital of the Ashanti Confederacy and the residence of its ruler. Thus the early Ashanti population node illustrates the correlation between high population density and state formation, a feature commented upon earlier.[25] However, the real boom period for Kumasi and the Ashanti population cluster has occurred during the 20th century

[25] Stevenson, *Population*, p. 167.

as European influences have been strongly felt. Two rail lines, built to connect Kumasi wth the coastal ports of Takoradi and Accra, have stimulated the commercial growing of cacao, with the result that Kumasi is now a vigorous commercial city second only to Accra in size, serving the chief cacao producing region of the country. Ghana's production and population are strongly concentrated within a south central region that extends from the coast inland to about the vicinity of Kumasi (on Fig. 7.7 see area enclosed by heavy line). Within this core region, where the average density exceeds 200 per sq mi, the population concentration is related in part to economic factors, since it contains all the mines, more than half the cacao, and four of the five most important ports. And although the region covers only about one sixth of the national area, it accounts for nearly one half the national population, three fifths of the towns, and four fifths of the urban inhabitants.[26]

The relatively empty Volta Basin, which comprises most of Ghana's Middle Belt, is a region of poor savanna woodland, plagued by a difficult environment that involves extensive areas of infertile sandy soils, a scarcity of water in the dry season and widespread flooding in the wet season, and a heavy infestation of tsetse fly. Large areas are uninhabited. The single important cluster of population has as its nucleus the town of Tamale, the largest urban center in the basin. It is the administrative center of the Northern Territories and a commercial town of some significance, located at the intersection of highways. The origin of the small Tamale population cluster is also related to an earlier state formation, since it was the political center of the Gonja people.[27]

Along the northern margins of Ghana, north of about the 10° or 10.5° parallel (where granites replace the Voltaian sandstones), population densities rise sharply, particularly in the northeast and the northwest, where settlement nodes are conspicuous. There the average density is about 130 per sq mi, and in parts it exceeds 200. Nucleated settlements are few, and only 3 percent of the people live in towns with more than 5000 inhabitants. The prevailingly subsistence agriculture shows only low yields, since soils are thin (although of somewhat better quality than the sandy ones overlying the sandstones of the Voltaian Basin), and little fertilizer is applied. Nearly every year many people are short of food during the dry season, a condition that stimulates an increasing out-migration toward the coast. As noted earlier, this concentration of people in the sudan savanna of northernmost Ghana is really the southern-

[26] Enid R. Forde, "The Population of Ghana." *Northwestern University Studies in Geography*, No. 15, 1968, pp. 12–15.
[27] Stevenson, *Population*, p. 169.

most sector of a much larger population cluster whose main center is in Upper Volta farther north. The Upper Volta-Ghana cluster as a whole corresponds rather closely to the territory of the Mossi Empire, which persisted politically and culturally for over 500 years, or down to the period of colonial conquest.

Westward from Ghana the triple-belt arrangement of population densities is much weaker or even disappears, and overall densities decline. The only fairly large areas with densities over 100 per sq km (260 per sq mi) are to be found in nodes around the old colonial centers of Abidjan in Ivory Coast, Freetown in Sierra Leone, Conakry in Guinea, and Dakar in Senegal. The seaward forested belt of high density is therefore much less continuous than in Ghana and eastward. The reasons are not so clear. In some degree this situation may relate to the fact that economic exploitation by Europeans was slower in getting under way along this western coast, usually not occurring until the late 19th century; consequently the stimulating effects of Western enterprise and medicine on economic expansion and population growth have been weaker there.

The *Ivory Coast* (4.3 million) and *Liberia* (1.2 million) provide the most extensive gap in West Africa's seaward forest belt of above-average population density. In fact, most of their coasts are conspicuously sparse in occupance. In the Ivory Coast commercial agriculture in the forest zone and port development along the coast have not prospered. The most populous and productive part of the country is its southeastern

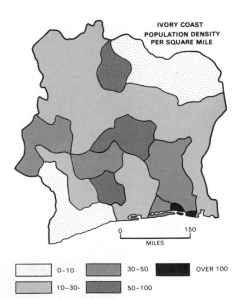

IVORY COAST
POPULATION DENSITY
PER SQUARE MILE

0   150
MILES

| | 0–10 | | 30–50 | | OVER 100 |
| | 10–30- | | 50–100 | | |

Fig. 7.8. Ivory Coast—population density. After map in *Focus* (American Geographical Society), October 1965.

sector, which includes the metropolis, capital, and port of Abidjan, a region that benefited through having been organized by the Ashanti state in the 18th and 19th centuries (Fig. 7.8). West of about Abidjan there is no evidence of the existence of any organized state; the meagerly settled southwest was widely but unfavorably known for its cannibal population.

Small *Sierra Leone,* with its estimated 2.6 million people, is one of Africa's more densely populated states, having a degree of crowding that is more than three times that of the continent as a whole and two to three times what it is in Liberia or the Ivory Coast. As a consequence the seaward population belt of West Africa is much better defined in Sierra Leone than it is in the two countries mentioned before. While population is by no means evenly distributed, still there are no extensive voids and no remarkable concentrations of settlement except in the vicinity of Freetown, the chief port and capital city. The map of rural settlement exhibits two somewhat amorphous and separate lobes of denser settlement and more rapid population growth, one in the west and the other in the southeast (Fig. 7.9). In both areas densities of 100–250 per sq mi are widespread, but steep population gradients are not a conspicuous feature. In both, the above-average densities are associated with a market-oriented agriculture—paddy rice and oil palm in the west and tree crops, including oil palm, cacao, coffee, piassava, and ginger, in the southeast.[28] The largest area of low density is in the northeastern dissected plateau section, where there has been a long history of intertribal wars, and in addition accessibility is difficult. Of the total population, about one quarter live in urban places with more than 1000 inhabitants; 24 percent of the urban population are in the capital city and port of Freetown.

Guinea (3.9 million people), which is much larger than either Sierra Leone or Liberia, extends deeper into the interior where savanna conditions prevail and settlement is relatively sparse. There on the savanna upland plains, the Malinke, a sudan Moslem people, dominate. The main concentrations of population are (1) in the super-wet western uplands back from the coast (the Fouta Djallon) and (2) to a lesser degree on the coastal lowland, especially in the vicinity of Conakry, the metropolis. The generally high population densities in the Fouta Djallon Massif appear to have some association with state organization in that region following the Fulani conquest of the mid-18th century.[29] Two

---

[28] John I. Clarke (ed.), *Sierra Leone in Maps.* University of London Press, London, 1966, pp. 42–43, 60–61, 76–81.
[29] Stevenson, *Population,* p. 171.

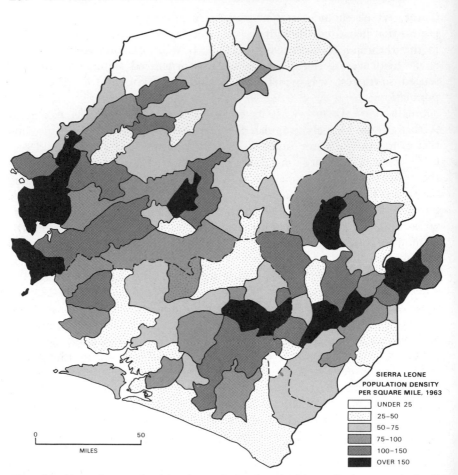

Fig. 7.9. Sierra Leone—density of population by chiefdoms. Redrawn and simplified from John I. Clarke, *Sierra Leone in Maps.*

· fifths of its population, mainly concentrated in the uplands, are Moslem Fùlani people of sudan origin. Their economy is associated with the keeping of tsetse-resistant Ndama cattle and the growing of subsistence crops. Negroes, formerly slaves of the Fulani, are crowded onto the trenchlike valley floors.

Senegal (3.9 million), unlike Guinea, has its main concentration of settlement in the country's seaward ports, with the main center around and just inland from the metropolis and port of Dakar. To an overwhelming degree the main food crop supporting the population is millet, while groundnuts, or peanuts, are virtually the exclusive cash and export crop.

The latter occupies about 40 percent of the cultivated area. Senegal's population cluster, while greatly accentuated by colonial influences leading to the establishment of ports, trade and administrative centers, and naval bases, did have a precolonial origin that was rooted in the state formation among the Serer, Wolof, and Tenme peoples.[30]

While the three very extensive Sahara-sudan states of *Mauritania, Mali,* and *Niger* have a largely desert climate, each extends far enough south to feel the effects of the brief high-sun rains characteristic of the sahel-sudan savanna belt. Mauritania, which reaches only to 15° or 16°S, is more exclusively desert than the other two. Its million or so inhabitants are concentrated along the Senegal River, where water is most readily available (Fig. 7.10). Mali, which reaches as far south as 10°N, has a much larger area within the subhumid-semiarid sudan savanna belt, with the consequence that it meagerly supports close to five million people. These are concentrated in the more humid southern and southwestern part of the country and more particularly along the Niger River and its tributaries, where annual flooding and irrigation make agriculture safer. Although southern Mali lies in the heartland of the old empires of Ghana and Mali, these earlier centers of political strength have not left behind them large residual clusters of modern population concentration. Niger's 3.8 million inhabitants are strongly concentrated along its southern or Nigerian border where the Kano-Katsina and Sokoto population clusters of its southern neighbor extend shallowly across the international boundary (Fig. 7.10). In Niger's extreme southwest there is a single, highly linear concentration of population that closely coincides with the floodplain of the Niger River.

Landlocked *Upper Volta's* estimated 5.4 million inhabitants are one of tropical Africa's most impoverished populations. The overall density of about 50 per sq mi greatly exceeds that of the much larger but drier states of Mauritania, Mali, and Niger, a feature reflecting Upper Volta's more favorable location exclusively within the sudan-guinea savanna where rainfall is generally adequate for unirrigated agriculture. Still, much of the country is unproductive and sparsely settled, because soils are usually thin and infertile, vast areas are subject to flood or are poorly drained, and the tsetse fly is widespread. Upper Volta's population is strongly concentrated in the country's geographical center (Fig. 7.10). Within this core region, containing the capital city of Ouagadougou, dwell about half of the state's total population—a fact that relates more to historical than to environmental causes, since, significantly, this population concentration corresponds rather closely with one of the two most

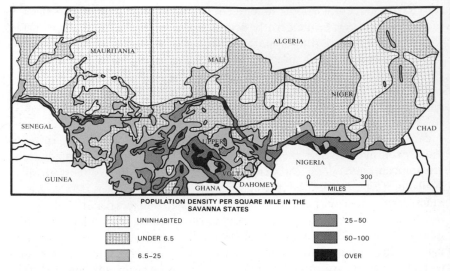

POPULATION DENSITY PER SQUARE MILE IN THE
SAVANNA STATES

UNINHABITED

UNDER 6.5

6.5-25

25-50

50-100

OVER

Fig. 7.10. Population density in the savanna states of Mauritania, Mali, Upper Volta, and Niger. Note that population is concentrated in the somewhat more humid southern parts of this belt. The Saharan central and northern parts are relatively empty of settlement. Simplified from a density map by Else Schmidt and Paul Mattingly in *Geographische Rundschau,* 1966, Heft 12.

durable savanna cultures in West Africa, that of the Mossi states. While the military power of the Mossi has waned since the late 15th century, that group has been able to retain its cultural and political integrity over half a millennium of time. So even today the territory of the old Mossi states continues to be reflected in the high-density parts of central Upper Volta and adjacent northern Ghana.

TROPICAL CENTRAL AFRICA

Somewhat arbitrarily, Central Africa is here considered to include the following political subdivisions: Chad, Cameroon, Central African Republic, Gabon, the two Congos, Angola, and Equatorial Guinea. Its estimated population in 1970 was about 36 million.

Overall vital rates in Central Africa are high (1970 estimate, birth rate 43, death rate 23) and therefore not significantly different from those in the other two large subdivisions of black Africa. Infant mortality is also excessively high. But one unusual regional feature of birth rates and of total fertility rates in Central Africa is the broad belt of relatively lower fertility that stretches from Gabon and most of Cameroon in the west, eastward through the northwestern and northcentral provinces of Congo (Kinshasa, formerly Leopoldville) and the central parts of the Central African Republic into southwestern Sudan. For example, northern and southeastern Cameroon have a birth rate of only 37.4 and 30.8 per 1000; Gabon, about 31; and five provinces of Congo, 26 per 1000 or below.[31] The reasons for this anomalous situation are obscure, but pathological sterility associated with venereal disease is undoubtedly one factor.

Already pointed out in an earlier chapter is the fact that the overall population density of Central Africa is well below that of either West Africa or East Africa—about one third that of the former and roughly 42 percent that of the latter (Fig. 5.3). The reasons for this generally lower density are not readily apparent. A contributing circumstance may be the fact that in this region state formation among native peoples never had the high incidence that it did in the sudan zone of West Africa or in the lake region of East Africa, and its time span was briefer as well.[32] In addition, depopulation associated with slave raiding and trading may have been more severe here than in either of the other two regions. Moreover, not only did the colonial period begin later in Central Africa than in most other tropical parts of the continent, but in addition European enterprises were not pushed as vigorously as they were in the coastal belt of West Africa, especially in the English colonies. Within Central Africa state formation was usually so bound up with the slave trade that depopulation in some areas, and population increase in others, went on simultaneously. Successful slave-trade centers had a tendency to become nodes of denser population; other less-favored areas, lacking state formation or advanced military organization, suffered depopulation through systematic raiding.[33]

Within only modestly populated Central Africa the modern distribution patterns of relatively high and low densities are less well-defined than in West and East Africa. If anything, they also appear even less rational. A reasonably conspicuous gross pattern, such as characterized West Africa, is absent. A northern sudan belt of higher density is largely lacking, while the seaward belt, instead of being a zone of high-density concentration as in West Africa, is actually one of diminished population. Over three quarters of the population of former French Equatorial Africa live more than 600 mi from the sea. European-induced export crops and port development are minimal in Central Africa. As a rule the regions

[31] Etienne von de Walle and Hilary Page. "Some New Estimates of Fertility and Mortality in Africa," *Population Index*, Vol. 35, No. 1, 1969, pp. 3–17.

[32] Stevenson, *Population*, p. 181.

[33] Stevenson, *Population*, p. 183.

relatively empty of settlement grade almost imperceptibly into others of higher density; an absence of steep population gradients is typical. Only along the eastern margins of Central Africa, in the vicinity of the Rift Valley and its lakes, are steep gradients present (Figs. 5.3, 5.4). Regions that stand out because of having above-average settlement density are as follows: (1) A small region in northern Cameroon, which is matched by a similar region of concentration across the international boundary in Nigeria. This may be thought of as a small eastern fragment of the sahel-sudan savanna zone. (2) A somewhat larger area in southwest Cameroon, located mostly inland from the coast. (3) A more extensive zone situated between about 4° and 8°S, which extends eastward from the Atlantic coast to nearly 25°E. It lies almost exclusively within the border of the Republic of Congo (Kinshasa). Nodular pattern is conspicuous. (4) A rather poorly defined, not too emphatic, and not completely continuous east-west belt along the northern margins of the same country. (5) A succession of very high-density nodes that forms an interrupted north-south band of high density along the northeastern border of Congo, south to about 3°S. It represents the densely settled western section of the Rift Valley highlands. This zone of higher density continues on eastward into East Africa, in Uganda, Rwanda, and Burundi. (6) The highlands of west-central Angola.

The more extensive near-empty areas are (1) Gabon and eastward into the northern half of Congo (Brazzaville); (2) the eastern part of the Central African Republic; and (3) southeastern and eastern Angola.

Rationalizing the above-described gross distribution pattern is difficult if not impossible. For the most part, association with environmental causative factors is weak. The east-west band of higher density in Congo according to Stevenson, appears to show some correspondence with what was the former Kingdom of the Kongo in the west and with the heartland of Luba-Lunda state toward the center. The same source relates the population concentration in the northeastern region of Congo to the state-building activities of the Azande people, supplemented by immigration from Sudan.[34]

Cameroon. This state occupies the hinge position between West and Central Africa. While its estimated population of some 5.8 million (1970) is only about one third that of the much larger Congo (Kinshasa), its overall population density is not only somewhat above the African average but also considerably the highest of all the Central African states. On the other hand, it is far below those of Nigeria and Ghana in West Africa. Population diversity is not only marked but also exceedingly

---

[34] Stevenson, *Population*, p. 180.

complex in the overlappings that occur among the various elements. Present Cameroon is made up of two former Trust Territories—the ten-times-larger eastern part, with about four fifths of the population, was French; the greatly smaller west was British. Accordingly, the bilingual character of the new state presents serious problems relating to political integration. Ethnic division also exists, since southern Cameroon is predominantly populated by Bantu and semi-Bantu Negroes, mostly Christian and considerably westernized, while the north is prevailingly Sudanese Negroes, Hamitic Fulani, and Arabs, who are largely Moslem or animist and less modernized.

Since 84 percent of the people live in rural environments, clearly it is the rural population that largely determines density in Cameroon. Four nodes of relatively dense population can be recognized, one located in the far north and three in fairly close juxtaposition in the southwest (Fig. 7.11). Two of those in the southwest are regions of in-migration; in the other two, out-migration predominates.[35] The northern cluster lying north of the Benue River, consists of two groups: (1) densely settled

[35] John I. Clarke, "Population Distribution and Dynamics in Cameroon," in Wilbur Zelinsky, Leszek A. Kosinski and R. Mansell Prothero (eds.), *Geography and a Crowding World.* Oxford University Press, New York, 1970, pp. 348–362.

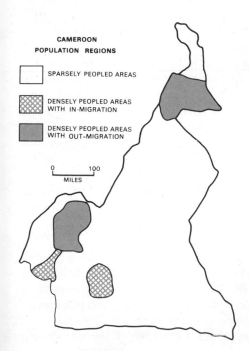

CAMEROON
POPULATION REGIONS

SPARSELY PEOPLED AREAS

DENSELY PEOPLED AREAS
WITH IN-MIGRATION

DENSELY PEOPLED AREAS
WITH OUT-MIGRATION

0   100
MILES

Fig. 7.11. Population density regions in Cameroon. After map by John I. Clarke. Later published in *Geography and a Crowding World*, Wilbur Zelinsky et al (eds), Oxford University Press, 1970.

Negroid peasant farmers in the humid hill lands and (2) more widely spaced pastoralists and cultivators on adjacent drier plains. Out-migration is on a modest scale. The southern node of relatively dense population, which is also characterized by out-migration, belongs to both East and West Cameroon. On the region's high plateaus with their fertile volcanic soils there is an intensive cultivation of both food crops and such commercial export crops as coffee and cacao. Rural densities exceed 250 per sq mi.

The more western of the two southern dense nodes with in-migration is the only one that reaches down to tidewater. It is composed of both lowland and upland and lies about equally within East and West Cameroon. On the region's fertile volcanic soils a modern plantation agriculture has developed. Its population benefits as well by having access to the main ports, especially Douala, which is also the country's metropolis and principal industrial center.

Farther to the east, inland and mainly on a plateau, is a fourth node of relatively dense population that is centered on the capital city of Yaoundé. Although here plantation agriculture is lacking, nevertheless this cluster of population does produce close to four fifths of the country's cacao output as well as a variety of food crops in large quantities.

No easy explanations can be suggested for the density variations in Cameroon; much of it seems irrational in terms of environment potential, which suggests that some of it must be rooted in historical causation, for which the records are scarce indeed.

Chad. The large state of Chad, which borders Cameroon on the northeast, has an estimated total population of only 3.7 million (1970). The Saharan part north of about 15°N is a relatively empty land, with probably only one person for every four or five sq mi. Highest densities are in the Chari-Logone Basin in the extreme southwest, close to northern Cameroon. Chad's proportion of urban population—only 3–4 percent—is one of the lowest in all Africa.

Central African Republic. Situated just south of Chad, the Central African Republic is estimated to have a population of only 1.5 million. It represents one of the most remote and underdeveloped parts of all Africa. Most of its people are concentrated in a few regions along the Ubangi River on the Congo border.

Congo (Kinshasa). This is the giant of Central Africa, both in area and in population, its estimated 17.4 million people (1970) making it the fifth most populous state in all Africa. Still its average density is low—only about 16 per sq mi. Like most African states, Congo's annual growth rate has moved rapidly upward over the past few decades—estimated at only 0.6 percent over the period 1925–1940, 1 percent during

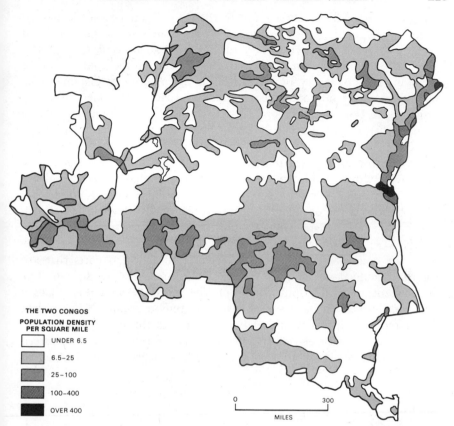

THE TWO CONGOS
POPULATION DENSITY
PER SQUARE MILE

UNDER 6.5

6.5–25

25–100

100–400

OVER 400

0   300

MILES

Fig. 7.12. The two Congos—density of population. Simplified from a density map by Else Schmidt and Paul Mattingly, in *Geographische Rundschau*, 1966, Heft 12.

1940–1950, but 1.9 percent in the 7 years 1950–1957. More recently the crude annual rate of natural increase has exceeded 2 percent. Recapitulating what was pointed out in an earlier section dealing with population distribution patterns for Central Africa as a whole, the highest densities in Congo are to be found, (1) in a north-south band coincident with the highlands on the western side of the Rift Valley where fertile but seriously eroded soils prevail and (2) in the lower Congo Valley where the capital and metropolis of Kinshasa (420,000, 1961) and the port of Matadi are located (Fig. 7.12). This latter concentration forms the westernmost part of a before-mentioned band of above-average density, which lies between about parallels 4° and 8°S. The existence of this zone, it has been pointed out, was probably influenced by earlier state building.

Congo (Brazzaville). With fewer than a million people, it has 70 percent of its population concentrated in the state's southern part, both along the lower Congo River and on the coastal lowland (Fig. 7.12). Urban people comprise an estimated 19 percent of the total, with 14 percent in the capital city of Brazzaville alone. Adjoining Gabon's half-a-million people, tend to concentrate along roads and waterways.

Angola. A Portuguese colony, it has an estimated population of 5.7 million (1970), including some 200,000 (1961) Europeans. Bantu-speaking tribes comprise the great bulk of the population. Unlike the situation in most of tropical Africa, many Europeans in Angola are small land holders who work their own farms, serve as unskilled laborers, and are engaged in various kinds of small-scale operations. The emptiest part of the country is the dry coastal lowland, especially the southern third, or south of Lobito, where aridity is most intense and the lowland narrowest (Fig. 7.13). On the extensive plateau, which includes much the larger part of the country's area, it is the eastern and southern parts that are meagerly occupied—in general by under 6.5 persons per sq mi. The main concentration of population is on the more elevated Bihe Plateau in the central-western part, particularly the region around Nova Lisboa and along the main east-west rail line that passes through that city and connects the port city of Lobito with the mining region of southeastern Congo. Thus Angola's core region of highest density (50–100 per sq

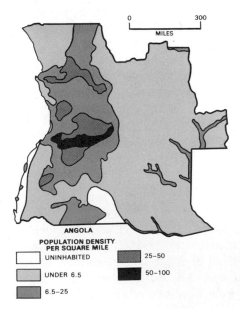

Fig. 7.13. Angola—population density. Rural settlement is concentrated mainly on the higher, cooler, and more humid central-western part of the plateau. Simplified from a density map by Else Schmidt and Paul Mattingly in *Geographische Rundschau*, 1966, Heft 12.

mi) has a distinctly linear shape. Much of the Bihe Plateau, characterized by both subsistence and commercial agriculture, has densities exceeding 25 per sq mi. With increasing distance from the Bihe core region, the natives are given more and more to shifting cultivation, and hence population density declines. But over large parts of the western upland densities still exceed 13 per sq mi.

REFERENCES

Adams, John. "A Population Map of West Africa," *Journal of the Geographical Association of Nigeria*, Vol. 12, December 1969, pp. 87–97.

Adams, J. G. U., and R. J. Harrison Church. "The Population of West Africa," in Paul F. Griffin (ed.), *Geography of Population*. Feardon Publishers, Palo Alto, California, 1969, pp. 209–226.

Agboola, S. A. "The Middle Belt of Nigeria: The Basis of Its Unity," *Nigerian Geographical Journal*, Vol. 4, No. 1, 1961, pp. 41–46.

Atlas of Population Characteristics, Accra, Ghana, 1964.

Barbour K. M. and R. M. Prothero (eds.), *Essays on African Population*. Routledge and Kegan Paul, London, 1961.

Barlet, Paul. "*La Haute-Volta* (Essai de presentation géographique)," *Études Voltaiques*, No. 3, 1962, pp. 5–77.

Birmingham, Walter, I. Neustadt, and E. N. Omaboe. *A Study of Contemporary Ghana*. Vol. I: *The Economy of Ghana*. Vol. II: *Some Aspects of Social Structure*. George Allen and Unwin, London, 1966.

Boateng, Ernest Amano. "Some Geographical Aspects of the 1960 Population Census of Ghana," *Ghana Geographical Association, Bulletin*, Vol. 5 (1960), pp. 2–8.

———. *A Geography of Ghana*. Cambridge University Press, New York, 1966.

Brass, W., et al., *The Demography of Tropical Africa*. Princeton, New Jersey, Princeton University Press, 1968.

Buchanan, Keith M. and Pugh, John Charles, "The Human Pattern," in *Land and People in Nigeria*. University of London Press, London, 1955, pp. 58–99.

Caldwell, John C. *African Rural-Urban Migration: The Movement to Ghana's Towns*. Columbia University Press, New York, 1969.

———. "Determinants of Rural-Urban Migration in Ghana," *Population Studies*, Vol. XXII, No. 3, November 1968, pp. 361–377.

Caldwell, J. C., and Chukuka Okonjo (eds.), *The Population of Tropical Africa*, Longmans, Green and Co., London, 1968, pp. 78–115, 238–245, 264–276, 278–296, 298–311, and 320–330.

Church, R. J. Harrison, *West Africa: a Study of the Environment and of Man's Use of It*. London, Longmans, Green, 1966, 5th ed; pp. 163–173.

Clarke, John I. (ed.). *Sierra Leone in Maps.* University of London Press, Ltd., London, 1966, pp. 36–51, pp. 60–61.

Clarke, John I. "Population Distribution and Dynamics in Cameroon," in Wilbur Zelinsky, Leszek A. Kosinski and R. Mansell Prothero (eds.), *Geography and a Crowding World.* Oxford University Press, New York, 1970, pp. 348–362.

Clarke, John I. "Sex-Ratios in Sierra Leone," *The Bulletin; the Journal of the Sierra Leone Geographical Association,* No. 9. May 1965, pp. 72–77. Map.

Dickson, Kwamina B. *A Historical Geography of Ghana.* Cambridge University Press, 1969, pp. 239–301.

Engmann, E. V. T. "Population Movements in Ghana; a Study of Internal Migration and its Implications for the Planner." *Bulletin of the Ghana Geographical Association,* Vol. 10, No. 1, January 1965, pp. 41–65. Maps.

Floyd, Barry. *Eastern Nigeria; A Geographical Review.* Frederick A. Praeger, New York, 1969, pp. 19–63.

Forde, Enid R. *The Population of Ghana: A Study of the Spatial Relationships of Its Sociocultural and Economic Characteristics.* Northwestern University Press, Evanston, Studies in Geography, No. 15, 1968.

Gaisie, S. K. "Dynamics of Population Growth in Ghana." *Ghana Population Studies,* No. 1. Legon, University of Ghana, Department of Sociology, Demographic Unit, 1959. xiv, 118 pp. and 2 folding tables.

Gleave, M. B., and H. P. White. "The West African Middle Belt: Environmental Fact or Geographer's Fiction?" *The Geographical Review,* Vol. LIX, No. 1, January 1969, pp. 122–139.

Grove, A. T. "Population Densities and Agriculture in Northern Nigeria," in K. M. Barbour and R. M. Prothero (eds.), *Essays on African Population.* Routledge and Kegan Paul, London, 1961, pp. 115–136.

Grove, A. T. *Africa South of the Sahara.* Oxford University Press, London, 1967, pp. 106–148 (scattered references to population).

Hill, Polly. *The Migrant Cocoa-Farmers of Southern Ghana.* Cambridge University Press, London, 1963.

Hilton, T. E., *Ghana Population Atlas,* University College of Ghana, Thomas Nelson and Sons Ltd., Edinburgh, 1960.

Hoffmann-Burchardi, Helmut. "Die Bevölkerungsballung in südost-Nigerien (Biafra): ein Forschungsbericht mit Bemerkungen zu den siedlungsgeographschen Arbeiten von Y. Karmon und R. K. Udo, "*Erdkunde* (Bonn), Vol. 22(3), September 1968, pp. 225–238. English.

Hunter, John M. "The Social Roots of Dispersed Settlement in Northern Ghana," *Annals of the Association of American Geographers,* Vol. 57 (2), June 1967, pp. 338–349.

Hunter, J. M. Regional Patterns of Population Growth in Ghana 1948–1960, in J. S. Whittow and P. D. Wood (Eds.), *Essays in Geography for Austin Miller,* Reading, England, 1965, pp. 272–290.

Jarrett, H. Reginald. "Population and Settlement in the Gambia," *The Geographical Review,* Vol. XXXVIII, No. 4, October, 1948, pp. 633–636.

Kayser, Bernard. "La démographie de l'Afrique occidentale et centrale." *Cahiers d'Outre-Mer* (Bordeaux), No. 18, January-March 1965, pp. 73–86.

Kuper, H. (ed.). *Urbanization and Migration in West Africa.* University of California Press, Berkeley, 1965.

Little, Kenneth L. *West African Urbanization: a Study of Voluntary Associations in Social Change.* Cambridge University Press, 1965.

Mabogunje, A. L. *Yoruba Towns.* Ibadan University Press, 1962.

Mabogunje, Akin L., *Urbanization in Nigeria.* University of London Press, London, 1968.

Mabogunje, Akin L. "A Typology of Population Pressure on Resources in West Africa," in *Geography and a Crowding World,* Wilbur Zelinsky et al. (eds.), Oxford University Press, New York, 1970.

Mason, Michael. "Population Density and 'Slave Raiding'–the Case of the Middle Belt of Nigeria," *Journal of African History,* Vol. 10(4), 1969, pp. 551–564.

218 THE LESS DEVELOPED REALM: A GEOGRAPHY OF ITS POPULATION

Mitchel, N. C. "Yoruba Towns," in K. M. Barbour and R. M. Prothero (eds.), *Essays on African Population*, Routledge and Kegan Paul, London, 1961, pp. 279–301.

Morgan, W. B. "Farming Practice, Settlement Pattern and Population Density in South-Eastern Nigeria," *The Geographical Journal*, Vol. CXXI, Part 3, 1955, pp. 320–333.

Morgan, W. B., and J. C. Pugh, *West Africa*, Methuen and Co., Ltd., London, 1969, pp. 3–61, 310–372, 421–466.

Morgan, W. T. W. "Urbanization in Kenya: Origins and Trends," *Transactions of the Institute of British Geographers*, Vol. 46, March 1969, pp. 161–172.

Mortimore, M. J. "Land and Population Pressure in the Kano Close-Settled Zone, Northern Nigeria," *Advancement of Science*, Vol. 23, No. 118, April 1967, pp. 677–686. Maps.

Mortimore, M. J. "Population Densities and Rural Economics in the Kano Close-Settled Zone, Nigeria," in Wilbur Zelinsky, Leszek A. Kosinski, and R. Mansell Prothero (eds.), *Geography and a Crowding World*. Oxford University Press, New York, 1970, pp. 380–388.

Prothero, R. M. "The Population of Eastern Nigeria," *The Scottish Geographical Magazine*, Vol. 71, No. 3, 1955, pp. 165–170.

Prothero, R. Mansell. "Population Movement in West Africa," *Geographical Review*, Vol. 47, 1957, pp. 434–437.

———. "Labour Migration in British West Africa," *Corona*, Vol. IX, No. 5, May, 1957, pp. 169–172.

———. "Migrant Labour in West Africa," *Journal of Local Administration Overseas*, Vol. I, No. 3, July, 1963, pp. 149–155.

———. *Migrants and Malaria*. Longmans, Green and Co., London, 1965.

Pullan, R. A. "The Concept of the Middle Belt in Nigeria—An Attempt at a Climatic Definition," *The Nigerian Geographical Journal*, Vol. 5, No. 1, 1962, pp. 39–52.

Simms, R. P. *Urbanization in West Africa*. Northwestern University Press, Evanston, Illinois, 1965.

Sociological Review, Special Number on *Urbanization in West Africa*, Vol. 7, No. 1, 1959.

Spengler, Joseph J. "Population Movements and Economic Development in Nigeria," in Robert O. Tilman and Taylor Cole eds. *The Nigerian Political Scene*. Published for the Duke University Commonwealth Studies Center (by) the Duke University Press and the Cambridge University Press, Durham, N.C., and London, 1962. 340 pp.

Stamp, L. Dudley (ed.), *Natural Resources, Food and Population in Inter-Tropical Africa*. Report of a Symposium held at Makerere College, Uganda, September, 1955, under the auspices of the International Geographical Union, London: Geographical Publications, Ltd., 1956.

Steel, R. W. "Land and Population in British Tropical Africa," *Geography*, Vol. XL, No. 187, January 1955, pp. 1–17.

Steel, Robert W. "Some Problems of Population in British West Africa," in Robert W. Steel and C. A. Fisher (eds.), *Geographical Essays on British Tropical Lands*, London, 1956, pp. 19–50.

Trewartha, G. T. "New Population Maps of Uganda, Kenya, Nyasaland, and Gold Coast," *Annals of the Association of American Geographers*, Vol. 47, No. 1, March, 1957, pp. 41–58.

Udo, R. K. "Patterns of Population Distribution and Settlement in Eastern Nigeria," *The Nigerian Geographical Journal*, Vol. VI, No. 2, December 1963, pp. 73–88. Maps.

U.N. Economic Commission for Africa. "The Demographic Situation in Western Africa." *Economic Bulletin for Africa (Addis Ababa)*, Vol. 6(2), July 1966, pp. 89–102.

Verrière, Louis. *La Population du Sénégal.* Université de Dakar, Dakar, July 1965.

Central Africa

Baker, Samuel J. K. "The Distribution of Native Population over South-East Central Africa," *Geographical Journal*, Vol. 108, 1946, pp. 198–210.

Clarke, John I. "Population Distribution and Dynamics in "Cameroon," in *Geography and a Crowding World*, Wilbur Zelinsky, Leszek A. Kosinski, and R. Mansell Prothero (eds.), Oxford University Press, New York, 1970, pp. 348–362.

Gourou, Pierre. *La Densité de la Population Rural au Congo Belge*, Brussels, 1955.

Mitchell, J. C. "Wage Labour and African Population Movements in Central Africa," in K. M. Barbour and R. M. Prothero (eds.), *Essays on African Population*, Routledge and Kegan Paul, London, 1961, pp. 193–248.

Romaniuk, Anatole, "The Demography of the Democratic Republic of the Congo," in Wm. Brass et al. (eds.), *The Demography of Tropical Africa.* Princeton University Press, Princeton, 1968, pp. 241–339.

Shaul, J. R. H., "Demographic Features of Central Africa," in K. M. Barbour and R. M. Prothero (eds.), *Essays on African Population*, Routledge and Kegan Paul, London, 1961, pp. 31–48.

Trewartha, Glenn T., and Wilbur Zelinsky, "The Population Geography of Belgian Africa," *Annals of the Association of American Geographers*, Vol. XLIV, No. 2, 1954, pp. 163–193.

van de Walle, Etienne, and Hilary Page. "Some New Estimates of Fertility and Mortality in Africa," *Population Index*, Vol. 35, No. 1, 1969, pp. 3–12.

Vennetier, Pierre. "La population et l'économie du Congo (Brazzaville)," *Cahiers d'Outre-Mer* (Bordeaux) Vol. 15(60), October-December 1962, pp. 360–380.

Vennetier, P. "L'urbanisation et ses conséquences au Congo (Brazzaville)," *Cahiers d'Outre-Mer* (Bordeaux), Vol. 16(63), July-September 1963, pp. 265–280.

Witthauer, K. "Die Bevölkerungsverteilung in der Zentralafrikanischen Republik." *Petermanns Geographische Metteilungen* (Leipzig), Vol. 111(4), 1967, pp. 309–311.

Tropical Africa: East Africa

The somewhat arbitrary region to which the name East Africa is here applied includes the eastern tropical part of the continent facing toward the South Atlantic and the Red Sea and reaching from the southern Sahara on the north to beyond the Tropic of Capricorn. At its northern extremity are the states of Ethiopia and (included with reservations) Sudan. In its far south are Zambia and Mozambique. It is larger in area than either West Africa or Central Africa; in population numbers it resembles West Africa and far exceeds Central Africa. But because of its greater area, East Africa's population density is only 75 to 80 percent that of West Africa, although it is far above that of Central Africa.

The gross distribution pattern of population in East Africa contrasts with those of the other two main regional subdivisions. Especially it lacks the recognizable belted arrangement that is present in West Africa. In this respect it more closely resembles Central Africa. But on the other hand, it is unlike the latter in that within East Africa sharp density contrasts are prevalent. The prevailing distribution pattern is one of extreme complexity, involving unevenly scattered population clusters of varying sizes and densities (Figs. 5.3, 5.4). Extremes of density and steep population gradients are characteristic of both highland and lowland locations.

Because of the highly irregular and intricate nature of the spatial population distribution in East Africa, it is difficult to set forth a simple gross pattern. There is a seaward belt of above-average population density, but it is not as well defined, as continuous, or as closely settled as is its counterpart in West Africa. Emphatically it is in the nature of a series of interrupted coastal nodes of high density but only modest size, which characteristically do not penetrate far inland. Much the greatest concentration of population lies well interior, in the complex lake and Rift Valley region, where there is a grouping of several distinct high-density nodes, the most important of which are (1) that around the margins of Lake Victoria, (2) another in Rwanda and Burundi just east of the Rift Valley, and (3) a third in the central highlands of Kenya. Eight or 10 distinct minor nodes are scattered throughout northern Tanzania. Three conspicuous small nodes lie within the Lake Nyanza Basin, one at the lake's northern tip and two within the southern parts of the basin.

While the origin of individual population clusters is a topic for later discussion, it seems appropriate at this point to remark that in East Africa as well as in the Central and West parts, there is evidence to support the hypothesis that some degree of correlation exists between high population density on the one hand and state formation, or political centralization, on the other.[1] Within the coastal zone of population concentration there are nuclear areas of dense settlement around the old port-of-trade city states and the coastal enclaves that grew up in response to Indian Ocean trade, a commerce that goes back at least 2000 years. Among the old nodes are the city states of Malinda, Mombasa, Dar es Salaam, Kilwa, and Quelimane. Later nodes grew up around the ports established by Europeans, of which Mozambique is one example. Several of the high-density nodes within the lake region of equatorial East Africa are related to major state systems, which include Buganda, Bunyoro, Rwanda, Burundi, and Ankole, all in the vicinity of Lake Victoria, and numerous lesser states as well. Some formerly populous states have been subsequently depopulated by sleeping sickness. Among the stateless tribal groups, densities of their mainly pastoral populations are usually low.

The native peoples of East Africa are highly varied, both ethnically and culturally. It is a fair generalization, however, that to the south of the equator Bantus strongly predominate. Over the northern half linguistic variety is much more striking, although the distinctions are less between individual languages than between families of languages— Sudanic, Nilotic, Nilo-Hamitic, and Bantu. Hence equatorial East Africa is a zone where the Hamitic and Negro culture realms show deep interpenetration, resulting in an observable meridional alignment of linguistic and ethnic distribution.[2] The Masai in Kenya and Tanganyika represent a southward intrusion of Nilo-Hamitic peoples that separates the coastal Bantu from those of the interior highlands.

Until recently the peoples of interior East Africa have had little contact with the outside; they had been affected scarcely at all by the foreign intrusions that occurred along the coast, and there had been less widespread exposure to either Christianity or Islam than had occurred earlier

---

[1] Robert F. Stevenson, *Population and Political Systems in Tropical Africa.* Columbia University Press, New York, 1968, pp. 174–180.

[2] S. J. K. Baker, "The Population Geography of East Africa." *The East African Geographical Review* (Kampala), No. 1, April 1964, p. 1.

in West Africa. Most of the interior's contacts with outside cultures that resulted in a stimulation of economic development, have been features of the 20th century.

The non-African population in East Africa, while small in absolute numbers, is a very effective minority economically, and in parts, politically. Tropical Africa's several hundred thousand Asians, mostly Arabs and Indians (including Pakistani), are to an overwhelming degree concentrated in East Africa, especially in Kenya, Tanzania, and Uganda. The factor of proximity to sources appears to account for this east-side concentration of the Asians; they make up about one quarter of the population in the city of Dar es Salaam. An important recent exodus of Asiatics as well as of Europeans has accompanied the postwar establishment of a number of independent native states in East Africa. European permanent colonists numbering between 100 and 200 thousand have been particularly numerous in the plateaus of Kenya, Rhodesia, and Mozambique, and in the island of Madagascar. Outside of these areas the thin and scattered European population has consisted almost wholly of transient personnel—administrators, merchants, and missionaries. Most of the non-Africans live in towns and cities. Unlike the situation in parts of West Africa, the cities in the other two major subdivisions of tropical Africa appear to be mainly of European and Asiatic origin.

REGIONS OF EAST AFRICA

Ethiopia and Somali. This northeasternmost section of East Africa, which includes the Abyssinian highlands and the Horn of Africa, is the part of the continent most destitute of any serviceable population figures. No data on vital rates are available for either Ethiopia or Somali; even those on total numbers of people are highly unreliable. No censuses have been taken. The Population Reference Bureau in 1970 estimated the Ethiopian population at 25 million, and that of Somali at 2.8 million, which makes Ethiopia by far the most populous country in East Africa, and, after Nigeria and Egypt, the most populous in all Africa. Ethiopia and Somali are among the poorest and most backward countries on the continent—some 95 percent of the Ethiopians are judged to be illiterate; the per capita annual gross national product is only $50–$60; and over 90 percent of the inhabitants are impoverished subsistence farmers and nomads. It is a land whose people, still organized into tribal societies, are encrusted with ancient customs and traditions that retard modernization. Bulwarks of Ethiopian culture are the Coptic Christian church, the "divinely endowed" emperor, and a feudal land system.

The core region of Ethiopia is the Abyssinian highland. On the upland dwell the Amharas, mainly Semites, who are a belligerent, warlike tribal group, although largely Christian. Farther downslope are mainly Hamitic tribes, the most powerful of which are the Galla, a light-skinned, predominantly Moslem people who may be even more numerous than the Amharas. It is the Galla who represent the main threat to Amhara dominance. Negro and Nilotic tribes occupy chiefly the dry, hot lowlands, with Somalis concentrated on the eastern slopes. Altogether the Ethiopian population is composed of perhaps 100 tribes, as many as 70 languages, and 2 important religions; understandably, divisive forces are strong.

A vertical zonation of both physical and cultural features characterizes the highland, with population and cultivation most concentrated in a temperate and humid middle zone located between about 6000 and 8000 feet (Fig. 8.1). Areas of rich volcanic soils attract the closest settlement. In the cooler, higher altitudes, rural densities gradually fall off, as they do in the drier lands below 6000 feet where pastoralism comes more and more to dominate.

The new state of Somali is ethnically highly homogeneous, because a great preponderance of its people are of one tribal group, the Hamitic Somalis. In this dry land an estimated three quarters of the inhabitants are nomads or seminomads; possibly only 12 percent are settled agriculturists. Meager rainfall causes about 40 percent of the country, mainly in the north and central parts, to be almost unoccupied (Fig. 8.1). Toward the south, where rainfall increases to about 20 in. (except along the drier coast) and there are two main rivers, settlement thickens, since grazing is better and some rain-grown crops can be raised, especially along the rivers where they benefit from supplementary water provided by flash flooding and irrigation. Bantu blacks are the chief cultivators of the riverine farms.

Sudan (16 million inhabitants). To an unusual degree the spatial distribution of dense rural population in Sudan is Nilotic in character (Fig. 8.2). In the desert region, north of about 14–15°N, or down-river from Khartoum, sedentary settlement is almost exclusively concentrated in a narrow alluvial strip along the Nile River. Here the pattern duplicates that in Egypt farther north, except that in Sudan the strip of irrigated floodplain and dense population is narrower and less continuous. Population densities of over 400 per sq mi characterize the riverine zone. Even farther south, where rainfall is greater and rural settlement less restricted, the riverine settlement strip continues to be evident, although it is less striking. In the dry north, away from the stream, the few inhabitants are nomads or seminomads.

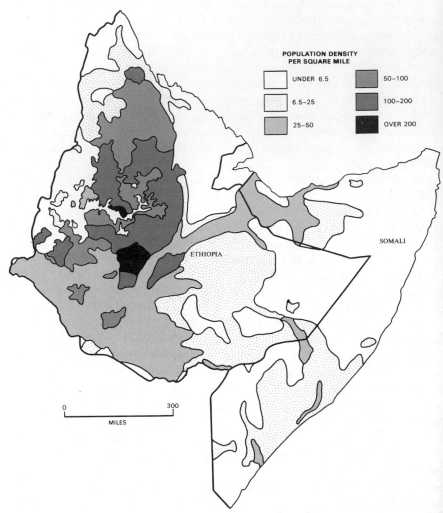

Fig. 8.1. Ethiopia and Somali—population density. Settlement is strongly concentrated in the cooler and more humid highlands of Ethiopia. Simplified from a density map by Else Schmidt and Paul Mattingly in *Geographische Rundschau*, 1966, Heft 12.

In the middle belt of the country, where rainfall is greater but still scanty, the pattern of population distribution has an east-west alignment, in contrast to the meridional arrangement in the desert north. Here it is within a broad belt bounded by approximately the 10° and 15° parallels that settlement is concentrated, but with the overall densities far below those attained on the Nile floodplain (Fig. 8.2), Lebon[3] points out that these two parallels approximately correspond with significant geographic divides. North of about 15°, as noted above, aridity makes rain-fed agriculture impossible. South of about 10°N is the animistic Negroid realm, which is socially and economically backward and in which population is sparser. In between is a wooded savanna zone inhabited mainly by Arabic-speaking tribes that have been agriculturally and commercially active over centuries of time. This more-populous zone, containing 50–60 percent of the total national population, is sometimes called the Central Rainlands. Within it rainfall increases from about 10 in. on the northern margins to some 30 in. in the south.

The part of the Central Rainlands that stretches from the west bank of the White Nile westward across lightly wooded plains with fixed sand dunes to the Chad boundary is known as the Qoz. With some modifications, a landscape similar to that of Qoz, called the Central Clay Plain, continues eastward across the White and Blue Niles and thence northeastward to the Red Sea. Although many of central Sudan's people are cattle nomads, rain-fed cultivation is still widely practiced. The inhabitants are a mixture of Arabs, Nubians, and other groups. Obviously, in such an environment the water supply is a prime determinant of settlement and land use, so that agriculture and population tend to cluster around small wells and ponds. Population thickens perceptibly within the Qoz at both its eastern and western extremities. In the east this involves the city of El Obeid as well as the more extensive cluster of population in the vicinity of the Nuba Mountains, one of several isolated massifs rising out of the monotonous plains that became places of refuge for the Nuba and Fur tribes at the time of the Arab invasions centuries back. The rainier Nuba Mountains and the adjacent plains where water is more easily available are mainly occupied by pagan Negro cultivators numbering about three quarters of a million. In addition there are more than a quarter million Arabs who are traders, pastoralists, and cultivators.

[3] J. H. G. Lebon, "Current Development in the Economy of the Central Sudan," in *Natural Resources, Food and Population in Inter-Tropical Africa*, A Report of a Geographical Symposium held at Makerere College, Kampala, September, 1955. International Geographical Union, Geographical Publications Ltd., London, 1956, pp. 57–66.

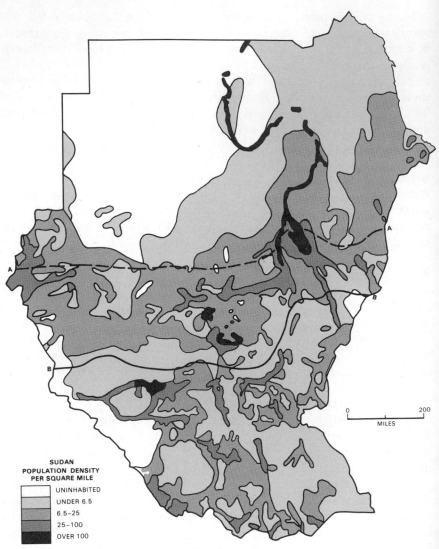

Fig. 8.2. Sudan—population density. Rural population is especially concentrated in a subhumid central belt; it is less so in the rainier southern parts. Settlement is particularly meager in the Saharan north, except for a strip along the Nile River. Dashed line (*A*) indicates northern limit of rain agriculture. Solid line (*B*) is the Arab-Negroid boundary. After Schmidt and Mattingly, Lebon, and Barbour.

Toward the western end of the Qoz are the Jebbel Marra highlands, another early Nuba refuge, where increased precipitation and greater water availability on the nearby lowlands have acted to attract a clot of denser settlement.

Where the Nile Oasis and the Central Rainlands belt intersect, as they do in the triangle formed by the confluence of the Blue and the White Nile, is located the heartland of Sudan and the focus of its political and economic life. At the apex of this triangle are three cities: Khartoum, the seat of government; Khartoum North, a growing industrial center; and Omdurman, which together contain over 40 percent of Sudan's whole urban population. Economic activity, and hence population, are concentrated in this vicinity for several interrelated reasons—it is the political center; it is centrally situated with respect to the main areas of commercial agriculture; and it is a focus of the sparse transportation lines of the country, both river and rail.

Within the angle formed by the two Niles is an important area of irrigated land, known as the Gezira, that figuratively is the economic powerhouse of Sudan and supports the main compact node of its population. Nearly one half of the country's total exports by value and a fifth of the government's revenue originate in the Gezira, where long-staple cotton is the main commercial crop. This small irrigated region contains some 7 percent of the national population.

The humid southernmost part of Sudan, south of about 10°S, is a region that is racially and culturally apart from the rest. Its Nilotic black people are more akin to those of Uganda and the Congo than to the inhabitants of the Arab-Moslem north and center. Although Christianity had earlier obtained an important foothold, over the last decade or two there has been a progressive Islamization and Arabization of the region. Large areas of this southland are annually inundated by the White Nile and its tributaries and thereby withheld from full use. Its tribal peoples keep cattle and raise food grains, but life is chiefly oriented toward the herds. Although it contains probably one quarter of the country's total population, the south is scarcely an integral part of the national territory and contributes little to the national economy.

The Equatorial Lake Region (Kenya, Uganda, Rwanda, and Burundi). On the lands tributary to Lake Victoria and in the vicinity of the Rift Valley Lakes to the west is one of Africa's greatest population concentrations. This area may support as many as 25 million people. Two distinct concentrations of settlement are to be observed, a more populous one on the rim lands of Lake Victoria, included within the states of Uganda, Kenya, and Tanzania, and a somewhat smaller one, roughly linear in shape, following the Rift Valley and its bordering high-

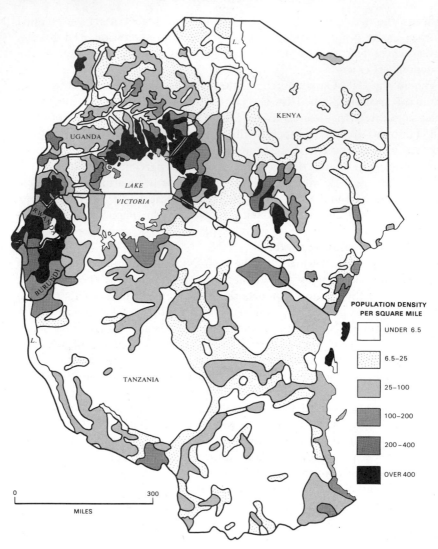

POPULATION DENSITY
PER SQUARE MILE

	UNDER 6.5
	6.5–25
	25–100
	100–200
	200–400
	OVER 400

Fig. 8.3. Population density in equatorial East Africa. Population in this region shows a strongly clustered pattern. Simplified from a density map by Elsa Schmidt and Paul Mattingly in *Geographische Rundschau*, 1966, Heft 12.

lands (Fig. 8.3). This second concentration falls mainly within four political units: Uganda, Burundi, Rwanda, and Congo (Kinshasa). Within the Lake Victoria ring of dense settlement, greatest crowding is in the northern sector, which is split between Kenya and Uganda. The less-densely populated southern part of the ring lies within Tanzania.

Kenya. According to the 1962 census, Kenya had a population of 8,636,000, all but about 270,000, or 3 percent, of which were Africans (including Somali). Of the three significant minority communities, Asians (Indo-Pakistani) represent 2 percent of the total population, Europeans 0.6 percent, and Arabs 0.4 percent.[4] The 1970 estimate of Kenya's population was 10.9 million, which provides an average density of about 50 persons per sq mi, a figure that is not too significant because of the great regional variations in density within the country. In 1967 only 7.8 percent of the people were urban, with that term defined as people living in communities with more than 2000 persons. But although only 5.3 percent of the Africans are urban, 84.8 percent of the non-Africans are so classified. Among the non-Africans, 93 percent of the Asians lived in towns and cities, compared with 63 percent of the Europeans.[5] Kenya has no statistics of birth and death registration, but from the 1948 and 1962 censuses it has been calculated that the average annual growth rate over the 14-year intercensal period was somewhere between $2\frac{1}{2}$ and 3 percent.[6] The present birth rate is estimated to be about 50 per 1000, the death rate about 20, and the current annual rate of growth about 3 percent.

From the superior population maps of Kenya[7] (scale 1:1,000,000; data from 1962 census) now available, it may be observed that this country, like most of East Africa, is characterized by striking inequalities in the areal spread of its people. The most noteworthy feature is the belt of high but variable densities that follows the humid highlands and extends from the northeastern shores of Lake Victoria in the extreme west in a southeastward direction to well beyond Nairobi (Fig. 8.3). Surrounding this populous belt on the north, east, and south are dry and relatively empty lands where herders rather than agriculturists predominate.

[4] W. T. W. Morgan and N. Manfred Shaffer, *Population of Kenya: Density and Distribution.* Oxford University Press, Nairobi, 1966, p. 4. See also Philip W. Porter, "East Africa—Population Distribution," Map Supplement, No. 6, *Annals of the Association of American Geographers*, Vol. 56, 1966. Map Scale: 1:2,000,000. Statistics on back of map.
[5] Morgan and Shaffer, *Population of Kenya*, p. 4.
[6] J. G. C. Blacker. "Population Growth in Kenya," *Inter-African Labor Institute Bulletin*, Vol. 12 (2), 1965, p. 247.
[7] Morgan and Shaffer, *Population of Kenya;* see also map by Philip W. Porter.

Isolated from the main population belt is a much smaller concentration of settlement along the coast in the vicinity of Mombasa.

In its broadest lineaments, then, Kenya's gross population pattern distinguishes between the extensive arid plains that represent 77 percent of the national area but only 11 percent of its population and the productive parts with adequate rainfall that support 70 percent of the population on only 11 percent of the area. Still, an environment-oriented explanation is inadequate to account for some features of the gross pattern just described, and particularly for many of the density variations within the general belt of above-average density.

In the precolonial period (up to about 1895), the population-density pattern was related to the distinction between pastoral tribes and those that depended largely on cultivation. The agricultural tribes were obliged to locate where physical conditions (climate, soil, terrain, and the like) made the land sufficiently productive to permit the sustaining of a family on a few acres (5–10) that the manpower could operate under the crude agricultural technology at its command. Typical would be areas with more than 40 in. of rainfall spread over 6 or more months. In such environments gross density could be of an order of 100–300 persons per sq mi.[8] On marginal lands the density of settled cultivators of necessity would be so low as to make protection against the marauding pastoralists ineffective. So the prevailing pattern came to be one of high densities on the agriculturally productive lands and low densities in the dry, less-productive areas used by pastoralists.

During the colonial period tribal locations were "frozen" and intertribal wars prohibited. But western influence, through lowering mortality rates, had the effect of speeding population growth so that population pressure on the land increased. Two tendencies became marked. Within the African areas where the original tribal compartments were maintained, the indigenous distribution pattern continued, but with increasingly higher densities. In the alienated region of the "White Highlands" lying northwestward of Nairobi, lands formerly occupied by the pastoral Masai or sparsely settled because of intertribal warfare, a large-scale native in-migration occurred that sought employment on new ranches and farms established by Europeans. Much of this region, while submarginal for African agriculturalists with their rudimentary technology, could be made to yield by Europeans with their more skillful methods. Thus developed a filling in of the Central (or White) highlands lying between populous western Kenya flanking Lake Victoria and the well-settled Eastern highlands containing Nairobi. Today these Central highlands sup-

[8] Morgan and Shaffer, *Population of Kenya*, p. 16.

port a multitribal population with moderate densities varying from 40 to 150 per sq mi.

The factors influencing present population distribution in Kenya are several. Rainfall is of prime importance because since much of tropical East Africa is relatively dry, localities with moderate-to-abundant rainfall are cherished by agricultural tribes. Altitude is related to population and agriculture mainly through the factor of rainfall. But at chilly elevations above 9500 feet there are few permanent settlements even though rainfall may be adequate. The influence of soils on population is most important on a local scale. Unusually striking contrasts in densities are often observed along sociopolitical boundaries, as for example those along the edges of reserved forests, between different tribes, or between tribal and alienated lands.

The over 80 percent of Kenya's population contained within the interrupted population belt mentioned earlier are largely concentrated within three nodes of high density: the Nyanza node in the extreme west; the Eastern highlands, or Nairobi, node in the center; and the coastal, or Mombasa, node in the extreme east (Fig. 8.3).

The Nyanza node on the western flanks of the highlands and reaching down to the margins of Lake Victoria contains slightly more than three million people on about 9000 sq mi of land. This is one sector of the fairly continuous belt of dense population encircling Lake Victoria. Here about 36 percent of Kenya's population are concentrated on 4 percent of the country's area, with an average density of 342 persons per sq mi. This crowding, highest for any of the country's population regions, has as its basis an intensive subsistence agriculture, which in turn is made possible by a relatively high-grade physical environment. Western Kenya has the largest area of high-potential agricultural land anywhere in the country. In the Department of Agriculture's system of land classification, 52 percent of Nyanza Province's area is given the highest rating of Al, defined as having adequate rainfall, good deep soil, and moderate temperatures.[9] Within the Nyanza population node there are conspicuous differentials in density. In one contiguous group of four small political subdivisions covering 170 sq mi, the average density (1962) was 1246 per sq mi. In another contiguous area covering 672 sq mi, the average density was 787 per sq mi. Such rural densities rival those of floodplains in Japan and China. But there are other parts of the Nyanza node where densities drop below 200 per sq mi.[10] Such variations are associated with combina-

[9] Morgan and Shaffer, *Population of Kenya*, p. 14. See also Glenn T. Trewartha, "New Population Maps of Uganda, Kenya, Nyasaland and Gold Coast," *Annals of the Association of American Geographers*, Vol. 47, 1957, pp. 50–51.

[10] Morgan and Shaffer, *Population of Kenya*, pp. 19–20.

tions of factors involving physical environment, tribal and ethnic groups, former state building, and character of land use.

The Eastern highlands population cluster also contains about three million inhabitants. They dwell in greatest numbers on the humid eastern flanks of the Kenya highlands and less densely on the adjacent drier hill country and plains to the east. Within this general concentration the average density of the rural population is about 172 per sq mi, or half that of the Nyanza node. Still, the intraregional density variations are great—only 47 per sq mi on the drier Kitui Plains to the east, but 598 on the southern and eastern lower slopes of Mt. Kenya and 479 in the Kikuyu subdivision.[11] Such high densities are made possible by the high and relatively reliable rainfall, together with the reduced evaporation at the higher altitudes, and in addition soils that, in the volcanic areas, are some of the best in Kenya. Still, no combination of physical factors is adequate to explain either the high average, or the regionally variable, densities. Formerly this populous highland belt was sparsely occupied by a hunting tribe known as the Doraba, and it was only when it was taken over by the agricultural Kikuyu in modern times that the resource base has been more fully exploited and population has greatly multiplied. On its western margins the abrupt termination of the somewhat linear but crooked belt of high densities is set by the establishment of forest preserves on the upper slopes of Mt. Kenya and farther south by the Aberdare Range.

Between the Nyanza and Eastern highlands clusters is the Central (White) highlands containing nearly 800,000 inhabitants and having a rural density (1962) of only 78.1 rural persons per sq mi (87.9 including urban persons). Thus its overall density is only about one quarter that of the Nyanza population node and one third to one half that of the Eastern highlands. So, while the Central highlands are a part of the general population belt, they lie outside the main nodes of that belt. The region is characterized by complex terrain and climate, but on the whole its rainfall of 25–50 in. is below those of the two nodal regions just described. Population patterns, like the physical ones, are too complicated for discussion here. As pointed out earlier, much of this region in the precolonial period was sparsely occupied by the pastoral Masai. Later the better parts were taken over and farmed by European settlers using native labor. These so-called White highlands have consequently been a region of recent rapid increase in immigrant native population.

Eastward from the Eastern-highlands population node is the Nyika region, a monotonous plain with low rainfall, most of it with an average

---

[11] Morgan and Shaffer, *Population of Kenya*, p. 9.

population density of only two persons or fewer per sq mi. Nyika, therefore, produces a complete break in the country's general population belt. Three small islands of higher population density are to be found within the otherwise barren Nyika; one of these, linear in shape, parallels the north-south valley of the Tana River; the other two coincide with small, isolated patches of rainier highland.

The third and smallest node of population in Kenya fronts on the sea and extends inland for 30 to 40 mi. It is fairly conincident with a littoral belt of heavier rainfall that is bounded on its land side by the 20–25 in. isohyet. Here there is a concentration of some 587,000 people (1962), or roughly one fifth the number contained in each of the other two nodes. A large majority of the population is coastal Bantu of various tribes. The region is culturally and economically distinct from the rest of Kenya in a number of ways, a condition that reflects its longer period of overseas contacts. These contrasts include a predominance of Islam; the use of Swahili as a first language; the presence of 85,000 non-Africans (including 46,000 Indian-Pakistani, 30,000 Arabs, and 7500 Europeans) who comprise over 13 percent of the total population; a sizable proportion (32.9 percent) of urban dwellers; and a relatively large nonagricultural labor force. In detail, rural population distribution is closely related to soil quality, water supply, and historical factors. The presently most densely populated part was the core of the Sultan of Zanzibar's domain during the period of British control.

Arid upland plains scantily peopled by Hamitic and Nilo-Hamitic herdsmen wrap themselves around Kenya's well-populated highland and lake regions on the north, east, and south. Average density on the dry plains is only 5.5 persons per sq mi. The highest overall density, and more than double the average for the dry plains, is in Masailand in the far south, located between the highlands and the Tanzania border. There rainfall is slightly higher and the wooded savanna provides better grazing than does the ordinary bushland. The number of livestock units per square mile is the highest for any of the large arid-land subdivisions.

Uganda.   Less than half as large as Kenya and with nearly 80 percent as many people (estimated 6 million, 1970), Uganda has an overall density that is nearly twice that of its much drier neighbor to the east. Only very small areas receive less than 20 in. or more than 60 in. of annual rainfall, while the general altitude of 3000 to 5000 feet tends to temper somewhat the tropical heat. A widespread vegetation cover consisting of tall grass with trees provides good grazing and by some is considered an indicator of better soils than those that develop under short grass and shrub. Altogether the environmental potential of Uganda for native agriculture is higher than that of Kenya.

Bantu blacks make up $\frac{2}{3}$ to $\frac{2}{3}$ of the total population; roughly $\frac{1}{5}$ are Nilotes who are Hamiticized Negroes speaking a sudan tongue, while Nilo-Hamites make up close to 14 percent. The Bantu are characteristically cultivators with whom cattle raising is secondary; the Nilotes are both cultivators and keepers of cattle, while the Nilo-Hamites are mainly pastoralists. As a rule, therefore, Bantu areas show the greatest crowding and those peopled by Nilo-Hamites the least. Bantus dominate in the southern half of the country, Nilotes on the west and north, and Nilo-Hamites in the east and the northeast.

Uganda contains portions of two of equatorial East Africa's main population concentrations; the more important one, and the nation's core area, forms the north and northwest sectors of the Lake Victoria ring of close settlement, and the other is coincident with the north-south Rift Valley and its bordering highlands (Fig. 8.3).[12] The lacustrine ring itself consists of three or four fairly conspicuous subnodes of population, separated from each other by more sparsely settled, poorly drained, riverine lands. In part the individual subnodes also seem to be related to state building. Thus, the main Buganda cluster, which dominates the region's economy and includes the metropolis of Kampala, relates to the powerful military state formed by the Baganda tribe. A recent development of commercial crops—coffee, sugar, and cotton—further strengthened Buganda's position. Another subnodal area of high density within the lacustrine population ring is coincident with the western and southwestern slopes of volcanic Mt. Elgon in easternmost Uganda, where the soils developed from basic lavas are unusually fertile.

Within Uganda's Rift Valley population belt, nodal areas are also conspicuous. Most striking is the one in the extreme southwest, situated in highlands south and east of Lake Edward, where the average density rivals those of the most crowded parts of the Lake Victoria population belt. In its southwestern districts, where density exceeds 800 per sq mi, dwell the Bakiga people, who have the reputation of being Uganda's most efficient Bantu farmers. Actually, this striking settlement cluster is the northernmost part of the larger Rwanda and Burundi population concentration centered farther south. Other nodes of relatively high density within Uganda's Rift belt are in (1) the extreme northwest along the Congo boundary and (2) the Ruwenzori area between Lakes Albert and Edward.

Rwanda and Burundi.   These two remote and pygmy-sized states are the most densely peopled countries in all Africa and also among the most impoverished. On any population map of Africa the high-density

---

[12] Map by Philip W. Porter.

node that includes not only Rwanda and Burundi but in addition adjacent parts of Congo and Uganda stands out prominently (Fig. 8.3). Within this cluster of dense settlement, coincident with plateaus and hills that lie astride the Congo-Nile watershed, cropland and pasture form a complex mosaic. The people tend to shun the lower levels and instead have chosen to concentrate at elevations between 2500–6500 feet; there, within their highland refuge, protected peripherally by lakes, swamps, streams, and mountains, they were for long shielded from Arab slave traders who ravaged and depopulated certain other more accessible parts of East Africa. Political solidarity under Tutsi rulers provided an additional element of protection. Some 98 percent of the people are considered rural; urban places are indeed scarce. Each of the two small countries has about 3.6 million inhabitants (1970 estimate), which indicates an average density of between 325 and 350 per sq mi. In parts, densities rise to 450–500 per sq mi. The serious crowding is reflected in the extensive out-migration and in the terraced fields on hillsides, where slopes inclined as much as 40° are under tillage.

Curious ethnic and social structures prevail in Rwanda and Burundi. About 80–90 percent of the people are Hutu, a Bantu tribe whose people are superior agriculturists. Most of the remainder are Tutsi, a pastoral group, noted for the remarkable tallness of its people, who, with their long-horned cattle, arrived in the region probably during the 15th century. The pastoral Tutsi came to occupy the peak of the country's social and political pyramid, while the Hutu formed the base. This caste system seems to have operated peacefully until recently, when a successful Hutu revolt resulted in thousands of Tutsi being slaughtered, while over 150,000 fled.

Tanzania. With a population of about 13.2 million (1970 estimate), Tanzania is one of the more populous countries in East Africa. But unfortunately these inhabitants are widely scattered in what appears to be a random pattern of more than 20 or more small, isolated, clusters, none large enough to provide a base for an important economic development. There seemingly is no genuine national heartland that furnishes the core area around which a strong state can develop. Large parts of the northeast and interior are semiarid and given over mainly to herders.

Probably the most productive and well-settled part lies peripheral to the southern half of Lake Victoria (Fig. 8.3). But Tanzania's sector of the Lake Victoria population ring is less closely settled and less continuous than its counterparts in Kenya and Uganda. The reason is not clear. The main lacustrine cluster has the town of Mwanza as its focus.

A second belt of concentrated settlement follows the ocean littoral, but it is scarcely continuous. Main clusters are (1) in the far north back of the port city of Tanga where sisal and coffee are important commercial crops, (2) in the vicinity of the metropolis and main port of Dar es Salaam and along the rail line leading to that port, (3) in the far south around the port of Lindi, (4) and on the islands of Zanzibar and Pemba.

Between the coastal and the Lake Victoria concentrations are half a dozen or more small population nodes, two of which are in dry country close to the Kenya boundary, where the elevations of nearby Mt. Kilimanjaro and Mt. Meru assure a water supply sufficient to permit of crop agriculture. Above-average densities also exist in the form of two tenuous bands, one extending inland from Dar es Salaam along the rail line leading to Tabora and Kigoma and the second following the highway southwestward from Dar es Salaam through Iringa to the dense cluster of settlement on the alluvial plain at the northern end of Lake Nyasa. The highway in turn follows an interfluve of higher land with somewhat heavier rainfall.

Zambia. The 4.3 million[13] (1970 estimate) people in Zambia, formerly Northern Rhodesia, are spread thinly but far from evenly, over the country's 288,000 sq mi. Europeans number only about 70,000 (1965), or a little over 2 percent of the total. A great preponderance of whites reside in cities. However, the small European farming population of about 1500, operating large tracts of a few thousand acres, probably account for one third of the country's total agricultural production. They and their farms are concentrated along the main north-south rail line that connects the cities of Livingstone, Lusaka, and Broken Hill with the group of seven copper-mining centers along the Congo frontier.[14] The railroad in turn follows the drainage watershed where groundwater can be readily tapped by borings, soils are above average, and the tsetse fly is absent.

Of the total African population, the 1963 census indicates that 75.4 percent were located in African rural areas, 4.8 percent were laborers in European farming areas, and 19.8 percent were in towns and cities.[15] Thus nearly one quarter of the Africans are to be classed as wage earners. The average population density for rural Zambia is only 9.5 per sq mi (1963). Nearly 16 percent of the total area is virtually uninhabited, since it contains only 0.3 percent of the total population. Regions of relatively

[13] The 1963 census counted 3,417,580.
[14] See Fig. 7, p. 34 in George Kay, *A Social Geography of Zambia: A Survey of Population Patterns in a Developing Country*. University of London Press, 1967.
[15] George Kay, *Maps of the Distribution and Density of African Population in Zambia*. University of Zambia, Institute for Social Research, Communication No. 2, 1967, pp. 5-6.

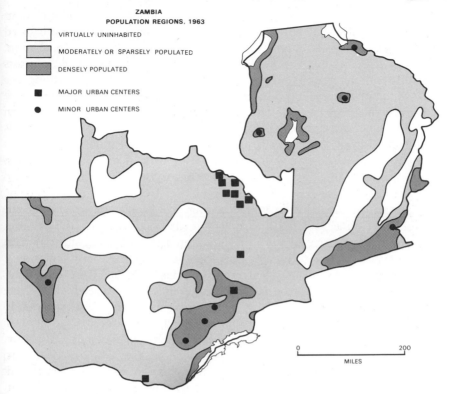

VIRTUALLY UNINHABITED

MODERATELY OR SPARSELY POPULATED

DENSELY POPULATED

■ MAJOR URBAN CENTERS

● MINOR URBAN CENTERS

0   200
MILES

Fig. 8.4. Zambia–population regions, 1963. *Densely populated* = 12.4 percent of area; average density 14.5 persons per sq km. *Sparsely populated* = 71.7 percent of area; average density 2.8 per sq km. *Virtually uninhabited* = 15.9 percent of area; average density 0.07 per sq km. After George Kay, *A Social Geography of Zambia*.

dense population comprise only 12.4 percent of the rural area but contain 47.3 percent of the total population.[16]

The economic, political and population heartland of Zambia is the watershed belt with its line of rail described previously. Within its southern half is the central, and a main, concentration of rural Africans (Fig. 8.4). A second focus is in the extreme west, along the main channel of the Zambezi River and some of its tributaries, where annual flooding of the rivers has provided fertile alluvial soils. East of the watershed heartland and also of the country's narrow waist are more than half a dozen isolated groupings of Africans. Two extensive regions of virtually

[16] Kay, *Maps of the Distribution*, pp. 18–22.

empty lands are to be noted, one to the east and the other to the west of the watershed rail line. Since these two groups of near-uninhabited regions extend almost from the northern to the southern boundaries of the country, they tend to separate the more densely populated clusters in both east and west from the country's core region aligned along the rail route in the center. The large expanses of "dead land" therefore intensify the remoteness and isolation of the population clusters in both the east and the west, as a result of which the country faces serious problems of geographic integration.[17]

At the time of the 1963 census nearly one fifth of the total population was classed as urban, while 25.4 percent of the adult males were so classified. These are relatively high figures for tropical Africa. Moreover, the process of urbanization is proceeding at a rapid rate, since over the period May-June 1963 to December 31, 1965, growth of the African population in the ten largest cities amounted to 15.2 percent, compared with only an 8.2 percent increase for the total African population.[18] Much the largest single concentration of urban Africans is in the copper belt along the Congo frontier, where seven closely spaced cities have a combined population of 439,000 (1963 census).

Malawi.   In Malawi, a small, linear, landlocked country located in the Shiré River Basin and along the west side of Lake Nyasa, some 4.4 million people (1970 estimate) occupy an area of only 36,000 sq mi. The overall density of about 120 per sq mi, is roughly 8 times that of Zambia and 3–4 times that of Tanzania. On any population map of Africa, Malawi, or more specifically its southern part, stands out because of its denser settlement compared with its surroundings. As in most of East Africa the spread of population is very uneven. Almost 50 percent of the total is concentrated in the southern third of this linear state. There the two main nodal areas are (1) the Shiré highlands at the country's southern extremity and (2) the Agoniland plateau west of the southern end of Lake Nyasa (Fig. 8.5). In parts of the humid Shiré highlands density exceeds 300 persons per sq mi. This high concentration of native peoples is of recent date, because late in the last century the Shiré highlands were still a region of sparse settlement. Subsequently much of the land was alienated for the use of Europeans, and it was the employment opportunities offered by their estates, specializing in cash crops, that attracted native laborers in large numbers. Crowding is now so great, however, that there is an important out-migration in search of employment. Malawi is one of Africa's poorest countries, the

[17] Kay, *Maps of the Distribution,* p. 20 and Fig. 2.
[18] Kay, *Maps of the Distribution,* pp. 6–7.

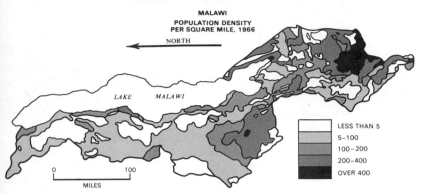

MALAWI
POPULATION DENSITY
PER SQUARE MILE, 1966

NORTH

LAKE   MALAWI

LESS THAN 5
5–100
100–200
200–400
OVER 400

0   100
MILES

Fig. 8.5. Malawi—density of population, 1966. After a map in *Focus* (American Geographical Society), November 1968.

average per capita annual gross national product amounting to only about $60.

Mozambique (Portuguese East Africa). Although 300,000 sq mi in area, this country supports only 7.7 million (1970 estimate) inhabitants, which represents a low average density of only about 25 per sq mi. Interior Mozambique is relatively unproductive and sparsely settled. Most of its inhabitants are concentrated in a littoral belt, but even that exhibits only moderate densities with frequent interruptions (Fig. 8.6). In this belt are Lourenco Marques and Beira, the two largest cities, each having populations over 150,000. Both are ports and rail terminals, so that they gain much of their importance from the overseas trade of adjacent interior countries with no ports of their own. Settlement is concentrated not only around the above two cities but also around a series of other smaller ports and the rail lines extending inland from them. The most developed and populous part of the coastal belt is that between Lourenco Marques and the tropic, which includes the lower Limpopo and Incomati valleys. A much smaller population cluster lies tributary to Beira and in the valleys of the Revué and Punguvé behind that port. The Zambezi Valley also carries a filament of settlement well into the interior. North from the Zambezi the coast is moderately well populated to within some 50–75 mi of the Tanzania boundary.

Rhodesia. Within tropical Africa Rhodesia stands out because of its larger than usual (217,000 in 1964) and powerful white minority who represent nearly 5.3 percent of the total population. In Kenya, by comparison, Europeans comprise less than 1 percent of the whole population; in Zambia the figure is 3.1 percent. Moreover, Rhodesia's whites represent

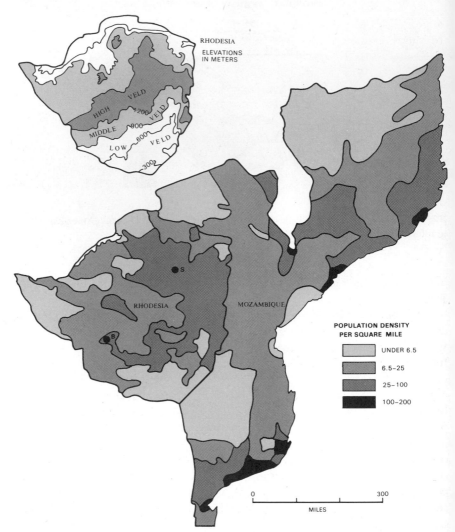

Fig. 8.6. Rhodesia and Mozambique—density of population. In Rhodesia, population has been attracted to the moister and cooler uplands and avoids the drier lowlands. Simplified from a density map by Else Schmidt and Paul Mattingly in *Geographische Rundschau*, 1966, Heft 12.

a political and economic power segment that is out of all proportion to their numbers. Not only have the Europeans appropriated the best agricultural lands, but their total land holdings amount to 84 percent of the area held by the Africans, whose numbers are 16 to 17 times as great. Average size of the European holdings is some 4000 acres, of which about 140 are arable (1958). African holdings are about 100 acres in size, of which only 9 are cultivated. Close to 68 percent of the whole national agricultural production is derived from European farms. Politically, the white minority dominates the country and seemingly is in no mood to diminish its degree of control within the foreseeable future.

Since 1951 Rhodesian whites have increased at an average compound rate of 6.5 percent per annum, a figure that derives both from a high rate of natural increase and from a net in-migration. Eighty-five percent of the adult whites are immigrants. With an average age of only 28.8 years, the Europeans represent a relatively young group in which nearly 77 percent of the adult female population is of childbearing age. Seventy-two percent of the whites live in urban places with 2500 or more inhabitants; 59 percent are in Salisbury and Bulawayo.[19] Although a majority of Rhodesia's European population is from Great Britain or South Africa, and it is they who form the top layer of the social hierarchy, still the white group as a whole represents great national and ethnic heterogeneity.

The overall density of population in Rhodesia is only about 33 per sq mi, which is similar to that of Tanzania, more than twice that of Zambia, but only one third that of Malawi or of Uganda. A strong nodal pattern of population distribution, a feature so conspicuous in the lake states of equatorial East Africa, is lacking. The gross distribution pattern of Rhodesia's 5 million (1970 estimate) people shows a strong relationship with altitude and associated physical features. Most of Rhodesia is plateau country of several thousand feet elevation. The main core of higher plateau, known as the high veld (over 2800 feet elevation) and representing nearly one quarter of the national area, forms the watershed between Zambezi and Limpopo drainage. Principal routeways, both rail and highway, follow this divide. Having lower temperatures, greater rainfall, and improved transportation facilities, it is the most favored region and for this reason it has been taken over largely by Europeans, who have made it the economic heartland of the country. But because of the extensive nature of the agriculture, the high veld's rural areas are only thinly populated, especially the southwestern two thirds where

[19] Peter J. M. McEwan, "The European Population of Southern Rhodesia," Civilisations, Vol. 13, No. 4, 1963, pp. 430–431.

farms are unusually large. On the other hand, along the high veld's Bulawayo-Salisbury axis and its rail line are located 80 percent of the country's urban population. Flanking the high veld zone is the middle veld (2100–2800 feet), representing a somewhat less desirable environment where rainfall is lower and temperatures are higher. Here there is a mixture of native and European farms, but with the former far more numerous. Below about 2100 feet is the low veld, comprising slightly more than one third of the country and located mostly in the drainage basin of the Zambezi along the country's northern and northwestern margins and on that of the Limpopo in the southeast.[20] In these lower lands aridity, high temperatures, and the presence of the tsetse fly discourage settlement.

Rural Africans, who make up a large majority of the total population, are concentrated in a broad arc overlapping both middle and high veld, that stretches from the national boundary south of Bulawayo, northeastward through Fort Victoria to Umtali and thence northwestward to Salisbury and beyond (Fig. 8.6). Within this arc population densities are characteristically higher on the tribal trust lands than in the alienated European areas. Noticeably, the population arc is much wider in its central and northern parts around Umtali and Salisbury, where rainfall is more abundant and reliable, while it narrows toward the drier southwest.

There are two kinds of rural population patterns resulting from the application of the native Land Husbandry Act, which in turn involves the transfer of landholding rights from the tribe to the individual. Where the Act has not been applied, the traditional riverine location and pattern of settlement prevail. Where it has been applied, arable blocks of territory have been consolidated and settlements are located within fairly regular boundaries at some distance from their former riverine situations.[21] The resulting pattern is a patchwork of blocks, with each block having a fairly uniform density of population.

Madagascar Island (Malagasy Republic). With a population of 6.9 million (1970 estimate) in an area of 228,000 sq mi, Madagascar is only sparsely populated (about 30 persons per sq mi). Like most countries in tropical Africa, this one has seen a recent acceleration in its population growth rate as the previously high mortality has been lowered. Over

---

[20] Rudolf Hellmeier, "Bevölkerungs-Geographische Studien en Rhodesian, ein Beitrag zur Bevölkerungs Verteilung mit einer Karte en Masstab 1:2 Mill," *Mitteilungen der Georgraphische Gesellschaft in München*, Band 21, 1966, pp. 135–181.

[21] J. R. V. Prescott, "Population Distribution in Southern Rhodesia," *Geographical Review*, Vol. LII, 1962, pp. 563–564.

the 10 years 1952–1962 population increased nearly 30 percent.[22]

A distinctive feature of the population arises from the fact that a substantial proportion of its inhabitants are of Malay-Polynesian origins. Indeed, there is reason for believing that the island's original culture was Indonesian, and even at present the crops grown are those of southeastern Asia, while rice is the staple food. The immigrants from across the Indian Ocean brought with them a language that subsequently developed into Malgache, the tongue now in use. And although Bantu arriving from the mainland have modified the ethnic composition, their cultural contribution has been small. As a rule, the Mongoloid strain predominates in the highlands and Negroid blood in the lowlands.

[22] Sauvy, Alfred. "La République de Madagascar: Population, Economie et Perspectives de Développement." *Population* (Paris), 17, July–September 1962, p. 444. See excellent population-density map, p. 446.

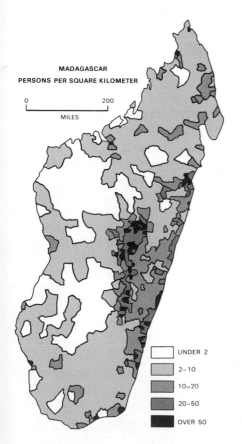

Fig. 8.7. Madagascar—population density. After Alfred Sauvy in *Population,* Vol. 17, 1962.

Population is asymmetrically distributed between east and west sides, with the windward humid east much more closely settled than the leeward, water-deficient west (Fig. 8.7). Within the former two distinct centers of relatively high density stand out. First, the heart of the country, is the central highland region, which contains Tananarive, the capital and metropolis. Despite a discouraging relief and low-grade soils, this rather inhospitable region supports some two fifths of the total inhabitants and includes over half of the irrigated crop acreage. Terraced fields are common. A second east-side region of fairly dense population is the eastern littoral, where a tropical wet climate prevails. There settlement occupies the low, flat coastal plain as well as a zone of foothills back of the lowland. In certain parts of the central highlands and of the east coast densities rise to over 125 per sq mi. Within Madagascar 60 percent of the inhabitants live on 20 percent of the surface.

REFERENCES

Baker, S. J. K. "The Population Geography of East Africa," *The East African Geographical Review* (Kampala), No. 1, April 1964, pp. 1–6.

Barbour, K. M. "Population, Land and Water in Central Sudan." in K. M. Barbour and R. M. Prothero (eds.), *Essays on African Population*. Routledge and Kegan Paul, London, 1961, pp. 137–156.

Barbour, K. M. "Population Shifts and Changes in the Sudan Since 1898," *Middle Eastern Studies*, Vol. 2 (2), pp. 98–122, 1966.

————. *The Republic of the Sudan: A Regional Geography*. London, University of London Press, 1961.

Blacker, J. G. C. "Population Growth in Kenya," *Inter-African Labour Institute Bulletin*, Vol. 12 (2), 1965, pp. 246–255.

Blacker, J. G. C. "The Demography of East Africa," in E. W. Russell (ed.). *The Natural Resources of East Africa*. D. A. Hawkins, Nairobi, 1962.

Davies, H. R. J. "Nomadism in the Sudan: Aspects of the Problem and Suggested Lines for Its Solution," *Tijdschrift voor Economische en Sociale Geografie*, Vol. LVII, No. 5, September–October 1966, pp. 193–202.

————. "The West African in the Economic Geography of Sudan," *Geography*, Vol. XLIX, No. 3, July 1964, pp. 222–235.

Delf, George. *Asians in East Africa*. Oxford University Press, 1963.

Demeny, Paul. "The Demography of the Sudan: An Analysis of the 1955–56 Census," in Wm. Brass et al., *The Demography of Tropical Africa*. Princeton University Press, 1968, pp. 466–514.

El-Sayed el-Bushra. "The Factors Affecting Settlement Distribution in the Sudan." *Geografiska Annaler*, Series B, Human Geography (Stockholm), Vol. 49 (1), 1967, pp. 10–24.

Elkan, Walter. "Circular Migration and the Growth of Towns in East Africa," *International Labour Review*, Vol. XCVI, No. 6, December 1967, pp. 581–589.

Federation of Rhodesia and Nyasaland. *Atlas of the Federation of Rhodesia and Nyasaland*. Salisbury, Federal Surveys Department, 1960–65.

Gourou, Pierre. *La Densité de la Population au Ruanda-Urundi; Esquisse d'une Étude Géographique*. L'Institut Royal Colonial Belge, Mémoires, Tome, XXI, 1952–1953, Bruxelles, 1953, appended map, scale 1; 750,000.

Gourou, Pierre. *Madagascar: Carte de Densité et de Localisation de la Population*. Brussels, CEMUBAC/ORSTOM, 1967.

Great Britain. *East Africa Royal Commission 1953–1955 Report*. London, H.M.S.O., Cmd. 9475, June 1955.

———. Colonial Office. *Land and Population in East Africa*. Colonial No. 290. London, H.M.S.O., 1952.

Grove, A. T. *Africa South of the Sahara*. Oxford University Press, 1967, pp. 175–234, 166–174, 83–91.

Hance, W. A. "The Gezira: An Example in Development," *Geographical Review*, Vol. 44, 1954, pp. 253–270.

Hance, William A. *The Geography of Modern Africa*. Columbia University Press, New York, 1964, pp. 142–162, 343–512.

Hartley, R. G., and Norris, J. M. "Demographic Regions in Libya. A Principal Components Analysis of Economic and Demographic Variables." *Tjdschrift voor Economische en Sociale Geografie* (Amsterdam), Vol. 60 (4), 1969, pp. 221–227.

Hellmeier, Rudolf. "Bevölkerungs-geographische Studien in Rhodesian; ein Beitrag zur Bevölkerungs. Verteilung mit einer Karte in Masstab 1:2 Mill," *Mitteilungen der Geographische Gesellschaft* in München, Band 51, 1966, pp. 135–181.

Herrick, Allison B., et al. *Area Handbook for Tanzania*. U.S. Government Printing Office, Washington, D.C., 1968, pp. 71–104.

Hollingsworth, Lawrence W. *The Asians of East Africa*. St. Martin's Press, New York, 1960.

Jensen, S. *Regional Economic Atlas, Mainland Tanzania*. Dar es Salaam, University College, Bureau of Resource Assessment and Land Use Planning, Research Paper No. 1, 1968.

Karmon, Yehuda. *A Geography of Settlement in Eastern Africa*. Jerusalem, Hebrew University, 1966.

Kay, George. "Population Pressure on Physical and Social Resources in Zambia," in Wilbur Zelinsky, Leszek A. Kosinski, and R. Mansell Prothero (eds.), *Geography and a Crowding World*. Oxford University Press, New York, 1970, pp. 363–379.

———. *A Social Geography of Zambia*. University of London Press, London, 1967.

———. "Maps of the Distribution and Density of African Population in Zambia," University of Zambia, Institute for Social Research Communication No. 2 (Lusaka), 1967.

Kenya. *Atlas of Kenya.* The Survey of Kenya, Nairobi, 1959.

Lebon, J. H. G. "Population Distribution and Land Use in Sudan," in *The Population of Sudan: Report on the Sixth Annual Conference, Held in the University of Khartoum, 16th and 17th January, 1958.* Khartoum, 1958.

Lury, D. A., "Population Data in East Africa," in John C. Caldwell and C. Okonjo (eds.), *The Population of Tropical Africa.* Longmans, Green and Co., London, 1968, pp. 44–70.

Martin, C. J. "Estimates of Population Growth in East Africa, with Special Reference to Tanganyika and Zanzibar," in K. M. Barbour and R. M. Prothero (eds.), *Essays on African Population.* Routledge and Kegan Paul, London, 1961, pp. 49–61.

Mather, D. B. "Migrations in the Sudan," in R. W. Steel and C. A. Fisher (eds.), *Geographical Essays on British Tropical Lands,* London, 1956, pp. 113–144.

McEwan, Peter J. M. "The European Population of Southern Rhodesia," *Civilisations* (Brussels), Vol. 13 (4), 1963, pp. 429–444. French summary.

McMaster, David N. "Toward a Settlement Geography of Uganda," *East African Geographical Review* (Kampala), Vol. 6, April 1968, pp. 23–36.

Morgan, W. T. W., and N. Manfred Schaffer. *Population of Kenya: Density and Distribution.* Oxford University Press, 1966.

Myburgh, C. A. L. "Migration in Relationship to the Economic Development of Rhodesia, Zambia, and Malawi," in U.N., *World Population Conference,* Belgrade, 1965. Vol. IV.

Ominde, S. H. *Land and Population Movements in Kenya.* Northwestern University Press, Evanston, Illinois, 1968.

Porter, Philip W. "East Africa—Population Distribution—as of August 1962," Map Supplement Number 6, *Annals of the Association of American Geographers,* Vol. 56, No. 1, March 1966, Map scale—1:2,000,000.

Prescott, J. R. V. "Population Distribution in Southern Rhodesia," *Geographical Review,* Vol. 52 (4), October 1962, pp. 559–565.

Russell, E. W. (ed.), *The Natural Resources of East Africa.* D. A. Hawkins, Nairobi, 1962.

Sauvy, Alfred, "Le République de Madagascar: Population, Économies et Perspectives de Développement," *Population* (Paris), Vol. 17(3), July–September 1962, pp. 443–458.

Scaff, Alvin H. "Urbanization and Development in Uganda: Growth, Structure, and Change," *Sociological Quarterly,* Vol. 8, 1967, pp. 111–121.

Soja, Edward W. *The Geography of Modernization in Kenya: A Spatial Analysis of Social, Economic, and Political Change.* Syracuse Geographical Series, No. 2, Syracuse University Press, Syracuse, 1968.

Southall, A. W. "Population Movements in East Africa," in K. M. Barbour and R. M. Prothero (eds.), *Essays on African Population.* Routledge & Kegan Paul, London, 1961.

Tanganyika. *Atlas of Tanganyika.* 3d ed. Dar es Salaam, Department of Lands and Surveys, 1956.

Thomas, I. D. "Geographical Aspects of the Tanzania Population Census 1967," *The East African Geographical Review*, No. 6, April 1968, pp. 1–12.

Trewartha, Glenn T., and Wilbur Zelinsky. "The Population Geography of Belgian Africa," *Annals of the Association of American Geographers*, Vol. XLIV, No. 2, June 1954, pp. 163–193.

Trewartha, Glenn T. "New Population Maps of Uganda, Kenya, Nyasaland, and Gold Coast," *Annals of the Association of American Geographers*, Vol. 47, No. 1, March 1957, pp. 41–58.

Trewartha, Glenn T., and Wilbur Zelinsky. "Population Patterns in Tropical Africa," *Annals of the Association of American Geographers*, Vol. 44, No. 2, June 1954, pp. 135–162.

Uganda. *Atlas of Uganda*. Entebbe, Department of Lands and Surveys, 1962.

United Nations. *The Population of Ruanda-Urundi*. New York, 1953.

———. *The Population of Tanganyika*. New York, 1949.

United Nations, Department of Economic and Social Affairs. "Population Growth and Manpower in the Sudan. A joint Study by the United Nations and the Government of the Sudan, Department of Statistics, Council of Ministers, The Republic of the Sudan, Khartoum." *Population Studies*, 37. ST/SOA/Ser. A/37. Sales No.: 64.XIII.5. New York, 1964. vii, 150 pp.

U.S. Army Handbook for Ethiopia, 2nd edition, June 24, 1964. U.S. Government Printing Office, Washington, D.C., 1964, pp. 52–86.

U.S. Army Area Handbook for the Republic of the Sudan. Second Edition, June 18, 1964. U.S. Government Printing Office, Washington, D.C., pp. 44–90.

Williams, Stuart. "The Distribution of the African Population of Northern Rhodesia." Rhodes-Livingstone Communication 24, Lusaka, 1962.

CHAPTER

9

Southern Africa

While that continental subdivision called Southern Africa includes nearly 1.1 million sq mi and has an estimated 23 million inhabitants, it is one state, the Republic of South Africa, with 43–44 percent of the area, that supports 90 percent of the inhabitants. Large but arid Southwest Africa and Botswana each have only about 600,000 people (1970 estimate), while the ministates of Lesotho and Swaziland, imbedded in South African territory and highly dependent on that country, have only one million and 400,000 inhabitants respectively.

While Southern Africa lies between about latitudes 17° and 35°, most of it is scarcely tropical, since altitude tends to ameliorate the effects of latitude. But, following the general world pattern of land climates for these latitudes, much of the region, especially its central and western parts, is moisture deficient. Only the east and the extreme south have adequate precipitation to permit rain-fed cropping. It is these humid parts that are the core area of Southern Africa and also of the Republic of South Africa.

A key feature of the 20.1 million (1970 estimate) inhabitants of South Africa is that they represent a plural society. Pluralism implies not only the multiple racial groups—Bantu, white, Asiatic, Colored—comprising South African society and the social division between them, but also the schemes for social, economic and political separation included in the coined term *apartheid*, meaning separate development. Apartheid permeates all aspects of living in South Africa, because there society and economy are legally stratified along color lines to a degree unknown in most parts of the world. The government's present apartheid policy of separate racial development also aims for the converting of the existing horizontal stratification to a future regional separation of South Africa into European (White Republic) and Negro (Bantu Reserves) areas. The latter include some 250 separate parcels of territory covering 13 percent of the national area.[1] Expectably, the Reserves are to be devel-

[1] M. Ernest Sabbagh, "Some Geographical Characteristics of a Plural Society: Apartheid in South Africa," *Geographical Review*, Vol. LVIII, January 1968, pp. 1–3.

oped into economically viable units. Accordingly the native areas will be obliged to support not only their present population of 4.5 million, but also the 6.5 million Bantu at present living within what are white regions, and at the same time they must provide for the future rapid increase in Bantu population. Up to the present the scheme of separate development has largely disregarded the Asiatics and Coloreds, who together comprise only 12 percent of the total population.

The Bantu Reserves are at present overpopulated with both people and livestock; the land is impoverished; little or no economic progress has occurred; minerals are largely absent; and the subsistence agriculture now practiced is primitive and unable to adequately support even the current Bantu population. During the past century the crowded Reserves have been able to survive economically only because large numbers of their inhabitants have left to work in the White Republic, a prosperous and technologically advanced state supported by a complex economy involving mining, manufacturing, commerce and agriculture.

The racial proportions of South Africa's population are shown in Table 9.1. Bantu make up over two thirds (68.6 percent) of the total population, Europeans slightly under one fifth. These proportions have not changed substantially over the half century preceeding 1960, and by means of apartheid the government hopes to maintain at least the white-Bantu proportions at about what they were in 1951—21 percent and 68 percent. Coloreds are half as numerous (9.5 percent) as whites, while Asiatics represent only 2.5 percent. Altogether, the nonwhites represent 80–81 percent of the total population; yet the European minority is all-powerful.

South Africa has a serious problem not only in the pluralism of its races but also in the fact that its society is bilingual. Boer descendants of Dutch immigrants speak Afrikaans, a Dutch dialect that includes many African words. The other language is English. By law, government officials are required to know both Afrikaans and English. It is believed that about 60 percent of the European population speak Afrikaans in their homes, and the rest speak English. As many as 60 percent are able to speak both languages. Afrikaans-speaking whites predominate in Orange Free State and in rural Transvaal. Those speaking English are more numerous in the south and east in what is Cape Province and Natal, and in urbanized Witwatersrand in the north.

Because of the racial plurality, average vital rates for the whole population mix are not very significant. The estimated birth rate for the African population is about 48 per 1000; for Europeans, about 17; for Coloreds, 34; and for Asiatics, 26. Death rates also show differentials between the races: Bantu, about 11 (1956); Europeans, 8–9; Coloreds, nearly 15; and Asiatics, 7–8. What becomes clear is that while the average current annual

TABLE 9.1   Demographic Structure of the South African Population

Population Group	Census of 1951			Census of 1960			Year 2000—Projection		
	Number	Percent of Total	Percent Increase	Number	Percent of Total	Percent Increase	Number	Percent of Total	Percent Increase
White	2,641,689	20.9	2.26	3,088,492	19.4	1.88	4,588,000	14.7	1.21
Bantu	8,560,083	67.7	1.93	10,927,922	68.6	3.07	21,361,000	68.4	2.39
Asiatic (Indian)	336,596	2.7	3.60	403,868	2.5	2.22	1,382,000	4.4	6.05
Colored	1,103,016	8.7	3.75	1,509,258	9.5	4.09	3,917,000	12.5	3.99
Total nonwhite	9,999,695	79.1	2.17	12,841,048	80.6	3.16	26,660,000	85.3	2.69
Total population	12,641,384		2.19	15,929,540		2.89	31,248,000		2.40

SOURCE: Sabbagh, "Some Geographical Aspects of a Plural Society: Apartheid in South Africa."

rate of population growth for the country is estimated to be about 2.4 percent, the non-European groups, and especially the Bantu and Asiatics, are multiplying faster than the whites. Thus between the censuses of 1951 and 1960 the rate of increase (natural plus migrant) was only 1.88 percent for whites but 4.09 for Coloreds, 3.07 for Bantu, and 2.22 for Asiatics. South Africa is progressively becoming more non-European. A realistic projection represents the percentage of the total population that is white as dropping from 19.4 percent in 1960 to 14.7 percent by the year 2000 (Table 9.1), with the Bantu just about maintaining their present proportion. If this change actually occurs, Bantu numbers 3 decades hence will be 5 times those of the whites. Asiatics and Coloreds will likely increase their proportions substantially.

Thus the rapid increase in overall population and the relatively greater increases within the non-European sectors have raised serious population problems, which eventually have dictated the racial policy of South Africa. Agriculture alone cannot support any one of the racial groups, hence the large-scale migration of Bantu and other non-Europeans to the cities to work in factories, mines, and other forms of urban employment. The Bantu in the Reserves are unable to make more than a bare living from their poor land, using their primitive methods of cultivation, so they tend more and more to rely on cash earned in mines and factories and as workers on farms owned by Europeans. Thus, overcrowding, unemployment, and appalling slums are serious problems in all cities, where each racial group is restricted by law to its own location. The government seeks to restrict migration to the cities, but this only aggravates the crowding in the rural areas, where the high rate of population increase taxes the resources of the native reserves.

SPATIAL DISTRIBUTIONS

Looking first at the spatial arrangement of total population, a ready observation is that the higher densities are skewed toward the east and south where rainfall is more abundant and reliable, altitudes are higher and temperatures reduced, and mineral wealth is more bountiful (Fig. 9.1). Settlement in the dry center and west is sparse indeed. Thus, the country west of the 20-in. summer-rainfall isohyet and north of the 10-in. winter isohyet is almost purely pastoral except for limited riverine strips. The more closely settled east and south are regions of diversified farming. Within them variations in relief, rainfall, the occurrence of mineral wealth, and a complex of other factors promoting industry and commerce have created marked contrasts in density.

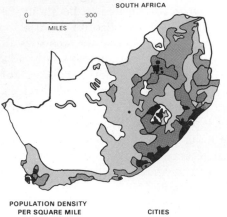

POPULATION DENSITY
PER SQUARE MILE

☐	UNDER 6.5
	6.5–25
	25–50
	50–100
■	OVER 100

CITIES

■	OVER 1,000,000
●	500,000–1,000,000
●	250,000 – 500,000
•	100,000 – 250,000

Fig. 9.1. South Africa—density of population; cities with more than 100,000 inhabitants are shown. Simplified from a density map by Else Schmidt and Paul Mattingly in *Geographische Rundschau*, 1966, Heft 12.

Rural and Urban Distributions. Depending on the definitions of rural and urban used, some 53 to 64 percent of the total population are classed as living outside of towns and cities. Distribution patterns of rural dwellers are exceedingly complex. By far the greatest concentration is in the eastern lowland and on the plateau slopes to the rear, within the sector situated between about Port Elizabeth on the south to well beyond Durban in the north (Fig. 9.1). Here the slope portions are characterized by great spurs, remnants of the eroded plateau surface, which rise abruptly above extensive level basins developed along river valleys. Within this eastern concentration, overcrowded Bantu reserve lands, including the large Bantu state of Transkei, cover extensive areas. A second important cluster of rural inhabitants is centered on the northeastern part of the plateau in the general environs of the country's greatest urban node, whose main focus in the metropolis of Johannesburg. The near-at-hand large urban market for farm products is no doubt a primary attraction for the sizable nonurban population. But this particular part of southern Transvaal and northern Orange Free State is also one of the country's main agricultural regions, where maize, wheat, and livestock are the primary products. A third and less compact rural-population aggregation lies in northeastern South Africa, in Transvaal, centered at about 23°N. This versant, like Transkei farther south, is a region of well watered slopes and of concentrated Bantu reserves. Whites are

TABLE 9.2   White and Bantu Urban Population, 1904 to 1960
(In Thousands)

Year	Total	White	Percent of Urban Total	Bantu	Percent of Urban Total
1904	1222	599	49.01	361	29.54
1911	1546	677	43.79	524	33.89
1921	1950	908	46.56	658	33.74
1936	3218	1367	42.48	1252	38.90
1946	4482	1793	40.00	1902	42.43
1951	5494	2089	38.02	2391	43.52
1960	7474	2575	34.45	3471	46.44

SOURCE: Statistical Year Book 1966, Bureau of Statistics, Pretoria, 1966.

few except in the towns. A fourth cluster, situated in the extreme south-west inland from Cape Town, has a large percentage of Coloreds in its population. The modest winter precipitation, plus the Cape Town market, makes this region agriculturally attractive. In various parts of the country the general population distribution is modified by intrusions of narrow bands of dense rural settlement along the main river valleys where irrigation permits a more intensive type of farming. Particularly noteworthy because of its meager human settlement is the Kruger National Park region in extreme northeastern South Africa, north of Swaziland.

As African states go, South Africa's 47 percent urban population is high, about the same proportion as that in Egypt. In 1960, 46.4 percent of the urban inhabitants were Bantu and 34.5 percent white; the remaining 19 percent were Asiatics and Coloreds. In spite of the fact that the Europeans are predominantly urban, the population of the cities is almost two thirds nonwhite (Table 9.2). The table also shows that over the past 50–60 years the cities have become decreasingly white and increasingly Bantu. This large-scale movement of Bantu into the cities in search of employment has been a matter of grave political concern. By 1960 whites were a minority in every South African city. Bantu concentration has increased most rapidly in the large industrial and mining centers where employment opportunities are greatest. A distinguishing feature of the Bantu urban population is its remarkable transiency. A study in Pretoria showed that 24 percent of the urban Bantu there were only temporary, while another 8 percent were classed as recently arrived.[2] Despite the heritage of almost a century of living and working in what is a fairly advanced technological environment, few of today's Bantu are skilled workmen. In the southern Transvaal less than 1 percent of the male Bantu labor force is classed as skilled (professional and technical). Legally, those Bantu living in the cities are there only by permit; they cannot possess land and must reside in specified locations. Resettlement of this huge racial group, as the policy of apartheid envisions, is a formidable undertaking indeed.

By far the greatest concentration of urban people is associated with the Witwatersrand industrial complex, the one genuine large conurbation in all Africa (Fig. 9.1). Covering less than 5000 sq mi, or only 1 percent of the country's area, it supported nearly 2.2 million inhabitants in 1960, or 14 percent of the nation's total. The primate city within the urban cluster is Johannesburg, with well over a million inhabitants, and in addition there are half a dozen lesser cities, including Pretoria, the capital. This urban nexus is very much the commercial and industrial core of South Africa, as well as the focus of its transport net. A prime factor in the development of the Witwatersrand industrial complex, with its large aggregation of people, was the unusual assemblage in that vicinity of mineral wealth (mainly in the form of gold, iron ore, coal, and subsurface water) located in close regional juxtaposition that provided a resource environment scarcely to be matched elsewhere. Gold has been of primary importance.

Other important but lesser concentrations of urban population have grown up around the ports of Cape Town and Durban, while still smaller ones focus on the ports of East London and Port Elizabeth, the mining town of Kimberley, and the much more numerous secondary cultural, trade, and administrative centers.

Distribution of Racial Groups. Regional variations in population density are also importantly connected with the distribution of the several racial groups. These in turn have been strongly influenced by official division of land, and grow out of the history and politics of the state. By 1910, at the time of Union, the broad patterns of racial distribution had already been set as a consequence of the course of settlement. Europeans held the Cape region west of about East London as well as the greater part of the plateau. Bantu occupied most of the land in Transkei and Ciskei in eastern Cape Province and in the former protectorates of Lesotho and Swaziland. Along the eastern slopes farther north, in Natal and Zululand, the land was divided between Bantu and whites. The Coloreds had become numerous in the Cape, as the Indians were

[2] Sabbagh, "Some Geographical Aspects," p. 17.

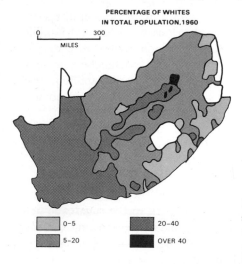

PERCENTAGE OF WHITES
IN TOTAL POPULATION, 1960

0   300
MILES

0-5

5-20

20-40

OVER 40

Fig. 9.2. Unshaded areas include the states of Lesotho and Swaziland, and also a game preserve and national park. After a map by Fair and Shaffer in *Economic Geography*, 1964.

in Natal.[3] After Union, in 1913, the above-described division of land between Bantu and whites was officially confirmed. Since then the native territory has been increased by 64 percent, most of this addition being in the northeast in Transvaal.

With certain important exceptions, the present distribution of Europeans and Bantu faithfully reflects the division of land between the two races. European people, who make up about 19–20 percent of the total population, live for the most part on the Highveld plateau and in the white sections of the eastern and southern coastal belt (Fig. 9.2). They are few in the Bantu territories. All population is sparse in the dry central and western parts, but those inhabitants that are there are mainly whites and Coloreds; Bantu are few. Probably the most striking and characteristic distributional feature of the white population is its high degree of concentration (83 percent, 1960) in urban places. It was the Europeans who established the cities, since urban organization was foreign to the African natives. Whites also are the initiators and leaders in all economic activities as well as the directors and overseers. A second noteworthy feature is the fact that 45–50 percent of the whites live in Transvaal in the northeast, and of these two thirds are concentrated in the Witwatersrand, or Johannesburg, conurbation. The second largest concentration of whites is in Cape Province.

The Bantu representing nearly 69 percent of the total population, are almost bound to have a distribution somewhat similar to that of the total

---

[3] Monica M. Cole, *South Africa*. E. P. Dutton and Co., New York, 1961, p. 656.

population. While about 70 percent are rural and agricultural, they are the predominant racial group in urban places as well. Some 4.5 million, or 41 percent, live in the native reserves, which means that they are mainly on the eastern slopes and South Atlantic coastal belt or in the northern Transvaal. The remaining 59 percent, or 6.5 million, reside in white areas, 3.47 million in urban places, and over 3 million on white farms and ranches. Most of the reserves (except for Transkei), while not so densely populated in an absolute sense, appear to be overcrowded economically in terms of the quality of the resource base. Within the reserves, population usually is distributed fairly uniformly.

The 404,000 Asiatics, mainly Indians, are highly concentrated in the city of Durban and along the Natal coast adjacent. And while they were originally brought to South Africa to work in the sugarcane fields, 75–80 percent of them now reside in cities, mainly those along the coast. Some have spread inland to towns along the rail line leading to the Transvaal and to the cities of the Johannesburg conurbation.

The 1.5 million Cape Coloreds are a highly varied group, mostly of mixed blood, but including as well descendants of pureblood Bushmen, Hottentots, and Malays. Strong contributors to the mixture were imported African slaves and itinerant sailors from the world over. Their cultural affinities are with the Europeans, but they are treated by the whites as inferiors. Nearly 90 percent are in Cape Province, especially its western and southern parts, where over extensive areas they constitute more than half the population, the remainder being mainly whites.[4] While over 65 percent of the Coloreds live in towns, especially Cape Town and environs, they, along with whites, are widely and sparsely spread over the dry interior as well, where Bantu are very few. In smaller numbers they have collected in the Johannesburg conurbation.

Changing Distributions. Not only does the present spatial distribution of people in South Africa show a strong concentration in a few core areas, but the process of concentration is also continuing with little diminution of momentum. It is the old story of "Unto those that hath shall it be given." This phenomenon of the clustering of economic activity and of population seems to be an inevitable concomitant of growth itself, since inequalities in regional growth are a universal phenomenon. Fair[5] divides the country into seven core regions (four major and three minor) and nine peripheral regions (three inner zones around the large cities

[4] Keith Buchanan and N. Hurwitz, "The 'Coloured' Community in the Union of South Africa," *Geographical Review*, Vol. XL, 1950, pp. 397–414.

[5] T. J. D. Fair. "The Core-Periphery Concept and Population Growth in South Africa, 1911–1960," *The South Africa Geographical Journal*, Vol. XLVII, 1965, pp. 59–71.

and six outer zones), and subsequently analyzes the growth performance of the several regions by noting how their shares of the total national population changed from 1911 to 1936 and to 1960. In addition Fair

Development Regions (after Fair)

Core Areas
Major
Southern Transvaal
Cape Town
Durban
Port Elizabeth
Minor
East London
Bloemfontein
Kimberley

Peripheral Areas
Inner Zones
Western Cape
Natal
Transvaal & N.O.F.S.
Outer Zones
Western Cape
Eastern Cape
Northern Cape
Transvaal
Natal
Southern O.F.S.

shows the relative size of the gains and losses in population, region by region, compared with the national rate of growth.

Of unusual significance is the fact that the four major core areas (Southern Transvaal, Cape Town, Durban, and Port Elizabeth) increased their combined share of the total South African population from 15.2 percent in 1911 to 31.0 percent in 1960 (Fig. 9.3). One of the peripheral areas, inner-zone Transvaal and Northern Orange Free State (N.O.F.S), which surrounds the Southern Transvaal major core area, also increased its share of the country's population—from 3.7 percent to 6.7 percent. By contrast, the Natal and Western Cape inner zones and all of the 6 outer zones declined relatively or remained stagnant. The outstanding

REGIONAL PERCENTAGE DISTRIBUTION OF SOUTH AFRICAN POPULATION, 1911, 1936, 1960

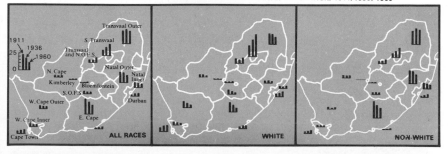

Fig. 9.3. South Africa—percentage distribution of population by regions in 1911, 1936, 1960. After maps by Fair in *South African Geographical Journal*, 1965.

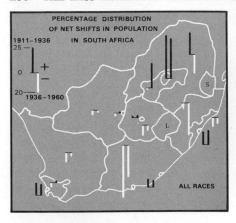

Fig. 9.4. South Africa—percentage distribution of net shifts in regional populations, 1911 to 1936 and 1936 to 1960. After maps by Fair in *South African Geographical Journal*, 1965.

regional growth occurred in the Southern Transvaal core area around Johannesburg and its peripheral inner zone of Transvaal and N.O.F.S. Together these two areas accounted for 12 percent of the total population in 1911 and 24.5 percent in 1960; for 23.4 percent of the whites in 1911 and 41.7 percent in 1960; and for 9.9 percent of the nonwhites in 1911 and 20.5 percent in 1960. Among nonwhites, relatively heavy losses occurred in Natal and the Eastern Cape regions that contain South Africa's most densely settled native reserves.

The seven core areas, major and minor, accounted for 77.2 percent of all the upward shifts ("extra" growth above the country average) of total population in South Africa between 1911 and 1936, and 73.6 percent between 1936 and 1960 (Fig. 9.4).[6] In the latter period, one of the peripheral areas (that around the core region of Southern Transvaal) accounted for 25.1 percent of the total upward shifts. For the remainder of the country the shifts in total population were generally downward, since their rates of growth were below the country average.

REFERENCES

Cole, Monica. *South Africa.* E. P. Dutton and Co., New York, 1961, pp. 653–667.

Fair, T. J. D. *The Distribution of Population in Natal.* Natal Regional Survey, Vol. 3. Oxford University Press, New York, 1955.

Fair, T. J. D., and L. P. Green. "Development of the Bantu-Homelands," *Optima,* Vol. 12, 1962, pp. 7–19.

[6] Fair, "The Core-Periphery Concept," p. 65.

Fair, T. J. D., and N. Manfred Shaffer. "Population Patterns and Policies in South Africa, 1951–1960," *Economic Geography*, Vol. 40, July 1964, pp. 261–274.

Fair, T. J. D. "The Core-Periphery Concept and Population Growth in South Africa, 1911–1960," *The South African Geographical Journal*, Vol. XLVII, 1965, pp. 59–71.

Flohr, Ernst Friedrich. "Bevölkerungsprobleme und die Politik der eigenständigen Entwicklung der Bevölkerungsgruppen der Republik Südafrika," *Mitteilungen der Geographischen Gesellschaft in Lübeck*, Heft, 51, 1965.

Houghton, D. Hobart. "Economic Dangers of Separate Bantu Development," *Optima*, Vol. 9, 1959, pp. 188–198.

Jones, J. D. Rheinallt. "The Effects of Urbanisation in South and Central Africa," *African Affairs*, Vol. LII, No. 206, January, 1953, pp. 37–44.

Nel, A. "Geographical Aspects of Apartheid in South Africa," *Tijdschrift voor Economische en Sociale Geografie* (Rotterdam), Vol. 53, 1962, pp. 197–209.

Sabbagh, M. Ernest. "Some Geographical Characteristics of a Plural Society: Apartheid in South Africa," *Geographical Review*, Vol. LVIII, 1968, pp. 1–28.

Schumann, C. G. W. "Die Afrikaans-sprechende Bevölkerung in Südafrika," *Afrika Heute* (Bonn), No. 16, September 1, 1965, pp. 216–220.

Smits, Lucas G. A. "The Distribution of the Population in Lesotho and Some Implications for Economic Development," *Lesotho (Basutoland Notes and Records)*, No. 7, 1968, pp. 3–19.

Strauss, C. B. "Population Growth and Economic Development," *South African Journal of Economics*, Vol. 31, June 1963, pp. 138–148.

Talbot, A. M., and W. J. Talbot. *Atlas of the Union of South Africa*. Pretoria, The Government Printer, 1960.

Wellington, John H. *Southern Africa: A Geographical Study*, Vol. II. Cambridge University Press, 1955, pp. 201–270.

Whittington, G. "Recent External Migration in the Republic of South Africa," *Tijdschrift voor Economische en Social Geografie*, Vol. 54, May 1963, pp. 135–138.

10

Asia

PROLOGUE: ASIA

Although Asia is one of a triad of LD continents, in reality only part so qualifies. Soviet Asia, which culturally identifies with Europe, is excluded. It is populous Asian Asia, comprising the eastern, southern, and southwestern rimlands of the continent, sometimes termed the *Asian Crescent*, that is properly designated as economically less developed. Yet even there, technologically advanced Japan and tiny Israel must be excluded.

In any discussion of population in the LD world, scale alone sets apart the Asian Crescent from Africa and Latin America, since Asian Asia of traditional societies (omitting Japan) probably accounts for as much as 53 percent of the earth's total inhabitants and over three quarters of those within the LD realm. The problems associated with modernizing this vast Asiatic population are staggering in their proportions, greatly transcending those presented by Latin America and Africa with their far fewer people.

Features other than a superabundance of humanity also mark the Asian Crescent. Here are the cores of some of the earth's most ancient and enduring civilizations whose historical roots extend far back into antiquity. Underpinning and supporting this huge segment of humanity is an intensive subsistence peasant agriculture, often described as hoe culture or garden culture. Moreover, Asiatic tillage is one based emphatically on the exploitation of cultivated plants; domesticated animals play only a minor role. Indeed, it is this agricultural specialization based almost exclusively on the vegetable kingdom that has permitted the development of extreme population density to the degree that now exists. A colonial background, long-continued foreign contacts, widespread poverty and economic retardation, but rising expectations—these too are features common to much of the Asiatic rimlands.

But while there are some elements of unity among the Asiatic traditional societies, great cultural diversity, scarcely matched elsewhere far more widespread. The inhabitants present an almost unbelievable variety of ethnic combinations, languages, religions, and forms of government. Originating from these population differences, four great realms are usually recognized within the Asiatic Crescent, described below.

Dry and subhumid *Southwest Asia* is the exception and in many ways unlike the other three. A degree of unity derives from its relative lower average density of settlement, its adherence to Islam, and a population featuring dry farming on oasis agriculture and nomadic herding.

South Asia, mainly the gigantic peninsula of Hindustan, obtains an element of unity from its strong Indian center of gravity, its inheritances from British rule (including present membership in the British Commonwealth), and its land isolation from the rest of Asia by highland bulwarks. In its core region there has emerged a culture known as Hindu, fundamentally religious in character and strongly permeated by the caste system.

Southeast Asia, positioned between India and China and influenced by the national cultures of both, is in the nature of a shatter zone, exhibiting a great diversity of languages, religions, and ethnic groups. Intermingling and intermixing have produced a hybrid people with a hybrid culture.

East Asia includes China, the ancient heartland of the region, where emerged a strongly unified culture characterized by a family-centered social system, ancestor worship, intensive tillage, and a high regard for learning. Japan, Korea, and Taiwan all bear the imprint of this Sinitic culture. Largely middle-latitude in location, much of the Far East's diversity is latitudinal and climatic in origin.

CHINA

It is a misfortune of the first order that for China, the earth's most populous country, including probably one fifth to one quarter of the earth's people, there is such a dearth of reliable population data. This is true not only for the country as a whole but even more so for its administrative subdivisions. Serious limitations thereby confront any attempt to analyze the spatial patterns of population distribution in China.

In an earlier publication,[1] the durability of East Asia and of China in particular as a main center of world population through two millenniums has been sketched. It remains now to amplify this sketch and,

[1] Glenn T. Trewartha, *A Geography of Population: World Patterns.* John Wiley and Sons, New York, 1969, pp. 15–16, 20–22, 32, 59–61, 69.

where possible, add features concerned with the intra-China arrangement of people and their characteristics.

Population Numbers. *Ancient China.* From the first purported census of China taken in 2 A.D. at the close of Western Han, Bielenstein concludes there may have been 12–13 million households, or 57–58 million individuals, residing within the Empire (55 million living within the 18 provinces of China proper).[2] Using the same census source, Durand arrives at somewhat different figures—71 million for China proper and 74 million for the Empire.[3] But whichever of the two estimates is accepted, by the beginning of the Christian era, when the earth's total population is inferred to have reached 133 to 300 million, China already represented one of the three great concentrations of humanity. Two millenniums ago it had probably outstripped the whole Roman Empire in numbers of inhabitants. And at least since the close of the medieval period it seems probable that China has been the earth's most populous national society. Throughout the modern period, in spite of China's remaining a thoroughly traditional and agrarian society, its population has been larger than that of any modern industrial society.

Bielenstein's map that purports to show population distribution within China as of two millenniums ago indicates a high degree of concentration in the northern parts, which had been the focus of the early Empire, and also of the still earlier feudal states (Fig. 10.1). Approximately three quarters of the people, or 43 million, were probably located in subhumid North China, north of the Ch'in Ling-Tapieh Shan highlands, a great majority of them on the delta plain of the Huang River or the North-China Plain.[4] There were lesser concentrations in the tributary valleys of the Huang, especially the Wei and the Fen, situated in the Loess uplands west of the great delta. Probably the whole low-lying northern part (Hopeh Basin) of the delta plain was a region of swamps plagued by floods, with only a modest occupance. The danger of flooding along the Huang tended to discourage settlement near that stream. The low-lying coastal belt of salt marshes bordering the Gulf of Po Hai was almost uninhabited.

[2] Hans Bielenstein, *The Census of China.* The Museum of Far Eastern Antiquities, Stockholm, Bulletin 19, 1947, pp. 126–133.

[3] John D. Durand, "The Population Statistics of China, A.D. 2–1953," *Population Studies,* Vol. 13, No. 3, 1960, p. 221.

[4] Bielenstein, *The Census of China,* pp. 157–158, Plate II. For still another population map of China based on the Han census of 2 A.D. see Wan Kuo-Ting "Population and Land Utilization in China, 1400 B.C.–200 A.D." (in Chinese), *Nanking Journal,* 1931. The map by Wan was reproduced in Percy Maude Roxby, "China as an Entity: The Comparison with Europe," *Geography,* Vol. 19, 1934, Fig. 2, p. 8.

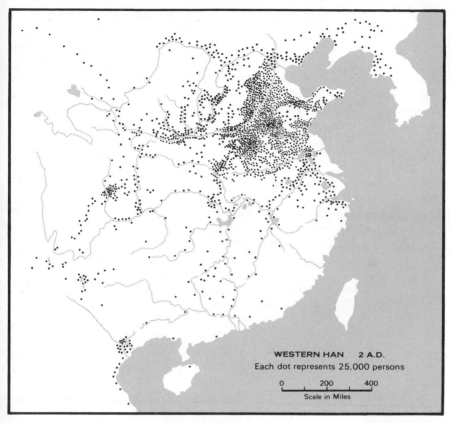

WESTERN HAN   2 A.D.
Each dot represents 25,000 persons

0   200   400
Scale in Miles

Fig. 10.1. China—population distribution as of about the beginning of the Christian Era. At this early date settlement was strongly concentrated in the north, especially so on the delta plain of the Huang, or Yellow, River. After a map by Hans Bielenstein, *The Museum of Far Eastern Antiquities*, Stockholm, Bull. No. 19, 1947.

Especially populous local areas are observable on Bielenstein's map in the vicinity of the Han capital, Ch'ang-an (Sian), and the Chou capital of Loyang. Along the country's northern frontier, and fairly coincident with the Great Wall, Bielenstein shows a conspicuous belt of above-average population density, composed mainly of military settlements. The overall region of greatest settlement concentration on the North-China Plain, however, is believed to have coincided with the higher, drier, well drained, and more fertile central part that acted as a bridge between Shantung peninsula and the Loess uplands of Shensi and Honan. There the slightly uneven and well-drained terrain reaches elevations of 150 meters, and the rivers are incised. The calcareous soils, composed of alluvial loess, are unusually fertile. The vegetation was originally one of semisteppe. This broad belt of slightly higher land forms the watershed between Huang and Huai drainage. Roxby[5] is of the opinion that the strong concentration of Chinese two millenniums ago on the great delta plain of the Huang and in its tributary valleys reflects in part the several favorable physical features that exist in combination in the slightly higher central part of that lowland.[6] But he and Bishop[7] note a second factor, namely one of location. They see the Great Plain, and especially its central part, as benefiting from its situation near the eastern portal of the Kansu Corridor through which were channeled the northern land routes across interior Asia, along which elements of early culture may have filtered eastward from the more ancient Western centers of civilization in Southwest Asia and the eastern Mediterranean. Bielenstein believes that the most populous parts of the North-China Plain two millenniums ago had densities nearly equal to those that prevail there in modern times.

Of the 14–15 million Chinese who may have resided in moderately peopled south China two millenniums previously, their patterns of linear distribution clearly reveal the routes of human migration along the river valleys. The hilly interfluves were only thinly occupied. The single most populous cluster, according to Bielenstein, was coincident with the Ch'eng-tu Plain in the Red Basin of Szechwan or the delta of the Min River.

Medieval and Modern China. Over the period of about a millennium and a half following the Western Han census of 2 A.D., China's population probably moved upward only slowly and erratically.[8] Ho conjectures that the numbers may have reached nearly 150 million by around 1600, or double to triple what they were at the beginning of the Christian era.[9]

With the advent of the modern period, beginning in the 17th century,

[5] Percy M. Roxby, "The Terrain of Early Chinese Civilisation." *Geography*, Vol. 23, 1938, pp. 225–236.

[6] The historian Arnold Toynbee views the situation differently. He sees the origin of Chinese civilization on the Huang delta as an example of what he calls "the stimulus of a harsh environment." Not because it offered special advantages, then, but rather because it presented challenging difficulties, particularly the dual scourge of flood and drought, did the Huang plain emerge as an early culture center.

[7] C. W. Bishop, "The Rise of Civilization in China With Reference to Its Geographical Aspects," *Geographical Review*, Vol. 22, 1932, pp. 617–631.

[8] Ping-ti Ho, *Studies on the Population of China 1368–1953.* Harvard University Press, Cambridge, Mass., 1959, p. 22.

[9] Ho, *Studies on the Population of China*, p. 264.

TABLE 10.1

China's Population (Millions)						Annual Rate of Increase (Percent)				
1750	1800	1850	1900	1950	2000	1750–1800	1800–1850	1850–1900	1900–1950	1950–2000
200	323	430	436	560	1034	1.0	0.6	0.0	0.5	1.2

SOURCE: John D. Durand, "The Modern Expansion of World Population."

there are indications of an upswing in the rate of population growth in China, the causes for which are not understood. Significant or not, a similar accelerated growth took place in Europe at about the same time, but likely for different reasons.

For the period 1741–1851 there is a record of officially reported annual totals of population for the Chinese Empire. Apparently these figures are derived from the *pao-chia* system of registers, but their reliability is known to be poor. Still, they are the best source that is available and in spite of their deficiencies Durand has used them in tracing China's modern population growth.[10] After 1851 the Chinese authorities were no longer able to obtain reports from all of the provinces.

Durand's medium estimates of China's modern population growth are indicated on Table 10.1. Most writers assume that following the establishment of the Manchu dynasty in the middle of the 17th century there was a long period of relative national prosperity, accompanied by a general and steady population increase that continued up to about the middle of the 19th century (Fig. 10.2). The most striking feature of China's

[10] John D. Durand, "The Modern Expansion of World Populations," *Population Problems, Proceedings of the American Philosophical Society*, Vol. 111, No. 3, June 22, 1967, pp. 141, 146–148.

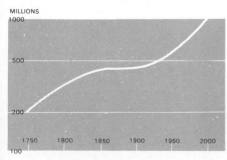

Fig. 10.2. Growth of population in Mainland China, "medium" estimates, 1750–1950 and projections to 2000. Especially noteworthy is the rapid growth during both the 18th and 20th centuries, but a near-static condition during the second half of the 19th century. Data from John D. Durand, "The Modern Expansion of World Population," *Proceedings of the American Philosophical Society*, Vol. 111, 1967.

population trend in the modern period is the seeming lack of growth during the second half of the 19th century, a feature on which historians seem to be fairly well agreed.[11] Such a stagnation probably has its explanation in the prevalent internal turmoil associated with wars, slaughter, property destruction, famines, and epidemics, which wiped out substantial sections of local populations, probably reduced the birth rates, and caused a total collapse of the *papo-chia* system of population registration.[12] This was the period of the Taiping Rebellion, the drawn-out Nien Wars, and the campaigns against the Moslems in the Northwest.

Using the *pao-chia* reports of the Ch'ing and the census of 1953, Irene Taeuber has constructed two maps showing annual rates of growth by provinces, 1749–1850 and 1850–1953.[13] In the earlier period, growth rates are consistently low in the north, except in Kiangsu. They are generally higher in the Yangtze provinces and southward. They are well above the country average in the Yangtze provinces of Chekiang, Hupeh, and Szechwan, and also in Yunnan in the far southwest. In the later period, 1850–1953, which includes the desolate second half of the 19th century, annual growth rates are low for much of the country. Five widely scattered provinces showed no gain. The largest gains were in the three southwestern provinces of Kwangsi, Kweichow, and Yünnan.

Present Population. Although the 1953 population census of China represents the most systematic and complete inventory of that country's people that has ever been made, still it has many serious deficiencies. It provides little published data that permit regional and provincial comparisons. The same is true of rural and urban categories. Data on age and sex were apparently collected but never released. Lacking also are official data that would permit a tracing of demographic change.[14]

According to the 1953 census, China had a population of 582.6 million on June 30, 1953. Chinese, or Han, peoples numbered 546.3 million, or 94 percent of the total, while over 35 million, or 6 percent, belonged to national minorities. It is believed that the census figure for total popula-

[11] Durand, "The Modern Expansion," p. 148. See also Ho, *Studies on the Population of China*, pp. 67–73.

[12] Ho, *Studies on the Population of China*, pp. 70–71.

[13] Irene B. Taeuber, "Population Dynamics and Population Pressures: Geographic-Demograpihc Approaches," Paper prepared for a Symposium on the Geography of Population Pressure on Physical and Social Resources, The Pennsylvania State University, September 17–23, 1967, Figs. 3a and 3b.

[14] On the topic of limitations of the official population data for China, see John S. Aird, "Population Growth and Distribution in Mainland China," in *An Economic Profile of Mainland China*. Studies Prepared for the Joint Economic Committee, Congress of the United States, U.S. Government Printing Office, Washington, D.C., 1967, Vol. 2, pp. 344–355.

tion probably represented an undercount of as much as 18 to 19 million, so that the actual population may have numbered closer to 601.3 million in June 1953 and 608.3 million by the eve of that year.[15] This represented between a fifth and a fourth of the earth's total inhabitants. Based on the assumption of an average birth rate of 44, a death rate of 20, and a natural increase of 24 per 1000 for the period 1953–1958, Aird judges that the population of China may have reached the astounding figure of about 723 million at year-end 1960.[16] By this latter date the annual natural increase could have reached 2.56 percent.

The unusually large size of China's population as reported by the 1953 census probably was as much a surprise to Chinese officials as it was to outsiders. When the Communists came to power in 1949 they used the population figure of 475 million, which was based on a release by the Nationalist Government in 1931. Nationalist figures published in subsequent years varied between 450 and 500 million, the last one, in 1948, being 468 million. Foreign sources were inclined to provide still lower estimates, ranging from 375 to 425 million. No source had come close to the 1953 census count of nearly 600 million.

Admittedly there can be no certainty regarding the magnitude of China's population at the present time. In the summer of 1964 there seems to have been one more effort to restore the population registers and to derive from them a current population figure. Apparently it turned out to be only a field check by security police, and if it was completed no results were ever released or published. In 1966 the figure of 700 million was restored to currency by Chinese Communist leaders. In Table 2 Aird[17] has summarized some estimates and projections of the population of China for selected years between 1953 and 1985, based on four different models. Each of the models embodies a different set of assumptions. The resulting population conjectures show striking variations. Model III, which embodies the most optimistic prospect for economic development, with falling birth and death rates, is shown in Table 10.2.

China, then, has been a main center of world population concentration for several millenniums. Its present first rank among nations in terms of number of people (probably 760 to 800 million by 1970) is not a late historical development; on the contrary it represents a persistent and enduring feature of the world's map of people.

[15] John S. Aird, "The Present and Prospective Population of Mainland China," in *Population Trends in Eastern Europe, the U.S.S.R. and Mainland China*. Milbank Memorial Fund, New York, 1960, pp. 122 and 129.

[16] Aird, "The Present and Prospective," pp. 127–129. A United Nations estimate for the late 1960's was 740.3 million. Other estimates range from 800–950 million.

[17] Aird, "The Present and Prospective," p. 363.

TABLE 10.2   Estimates and Projections of the Population of
Mainland China, for Selected Years, 1953–1985[a]

China's Model III Series	1953	1955	1960	1965	1970	1975	1980	1985
Census-based series	577	601	672	734	814	904	1003	1104
5-percent undercount series	607	633	708	772	857	951	1056	1162
10-percent undercount series	641	668	747	815	904	1004	1114	1226
15-percent undercount series	679	707	791	863	957	1063	1180	1298

SOURCE: Aird, "Population Growth and Distribution in Mainland China."
[a] Figures are given in millions.

It seems natural to inquire how it has happened that a fifth to a quarter
of the earth's total population are concentrated in China, while at the
same time retaining their rural and agricultural complexion. Among the
large subdivisions of the earth, this feature of vast rural numbers and
their high densities is unique to the rimlands of eastern and southern
Asia, a region that has the distinction of supporting more than half the
planet's people, and of which China is a representative part.

One reason for China's incredibly numerous and essentially rural and
agrarian population stems from the nature of its civilization, defined as
the technology employed to utilize nature and the aptitude of a people
to organize its national space. Thus, the civilization of China and of
most other countries within the rimlands of eastern and southern Asia—
some of which have drawn their inspiration from China—is based on
the vegetable kingdom. Most important of all, the Chinese subsist very
largely on a vegetarian diet; animals play only a small part in their work
as well as in their diet. In addition, the clothing of the Chinese is made
from vegetable fibers, their utensils are of plant origin, and their houses
have a wooden framework. About 98 percent of the caloric content of
the diet is of vegetable origin. It is these habits, pointing to a dependence
on the vegetable kingdom, that to an important degree determine the
character of the rural landscape, since a vegetarian diet exercises a determining influence on the number of people that can be supported.[18]
A population whose diet is very largely one of cereals, vegetables, tubers,
and fruits can become ever so much more numerous than one whose

[18] Pierre Gourou, "The Development of Upland Areas in China," in The Development of Upland Areas in the Far East, International Secretariat, Institute of Pacific
Relations, Vol. I, Part I, 1949, pp. 8, 11–13.

diet represents a balance between vegetable and animal products. Thus, a unit area of wheat or rice affords at least five times more calories than the same unit area of grass or forage supporting dairy cattle. For this reason subsistence peasant farmers living on a mixed animal-vegetable diet can never become as numerous in the producing area as can societies that are almost exclusively vegetarian. Moreover, the latter must rely for their food supply wholly from tilled fields, while the former derive sustenance from more extensive areas, which include natural grasslands. Thus the vegetarian diet typical of the Far East has been a principal factor permitting the large population. Moreover, once an agricultural population has attained such large numbers and a resulting high density based on a vegetarian diet, it is almost impossible to subsequently modify the diet so as to include a large amount of animal products. The population operates in an economic strait jacket that compels it to continue to produce the maximum amount of food through creating and subsisting on vegetable products, the only alternative being starvation.

What may be the origin of this vegetarian diet, which is only one element of a whole civilization whose techniques for exploiting nature are almost completely oriented toward the vegetable kingdom, is not entirely clear. It is dubiously related to religious influence, since although Buddhism teaches respect for animal life it does not frown on the use of milk and its products. Moreover, the people's vegetarian habits preceded the advent of Buddhism in eastern Asia. Neither can a case be made for the physical environment acting in such a way as to induce large agricultural populations with a predilection toward a vegetarian diet. Nor did an already-dense population subsequently compel the Chinese to adopt a vegetarian diet, since as far as can be determined from historical records, the cultural factor preceded the demographic one.[19] Since neolithic times the Chinese people have evidenced a remarkable propensity toward a vegetarian type of civilization and a lack of interest in animal husbandry.

The delta of the Huang River (North-China Plain) and the tributary valleys in the Loess uplands to the west represent the original hearthland of China. From this ancient culture center Chinese influence spread early to the south and east, where the physical environment was favorable for intensive agriculture, which already had become a Chinese way of life. In part the expansion involved a movement of Chinese people, but it represented as well an assimilation of Chinese culture by peoples who were ethnically different. A similar expansion from the hearthland to the north and west was obstructed by adverse climatic conditions, by

[19] Gourou, "The Development of Upland Areas," pp. 12–13.

the inability of Chinese farmers to compete with the resident herders and nomads, and by the hostility of these native peoples. Such areas were unfit for the traditional Chinese agriculture, and the culture itself was too stagnant and inflexible to make the required adjustment. Even in those periods when Chinese armies were able to unify vast areas of eastern Asia, there has never taken place a type of migration such as that which settled the American West. "The fundamental fact in the demography of the Chinese has been the expansion of the area of utilization and the generation of high densities of population in the parts of those areas capable of utilization by Chinese agricultural techniques under Chinese forms of familial and larger social organization."[20]

Future Numbers. Any projection of China's future population is especially hazardous, since this country is still subject to subsistence crises that may interrupt the current trends in both fertility and mortality. The demographic future of China is mainly dependent on two unknowns: the outcome of the struggle for increased food production and the direction and effectiveness of the government's population policy. The assumed present rate of increase would enlarge China's population to about 1.7 billion by the year 2000, less than 4 decades hence. Under all but the most pessimistic expectations, the population of China will surpass 1 billion by 1985.

Characteristics of China's Population. The census of 1953 provides only meager information concerning the characteristics of the total national population. It gives still less for those of smaller administrative subdivisions, such as would permit some inference regarding spatial variations. Consequently, a geography of China's population characteristics is impossible to attain at the present time.

Vital Rates. On the basis of a sample study of 30 million inhabitants, the census of 1953 announced an overall birth rate of 37 per 1000 and a death rate of 17 per 1000, which would provide for a national increase of 20 per 1000 (2 percent per year). Official vital rates in 1957 were given as birth rate, 34; death rate, 11; and natural increase, 23. These ratios appear to have been based on a sample of reporting areas in which urban conditions predominated, and so are probably a defective measure of birth and death rates for the country at large. For 1953, the official vital rates were probably too low. Aird concludes that a national birth rate of about 40 and a death rate of 20 would seem to be more realistic.[21] The present rates are unknown, but they are probably lower. The Popula-

---

[20] Chia-lin Pan and Irene B. Taeuber, "The Expansion of the Chinese: North and West," *Population Index,* Vol. 18, No. 2, 1952, p. 91.

[21] Aird, "Population Growth and Distribution," Table 4, p. 364.

tion Reference Bureau's 1970 estimates were 34 per 1000 for births, 15 for deaths, and 18–19 for natural increase. Scattered and fragmentary data suggest that there are regional variations of considerable magnitude in the birth rate, ranging from the low 30's to the high 40's, but information is inadequate to permit a geographical distribution to be made.

Age Structure. As might be expected in a country with vital rates as described above, young people predominate and oldsters are relatively few. According to the official figures produced by the 1953 census, 35.9 percent of the population were under 15 years of age and 7.3 percent were 60 years old and over. According to Aird's estimates the official figures are somewhat too low for the young and slightly too high for the old. But in any case, the dependent group (young plus old) is proportionately large (46 to 47.5 percent) in comparison with that of labor-force age. Having such a large proportion of the total population in the relatively nonproductive ages places a severe burden on the national economy. Data on regional variations are lacking.

The actual and potential labor force is immense, military manpower is huge, and the children of school age are multitudinous. The combined population of those in primary and secondary school ages was roughly 145–175 million in 1953 and 200–250 million in 1965, and it will be 180–350 million by 1985. In 1965 the annual increment in the population of primary school ages was increasing at the rate of 1.6 to 3.0 million each year; by 1985 this could rise to 3.5 million. Assuming universal education through the secondary level, the schools of China might have to accommodate over 6 million new pupils annually, under the most optimistic projections. The number of new persons entering the labor-force ages each year was 11–13 million in 1953 and will rise to 15–26 million by 1985.[22] These figures relating to age structure, in combination with those on the size and rate of growth of the total population, indicate something of the magnitude of China's problem in regard to the economic, social and political planning that must take place in order to provide the food, clothing, housing, education, employment, health care, welfare services, and other essential goods and services needed by such a population.

Sex Ratio. The 1953 census gave an overall sex ratio for China of 107.6 males per 100 females. This would mean that males exceeded females by over 20 million. But Aird's models of age-sex distributions used in constructing his estimates and projections, include varying allowances for high mortality among males in wars, civil disturbances, and political executions over the century prior to 1953. Thus adjusted, the data show sex ratios well below that of the 1953 census: 102.3 under one set of

[22] Aird, "Population Growth and Distribution," pp. 367–368.

assumptions and 100.6 under the other.[23] Data are lacking for provincial or other regional variations.

Occupational Status. Nothing in the 1953 census provides direct information concerning the occupational structure of the Chinese population. Nevertheless, the fact that nearly 87 percent were reported as having rural residence indicated indirectly the overwhelming predominance of people engaged in agriculture. Most authorities on China suggest that roughly three quarters of those gainfully employed in that country are probably engaged in tillage, a figure that places China among the most strongly agrarian of the earth's nations. To what extent, and how rapidly, this population characteristic will change as the country continues its industrialization is problematical. Although an absolute decline in the agricultural population is unlikely, its relative importance may gradually wane.

Urban-Rural Residence. The *proportion* of a country's total population that resides in cities and towns indicates its degree of urbanization. This proportion is also a rough indicator of the state of its economic development. In a strongly urbanized society the economy is usually well advanced and modern. Domestic agriculture is mechanized and efficient, or industry and commerce are so well developed that an im-

[23] Aird, "Population Growth and Distribution," p. 367.

TABLE 10.3 Size and Rate of Growth of the Population of Mainland China: by Urban and Rural Residence, 1949–56[a]

	Total		Urban		Rural	
Year	Number	Percent Increase During Year	Number	Percent Increase During Year	Number	Percent Increase During Year
1949	541,670	—	57,650	—	484,020	—
1950	551,960	1.90	61,690	7.00	490,270	1.29
1951	563,000	2.00	66,320	7.50	496,680	1.31
1952	574,820	2.10	71,630	8.00	503,190	1.31
1953	587,960	2.29	77,670	8.43	510,290	1.41
1954	601,720	2.34	81,550	4.99	520,170	1.94
1955	614,650	2.14	82,850	1.59	531,800	2.24
1956	627,800	2.14	89,150	7.60	538,650	1.29

SOURCE: Aird, "Population Growth and Distribution in Mainland China," p. 364.
[a] Absolute figures are in thousands and relate to the end of the year.

portant part of the food supply is obtained from outside sources. By contrast, where a large proportion of a population is engaged in agriculture, and lives in rural areas, the economy is characteristically backward and living standards are low.

The proportion of people in China that is urban now or was so in the past cannot be accurately determined for lack of reliable data. In Table 10.3, estimates for the eight-year period 1949–1956 are provided. Although the census of 1953 reported 77.3 million Chinese, or 13.3 percent of the total population of 582.6 million, as residing in urban places, no census definition of what constituted an urban community was made public, so doubts remain as to what the figures signify. Moreover, there never had been a uniform standard definition of the term "urban" used in any of the earlier estimates. Between 1917 and 1946 Orleans lists 7 different estimates of the size of China's urban population, ranging from a low of 100 million to a high of 141.[24]

Since the publication of the 1953 census, the government of mainland China has officially defined an urban place as one that meets any one of the following criteria:

1. Seat of a municipal people's committee above the *hsien* (county) level.

2. A resident population of 2000 or more, of whom 50 percent or more are nonagricultural.

3. A resident population of 1000–2000 of whom 75 percent are nonagricultural.

Whether these criteria are being used at present or were used at the time of the 1953 census is a disputed question.[25]

Depending on whether the urban population of China is viewed in a relative or an absolute sense, it can be concluded either that it is small or that it is large. On a world map representing the distribution of urban population as a *proportion* of the total population, China, like most of eastern and southern Asia (except for Japan)—in fact, like the LD world in general—is characterized by a low degree of urbanization. But this is because China's total population is so large, since in an *absolute* sense

[24] Leo A. Orleans, "The Recent Growth of China's Urban Population," *Geographical Review*, Vol. 49, 1959, p. 46.
[25] Orleans, "The Recent Growth," pp. 46–47; Lawrence Krader and John S. Aird, "What Do We Know about the Population of Mainlaind China?" Paper read at the meetings of the Population Association of America, in Chicago, May, 1958; Ernest Ni, *Distribution of the Urban and Rural Population of Mainland China 1953 and 1958.* U.S. Bureau of the Census, International Population Reports, Series P-95, No. 56, October 1960, p. 31.

that country's officially stated 77.3 million urban dwellers in 1953 (estimated at 104.7 million in 1960, or 15.4 percent of the total population)[26] represented an unusually large national urban group, approximately equal to that of the U.S.S.R. and exceeded only by that of the United States.

Even in the absence of reliable data, some conclusions can be drawn concerning the trend of urbanization in China, using a variety of sources (see Table 10.3). A long upward trend in urban growth was already in progress before 1949, but urbanization in the Western sense, where it is linked to industry and trade, at that time was largely confined to the treaty ports and Manchurian cities. However, after 1949, the resumption of urban growth involved interior as well as seaboard locations and included administrative centers and new industrial and mining cities stimulated by the First Five-Year Plan and by U.S.S.R. assistance. Since 1949, the cumulative evidence is strong that the rate of urban population increase, at least through 1956, was markedly greater than that of either the total population or the rural population. According to Table 10.3, the annual rate of urban increase for the 8-year period 1949–1956 was 6.36 percent, compared with 2.13 percent for the whole population and only 1.54 percent for the rural sector. Not all recent urban growth represents increased industrialization. Some is a result of expansion of traditional marketing functions and the providing of specialized services for the vast agricultural population. A part has resulted from the ruthlessly enforced collectivization in the rural areas as well as the drift of population from the overcrowded and poverty-ridden agricultural countryside into the cities in a desperate search for improved living conditions. The government soon realized the dangers associated with this movement toward the cities, aptly described by Chinese newspapers as a "blind infiltration," and steps were taken to slow it down. As a consequence the rate of growth in urban population was retarded shortly after 1953, although it still continued to be greater than that of the total population.

Since 1957 no precise figures for urban population have been disclosed by Chinese officials. It has been noted earlier that Orleans estimated the total to be about 104.7 million in 1960, or 15.4 percent of the total population. Po I-Po, in an interview with Anna Louise Strong in 1964, indicated that as of some unspecified earlier date China's urban population had reached 130 million, but stated that it must be reduced to 110 million.[27] Since the end of the disastrous "Leap Forward," and as the crisis of 1959–1962 deepened, further restrictions on urban growth were imposed, with the result, so Aird believes, that the proportion of China's total

[26] Orleans, "The Recent Growth," p. 57.
[27] Aird, "Population Growth and Distribution," pp. 382, 388.

population residing in urban places as of the middle 1960's may have
been smaller than it was in 1958. Actually, "the urban population of
China is probably declining now in relative if not in absolute terms,
and there is no immediate prospect for a return to rapid urban growth."[28]
China may be the earth's single major LD country in which urbanization,
or the relative *proportion* of city dwellers, is not at present increasing.

   While the focus of this discussion is primarily on urban population
en masse, especially compared with total or rural numbers, and not so
much on cities and towns as settlements, it may not be out of place
to comment briefly on urban places by size classes (Fig. 10.3). According
to the 1953 census, there were in China 420 urban places of 20,000 or
more population.[29] This group accounted for about two thirds of the
total number of urban inhabitants; about one third dwell in smaller places.
If the 420 larger urban places having population in excess of 20,000,
164 were designated as municipalities. These included places with 100,000

[28] Aird, "Population Growth and Distribution," p. 378.
[29] For the geographical location and distribution of these 420 urban places by
size classes in 1953, see Fig. 2 in Aird, "Population Growth and Distribution in
Mainland China," pp. 378–379.

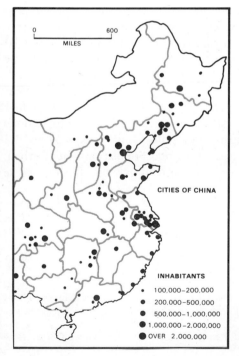

Fig. 10.3. Urban places in China with
50,000 or more inhabitants, 1953. After
map by Morris B. Ullman, in, *Cities of
Mainland China; 1953 and 1958,* U.S.
Bureau of the Census, International
Population Reports, 1961.

or more inhabitants, and in addition some important industrial and mining centers with less than 100,000 population. In 1953 the 164 municipalities accounted for about 56 percent of the total urban population.[30] By the summer of 1958 the number of municipalities had increased to 180–190, 20 of which were new cities.[31] Of these 180–190 municipalities, some 160 had their origin as *hsein* (county) capitals, in which administrative functions were important.[32]

Distribution of Urbanization. From the data supplied by Ni[33] on urban population of China by provinces for 1953 and 1958, it is possible to make a few crude distribution maps of that country's city dwellers. As of 1958 (and therefore just before the disastrous effects of the Leap Forward developed), when the urban population is estimated to have been about 96.1 million, or 14.7 percent of the total for the whole country, provincial percentages of the population that was urban ranged from a high of 42.2 percent to a low of 4.9 percent. If about 15 percent (actually 14.7 percent) is accepted as the country average for degree of urbanization, then only six provinces exceeded this average (Fig. 10.4). With one exception, Kiangsu, which includes the lower Yangtze Valley, they are all in north China. Three of the six, and also the three with the highest percentages, are in Manchuria. Two of the latter have urban percentages of over 35. This relatively strong urbanization in Manchuria reflects the more extensive and more commercial nature of the agriculture there, as well as the Northeast region's position as the foremost industrial area of China. Its beginnings in manufacturing can be attributed to the Japanese and the Russians, who held spheres of influence in the south and in the north of Manchuria respectively. After the Pacific War Manchuria continued to maintain its prime position in industry, first under the Nationalist government and later under the Communist regime. Hopeh in north China and Kiangsu in middle China rank next to the Manchurian provinces in percentage of the total population that is urban, and at the same time are well above the national average. Both of these

---

[30] For further discussion of numbers, sizes, and classification of Chinese cities, see the following: Theodore Shabad, "The Population of China's Cities," *Geographical Review*, Vol. 49, 1959, pp. 37–42; Ni, *Distribution of the Urban and Rural Population of Mainland China; 1953 and 1958*, and Morris B. Ullman, *Cities of Mainland China: 1953 and 1958*. U.S. Bureau of the Census, International Population Reports, Series P-95, No. 59, August, 1961.

[31] Shabad, "The Population of China's Cities," pp. 37–42.

[32] Sen-dou Chang, "Some Aspects of the Urban Geography of the Chinese Hsien Capital," *Annals of the Association of American Geographers*, Vol. 51, 1961, pp. 43–44.

[33] Ni, *Distribution of the Urban and Rural Population of Mainland China: 1953 and 1958*.

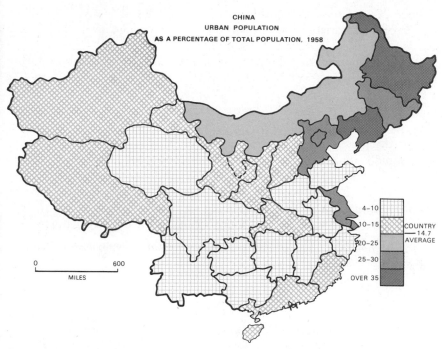

CHINA
URBAN POPULATION
AS A PERCENTAGE OF TOTAL POPULATION, 1958

4–10
10–15   COUNTRY
           — 14.7
20–25   AVERAGE
25–30
OVER 35

0   600
MILES

Fig. 10.4. Data from Ernest Ni, *Distribution of the Urban and Rural Population of Mainland China: 1953 and 1598;* U.S. Bureau of the Census, International Population Reports, 1960.

front on the sea and have important maritime interests. Hopeh contains the two great metropolises of Peking and Tientsin, and Kiangsu those of Shanghai and Nanking. Both are also industrial regions of long standing. Within the much more extensive part of China where the urban percentages are below 15 (the country average), 2 subdivisions are recognized, a moderate substandard type with percentages of 10–15 and a low substandard type with percentages between 4 and 10. The first of these includes the semiarid and arid provinces in the north and northwest Shansi, Shensi, Kansu, and Sinkiang). In addition there are Hupeh in middle China, containing Wuhan, an industrial city of over 2 million located on the Yangtze, and Fukien and Kwantung in southeastern China. Both of the latter front on tidewater and have important maritime interests. Kwantung contains the metropolis of Canton, a city approaching 2 million in population. In the low substandard class are 2 provinces in southern north China, 8 in south China, and the subdivisions of Tibet-Chamko and Tsinghai in the western interior.

Since Ni presents data both for 1953 and 1958, it is also possible to show regional variations in urban population change over this 5-year period just preceding the crisis beginning in 1959.

On the map portraying the percent increase in urban population during 1953–1958, derived from Ni's Table 3,[34] it can be seen that of the 24 main provinces or regions, 12 show urban growth above the country average of about 24 percent (actually 24.4 percent) and 12 are below (Fig. 10.5). As a useful generalization it may be pointed out that it was in the northeast, north, and northwest that urbanization proceeded most rapidly, only two provinces within those parts having percentage increases in urban growth that were below the country average. Significantly, both of these were in Manchuria, still China's main industrial region, but one that is not experiencing the rapid expansion true of some other parts of the country. In south China, with only two exceptions,

[34] Ni, *Distribution of the Urban and Rural Population, of Mainland China*, p. 13.

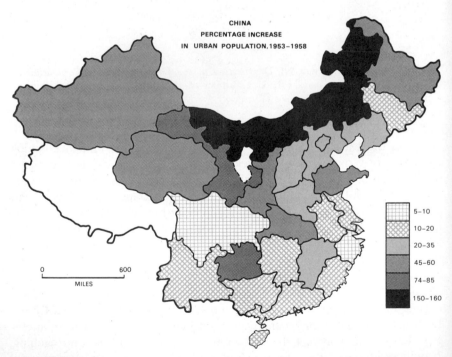

Fig. 10.5. Rate of increase in urban population, 1953–1958, by provinces. Data from Ernest Ni, *Distribution of the Urban and Rural Population of Mainland China; 1953 and 1958;* U.S. Bureau of the Census, International Population Reports, 1960.

all provinces showed urban growth rates below the country level, and in a distinct majority of them it was well below. One of the exceptions was Hopeh, with a 45 percent increase; it includes the large and rapidly expanding urban industrial complex of Wuhan. The large (85 percent) increase in hilly Kweichow may be related to the extensive railroad construction and subsequent development of mining and metallurgical industries occurring in that region.

If the map of percent increase in urban population during 1953–1958 is supplemented by another depicting change in the percentage of the population that was urban between 1953 and 1958,[35] many of the former generalizations are substantiated. For the country as a whole, over the 5-year period urban population rose from 13.3 percent of the total to 14.7 percent, or a gain of 1.4 percent. Twelve of the provinces showed gains equal to or exceeding the national average. All but two of these are in the north. The south, in general, is a region of very modest change in percent urban population; four provinces actually showed negative values, indicating that urban population was growing less rapidly than rural population.

The Ethnic Minorities. From the standpoint of language affiliation, China's population is highly homogeneous, with the Han Chinese ethnic group, according to the 1953 census, comprising 94 percent of the total. Still, the scant 6 percent non-Chinese minority represents a total of about 35 million persons, which in an absolute sense is large (Table 10.4). While throughout the Chinese-language group and area there is a uniform written language, the spoken language has important regional differences. It is especially in eastern China south of the Yangtze that the regional dialects differ from Mandarin Chinese, which is known as the national language and is prevalent in northern and southern-interior China.

[35] Ni, *Distribution of the Urban and Rural Population of Mainland China,* Table 2, p. 12.

TABLE 10.4   Population Numbers of Important Minority Groups in China According to the 1953 Census

Ch'uangs	6,611,455	Miaos	2,511,339
Uighurs	3,640,125	Manchus	2,418,931
Hui	3,559,350	Puyis	1,247,883
Yi	3,254,269	Koreans	1,120,405
Tibetans	2,775,622	Others	6,728,025

SOURCE: Aird, "Population Growth and Distribution in Mainland China," p. 393.

HAN PEOPLES CHAUNG-TUNG PEOPLES
MONGOLS MIAO-YAO PEOPLES
KOREANS TURKIC PEOPLES
TIBETANS UNPOPULATED AREAS
HUI (MUSLIMS)

0 600
MILES

CHINA'S MAIN ETHNIC GROUPS

Fig. 10.6. Note that the ethnic minorities are located along the perimeter of China, adjacent to the country's land borders. After map by S. I. Bruk, U.S.S.R. Academy of Sciences, Moscow, 1959.

Gradually the confusion resulting from various dialects is diminishing as a consequence of the effects of radio, cinema, and the required use of Mandarin Chinese in the schools.

Significantly the minority peoples, with few exceptions, have a peripheral location with respect to the preponderant Chinese, who occupy the physically more desirable eastern parts (Fig. 10.6). Thus, the non-Han peoples are concentrated in the territory adjacent to China's land borders. They mainly occupy low-grade environments, chiefly dry lands, but likewise cold lands of both the high-altitude and high-latitude varieties, as well as regions of rugged terrain. This locational differentiation of the Han Chinese and the minority groups, with the latter mainly in the frontier regions, is a durable historical pattern that has persisted through millenniums of time. The fact that the Chinese part of the nation's population is so overwhelmingly greater than the border peoples suggests that over the centuries the balance between births and deaths differed between the two groups. This in turn reflects contrasts in their physical environments, types of economy, and density of settlement.[36] Over thousands of miles the corporeal evidence of the zone of demarcation between Han and non-Han peoples is the Great Wall. The boundary has been far from static, however, since at times eastward and southward thrusts of minority power have seen Mongol and Manchu dynasties in control of eastern China, while other periods have witnessed the deep penetration of Chinese power and settlements beyond the limits set by climate for indigenous Han agriculture.[37]

There are more than 50 minority groups in China, distinguished from

[36] Pan and Taeuber, "The Expansion of the Chinese," pp. 90–91.
[37] Pan and Taeuber, "The Expansion of the Chinese," p. 90.

the dominant Han people by language, culture, race, religion, or occupation, or by some combination of these features. Reservations concerning the accuracy of the 1953 census data for the ethnic minorities are greater than for the Han Chinese. Estimates rather than actual field enumerations were common for the minority peoples.

Most of the minorities are concentrated to some degree in a particular part of China, although the degree of compactness is variable. Even in the areas of greatest concentration, most of the minority groups do not form a majority of the local residents. Han Chinese outnumber the minority populations in every provincial unit except Tibet and Sinkiang.[38] In some regions, particularly in the southeast, several different ethnic groups interpenetrate geographically, even though they maintain their separate identities. Not only language and culture differences but also economic functions may serve to distinguish the interpenetrated ethnic groups.

The alleged doctrinal basis of Communist China's policy with respect to national minorities asserts the equality of different nationalities and the need for regional autonomy in order to permit the preservation of language, customs, or religious beliefs. Actually, minorities are permitted to preserve only the aspects of their culture that are picturesque and do not interfere with Party objectives.[39]

Representing the complex distribution of the main ethnic minorities on a small-scale map presents a serious problem.[40] A high degree of generalization is required. In Fig. 10.6, based on Bruk's map, only major ethnic groups with distinct regions of concentration are shown. It will

[38] Aird, "Population Growth and Distribution," p. 391.
[39] Details concerning the names, locations, and total populations of the various minorities can be found in Theodore Shabad, *China's Changing Map*, New York, 1956, pp. 31–35, 39–48. A general distribution of the minority peoples can be observed in the pattern of Communist autonomous regions of different ranks shown on Plate 2, in *China Provisional Atlas of Communist Administrative Units*, prepared by the Central Intelligence Agency, Washington, D.C., 1959.
[40] The most detailed density map of China is that by S. I. Bruk, *Karta Narodov Kitaya MNR, i Korei (Map of the Peoples of China, The Mongolian People's Republic, and Korea)*, in color, scale 1:5,000,000, Akademiya Nauk SSSR Moscow, 1959. Bruk's map is based on a Chinese Communist secondary-school population density map, several Chinese maps on the distribution of ethnic groups, and a variety of other publications, as well as on consultations with Chinese ethnographers. The text explaining the map is available in translation as Solomon I. Bruk, *Naseleniya Kitaya MNR, i Korei (The Peoples of China, the Mongolian People's Republic, and Korea)*, Publishing House of the U.S.S.R. Academy of Sciences, Moscow, 1959, translated in *U.S. Joint Publications Research Service*, No. 3710, August 16, 1960. A small, generalized edition of Bruk's map is available in Aird, "Population Growth and Distribution in Mainland China," p. 392.

facilitate description to begin in the northeast and proceed counterclockwise around the land frontiers of China where the minority peoples are concentrated.

Following this procedure, the first major minority is the Korean group, numbering over a million, which is concentrated just north of the Korean-Chinese border at its eastern end. These people are relative newcomers to the region. They are mainly farmers engaged in growing paddy rice.

Scattered throughout Manchuria are some 2.4 million Manchus. Since these have been assimilated into the much larger Chinese community and speak Chinese, they do not have a separate ethnic existence, and therefore are not shown on the map (Fig. 10.6).

Some 1.5 million of China's people speak a variety of Mongolian languages; many of these are also adherents of Lamaist Buddhism. Most of the Mongols are nomadic tribal peoples. Although outnumbered by the Han Chinese in much of their domain, their identity has been maintained because of their nomadic habits. Their main region of concentration is the vast dry lands of the Inner Mongolian Autonomous Region, situated to the west of Manchuria along the northern perimeter of China and to the south of Mongolia, a Soviet satellite. Smaller numbers are to be found in several autonomous *chow, hsien,* and *banners* located in western Manchuria, northern Sinkiang, and western Kansu.

Chinese Moslems, known as Hui, number about 3.6 million. They arrived in northwest China from central Asia during the Middle Ages. While Moslem colonies are widely dispersed in northern and western dry China, their greatest concentration is within the Ninghsia Hui Autonomous Region, in what was formerly northeastern Kansu. Although they speak Chinese, their strong adherence to Islam has usually caused them to live apart from their Han neighbors.

Turkic peoples (Uighurs, Kazakhs, and Kirghiz) occupy China's dry northwestern sector. The Uighurs are mainly irrigation agriculturalists, clustered around oases; the other two groups are nomads. Their isolation and their Moslem faith have preserved their separate identity, even though their relative numbers are shrinking as more and more Han Chinese move in. The recent Chinese settlement has both economic and political motives. It is politically significant that both the Mongol and the Turkic border regions of China are paralleled by similar concentrations of these same minority peoples along the Soviet side of the boundary separating China and the U.S.S.R. As Sino-Soviet antagonisms have multiplied in recent years, a rivalry between the two countries for influence among the Turkic minority groups divided by the international boundary has intensified.

ASIA 283

The Tibetans, and the closely related Yi peoples, are distributed throughout not only Tibet but also Szechwan, Kweichow, Yünnan, Tsinghai, and Kansu provinces. Lama Buddhism is the main religion of the Tibetans. The Chinese have succeeded in incorporating Tibet into the state only by force of arms.

The Ch'uangs and the linguistically related Puyis comprise the most numerous of China's minority groups. They are mainly located on the Chinese border where it makes contact with North Vietnam, but they also extend far to the south and southwest of the border as well. Their religion is animist, and paddy rice is their main crop.

The important Miao-Yao minority group is widely distributed throughout the south and southwestern provinces, but with a main concentration in Kweichow. Their language, related to that of the Tibetan-Burmese peoples, is the main feature distinguishing them from the Han Chinese.

China's essential unity in language and religion makes for national cohesiveness. Nowhere are the linguistic and religious minorities numerous and economically strong enough to constitute a threat to national unity. In this respect China differs from India, where the multiplicity of languages, the religious differences, and the prevalence of caste create divisive influences.

Population Distribution. Throughout most of historic time there has been a long-term shift of population from older northern centers toward the south. But in recent centuries the drift has been reversed and is toward the north. Still more recently, and in limited volume, the movement has been to the northwest and west.

Elements of Redistribution. It seems unlikely, however, that the general features of spatial population distribution have altered much over the past several decades, although, to be sure, densities have changed as the country's population has increased in numbers, and some regions have grown more rapidly than others. No doubt, also, there are regional variations in the vital rates that would make for some changes in relative density over the past half century and more, but the data are inadequate to permit the portrayal of these changes on a map. Also, there have been migrations of some consequence that must have resulted in regional differentials in population growth. In recent centuries most large-scale migrations have been associated with calamities of a natural, social, or political origin. With few exceptions, it was the "push" rather than the "pull" factors that instigated these migrations, and as soon as the conditions in the source regions improved, the people returned to their original home areas.

The most important of the migrations in recent history, and the one that is the exception as it relates to the push and pull factors stated above, is the settlement in large numbers of Han Chinese in Northeast China, commonly known as Manchuria. Here there were the attractions of good quality virgin farm land and of employment in the expanding mining and industrial enterprises. Thus, Manchuria increased disproportionately in population as a consequence of migration. In spite of an imperial decree by the Manchu rulers banning Chinese settlement in Manchuria after 1668, a surreptitious limited migration continued, so by 1900 the population there may have been 80 percent Chinese. These early migrants were mainly agricultural settlers. With the beginning in the 19th century of large-scale investment by the Japanese in mining and industrial development in Manchuria, not only did Chinese migrants increase in numbers, but the incentive became less the land and more the urban employment opportunities. Within the 1910 boundaries of Manchuria, population is thought to have more than doubled between 1910 and 1940, expanding from 18.5 to 38.4 million. About half of this nearly 20 million increase was attributed to migration.[41] In the 20 years from 1923 to 1943 the official records indicate an average net increase by migration in the population of Manchuria of about 1 percent per year. By the end of World War II, population in Manchuria had expanded to 44–45 million, but it fell off by several million in the years of turmoil and confusion following the conflict. After 1950, in-migration was again heavy, probably averaging around a million a year.[42]

The reasons why the Chinese have not, to a greater extent, spilled over into the sparsely settled lands to the west and north are at least threefold. First, there are the natural handicaps, especially the low and variable rainfall. Second, there is the immobilizing effects of Chinese cultural and social structures such as the strong attachment to the family and the native village, the veneration of ancestors, the language differences, and a lack of appreciation of upland sites and their nonirrigated type of agriculture in which grazing and feeding of animals would play a part. And third, there is the economic factor, which makes it difficult for the peasant, who has always been close to destitution and starvation, to move a long distance.[43] The result has been a relative stability in

[41] Waller Wynne, Jr., *The Population of Manchuria*. U.S. Bureau of the Census, International Population Statistics Report, Series P-90, No. 7, 1958, p. 1. On this topic, see also Leo A. Orleans, "The 1953 Chinese Census in Perspective," *Journal of Asian Studies*, Vol. 16, 1957, pp. 568, 572–573, and "Manchuria as a Demographic Frontier," *Population Index*, Vol. 11, 1945, pp. 260–274.

[42] Wynne, *Population of Manchuria*, p. 1.

[43] Leo A. Orleans, "Population Redistribution in Communist China," in *Population Trends in Eastern Europe, the U.S.S.R. and Mainland China*. Milbank Memorial Fund, New York, 1960, pp. 141–142.

the pattern of population distribution, despite the fact that an overwhelming proportion of the people are crowded onto the small percentage of the land that is cultivated and can be utilized in the Chinese cultural tradition, while a genuine sparseness of people exists elsewhere.

Regrettably the official provincial population figures over the last half century are not of a quality that will permit a discerning analysis of regional population changes. Moreover, there have occurred rearrangements of provincial and *hsien* boundaries, so that comparisons through time are made difficult. Orleans[44] has prepared tables showing 20 sets of provincial population figures in chronological order, starting with the 1909–1911 census. His Table 1 represents absolute numbers, and his Table 2 the percentage of the total national population that each province represents. Population data thus arranged in a time sequence ordinarily follow a regular pattern of development, but that is not consistently true of these provincial figures for China. Rather, there are a number of erratic changes in the data, and in view of their known or presumed deficiencies, this is not unexpected. Still, there is a certain basic consistency in the provincial data, and the range of the variation for the individual provinces through nearly half a century are generally not very large. In some provinces the percentage figures are relatively stable and in others the range of variation narrows considerably if a few extremes are eliminated. Among the 18 provinces of China proper, the 1953 census figure of population was lower than any previous estimate in 9 instances and higher in 9. Expectably it should be higher in almost all, since the national total was so much greater than in any previous count.

Since the Communists took over in 1949 there have been a few types of population redistribution that warrant mentioning, even though their overall effects on the durable spatial arrangements of people have been slight.

Stemming from the confusion in the countryside resulting from agricultural reorganization imposed by the Communist government, some 20 million people are estimated to have moved from the country to the city between 1949 and 1956.[45] Most of this movement was local in character and did not extend across provincial boundaries.

In addition to the rural-urban migration there were movements of people resulting from state planning for increased industrialization and agricultural output. Partly as a defense measure but also with the idea of correcting what was felt to have been an unreasonable concentration

[44] Orleans, "The 1953 Census in Perspective," pp. 565–573.
[45] Orleans, "Population Redistribution in Communist China," p. 144.

of industry in the coastal provinces, the Government set out to redistribute manufacturing so as to utilize unused resources in the interior and build up industrial complexes in the hinterland. In 1949, 77 percent of the industrial output, (excluding handicrafts) originated in 7 coastal provinces, a large part of it in a few cities such as Shanghai, Peking, Tientsin, and Canton. This proportion decreased to 70 percent in 1952 and 60 percent in 1955 as interior developments were emphasized.[46] The industrial buildup of the interior is reflected in the sharp rise in the proportion of urban population in some of the inland provinces between 1953 and 1958: the Inner Mongolian Autonomous Region from 10.7 to 21.3 percent; Kansu, 8.6 to 13.3 percent; Shensi, 9.9 to 13.6 percent; and Kweichow, 3.9 to 6.3 percent.[47] Individual interior cities likewise experienced phenomenal growth in industry and population. Much the larger part of this planned urban growth was not contributed by interregional migration but resulted rather from local influxes of peasants from the surrounding countryside. Some skilled labor was moved interior from distant provinces, but although the precise volume of this westward migration resulting from hinterland industrial development is unknown, it is unlikely that it exceeded one million persons.

A second state program resulting in a degree of population redistribution is related to agricultural expansion, more precisely the reclamation of new lands in the west and north, especially in northern Manchuria. The numerous reports on the extent of lands reclaimed during individual years of the last decade vary, but a generous estimate suggests an annual average of 1.5 million acres.[48] Between 1949 and 1957 the Communists reportedly moved 1.3 million persons, many of them in family units, to settle on these new agricultural lands. Based on reported current reclamation rates, the number probably did not exceed half a million in any year.[49]

Other planned activities, such as the settling of Han Chinese in areas populated by minority nationalities primarily to strengthen political control and the development of large-scale work programs associated with road, railroad and dam building, and irrigation projects, have also resulted in some degree of population redistribution, but its total permanent effect was small indeed. Certainly this is true when the total migration is viewed against the great mass of 700 to 800 million lowland Chinese and their

---

[46] Orleans, "Population Redistribution in Communist China," p. 146.

[47] Ni, *Distribution of the Urban and Rural Population of Mainland China*, p. 12.

[48] Orleans, "Population Redistribution in Communist China," p. 148.

[49] Orleans, "Population Redistribution in Communist China," p. 148. See also Leo A. Orleans, *The Volume of Migration in Relation to Land Reclamation in Communist China*, REMP Bulletin (Research Group for European Migration Problems), April-June 1958, Vol. 6, No. 2, pp. 25–26.

probable annual increase of 14 to 17 million. To be sure, excluding the local intraprovincial migrations that involve by far the greatest numbers, the long-distance movement of several million people to the north and west has resulted in significant changes in the economies of the regions of in-migration. By contrast, the regions of exit have not been noticeably affected, and the overall population distribution remains unchanged.

Population Distribution and Density as of About 1953. Since no field enumeration or controlled registration of China's inhabitants has ever been made it is not possible to map and subsequently analyze their spatial distribution and their redistribution through time in the same detail as can be done for Japan's and India's populations, or for those of most advanced Western nations. Moreover, while the 1953 census doubtless provides the most accurate count of the Chinese people that has ever been made, its data are rendered less useful for the construction of detailed distribution maps, since they have never been published for civil divisions smaller than the provinces, that is, by *hsien* or counties. Consequently foreign scholars in their construction of population distribution maps of China are faced with two unsatisfactory alternatives: (1) either use the pre-Communist 1947–1948 estimates, which have the advantage that the data are available by *hsien*, but which suffer because of being older, less accurate, and clearly representing a deficiency of 100 to 200 million, or (2) use the more recent and more accurate 1953 census data, for which published *hsien* figures are not available, with the consequence that distribution can only be represented by the very large provincial subdivisions.

The only other solution is to rely on population maps using 1953 data, constructed by Chinese and Russian scholars, who most likely had access to unpublished sources of population data by *hsien*, not available to non-Soviet Western scholars. Here the primary source is a "Wall Map of the Population Density of China," scale 1:4,000,000, 1955, in color, published in China by the Map Publishing House (Ti-t'u Ch'u-pan She). A copy of this map is in the Library of Congress. A description of how the map was made is contained in the following source: "On the Explanation of the Wall Map of the Population Density of China," in *Geographical Knowledge* (Ti-li Chih-shih), November 1956, pp. 502–504. While in this explanatory article it is not explicitly stated that unpublished hsien population data were available to the authors, it may be inferred from a description of the procedures used in making the map that such was the case. On the Chinese population map all places of 20,000 or more inhabitants are represented by size classes. Consequently, the part of the nation's population represented by these cities, amounting to about 51.3 million,[50] is not included in the density computations. But on the other hand, the urban population contained in places smaller than 20,000, amounting to nearly 25.9 million, are included. In addition, where the suburbs of the larger cities are unusually big, the agricultural population in such suburbs are subtracted from the city populations and these amounts are included in computing the density categories. This agricultural population living in urban places probably amounted to about 10.4 million. Thus, the Chinese wall map appears to represent the distribution of 51.3 million urban people by graduated circles, while some 531.3 million others, chiefly rural (but also including urban people residing in places of under 20,000), and likewise rural suburban people of larger cities, are represented by density categories. The density map was constructed by first preparing a dot map of distribution, with, in most regions, one dot representing 10,000 persons, but one dot for every 1000 persons in the sparsely occupied dry and high western regions. The base used for the population dot map was a physical map showing *hsien* subdivisions, scale 1:2,500,000. To convert the dot map into a density map a unit of 400 sq km was used (1600 sq km where population was very sparse) and the dots were counted and population densities determined for squares of 20 km latitude distance.

A second and more recent (1959) map showing population distribution in mainland China based on the census data of 1953 is *Ethnic Map of China, Mongolian People's Republic, and Korea*, scale 1:5,000,000, 1959, in color, prepared by S. I. Bruk and published by the Academy of Sciences, U.S.S.R., Institute of Ethnology, Moscow. The Bruk map was referred to in an earlier section on minority groups. Although Bruk's is primarily a map of ethnic groups, which are shown by color shadings, population density categories are also represented, but by various line and dot patterns in black. The latter are rendered somewhat obscure because of the dominating colors. But by dint of considerable labor the density patterns were copied onto a separate map and subsequently emphasized by color to produce a very legible population density map.

In a brochure (in Russian) accompanying the Bruk ethnic map, acknowledgement is made of the Chinese 1955 map as the principle source used in determining population density, for which map it is noted *hsien* data appear to have been used. Among other sources employed by the Russians were data by *hsien* of some autonomous districts, regions, and provinces scattered throughout various Chinese publications. The discussion of population distribution to follow is based on the evidence provided by the Chinese (1955) and Russian (1959) population density maps, described above. A supplement to these is another map of China's popula-

[50] Morris B. Ullman, *Cities of Mainland China: 1953 and 1958*. U.S. Bureau of the Census, International Population Reports, Series P-95, No. 59, August, 1961, p. 8.

tion for the period 1945–1948, using the dot or point method of representation (scale, roughly, 150 mi = one in.).[51]

Other than the fact of prodigious numbers, the next most striking feature of population in China is its highly unbalanced and uneven spatial distribution. Obviously the inhabitants of China are to an unusual degree concentrated on the 10–15 percent of the country's area that is under cultivation, while the lands that are unsuitable for the type of tillage agriculture practiced by the Chinese have remained unoccupied or only sparsely occupied (Fig. 10.7). The most striking feature of popu-

[51] Glenn T. Trewartha, "New Maps of China's Population," *Geographical Review*, Vol. 46, 1957, Plate I, facing p. 234.

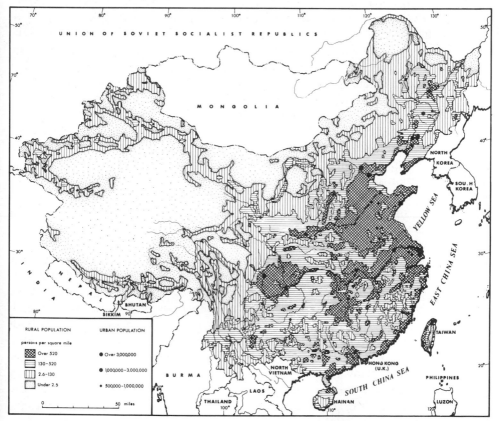

Fig. 10.7. Mainland China—population densities, 1953. Mainly after a map by S. I. Bruk, U.S.S.R. Academy of Sciences, Moscow, 1959. Reprinted from Paul F. Griffin, Ed., *Geography of Population*, Copyright 1969, by Feardon Publishers. Used with the permission of Feardon Publishers.

lation unbalance, because it is on such a large scale, is the contrast between the crowded lands of the coastal and eastern provinces and the relatively empty lands of the interior and west (Table 10.5). Thus, if a straight diagonal line is drawn from about Aigun on the Amur River in Heilungkiang Province in northern Manchuria to Tengyueh in Yunnan Province in the southwest, then the humid area to the east and south of that line (although representing only about 36 percent of the nation's area) does, on the other hand, support roughly 96 percent of its population. Doubtless it is the physical handicap of meager and unreliable rainfall in the western interior that presents the greatest single handicap there to the Chinese agriculturist, although cool summers and a short growing season at high elevations and in the higher latitudes, together with rugged terrain and steep slopes in other areas, are additional handicaps. It is the above unbalanced distribution of people that causes the overall arithmetic density figure of over 200 per sq mi (1970) to be of little significance. By contrast, the physiological density, or number of people per sq mi of arable land, in China is roughly 1400, and the agricultural density (agricultural population per sq mi) is 1190. The above density figures emphasize not only the large amount of unoccupied or meagerly occupied land in China, but also the small proportion of the total area that is densely populated, as well as the great preponderance of the population engaged in agriculture. China's present population distribution reflects the complex interaction of a number of factors, both physical and cultural. Moreover, it represents a particularly mature arrangement, resulting from continuing adjustment to the living area over millenniums of time.

A highly uneven distribution of settlement also prevails within the humid and populous east. There a strongly clustered or clotted pattern of distribution prevails, with extraordinary concentrations of numbers and abnormally high densities of rural people, coinciding with lowland plains, chiefly those composed of new alluvium. The hill lands with their steep slopes and thin and/or infertile soils that prevail over much of eastern China are avoided. The chief exceptions to the rule that dense population coincides with lowlands are the crowded hill lands of the Szechwan Basin and of parts of Shantung. On the other hand, the outstanding exception to the other rule, that lowland plains are densely populated, is parts of the great Manchurian Plain of northeastern China.

The essential fact is that the people of China have continued to pile up on the limited areas of good agricultural land and have not encroached strongly on the lands of marginal quality, especially the unirrigable up-

TABLE 10.5 Official Population, Area, and Population Density, by Province and Region, 1953 and 1957

Province and Region	Population (Thousands)		Area (Sq Mi)	Persons Per Sq Mi	
	1953	1957		1953	1957
Mainland China	582,603	646,530	3,711,889	157	174
Southern region	344,125	376,740	1,029,033	334	366
Kiangsu	47,137	52,130	41,699	1,130	1,250
Anhwei	30,663	33,560	54,015	568	621
Chekiang	22,866	25,280	39,305	582	643
Fukien	13,143	14,650	47,529	277	308
Hupeh	27,790	30,790	72,394	384	425
Hunan	33,227	36,220	81,274	409	446
Kiangsi	16,773	18,610	73,629	264	292
Kwangtung	36,740	37,960	82,857	443	458
Kwangsi	17,591	19,390	91,583	192	212
Szechwan	65,685	72,160	219,150	300	329
Kweichow	15,037	16,890	67,181	224	251
Yunnan	17,473	19,100	168,417	104	113
Northern region	210,388	237,020	653,118	322	363
Hopeh	43,348	48,730	84,316	514	578
Shansi	14,314	15,960	60,656	236	263
Liaoning	20,566	24,090	57,683	357	418
Kirin	11,290	12,550	72,201	156	174
Heilungkiang	11,897	14,860	178,996	66	83
Shensi	15,881	18,130	75,598	210	240
Shantung	48,877	54,030	59,189	826	913
Honan	44,215	48,670	64,479	686	755
Western region	28,090	32,770	2,029,736	14	16
Inner Mongolia autonomous region	7,338	9,200	501,930	15	18
Kansu and Ninghsia	12,928	14,610	135,298	96	108
Tsinghai	1,676	2,050	278,378	6	7
Sinkiang	4,874	5,640	641,930	8	9
Tibet	1,274	1,270	472,200	3	3

SOURCE: John S. Aird, "Population Growth and Distribution in Mainland China."

lands and the dry lands. The durability of that pattern over the centuries relates closely to two characteristic features of Chinese agriculture: (1) the emphasis on hand labor in most of the farm operations and (2) the importance of tilled crops, mainly for food, to the near exclusion of livestock and silviculture. The failure of the Chinese to utilize natural pastureland and forests, and to grow forage and feed crops for animals, still further accentuates their tendency to neglect the less desirable upland areas and concentrate their efforts instead on the raising of food crops on fertile lowland sites. Extraordinarily high densities of population in the areas that can be utilized within the framework of the Chinese cultural tradition of intensive cereal cultivation by hand-labor methods, and the near absence of people elsewhere, has been an enduring feature of China's population geography. In this connection it should be remembered that in China, unlike the industrial West, the high densities are mainly those of traditional agricultural peoples and not urban dwellers engaged in secondary and tertiary occupations. Thus, densities of population in China are to an unusual degree a function of the agricultural productivity of land as it relates to cereal crops.

Since in China most of the essential farm tasks have always been preformed by hand instead of by animals or machines, there is a limit to the area of land that can be cultivated by a farm family—at most a few acres. Thus a Chinese farmer can eke out an existence on 2–3 acres of good alluvial land, but he will starve on 50 acres of marginal land. Since it requires as much hand labor to till inferior land as it does fertile soil, the Chinese peasant is obliged to concentrate his labor very largely on the best lands, which reward intensive human effort, and to neglect the mediocre lands, exploitation of which often requires extensive methods involving the use of machinery and nonhuman power.

By far the most extensive cluster of dense population coincides with the country's largest alluvial plain, the delta of the Huang River, together with the adjacent broken hill lands of Shantung (Fig. 10.7). On the great plain, whose area is about 125,000 sq mi, there probably dwell more than 125 million people, or roughly one sixth of China's total. Its overall density, therefore, must approach 1000 per sq mi (385 per sq km). But there are extensive areas, chiefly in the central and southern parts, where the density rises to 400 to 600 per sq km (1040 to 1560 per sq mi), with very restricted spots of over 600. A somewhat isolated node of dense population, belonging equally to the Yangtze and Huang clusters, is that of the Han Basin, drained by the Han River, a tributary of the Yangtze. It appears as a southwestern extension of the Huang, or North-China Plain population cluster. In general, the less-well-drained northern parts of the Huang lowland support somewhat below-average densities; there are isolated areas of some magnitude where they drop below 200 per sq km. Particularly conspicuous are the lower densities along the seaward margins of the great plain, both to the north and south of Shantung peninsula. Here the amphibious character of the coastal terrain makes agricultural occupance difficult, and coastal urban settlements are nearly lacking. This situation is in contrast with that in hilly Shantung peninsula, where population, both rural and urban, is concentrated along the littoral. Smaller areas of relatively low density on the Huang Plain, most of them not evident on a small-scale population map, are coincident with inferior local agricultural environments, mainly in the form either of poorly drained spots or of sandy, droughty soils. The latter are probably remnants of beach ridges and dunes that existed along earlier coast lines, or are relics of old stream courses. Along most of its southern margins the Huang cluster of high-population density is separated from another concentration of high density coincident with the Yangtze lowlands by the hill lands of Tapieh Shan. Close to the sea the hills fade out, and the high densities of the Huang Plain merge with those of the Yangtze delta.

The population concentration on the delta and floodplain of the Yangtze and its main tributaries in South China is far less compact than that on the Huang Plain (Fig. 10.7). Although in area the Yangtze lowland is only about 75,000 sq mi, its total population may number 110 million or even more. Its overall density of around 1500 per sq mi is higher than that for any other extensive region of China, a fact that signifies unusual crowding. On the Bruk map of population density, it may be observed that the Yangtze delta shows the largest area in China with a rural density of over 600 persons per sq km. Three principal subsidiary regions of high density lead off to the south from the Yangtze's populous east-west belt, a larger one coincident with the tributary basin of the Hsiang and the smaller ones following the valleys of the Kan and Fu rivers. In these, densities of 200–400 per sq km are characteristic.

Still a third huge cluster of high density and one that is well isolated from the others is the one coincident with the Szechwan Basin (Red Basin) of deeply interior Szechwan Province (Fig. 10.7). Although traversed by the Yangtze and its tributaries, the Szechwan Basin, together with its population node, is separated from the Yangtze lowland and its population belt by intervening highlands that are crossed by the main stream in a deep gorge. It is estimated that in 1957 there lived within the Szechwan Basin (whose area is about 75,000 sq mi) some 66 million people, or nearly one third of the total population of the United States. The overall density was close to 880 per sq mi, or 340 per sq km. It must be appreciably higher at present. As noted earlier, the Szechwan

Basin is one of the few populous areas in China that are not coincident with a lowland plain. Probably not more than 5 percent of its area can be classed as even moderately level. Surrounded on all sides by mountains, the basin's typical topography is one of hill land, characterized by several hundred, and in parts over 1000 feet of local relief. Most of the basin is underlain by lime-enriched soft sandstones and shales that weather into relatively fertile residual soils. Nowhere else in China are artificially terraced tilled fields so widespread as in the Szechwan Basin. The most extensive plain within the Basin, the Cheng-tu, located in the northwestern part, is composed of the alluvial deposits of the Min River. There population densities rise to over 600 per sq km.

Smaller high-density clots of population are to be noted along the southeast coast, where each cluster is coincident with an expanded area of level alluvial land in the form of delta-floodplain deposits of a number of streams of modest size. Much the largest of these is the delta of the Si, or West, River, which supports the metropolis of Canton. The smaller, but still important, cities of Swatow, Amoy, Foochow, and Wenchow are the local metropolises of the other populous small deltas.

Although rivaling the North-China Plain in extensiveness, the Manchurian Plain, including adjacent hill lands on its southeastern margins, supports a population cluster whose numbers and density are of a lower order than those coincident with the alluvial deposits of the Huang (Fig. 10.7). Unlike the other principal plains of China, this one is structural rather than depositional in origin. Nevertheless, its grassland soils, mainly residual, are unusually fertile. In 1957 the three provinces comprising Northeast China, the Western name for which is Manchuria, had an estimated population of 50–55 million. But this figure, of course, was for a political region whose area is more than double that of the Manchurian Plain, which is its nuclear area. Moreover, the proportion of the Northeast's population that was included within the plain and its marginal hill lands is hard to determine, but it certainly must have been over one half, and 30–40 million inhabitants would seem likely. A reasonable assumption for the overall density of the plain, then, might be 200–300 per sq mi, or, as a conjecture, one fifth to one fourth that of the North-China Plain.

The average lower density of the Manchurian Plain reflects in part the modest and variable rainfall, especially in its western parts, and a discouragingly short growing season toward the north. In part, also, it is the result of a much later agricultural settlement. During none of the pre-Manchu dynasties had the rulers of China been able to establish their sedentary-village type of agriculture in Manchuria except in the southernmost parts. Even during early Manchu rule, which began in

1644, most of Manchuria beyond its southern littoral continued to be maintained as the domain of herders and hunters, and it was not until 1744 that the restrictions on voluntary Chinese immigration into Manchuria were relaxed. Even then it was the severe famines in north China that provided the main stimulus for an exodus to Manchuria. But after 1875 actual government encouragement in the form of land grants, subsidies, and exemption from taxation was given to Chinese immigrants.

It is noteworthy that the area of highest density in Manchuria is a north-south belt that coincides with the more humid eastern margins of the plain and spreads shallowly into the adjacent hill lands, where variable amounts of tillable lowland are present. In these same marginal hill lands important deposits of coal and iron ore have attracted population elements associated with mining and industry. And in order to effectively serve the agricultural, mineral, and industrial enterprises of the meridional population belt, the main north-south trunk rail line was built to coincide with the productive eastern margins of the plain; this in turn has further concentrated population within the earlier main settlement zone. Bruk's map of rural population density shows a fairly narrow belt with densities between 100 and 200 per sq km that extends from southernmost Liaotung peninsula northward to well beyond Haerhpin (Harbin). There are a number of areas within the belt where rural densities rise to 200–400 per sq km.

Throughout the hill lands and uplands of China, overall population densities are much lower than on the lowland plains. Thus, in the extensive hill lands of south China, south of the Yangtze, rural densities usually average only 10 to 100 persons per sq km. But in spite of relatively low arithmetic densities, the number of people per unit area of cultivated land (nutritional density) in this hilly region is exceedingly high. While it is not readily observable on a density map, a dot map reveals an intricate dendritic pattern of settlement throughout hilly south China, with the agricultural population highly localized in the river valleys.

In the relatively dry loess-mantled upland regions of Shansi, Shensi, and eastern Kansu, situated westward from the North-China Plain, overall population densities are also only low to moderate. Still, there are notable exceptions. Most conspicuous are the several linear concentrations of dense settlement in some of the larger river valleys, especially those of the Fen and Wei, but also of the Ching and Lo rivers (all tributaries of the Huang), where water for irrigation is available. Much less striking is any dense riverine type of settlement along the primate stream, or Huang, as it negotiates its remarkable northward loop around the barren Ordos Desert. Only along two segments of its course are there striking settlement concentrations, one near Lanchow, in eastern Kansu, and the other in the vicinity of Yinch-uan in Ninghsia. In its 400-mi southerly course along the east side of Ordos, the Huang flows in a gorge where little use can be made of its water for irrigation purposes.

Throughout the immense, dry, western region of interior China including Inner Mongolia, parts of Kansu-Ninghsia, Tsinghai, Sinkiang, and Tibet, the 30–35 million inhabitants are highly concentrated with respect to water supplies, which are mainly piedmont oases.

From the head of the Wei Valley in eastern Kansu Province, a conspicuous linear concentration of population thrusts westward into the genuinely dry area for nearly 500 mi (Fig. 10.7). This narrow zone of settlement follows the ancient Kansu Corridor route of military and commercial fame lying along the northern base of the high Nan Shan Range. From these snow-covered mountains is derived a year-round water supply that supports an important oasis agriculture whose centers of development coincide with the piedmont alluvial fans. The city of Lanchou is situated at the eastern end of the corridor, and Yümen at its western extremity. A westward extension of the Great Wall guarded this highly important route and the piedmont settlements along its northern margins.

A second belt of linear settlement, and the most northern one, follows a string of piedmont oases along the southern margins of the Dzungarian Basin at the base of the Tien Shan Mountains (Fig. 10.7). This conspicuous nodular strip of population runs all the way from the Soviet border to the western end of the Kansu Corridor. A third linear band of settlement reaches eastward from the Soviet border and joins the second one just below the western margin of Mongolia (Fig. 10.7). It is coincident with oases concentrated in a belt along the northern rim of the arid Tarim Basin, which are supplied with water from the numerous intermittent streams descending the southern flanks of the Tien Shan. A fourth belt of piedmont oases and settlement follows the southern margins of the western Tarim Basin, but it gradually fades in the eastern Tarim. Here the water supply is from the northern flanks of the Tibetan highlands. Far to the south in southern Tibet still another linear zone of population occupies mainly the valley of the Brahmaputra River.

TAIWAN

Taiwan is particularly noteworthy in terms of population because it is one of the few LD countries in which within the last decade, a well-documented fertility decline has occurred.[52] It may be one of the first

---

[52] Ronald Freedman and Joanna Muller, "The Continuing Fertility Decline in Taiwan: 1965," *Population Index*, Vol. 33, No. 1, 1967, pp. 3–17.

high-fertility traditional societies to experience a fall in its birth rate to moderate, or possibly even low, levels since the Pacific War. The current fertility decline began in 1957. From 1959 to 1965 there was a slump of 22 percent in the crude birth rate and 20 percent in the total fertility rate. The average birth rate, which was 44.9 per 1000 in 1955, was down to 36.2 in 1963, probably 32.5 by 1967, and an estimated 29 in 1970. The fall in fertility has been most pronounced and consistent among women 30 years of age and over.

Significantly, the drop in average fertility noted above is evident throughout the entire island; it is not restricted to a few of the larger cities or more important regions. To be sure, the late trend toward lower fertility appears to have started in the cities, but very recently it is the rural townships that have shown the greatest declines. It seems likely that the current downward trend in births will continue at the present rate, or even accelerate, during the next few years.[53]

Taiwan's estimated total population as of 1970 was 14 million. With the unusually low death rate of about 6 per 1000, even the declining fertility rates have permitted large natural increases, at the present time about 2.3 percent per year. Such a rate allows a doubling of the population in 26 years. Life expectancy at birth, now 65–70 years, is unusually high for a traditional society; in fact, it is not much below those of Europe and Anglo-America. The infant mortality rate of 22.2 per 1000 live births is very similar to that in the United States and Canada.

Other characteristics of Taiwan's population also reflect a country in the process of modernization. Its age structure points to a predominance of the young; 44 percent of its people are under 15 years of age. Illiteracy has been reduced to 35–40 percent, a figure well below the average for traditional societies in general and resembling more the situation in Latin America than in Asia. Only slightly more than half of the labor force is engaged in primary industry, mainly agriculture. Again, this figure is low for the LD realm and is low indeed for Asia. As in many other LD countries with a high population density and an overcrowded countryside, there has been a steady migration from the farms to the cities to seek work in factories and other urban occupations. As late as 1920 Taiwan is estimated to have had only 7 percent of its population living in places with 20,000 or more inhabitants. The figure had risen to 21 percent by 1940 and 29 percent by 1960. This is to be compared with only 13–14 percent for mainland China. There were 58 percent in Taiwan's urban places as nationally defined.[54] As elsewhere, this large-

[53] Freedman and Muller, "The Continuing Fertility Decline," p. 11.
[54] *Urban and Rural Population Growth, 1920–1960, With Projections*, United Nations, Population Division, Working Paper No. 15, September 1967, pp. 118, 123.

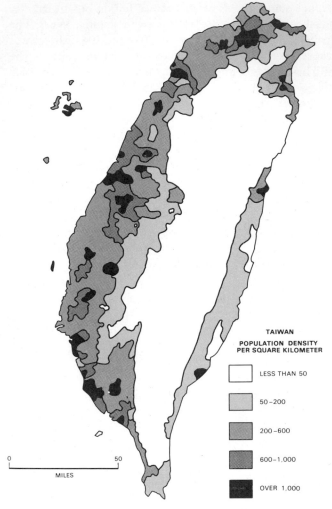

TAIWAN

POPULATION DENSITY
PER SQUARE KILOMETER

LESS THAN 50

50-200

200-600

600-1,000

OVER 1,000

Fig. 10.8. Taiwan—density of population. Simplified after map in National Atlas of China.

scale trek to the cities has created serious social and economic problems. Average per capita national income in Taiwan is estimated to be about $250, a relatively high figure for a LD country and more than double that of mainland China or India.

The current overall population density exceeds 1000 per sq mi, one of the highest national densities of the earth, greatly exceeding that of Japan and even that of the industrialized and urbanized Netherlands.

Such a high density is all the more remarkable in view of the fact that so much of the island's area is hilly and mountainous.

Spatial distribution of population is strongly influenced by the arrangement of mountains, hills, and lowlands. Five longitudinal geomorphic subdivisions are conspicuous. Dominating is a folded mountain axis that extends the whole length of the island. This is flanked on the west by a belt of hill land and it in turn by an alluvial coastal plain. On the east the central mountain belt reaches down to the sea on the north and south, but in its midsection it is flanked by the narrow Taitung Rift Valley, which in turn is bordered by the high and rugged coastal Taitung Ranges. Settlement is strongly oriented toward the west side, where it is remarkably concentrated on the coastal plain and in four separate basins—Tapei and Ilan in the north, Taichung in the midsection, and Pitung in the south (Fig. 10.8). The belt of hill country inland from the western plain, while well-peopled, does not experience a crowding equal to that of the coastal lowland. The highest rural densities are in those lowland parts benefiting from particularly efficient irrigation systems, which in turn permit unusually intensive cropping. On about 60 percent of the island's cultivated area, more than one crop is harvested annually. Within the interior highlands settlement is sparse, and the same is true of the eastern versant except in the Ilan Basin in the extreme northeast, which was mentioned earlier, and within a narrow elongated belt coinciding with the Taitung Rift Valley.

KOREA (South and North)

With its estimated 46 million inhabitants in 1970 and an average population density of nearly 550 per sq mi (212 per sq km), the Korean peninsula is in accord with the rest of humid East Asia in its degree of human crowding. But in a region that is so predominantly agricultural, simple arithmetic density scarcely reflects the intensity of real crowding. Here, where more than four fifths of the total area is so high or so rugged as to discourage tillage, the human congestion may reach 2500 per sq mi (1000 per sq km) of cultivated land.

The Koreans are a Mongoloid people, characterized by ethnic homogeneity and a common and ancient culture. International rivalries leading to a disastrous war have resulted in an unfortunate division of this homogeneous people and their country into a north and a south, between which at present there exists bitter hostility. Korean population was relatively stable until after the Japanese occupation beginning in 1910. Subsequently the growth rate soared as mortality rates were brought down, until at present they are estimated at only 11 per 1000. It is this lowered mortality, plus the continuing high fertility (estimated 39 per 1000 in the north; 36 in the South) that results in a high natural growth rate of 2.5–2.8 percent per year. Such a rate requires only a quarter of a century for the population to double.

Korea's pattern of settlement distribution resembles that of the Far East of which it is a part, since density variations in both reflect mainly the differential productivity of the land for agriculture. Therefore, population is highly concentrated on the plains of new alluvium, where soils are relatively fertile and water is available for irrigating the main crop, paddy rice. People crowd the best lands where the most food can be produced per unit of area. Population maps for the whole peninsula bear out this generalization, since there is a strong contrast between overcrowded southern and western Korea where terrain is more subdued, alluvial plains more abundant, and climate milder, and the less closely settled north and east where lowlands are fewer, the terrain more rugged, and the climate more severe.[55] However, the details of the spatial distribution of settlement are exceedingly complex, since the country cannot be readily broken down into a few main population regions. Instead there are almost innumerable small valleys, basins, and highland ranges, causing a bewilderingly complex arrangement of rural settlement. Still, a few main groupings can be distinguished. Most important is the series of population clusters located on, or close to, the littoral—on deltas, coastal plains, the broad lower ends of valleys, and the myriads of islands bordering the coast. This type is best represented along the southwest coast, where there is an almost continuous zone of dense settlement, but it is notable along the northwest and south coasts as well (Fig. 10.9). Narrowing bands of close settlement penetrate inland following major valleys. Along the mountainous east coast, settlement clusters are usually small and widely spaced.

A second but less important class of population concentration includes those that coincide with the few interior river basins. Most significant of these by far is the one within the north-south Naktong Basin in the southeast, but there are also some half a dozen others. Along the northern frontier there are lesser concentrations within the Yalu and Tumen valleys.

Most of the remaining population is scattered among the innumerable small valleys and basins of the hilly interior. But even in the most forbidding mountainous parts, nearly every patch of potentially arable land

[55] Glenn T. Trewartha and Wilbur Zelinsky, "Population Distribution and Change in Korea 1925–1949," *Geographical Review*, Vol. 45, 1955, pp. 5–7.

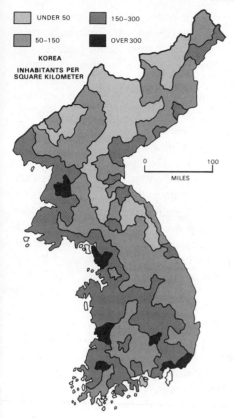

UNDER 50		150–300	
50–150		OVER 300	

KOREA
INHABITANTS PER
SQUARE KILOMETER

0   100
MILES

Fig. 10.9. Korea–density of population. *After Standard Atlas of Korea and Focus* (American Geographical Society), December 1961.

has been reclaimed; even the sparsely occupied minor political subdivisions have overall densities of 50–150 per sq mi. The least-populous tracts are most numerous and largest in the north and northeast and also along the peninsula's main spine of highland that lies just behind the eastern littoral.

The Korean War of the early 1950's resulted not only in a division of the peninsula into the two states of North Korea and South Korea but also in great dislocations of population. While no reliable records on population movements between north and south during the war years are available, official estimates indicate that South Korea probably experienced a net gain of about one million people in the exchange; but several thousand persons also went north. At least one million males and 800,000 females are believed to have lost their lives during the tragic war.

Of the two Korean states South Korea is somewhat smaller in area but much more populous. North Korea's estimated 13.9 million people result in an average arithmetic density of only 294 per sq mi; South Korea's 32.1 million produce an overall density of 845, or nearly three times that of the north and even somewhat higher than Japan's.

Only for South Korea are estimates available for a number of population characteristics. Adult illiteracy still remains high (55–60 percent). Per capita annual national income is only about $160, which is below the Asian average. The country is still predominantly rural, with 67–68 percent of the total population being so classed in 1965. Sixty-seven percent of the employed persons are engaged in primary industry, which means essentially agriculture. Significantly, this percentage has been waning over the past few decades—82.9 percent in 1949, 79.5 percent in 1955, 72.8 percent in 1963, and 67.4 percent in 1965. Only 9.2 percent of the laboring population was employed in secondary industry in 1965.[56] Conversely, as the rural and agricultural populations have declined relatively, so has the urban sector risen. A United Nations estimate indicates that 29 percent of South Korea's population resided in places of 20,000 or more inhabitants in 1960. A Korean source provides the figure 32.3 percent for 1965, with no definition of urban stated.[57] This is a relatively high figure for a traditional society. Both the rapid urbanization that has occurred in recent decades and the fairly high proportion of the population that is now urban, reflect several features of South Korea's recent history. One such is Japan's industrialization program for the country during the 1930's and early 1940's, a feature that attracted considerable numbers to the cities from rural areas. Urban growth was also stimulated by the repatriation, after the close of the Pacific War in 1945, of 1.2 million Koreans living in Japan and elsewhere, many of whom collected in the cities. War refugees seeking a haven in the cities had a similar effect in the 1950's.

REFERENCES

China

Aird, John S. "Population Growth and Distribution in Mainland China," in *An Economic Profile of Mainland China*. Studies prepared for the Joint Economic Committee, Congress of the United States, Vol. 2. U.S. Government Printing Office, Washington, D.C., 1967, pp. 341–401.

Aird, John S. *The Size, Composition and Growth of the Population of Main-*

---

[56] "Population Distribution and Internal Migration in Korea," Bureau of Statistics, Economic Planning Board, Seoul, Korea, 1966, pp. 43 and 53.

[57] "Population Distribution and Internal Migration," p. 43.

land China. U.S. Bureau of the Census, International Population Statistics Reports, Series P-90, No. 15. U.S. Government Printing Office, Washington, D.C., 1961.

Aird, John S. "The Present and Prospective Population of Mainland China," in *Population Trends in Eastern Europe, the USSR and Mainland China*, Milbank Memorial Fund, New York, 1960, pp. 93–133.

Bishop, C. W. "The Rise of Civilization in China with Reference to Its Geographical Aspects," *Geographical Review*, Vol. 22, 1932, pp. 617–631.

Chandrasekhar, Sripati. "Communist China's Demographic Dilemma," in S. Chandrasekhar (ed.), *Asia's Population Problems*, Praeger, New York, 1967, pp. 48–71.

Chang, Sen-dou. "The Distribution and Occupations of Overseas Chinese," *Geog. Rev.*, Vol. 58, 1968, pp. 89–107.

Chang, Sen-dou. "The Historical Trends of Chinese Urbanization," *Annals of the Association of American Geographers*, Vol. LIII, 1963, pp. 109–143.

Chang, Sen-dou. "Some Aspects of the Urban Geography of the Chinese Hsien Capital," *Annals of the Association of American Geographers*, Vol. 51, 1961, pp. 23–45.

Durand, John D. "The Population Statistics of China, A.D. 2–1953," *Population Studies*, Vol. 13, 1960, pp. 209–256.

Gourou, Pierre. "The Development of Upland Areas in China," in *The Development of Upland Areas in The Far East*. Vol. I. International Secretariat, Institute of Pacific Relations, New York, 1949, Part I, pp. 1–24.

Ho, Ping-ti. *Studies on the Population of China, 1368–1953*. Harvard East Asian Studies, No. 4. Harvard University Press, Cambridge, Mass., 1959.

Hung, Fu. "The Population of China and Present Means of Subsistence," in *Proceedings of IGU Regional Conference in Japan, 1957*, Tokyo, 1959, pp. 332–340.

Krader, Lawrence and John S. Aird. "What Do We Know About the Population of Mainland China?" Paper read at the Population Association of America Meeting, Chicago, May 3, 1958.

Murphey, Rhoads. "The Population of China: An Historical and Contemporary Analysis," in Paul F. Griffin (ed.), *Geography of Population: a Teacher's Guide*, National Council for Geographic Education Yearbook 1970, pp. 117–134.

Ni, Ernest. *Distribution of the Urban and Rural Population of Mainland China: 1953 and 1958*. U.S. Bureau of the Census, International Population Reports, Series P-95, No. 56. U.S. Government Printing Office, Washington, D.C., October 1960.

Orleans, Leo A. "The Population of Communist China," in Ronald Freedman (ed.), *Population: The Vital Revolution*, Aldine Publishing Co., Chicago, 1964, pp. 227–239.

Orleans, Leo A. "Population Redistribution in Communist China," in *Population Trends in Eastern Europe, the USSR and Mainland China*, Milbank Memorial Fund, New York, 1960, pp. 141–150.

Orleans, Leo A. "The Recent Growth of China's Urban Population," *Geographical Review*, Vol. 49, 1959, pp. 43–57.

Orleans, Leo A. *The Volume of Migration in Relation to Land Reclamation in Communist China*. REMP Bulletin (Research Group for European Migration Problems), April-June, Vol. 6, No. 2, 1958.

Orleans, Leo A. "The 1953 Chinese Census in Perspective," *Journal of Asian Studies*, Vol. 16, No. 4, August 1957, pp. 565–573.

Orleans, Leo A. "Propheteering: the Population of Communist China," *Current Scene*, Vol. 7, December 15, 1969, pp. 13–19.

Pan, Chia-lin and Irene B. Taeuber. "The Expansion of the Chinese: North and West," *Population Index*, Vol. 18, 1952, pp. 85–107.

Pritchard, Earl H. "Thoughts on the Historical Development of the Population of China," *Journal of Asian Studies*, Vol. 23, November 1963, pp. 3–20.

Roxby, Percy Maude. "The Terrain of Early Chinese Civilisation," *Geography*, Vol. 23, 1938, pp. 225–236.

Roxby, Percy Maude. "China as an Entity: The Comparison with Europe," *Geography*, Vol. 19, 1934, pp. 1–20.

Taeuber, Irene B., and Nai-chi Wang. "Questions on Population Growth in China," in *Population Trends in Eastern Europe, the USSR and Mainland China*, Milbank Memorial Fund, New York, 1960, pp. 263–301.

Taeuber, Irene B. "Manchuria as a Demographic Frontier," *Population Index*, Vol. 11, 1945, pp. 260–274.

Trewartha, Glenn T. "New Maps of China's Population," *Geographical Review*, Vol. 47, 1957, pp. 234–239.

Ullman, Morris B. *Cities of Mainland China: 1953 and 1958*. U.S. Bureau of the Census, International Population Reports, Series P-95, No. 59, U.S. Government Printing Office, Washington, D.C., August, 1961.

Wynne, Waller. *The Population of Manchuria*. U.S. Bureau of the Census, International Population Reports, Series P-90, No. 7. U.S. Government Printing Office, Washington, D.C., 1958.

Taiwan

Chen, Cheng-Siang. "Population Distribution and Change in Taiwan," in *Proceedings of the IGU Regional Conference in Japan, 1957*, Tokyo, 1959, pp. 290–295.

Freedman, Ronald, and Joanna Muller. "The Continuing Fertility Decline in Taiwan: 1965," *Population Index*, Vol. 33, 1967, pp. 3–17.

Hsu, Mei-Ling. "Taiwan Population Distribution, 1965," Map Supplement No. 11, *Annals of the Association of American Geographers*, Vol. 59, No. 3, September 1969.

Petersen, William. "Taiwan's Population Problem," in S. Chandrasekhar (ed.), *Asia's Population Problems*, Praeger, New York, 1967, pp. 189–210.

Korea

Cho, Lee-Jay, and Hahm, Man Jun. "Recent Change in Fertility Rates of the Korean Population," *Demography*, Vol. 5, No. 2, 1968, pp. 690–698.

Haller, Joanne E. *Population Trends and Economic Development in the Far East.* George Washington University, Washington, D.C., 1965, pp. 28–38.

Kim, Moon-Mo. "The Outline of Population Trends for Korea, 1945–1964," *Journal of Population Studies* (Seoul), No. 1, 1965, pp. 72–98. In Korean; English summary, end pages, 18–20.

Kwon, E-Hycock, and Kim, Tae-Ryong. "The Population of Korea," *Journal of Population Studies* (Seoul), No. 7, 1968, (Korean summary), pp. 113–383.

Lee, Chun Myun. "Recent Population Patterns and Trends in the Republic of Korea." Doctoral dissertation, University of Michigan, Ann Arbor, 1960.

McCune, Shannon. "The Korean Population Pattern," in *Korea's Heritage: A Regional and Social Geography*, Charles E. Tuttle Co., Rutland, Vermont, 1956, pp. 56–66.

Population Distribution and Internal Migration in Korea. Bureau of Statistics, Economic Planning Board, Seoul, Korea, 1966, 133 pp., plus tabular index.

"Population Increase in Korea: Its Possible Solution (A Symposium)," *Korean Affairs*, Vol. 3, July 1964, pp. 179–226.

Taeuber, Irene B. and George Barclay. "Korea and the Koreans in the Northeast Asian Region," *Population Index*, Vol. 16, 1950, pp. 278–297.

Trewartha, Glenn T., and Wilbur Zelinsky. "Population Distribution and Change in Korea, 1925–1949," *Geographical Review*, Vol. 45, No. 1, January 1955, pp. 1–26.

Zaichikov, V. T. "Population," in *Geography of Korea*, International Secretariat Institute of Pacific Relations, New York, 1952, pp. 35–53.

CHAPTER

11

Southeast Asia

Southeast Asia (a new regional name coined during the Pacific War) refers to the extensive peninsular and insular region that occupies the space between China on the north, the Indian subcontinent on the west, and Australia on the southeast. Its land area of some 1.73 million sq mi (including West New Guinea) is about 55 percent of the size of the conterminous United States. But because of its great fragmentation, it is spread over a far more extensive area, if the intervening seas are included.

Southeast Asia is a shatter zone of almost unparalleled diversity. This variety exists both in physical qualities, especially terrain, and in cultural attributes as well, including ethnic types, languages, religions, stages of economic development, and ranges of population density. It is no wonder that until recently Southeast Asia lacked a regional name. But in spite of important differences there is a basic underlying similarity in culture (as evidenced in the folklore, traditional architecture, sociopolitical organization, and methods of cultivation) and in the physical characteristics of the native population. The people have predominantly Mongoloid facial features, yellow-brown skin color, short stature and slender build.

The fact that the region has operated as both a bridge and a barrier to the movement of peoples and their cultures is mainly responsible for the present diversity of population attributes. In prehistoric times, before the Pleistocene land surface was partially submerged and made into an archipelago, there was an unbroken land route for migrants between Asia and Australia. And even after the foundering of the land bridge, there still remained numerous island stepping stones. Thus Southeast Asia has been aptly likened to a huge funnel whose flared northern end received successive trickles of humanity from mainland East and South Asia, which subsequently filtered southward as constrained by the grain of the meridional mountain ranges. These long-continued, small, separate migrations left their imprint in the form of the unusual variety of ethnic, linguistic, and religious differences mentioned earlier (Figs. 11.1, 11.2).

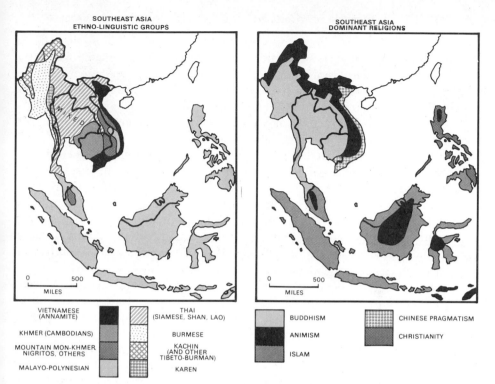

SOUTHEAST ASIA
ETHNO-LINGUISTIC GROUPS

SOUTHEAST ASIA
DOMINANT RELIGIONS

VIETNAMESE (ANNAMITE)	THAI (SIAMESE, SHAN, LAO)
KHMER (CAMBODIANS)	BURMESE
MOUNTAIN MON-KHMER NIGRITOS, OTHERS	KACHIN (AND OTHER TIBETO-BURMAN)
MALAYO-POLYNESIAN	KAREN

BUDDHISM	CHINESE PRAGMATISM
ANIMISM	CHRISTIANITY
ISLAM	

Fig. 11.1. Ethnolinguistic groups in Southeast Asia. Modified after maps by Le Bar, Hickey and Musgrave, and C. A. Fisher.

Fig. 11.2. Dominant religions of indigenous peoples. Modified after maps by C. A. Fisher, Joseph E. Spencer, and others.

Formidable highland barriers on the north made entry of migrants from China and India into mainland Southeast Asia difficult, a feature that reduced the magnitude but not the variety of the overland human migration into that region.[1] This southward drift of peoples through the mainland corridors was in the nature of successive spillovers from the vast ancient accumulations of humanity in the China-India sectors, which continued down to historic times. Many of the migrant groups became isolated within the complex mountain terrain, in whose basins and valleys they tended to perpetuate their original differences or to evolve along specialized lines.

During historic times the mountainous peninsula of Southeast Asia, plus Tibet, has functioned mainly as a barrier separating the populous lands of China and India, since the land routes, which were obliged to cut across the grain of the intervening mountain corrugations, were discouragingly difficult ones. Hence the long southern sea route around

[1] Charles A. Fisher, *South-east Asia: A Social, Economic and Political Geography*, Methuen and Co., London, 1964, p. 63. Grateful acknowledgement is made of the wide-ranging use to which this source has been put in preparing the chapter on Southeast Asia.

the Asiatic land barrier, by way of the Malacca and Sunda Straits, offered distinct advantages. Historically, Southeast Asia became a zone where the frontiers of Indian and Chinese cultures met, and as a consequence of sea routes, a crossroads between the Asiatic Far East and the European West.

Two main strata are represented in the native population. First there is an earlier primitive, and now small, component composed of Negrito and Australoid strains, at present chiefly confined to the highlands. A second and somewhat later stratum, now dominant almost everywhere, was originally made up of the ancestors of the present Burmese, Siamese, and Indochinese. These people occupy mainly the coastal and riverine lowlands. Two sublayers are recognized, an Indian strain that came by way of Assam and Burma and a Mongoloid one from what is now southern China. Centuries of later migrations involving Arabs, Indians, Chinese, and Europeans have further complicated the cultural and racial mixture.

For the first 1500 years of the Christian era, the total number of aliens in Southeast Asia was probably small. Still it was the aliens, mainly Indians and Chinese, who furnished the stimuli for most of the achievements that occurred during this premodern period. These were chiefly in the realms of writing systems, religion, and political organization. Southeast Asia resembled a frontier zone that was in the process of being penetrated by the more advanced cultures of the two ancient civilizations, Indian and Chinese. The parts affected were chiefly coastal. Indian influence, while more widespread, was also more dilute. Chinese influence was largely confined to Indochina east of the Annam highlands or what is now the Vietnams.

The large-scale immigration during the last 150 years, instigated by economic developments fostered by Europeans, has resulted in an addition of some 10 million Chinese, perhaps 1.5–2.0 million Indians, and much smaller numbers of Occidentals. Most of the latter are not permanent residents. The result is a pluralistic type of society with all of the problems that may derive from such ethnic, linguistic, and religious variety. It is especially in the cities, to which these new immigrants have been mainly attracted, that the frictions associated with pluralism are most noticeable. As a rule, the natives have been at the bottom of the economic ladder and are resentful of the more prosperous and economically powerful alien groups.

THE PRE-EUROPEAN PERIOD

Little can be conjectured about the magnitude and spatial distribution of population in Southeast Asia during the first millennium and a half of the Christian era. Fisher sees no reason for assuming that numbers were larger in ancient and medieval times than they were in the early 19th century when European control first began to have marked effects. Continuous political instability argues against an important growth. The changes that did occur were usually the result of movements of new people into Southeast Asia. But terrain must have strongly influenced human distribution through its effects on the evolution of states and their boundaries. Thus, it was mainly in the valleys of the great rivers and on the fertile and accessible coastal lowlands that the core areas of the more powerful states emerged, since the lowlands permitted a greater density of population as well as ease of communication, both of which fostered regional trade.[2]

It can probably be assumed, then, that in the early centuries of the Christian era the relatively modest total population of Southeast Asia was centered in the stronger states whose core areas coincided with coastal and riverine lowlands. One such center was the Red River delta in northeastern Indochina. It represented a southward extension of Chinese influence. Others were coincident with the core areas of a number of Indianized states, situated in the deltas of the Menam, Mekong, and Irrawaddy Rivers and in the Kra Isthmus, all of which benefited by location on the coastal sea route between India and China. By the 9th century a new Burman kingdom was centered in the dry zone of the middle Irrawaddy (or Mandalay) Basin. Outside mainland Southeast Asia, in the archipelago to the south, population nodes mainly coincided with small Indianized coastal kingdoms concentrated along sea routes. Prominent among these was the one coincident with a fairly powerful state located in east-central Java, where the river basins were so exceptionally fertile that they were able to support relatively large and compact population clusters whose densities markedly exceeded those in the other islands.[3]

THE IMPACT OF THE WEST

While, during the first millennium and a half of the Christian era, it was Southeast Asia's general location astride the sea routes between India and China and the particularly favored lowland sites along these routes that determined the location of the major kingdoms and their population cores, after the 16th century differential rates of population growth within the region became increasingly bound up with the impact

[2] Fisher, *South-east Asia*, p. 102.
[3] Fisher, *South-east Asia*, p. 107.

of Western influence, mainly European. Yet although the first contacts were made in the late 15th century, it was not until the 19th, with the growing demand of the Occident for markets and raw materials, the invention of the steamship, and the opening of the Suez Canal, that the influence of the West on the economy, and so on population growth and redistribution, was strongly felt.

Population estimates, of somewhat questionable validity, are provided for most parts of Southeast Asia as of about 1830, through the writings of John Crawfurd and Hugh Murray.[4] Supplementing Crawfurd's more comprehensive estimates with those of Murray for Burma, we arrive at a total population of about 25.8 million for the whole Southeast Asia region. This was divided among the various parts as shown in Table 11.1.[5] It can be inferred that the main population concentrations of nearly a century and a half ago were in east and central Java, the Red River delta in northernmost coastal Annam, and the Mandalay Basin in Burma.

Circumstantial evidence suggests that the above estimates of population in Southeast Asia are not greatly in error. If such is the case, then there

[4] John Crawfurd, *Journal of an Embassy From the Governor-General of India to the Courts of Siam and Cochin-China*, Vol. 2, 2nd edition, Henry Colburn and Richard Bentley, London, 1830; Hugh Murray, *The Encyclopedia of Geography*, Vol. II, Carey, Lea and Blanchard, Philadelphia, 1837. E. H. G. Dobby in his book, *Southeast Asia*, p. 385, estimates the population of Southeast Asia to have been only about 10 million in 1800. For comparison, a "medium" estimate of China's population in 1800 is 323 million, and of India 195 million.

[5] See comprehensive tables in Fisher, *South-east Asia*, pp. 174–175.

TABLE 11.1   Population in Southeast Asia (c. 1830)

1834	Burma	4,000,000	
c. 1830	Thailand	2,730,000	(4,000,000+)
c. 1830	Indochina	5,194,000	
1826	Malaya	350,000	
c. 1830	Indonesia	11,000,000	
	(Java 6,000,000)		
	(Outer Islands 5,000,000)		
c. 1830	Philippines	2,500,000	
Total		25,774,000	

SOURCES: Crawfurd, Murray, and Fisher; Second Thailand figure from Sternstein, *Pacific Affairs*, Vol. 6, 1955, p. 17.

has been a remarkably rapid rate of growth over the last 140 years, amounting to an increase of nine times. It may well be that the greatest differentials in population numbers and densities between Southeast Asia on the one hand, and East and South Asia on the other, existed during the early 19th century. After that the impact of the West wrought great political, economic, and cultural changes in Southeast Asia, one of the most important of which was the initiating of the recent period of soaring population growth.

The usual assumption is that the accelerated growth resulted from a declining death rate in conjunction with continuing high fertility. The waning mortality may have been related to a variety of causes, one of which was the suppression of internecine warfare and the establishment of law and order by the Western colonial powers. The best evidence for the effectiveness of this factor is that the earliest rapid growth occurred in Java and the Philippines, where effective European control was widespread by the early part of the 19th century. Such control came to the other parts only 50 to 100 years later, but when it did arrive they too showed a spurt in population growth. A second factor was the creation of new economic opportunities for the native peoples by the Occidentals. This included not only the opening of new lands for subsistence farming but also the development of commercial agriculture, mining, and other means of employment. Cash crops and mining, together with a variety of urban functions, attracted a large influx of alien immigrants as laborers, which accentuated population growth. All of these new economies directly and indirectly reduced mortality stemming from malnutrition. And finally, in the 20th century, there occurred a widespread dissemination of Western hygiene, sanitation, and medicine, which drastically lowered the death date still further. As a consequence the rate of population increase soared even more rapidly.

But while a degree of Westernization had the effect of dramatically reducing mortality among native peoples, it resulted in no significant decline in fertility; the large-family system is still the traditional way of life. With birth rates between 40 and 50 per thousand—among the highest on earth—and an average death rate that may now be as low as 18–20, the recent annual rate of natural increase could be about 22–26 per 1000, or 2.2–2.6 percent per year. This would result in a doubling of population every 29 years.

As a consequence of the soaring growth rates over the past 50–150 years, the population map of Southeast Asia has been significantly altered from what it probably was in about 1830. One striking feature has been the flocking of large numbers of people to the great southern deltas of the mainland—Irrawaddy, Menam, and Mekong—as their lands have been progressively reclaimed for paddy rice. In addition, there has been a rapid filling in of settlement in Java and the northern and central Philippines. And finally, for a variety of reasons, an increasingly larger proportion of the population has concentrated in cities.

It is the alluvial lowlands and coastal margins that have been absorbing an ever-increasing proportion of the swelling population. Consequently, regional differentials in population density grow stronger and gradients steeper, thereby causing the population-density map of Southeast Asia to more and more resemble those of China, Japan, and India. A crowding of people on the best lands is the rule, with the result that there has evolved a sharply delineated pattern of discontinuous high-density clusters separated by relatively empty spaces representing the poorer or less accessible lands. It is estimated that more than six sevenths of Southeast Asia's people are concentrated on about one sixth of the total land area.[6] But in spite of a rapid recent growth of population, average densities on the great southern deltas of mainland Southeast Asia are still only one quarter to one half what they are on the new-alluvium plains of East and South Asia. It is mainly on the Red River, or Tonkin delta in North Vietnam, in large parts of Java, and on a few Philippine lowlands that the densities match those of China and India.

THE SOUTHEAST ASIA POPULATION ANOMALY

A salient fact concerning the population geography of Southeast Asia is that numbers are fewer and overall density distinctly less than in either East Asia or South Asia. As of 1970, Southeast Asia's population is estimated to have reached 287 million—no small number, to be sure, but still far less than East Asia's 930 million or the more than 700 million of South Asia. The regional differential in numbers is further emphasized by the contrasting population densities; that of Southeast Asia is only roughly one third that of China proper (excluding the western territories) or India, and one sixth that of Japan.

The population anomaly in Southeast Asia has its roots in the past. Indeed, the density differentials between China and India on the one hand and Southeast Asia on the other were probably far greater in the early 19th century and before than they are today, since the last 150 years have witnessed a catching-up process on the part of Southeast Asia as the *rate* of population growth there has outdistanced those of China and India, whose total populations are still far greater.

[6] Fisher, *South-east Asia*, p. 177.

If we may accept the contemporary estimates of John Crawfurd and Hugh Murray, Southeast Asia as of about 1830 had a population of only about 26 million, or 9 to 10 percent of what it is 140 years later. The best estimates indicate that China, India, and Japan may have roughly trebled their population numbers over the same period. The indication of such a phenomenally high rate of increase for Southeast Asia might lead us to question whether Crawfurd's figures for about 1830 are underestimates. That they may not be too far out of line is suggested by the count of 4.8 million inhabitants for Java-Madura by the Raffles census of 1815. This is quite in accord with the Crawfurd estimate of 6 million as of about 1830.

Two questions, then, present themselves for answers: (1) Why had Southeast Asia lagged so far behind East and South Asia in population numbers, density, and growth rates down to the early 19th century and (2) why has the population growth rate in Southeast Asia been so much more rapid than those of China and India over the last century or two?

In regard to the first question, Fisher is of the opinion that the primary reason why Southeast Asia was, as late as 1830 (and continuing to this day), far less crowded than the other parts of Monsoon Asia, is related to the difficulty of entry on the north. There high mountain barriers make the land approaches so difficult that Southeast Asia remained a backwater, far more remote and insulated than either China or India from the great centers of human dispersal in interior Asia. The highland barrier is most formidable, and the approaches most difficult, toward the west along the Burma frontier as the Tibetan-Himalayan system is approached. Altitude declines eastward. A seeming weakness of the above explanation is that in spite of the barrier on the north, archeological evidence strongly supports the theory that it was via the northern land route into Indochina that Southeast Asia was peopled. Indeed, it became a persistent human corridor for successive trickles of small groups of people shifting slowly southward along the meridonal valleys and interfluves and living off the land. A further perplexing feature is that a greater volume of prehistoric and historic land migration from the north into Southeast Asia was feasible by the much easier water-level Annam coastal route. Yet for some unknown reason that easier passageway appears to have been little used. The Red River delta in Tonkin, located at the northern end of the easy coastal route from the north into Indochina, is also the region of most ancient and stable paddy rice culture. Such could scarcely have developed along a route subject to frequent invasions.

Perhaps more important than terrain obstacles in accounting for the small (by Asian standards) population of Southeast Asia in the early

19th century was the prevalence there of political turmoil over long periods of time, a condition not conducive to an enduring paddy-rice culture with its associated dense population. It seems safe to accept as a premise the statement that "the density of settlement in the deltas is a function of the stability or antiquity of a stable rice culure."[7] According to this dictum, differentials in the antiquity and stability of the various rice cultures in Asia would go far toward explaining the regional differentials in population numbers and densities. Throughout antiquity there appears to have prevailed a striking contrast between the greater political and military stability of the extensive empires of China and India on the one hand and the turmoil characteristic of much more politically and culturally fragmented Southeast Asia on the other.[8] The latter region suffered from a rapid succession of kingdoms, some of them ministates and others of modest size. The smallness of the core regions of most Southeast Asian states operated against a durable stability. Large empires with strong central governments capable of maintaining law and order, like those of China and India, were absent. Most states in Southeast Asia were short-lived, and even those of greater durability suffered periods of rapid shrinkage and expansion of their territories. A succession of interstate wars and intrastate struggles prevailed, many of which involved violent displacements of the resident peoples by invaders, who in turn occupied the defeated group's lands. By contrast, although China and India were certainly far from being peaceful domains, still in both, the eras of tranquility were long enough for the farm population to become so deeply rooted that the invaders did not bodily displace the peasant cultivators. The tillers of the soil and their offspring were able to persist in spite of a change in masters and to maintain their paddy-rice agricultural system. But in Southeast Asia, the more frequent displacement, sometimes even extermination, demanded a repeated large-scale rebuilding of the whole agricultural structure.

Just what factors were responsible for the greater premodern political instability in Southeast Asia than in China and India is not so clear. It may be that in some regions isolation operated to increase stability. This is suggested by the antiquity of rice culture in an island empire like Japan. In mainland Asia, China is protected from easy invasion on its land side by vast barren lands of both high and dry varieties. The earth's mightiest mountain-plateau ramparts guard India on its northern flanks; the only important land approach is along the subcontinent's north-

[7] "French Indo-China: Demographic Imbalance and Colonial Policy," *Population Index*, Vol. 11, No. 2, April, 1945, p. 79.

[8] Wilbur Zelinsky, "The Indochinese Peninsula: A Demographic Anomaly," *The Far Eastern Quarterly*, Vol. 9, 1950, pp. 137–141.

western frontier, and even there an invader must traverse extensive high-lands and deserts. Still, it was by way of these northwestern routes that the great historic invasions of India did occur, and these were frequent enough to make the maintenance of prolonged stability no easy matter. But at any rate, the invasion of either China or India would be almost prohibitively difficult for any but large and well-organized groups supported by strong military contingents. Such was scarcely the type of land invasions experienced by mainland Southeast Asia; these characteristically took the form of dribbles of various small groups of human migrants filtering southward through mountain valleys. It might be argued, of course, that the fact that Red River delta of Tonkin is the region of most ancient stable rice culture in the mainland part and yet is located on the easiest entry route from the north, acts to weaken the hypothesis that isolation makes for stability. But, as noted earlier, evidence is weak that the Annam coastal route actually was an important corridor used by large numbers of migrants from the north.

Still another possible explanation for the modest size of the precolonial population of Southeast Asia has its roots in the cultural background of the area's immigrants. It is believed that the dominant ethnic groups seeping in from the north were backward hill peoples who were experienced in the techniques of rain-fed shifting agriculture but much less so in the cultivation of paddy rice. Most of the immigrants were probably unacquainted not only with wet-rice culture but even with any form of sedentary agriculture. To these more primitive cultivators the great southern deltas of the mainland with their fertile soils, periodic inundations, and requirements for large-scale engineering works for drainage, flood control, and irrigation, were far from being attractive lands for settlement. Consequently, at the time the Europeans arrived, the great deltas of the Irrawaddy, Menam, and Mekong were very sparsely settled; large parts of their surfaces were still forested wilderness. The lateness of the changeover from shifting-field and dry-crop tillage to sedentary paddy-rice cultivation could only retard population growth. Perhaps it is significant that the oldest large center of population concentration in Indochina (excluding the Tonkin delta) is in the subhumid Mandalay Basin of Burma, on whose broken surface only about 19 percent of the cropped area is irrigated, and that mainly planted to paddy rice. There dry crops predominate, not paddy.

REGIONS OF SOUTHEAST ASIA: THE MAINLAND

As a geographical entity, mainland Southeast Asia is the broad peninsula that includes the states of Burma, Thailand, and the former French colony

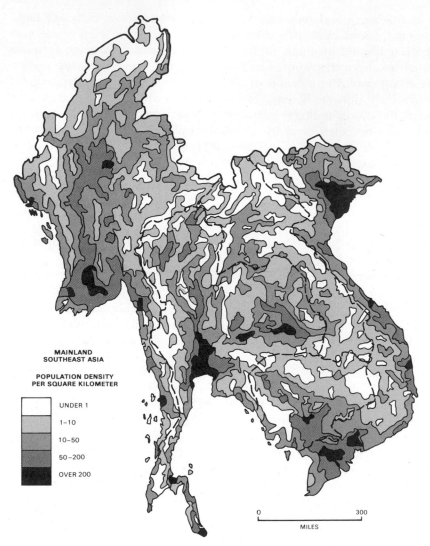

MAINLAND
SOUTHEAST ASIA

POPULATION DENSITY
PER SQUARE KILOMETER

UNDER 1

1–10

10–50

50–200

OVER 200

0   300
MILES

Fig. 11.3. Greatly simplified and otherwise modified from *Map of the Peoples of Indochina* (ethnic and density), scale, 1:5,000,000, Institute of Ethnography, Academy of Sciences, U.S.S.R., Moscow, 1959.

of Indochina. The latter is now divided into the four new states of Cambodia, Laos, North Vietnam, and South Vietnam. The whole embraces an area of close to 800,000 sq mi, and includes somewhat more than 100 million inhabitants. A preponderance of the population is concentrated in five great clusters (Fig. 11.3). Four of the five are coincident with coastal deltaic lowlands—the Irrawaddy of Burma, the Menam of Thailand, the Mekong divided between South Vietnam and Cambodia, and the Red River delta of North Vietnam. The fifth population cluster, located in the inland dry zone of central Burma, is not on a delta, although this Mandalay Basin does have a modest amount of alluvial plain. Thus, in population pattern, Thailand and North Vietnam are unimodal states and Burma is bimodal, while one population cluster, the Mekong, is bisected by an international boundary. Two of the population clusters, that of interior Burma and the one coincident with the Red River delta in North Vietnam, are relatively ancient and of long duration. That in the Mandalay Basin is the old heartland of the Burman state dating from early in the ninth century; the North Vietnam cluster antedates the Christian era. The three great southern deltas had really never been extensively settled and brought under cultivation until after the middle of the 19th century. Only the settlement cluster in North Vietnam has rural population densities that approach those of the Chinese and Indian deltas. All of the delta population clusters are supported by a monocultural wet-rice economy. That in the Mandalay Basin dry zone is the single exception.

Burma. Burma (262,000 sq mi; 27–28 million inhabitants; average density 100+ per sq mi), as noted earlier, is the only one of the mainland states characterized by a bimodal population concentration (Fig. 11.3). At present the center of gravity of the state, in population numbers as well as politically, is coincident with the Irrawaddy-Sittang delta and lowland where 50–60 percent of the people live. But such has not always been the case, since over the centuries the power center has oscillated between the old heartland in the interior dry zone and the "entrance zone" in the delta. The meridional lowland belt with its dual population nodes is surrounded on all except the sea side by sparsely populated, malaria-infested highlands.

As of about 1834, when Hugh Murray estimated the population of Burma to be around four million, the interior dry zone, the original nucleus of the Burmese state, was still by far the most highly organized and populous part of the kingdom. Although at that time Burman control already extended over the Irrawaddy delta, much the greater part of that lowland was unreclaimed wild forest land. At first it might seem that the interior dry zone, or Mandalay Basin, with its modest (generally under 40 in.) and variable rainfall, did not provide a particularly desirable environment for agricultural settlement. But there were offsetting factors. The forest cover was light and easily cleared. A broken terrain composed of undulating plains, low hills, and narrow alluvial lowlands provided a mixed environment suitable for a variety of crops. The narrow valleys offered considerable opportunity for irrigation, while the varied soils, most of them light, could be readily cultivated. Moreover, this was the first lowland encountered by the migrant Burmans coming from the north, and to them it must have appeared relatively attractive. It had the further advantage of being a natural focus of riverine routes, so that transport and communication were relatively easy.

To the Burman migrants, coming from the highlands to the north and bringing with them agricultural concepts based mainly on the cultivation of dry upland crops rather than of irrigated lowland rice, the variegated dry zone presented an environment that lay within their technological capacities. Accordingly, they developed a diversified subsistence agriculture, mainly based on unirrigated crops, but including some paddy rice in the irrigable valleys, or in areas where ponds could readily be constructed. Such a mixed agriculture, with emphasis on dry crops, prevails even today. Not only did the dry zone offer a more inviting environment than that provided by the highlands from which the migrants had come, but it also posed a less formidable task than that involved in subduing the great southern delta with its swamps, summer floods, and dense forests. However, the population-carrying capacity of the dry zone is not unusual, so that even by the latter half of the 19th century its population limit was being approached. After the country came under British control, population growth in the dry zone was slower than in the delta and along the Arakan and Tenasserim coastal margins.

At the time of British annexation (1824–1826), the great southern delta was largely a land of swamps and forest, and repellant to the Burmans as a potential settlement region. The English, eager to develop the country as a market for textiles, saw the need for a cash crop that would permit the native people to earn a money income. It was at this time that the unusual potentialities of the delta as a rich rice-exporting region were first clearly recognized. When the Civil War in the United States cut off Europe's supply of Carolina rice, and at about the same time the Suez Canal was cut, Britain turned to the Irrawaddy delta as the main source of her rice supply.

Active penetration of the delta began about the middle of the 19th century, but until approximately 1870 there is only meager reliable information relating to the progress of reclamation and settlement. Rice acreage in lower Burma expanded from 1.44 million acres in 1865 to

5 million by 1896 and 9.91 million in 1930.[9] Population in the delta likely soared accordingly. It is known that the mass migration southward of people drained from other parts of Burma was so great after the 1860's that, within the space of a few decades, the delta became the most densely populated region in all Burma. Significantly, the pioneering of the swampy rice lands of the Irrawaddy occurred at nearly the same time as the opening up of the world's subhumid wheat lands.

One principal problem in settling the delta was water control, because during July and August the flooding of the rivers, combined with the heavy local rainfall, placed such an excess of water on the land that injury to the rice crop resulted. It was only after 1860, when British engineers successfully raised a series of great embankments along the natural levees of the parent stream and its main distributaries, that rapid settlement of the delta began.[10] But except for the engineering work on the levee embankments, the local tasks associated with jungle clearing, reclamation, and the enclosure and diking of individual rice fields were done by the settlers themselves.

To attract settlers, the British authorities allotted as many as 15 acres free to each immigrant family. So it developed that rice culture in lower Burma came to differ in at least two respects from that in China and India—the crop was grown more extensively and it was raised for export. But while the delta soon became the most populous part of Burma, its densities remained far below those of the great rice-growing deltas of China and India, where farms were smaller and cultivation more intensive. Present population densities vary considerably within the Irrawaddy delta, being highest (250–500 per sq mi) in the upper, longer-settled parts, roughly within a triangle at whose apexes are Henzada, Bassein, and Rangoon. The rest of the delta and the Irrawaddy Basin north to Thabeikkyin have densities of only 125–250 per sq mi, and the same is true along the Arakan coast.

Burmans comprise roughly two thirds of the country's population. The remaining one third is made up of indigenous and foreign minority groups. Indians and Pakistanis may number as many as 800,000; some of them are low-wage laborers, while others are active in commerce and the professions. The Chinese minority, estimated at about 350,000, are chiefly miners, market gardeners, and small shopkeepers. But altogether the foreign element comprises only 4–5 percent of the total population.

The indigenous minority is much more numerous and presents more

[9] Dobby, *Southeast Asia*, p. 173.
[10] Fisher, *South-east Asia*, p. 437.

serious problems for the state. The Union of Burma is composed of six constituent units, Burma proper and five minority states. Each of the latter has its own council of state with local control over internal matters, and also representation in the upper house of the Union Parliament. Two of the largest minority groups, the Karens and the Shans, have proved difficult to accommodate within the Burma Union. As a useful generalization, Burmans are concentrated in the great central meridional lowland and along the Arakan and Tenasserim coasts; the native minorities occupy the surrounding hill lands.

Thailand. With only four fifths of Burma's area but 7–8 million more people (1970 estimate, 36.2 million), Thailand's average population density is two thirds again as great. The gross pattern of distribution is also somewhat different in the two countries, since Thailand has only one nuclear region of economic development and population concentration—the central plain (including the more restricted delta) drained by the Menam River (Fig. 11.3). There is no compact interior population cluster comparable to that in the Mandalay Basin in Burma. As early as 1350 the central plain, and especially the Menam delta, had already become firmly established as the single nuclear region of the kingdom, and so the pattern has remained. Crawfurd estimated Thailand's population in 1830 to be about 2.73 million, and Ingram judged it to have been some 5–6 million by 1850–1855.[11] Since then the numbers have multiplied five to six times. But although the Menam delta, even by the mid-1800's, had already become the most densely settled part of the country, the greater share of it was still uncultivated. Its tilled sections were at that time largely given over to subsistence paddy culture.

The great expansion of commercial rice growing in the Menam delta, including the attendant swelling of that region's population, occurred several decades later than it did in the Irrawaddy delta. No doubt this lag reflects the fact that colonial influence was much less in sovereign Siam. To be sure, the problem of flood control over extensive areas was less serious in the Menam than in the Irrawaddy delta, for rainfall is markedly less in the former (Bangkok 56 in., Rangoon 100 in). Still, the flooding problems were far from minor, while the rainfall deficiency compounded the difficulty of rice growing. The deficit was largely supplied by Menam flood waters.

It was the influx of Western manufactures that provided the stimulus for a large-scale expansion of rice growing in Thailand, as it did in Burma. From the 1870's to the 1930's the annual rice export multiplied

[11] Crawfurd, *Journal of an Embassy;* James C. Ingram, *Economic Change in Thailand Since 1850*, Stanford University Press, Stanford, California, 1955, p. 7.

TABLE 11.2 Thailand: Estimated Population Numbers and Density, and Proportion of the Total Population, by Regions, 1960

Region	Population (Thousands)	Density (Per Sq Km)	Percent of Total Population
Eastern (Korat) plateau	8781.0	55	33
Northern ranges	4462.7	26	17
Central plain (delta)			
1. Outer plain	3644.3	65	14
2. Inner plain	4286.2	348	16
Southeast upland and coastal plain	1421.4	42	5
Southern ranges	1500.8	29	6
Southern central plain	2161.5	70	8
Total	26,257.9	51	100

SOURCE: Larry Sternstein, "A Critique of Thai Population Data," *Pacific View Point*, Vol. 6, 1965, p. 23.

six or seven times, with three quarters of the total export originating in the Menam's alluvial lowlands. But for all the spurt in rice growing and in the number of rural inhabitants, the density of population per square mile of paddy in the Menam delta still remains less than one third what it is in the Tonkin delta of North Vietnam, with its intensive subsistence rice culture. The average population density for the delta, or central plain, is 250–300 per sq mi, which is by far the highest for any region of the country (see Table 11.2). Density on the inner plain is abnormally high because of the concentration there of a large urban population, including that of Bangkok, a city of over 1.3 million inhabitants.[12]

Besides the nuclear delta region, the only one of the outlying subdivisions supporting a major proportion of the population is the extensive Korat plateau, which is coincident with the great eastern bulge of the country. Korat includes about one third of the country's population, although its average density only slightly exceeds the national average. Essentially Korat is a low sandstone upland composed of flattish, poorly drained interfluves, with incised flat-bottomed valleys. Climatically Korat resembles the Burma dry zone, but in contrast to the dry zone it lacks

[12] Larry Sternstein, "A Critique of Thai Population Data," *Pacific Viewpoint*, Vol. 6, 1965, pp. 23, 27, 30.

a great river, its sandy upland soils are distinctly inferior, and irrigation water is less available. Rural living standards here are probably the lowest in the country. Only 7 percent of the area is under cultivation. The chief areas of rice culture are in the larger stream valleys, and it is from these floodplain paddy fields of Korat that 20–30 percent of the country's rice export is derived.

Compared with Burma, Thailand's indigenous population is ethnically somewhat more homogeneous. However, the alien Chinese minority, estimated at around three million, is the second largest in Southeast Asia, and the Thai government is apprehensive concerning the loyality of this group. Consequently, the political and economic activities of the Chinese have been restricted and new immigration has been limited.

Indochina. The geographical expression, "Indochina" (now the combined territories of the new states of North Vietnam, South Vietnam, Laos, and Cambodia), while somewhat obsolete, still has some validity, since it designates the area of a former French colony that continues to retain a veneer of French culture. But on the other hand, Indochina lacks indigenous homogeneity, since it lies astride the fundamental cultural boundary separating the Indianized lands of Cambodia and Laos to the west from the strongly Sinicized Annamite realm of the two Vietnams facing on the South China Sea.

Population numbers are somewhat uncertain, but the total is estimated to be about 49 million in 1970 (North Vietnam, 21.2 million; South Vietnam, 18.0 million; Cambodia, 7.1 million; and Laos, 3.0 million). There are two main clusters of population concentration, a northern one coincident with the Tonkin delta in North Vietnam and a southern one, bisected by the South Vietnam-Cambodia boundary, that focuses on the Mekong delta and the adjacent Tonle Sap-Mekong plains. Joining these two great population nodes is a narrow, discontinuous belt of high density that coincides with the narrow Annam coastal lowland (Fig. 11.3). While the total number of inhabitants on the northern and southern delta plains may not be greatly different, their densities are different, since the much smaller but more crowded Tonkin delta (5800 sq mi) is a strongly Sinicized region of ancient and stable rice culture. By contrast, extensive parts of the lower Mekong delta (14,000 sq mi) have been settled only during the present century.

The Tonkin lowland is a fertile region devoted to an intensive, subsistence wet-rice culture. This was the original core area of the old Annamite kingdom. During the millennium between 111 B.C. and 939 A.D. it was a part of Imperial China, during which period it was obliged to adopt the hydraulic culture of China, involving elaborate diking, irrigated wet-rice cultivation, and the use of green manure and animal and human excreta for fertilizer. Following the Chinese practice, over half the paddy land bears two successive crops of rice a year, while much of the remainder supports one crop of summer rice and a second dry crop in winter. Winter cropping is possible, since the cool months receive about 5–6 in. of rainfall. Dikes and embankments are used for bush and tree crops. As a result of the intensive land use, per-unit-area yields are high and large numbers of people can be fed. Tonkin is, therefore, in the nature of an agricultural and demographic southward extension of mainland China, and is unlike the rest of Indochina. The average population density approaches 1200 per sq mi, rises to 2500 in some rural sections, and reaches 3500 and over in the most fertile areas of new alluvium along the main rivers and near cities.[13] Yet, in efficiency, the Annamite farmers are not quite the equals of Chinese cultivators. Significantly, southward along the coast as Chinese influence becomes increasingly remote, population densities decline. It was only after their successful revolt against China (939 A.D.) that the Annamites began their advance south of the 18° parallel. In the more northerly of the small coastal deltas, densities already are less (500–750 per sq mi), and there is a further decline south of Cape Varella (12.58°N), beyond which Annamite settlement did not reach until the end of the 15th century.[14]

Over the Mekong delta, two or three times larger than the Tonkin, average population density is only about 250 per sq mi, or roughly one fifth to one quarter that of the northern lowland. Local variations are considerable, however—from around 500 per sq mi in the central parts between My Tho and the Bassac River to under 100 in the more remote west and down to 25 in the amphibious southern swamp lands.[15] These variations are frequently related to the recency of settlement.

The overall population-density differential between the Mekong and Tonkin deltas is not primarily a consequence of environmental contrasts. Rather, it stems from the more recent settlement of the southern delta and its less intensive type of rice culture. In addition, there is little or no annual double-cropping of rice, partly due to the fact that winter is a dry season. It is not quite true that settlement and rice growing in the Mekong delta are exclusively recent. In fact, the Indianized Funan Kingdom was centered there as early as the 3rd to the 5th centuries, and rice culture was practiced at that time and later by the farmers of subsequent delta states. But its cultivation was always by less efficient methods, which did not result in high densities of population. With the

---

[13] Fisher, *South-east Asia*, pp. 531–532.
[14] Fisher, *South-east Asia*, p. 532.
[15] Fisher, *South-east Asia*, p. 532.

entering of Annamite peoples in the 18th century, cultivation methods improved, but that group had occupied only a small part of the entire delta prior to annexation by France. Even as late as 1862 the delta's average density of population was only 50–60 per sq mi, a canal and diking system like that of Tonkin was lacking, and the paddy rice depended mainly on direct and often insufficient rainfall, supplemented by uncontrolled inundation from river floods during the wet season.

The first parts of the Mekong delta to feel the beneficial effects of French planning and engineering were the near virgin lands west and south of the Bassac River. There, beginning in 1870, a system of large canals for drainage and transport was constructed. The results were almost spectacular, since during the 70 years following, the rice acreage showed more than a fourfold increase.[16] Large land holdings were characteristic, and tenants comprised two thirds of the rapidly increasing total population.

On the Cambodian Plain lying just north of the Mekong delta, although rice is still the main crop, its cultivation is discontinuous because of terrain irregularities and insufficient water for irrigation. As a result, overall population density is less than that farther south, although it still continues to be moderately high in the parts along the Mekong River and the Tonlé Sap where rice culture prevails.

MALAYA[17]

Evolution of the Population Pattern.   In prehistoric times the bridge function of Malaya was paramount; the peninsula was the narrow exit of the funnel through which migrants coming from mainland Southeast Asia and farther north were channeled southward. Earliest of these migrants were the Negrito people, a few ten thousands of whose descendants still lead an ancient marginal existence based on hunting and gathering in the highlands. The chief Malay parent stock probably entered the peninsula between 1500 and 2000 B.C., expelled the earlier settlers from the choice lowlands, and in turn occupied them.

As of the immediate pre-British period, around 1830, the total population of the peninsula is estimated to have been several hundred thousand.

---

[16] Fisher, *South-east Asia*, p. 539.

[17] The term "Malaya" includes both the Federation of Malay States and the island of Singapore before 1964. After that date the new State of Singapore is excluded. The present state of Malaysia includes not only Malaya on the peninsula with the same name but also the outlying provinces of Sarawak and Sabah in northern Borneo.

Except for perhaps 10,000 aboriginal hill people, the remainder were lowland, or coastal, Malays, descendants of the proto-Malays but modified somewhat by foreign strains, including Chinese, Indians, Thais, and Arabs.

The foci of settlement were the river mouths, from which locations settlers spread inland along the streams and also along the coast.[18] Because river-mouth location commanded both coastal and river routes, it was advantageous for both economic and military reasons. The consequences was a development of numerous small riverine polities, separated from each other by swampy forested interfluves. River and coastal waters were used not only as routes of travel but also as sources of food and for bathing, while the streams provided potable water.

During the early and middle 19th century, which saw the acquirement by Britain of the four Straits Settlements of Penang, Province Wellesley, Malacca, and Singapore, the earlier population pattern of Malaya changed only modestly. The most significant feature was the small beginning of the Chinese and Indian immigration, a forerunner of the migrant flood that in later decades so completely altered the peninsula's population composition. Already by 1830 there were 15,000 to 20,000 Chinese, mainly miners and traders, in the Malay States. In 1850, Singapore, with a total population of about 53,000, included some 28,000 Chinese. By 1871 the immigrant population of 149,000 in the British Straits Settlements was numerically nearly equal to the indigenous Malays.

Extension of British rule to the Malay States beginning in 1874 and the imposition of colonial law and order there prepared the way for an accelerated economic development and with it a swelling tide of alien migrants. Immigration was actively encouraged by the British, who considered an expanded labor force composed of aliens to be essential to rapid economic expansion. The resulting influx of Chinese, Indians-Pakistanis, and Indonesians occurred in such numbers that Malaya's patterns of population composition and distribution were markedly changed. By 1941, or at the begining of the Pacific War, the total population, including Singapore, was 5,545,000, of whom only 40.5 percent were classed as Malays; nearly three fifths were immigrants and belonged to alien races. The Chinese element alone exceeded in numbers the indigenous Malays. Even at present Malays make up only about half of the total national population (Table 11.3).

The pluralistic nature of Malaysia's population has been a source of continuing friction and on occasions of grave concern to the state. For

[18] Jin-Bee Ooi, *Land, People and Economy in Malaya*, Longmans, Green and Co., London, 1963, p. 105.

TABLE 11.3   Composition of the
Population of Malaysia, June 1965
(Excluding Singapore)

Race	Number
Malays	4,027,963
Chinese	2,953,641
Indians	896,084
Eurasians and others	157,842
Total	8,035,530

SOURCE: Annual Bulletin of Statistics:
Malaysia, 1965, p. 1.

the most part the immigrant Chinese and Indians have remained apart from the Malays. The latter are suspicious of the alien peoples, partly because of their large numbers but also because they are better educated, more industrious, and non-Moslem. In addition, the non-Malay rates of natural increase are higher, which portends a still greater proportion of alien peoples in the future. It was the strong predominance of the Chinese element in the population of Singapore that recently led to the formation of the separate states of Malaysia and Singapore. But even in the present Malaya and Malaysia, interracial disagreement is rife, and envy and fear on the part of the Malay group is strong. This fear is reflected in a variety of ways. For example, Malay has been made the state language, and neither Chinese nor Indian languages may be used in Parliament. And while Malaysia is avowedly a secular state, it is nevertheless specified that Islam is the state religion. As one writer has commented, Malaysia is far from being an Asian Switzerland.

Apprehension concerning the Chinese element and its loyalty was intensified during the Communist uprising and terrorism of 1948–1960, known as the "Emergency." During the Japanese occupation of 1942–1945, thousands of Chinese left the cities and returned to the land, where they could grow their own food and escape Japanese control. Many of them remained rural even after the war ended. Some of these Chinese squatters and small rubber growers became a source of aid to the Communist guerrillas during the Emergency. To eliminate this threat, the government settled numerous rural Chinese, plus some Indians and Malays, in "new villages" situated on main roads, where they could be both protected and watched. In this process 580,000 rural dwellers were resettled in 536 new villages.

The Immigrant Peoples. Chinese migration to Malaya was economically motivated and was not intended to be permanent. The aim was to accumulate a modest fortune and then return to the homeland. Chinese migrants had no interest in subsistence farming involving rice culture, since it did not yield a cash income. The primary attraction at first was the employment provided by tin mining and trade; somewhat later employment on rubber plantations and in other commercial agricultural projects was added. Although the British, stimulated by the need for plentiful cheap labor, actively encouraged immigration, still it was not of a planned or organized type. The native Malays were little interested in hard labor for cash, and so remained paddy growers and predominantly rural. Because the export economies of tin and rubber were subject to marked price fluctuations, so also were their labor requirements; this resulted in a striking ebb and flow of migrants. It is estimated that 5 million Chinese entered Malaya during the 19th century and 12 million more between 1900 and 1940. A large majority of them eventually returned to China, but still in 1941, just before the Pacific War, the Chinese numbered about 2,419,000, or 44 percent of the total population.[19]

Indian immigration was much more closely linked to rubber than to tin. And while at the beginning of the 20th century, and therefore antedating the rubber boom, there were already some 116,000 Indians in Malaya, the great influx occurred after 1905 as the acreage in rubber soared. Indifference on the part of the Malays to cash wages and preoccupation of the Chinese with mining and trade obliged the British to turn to Indian workers for labor on the rubber plantations. Unlike Chinese migration, that of the Indians was organized in character and involved a contract. Three years was the average length of service. In 1941 Indians comprised about 14 percent of the total population.

Because of the temporary character of much Chinese and Indian immigration, the sex ratios of these migrant groups strongly favored males. Among the Chinese in Malaya in 1911 there were only 247 women per 1000 men; among Indians the comparable figure was 308. Such a situation could only result in a small proportion of both Chinese and Indians being Malaya-born—in 1920, only 20 percent of the Chinese and 12 percent of the Indians.

Less well documented is the modern immigration from Indonesia to Malaya. For one thing, most Indonesian migrants were physically indistinguishable from the native Malays. Moreover, they came in smaller groups, often entered at other than the main ports, and were attracted mainly by opportunities for settling on the land as peasant farmers. In

---

[19] Ooi, *Land, People and Economy in Malaya*, p. 113.

1931 it was estimated there were 244,000 Indonesians in the Federated Malay States who were either new immigrants or descendants of immigrants who entered the country between 1891 and 1931.[20]

Spatial Distribution Patterns. The Malay peninsula has two main belts of population concentration, one along the east coast and the other along the west (Fig. 11.4). Relatively few inhabitants and low densities are characteristic of the highland interior. Of the two coastal concentrations, the western one is by far the more important. It forms a fairly continuous belt 25–75 miles wide running the whole length of the peninsula. And although it includes only 30 percent of the region's land area, it supports fully three quarters of its people and has an average population density of over 310 persons per sq mi, or about 2.5 times the country average. Malays, Chinese, and Indians are all well, though variably, represented.

The east-coast population belt is much more limited in extent, since it is largely confined to the northeastern littoral. The southern three quarters of the coast has no genuine population concentration. The focus of settlement along the northeast coast is mainly on two deltas, Kelantan and Trengganu, where roughly 3 percent of Malaya's land area supports about 8 percent of its total population. Within this relatively isolated northeastern part, the population is overwhelmingly composed of Malay peasants engaged in subsistence paddy agriculture. Chinese and Indians comprise less than 6 percent of the total population, since the prevalent noncommercial type of economy does not attract immigrant labor.

The coastal asymmetry of population concentration in Malaya was a feature of the country's geography well before the advent of British control and the modernization of the economy. However, this demographic contrast has been markedly accentuated as a consequence of economic developments occurring within the last century and a half.

A partial explanation for the much larger buildup of population in the west than in the east, both in the pre-British period and later, is related to the greater natural assets possessed by the west. The west coast is protected by the peninsula's mountain spine from the boisterous winds and surf associated with the northeast monsoon, and from the weaker southwest monsoon of summer by the gigantic island of Sumatra. Thus the side fronting on the Malacca Strait has always been more attractive to settlement than the exposed east-side backwater on the South China Sea. The sheltered, quieter waters along the Strait side, together with the deeper harbors there, purged by tidal scour, attracted more shipping than did the rougher waters and shallower harbors of the less-

---

[20] Ooi, *Land, People and Economy in Malaya*, p. 119.

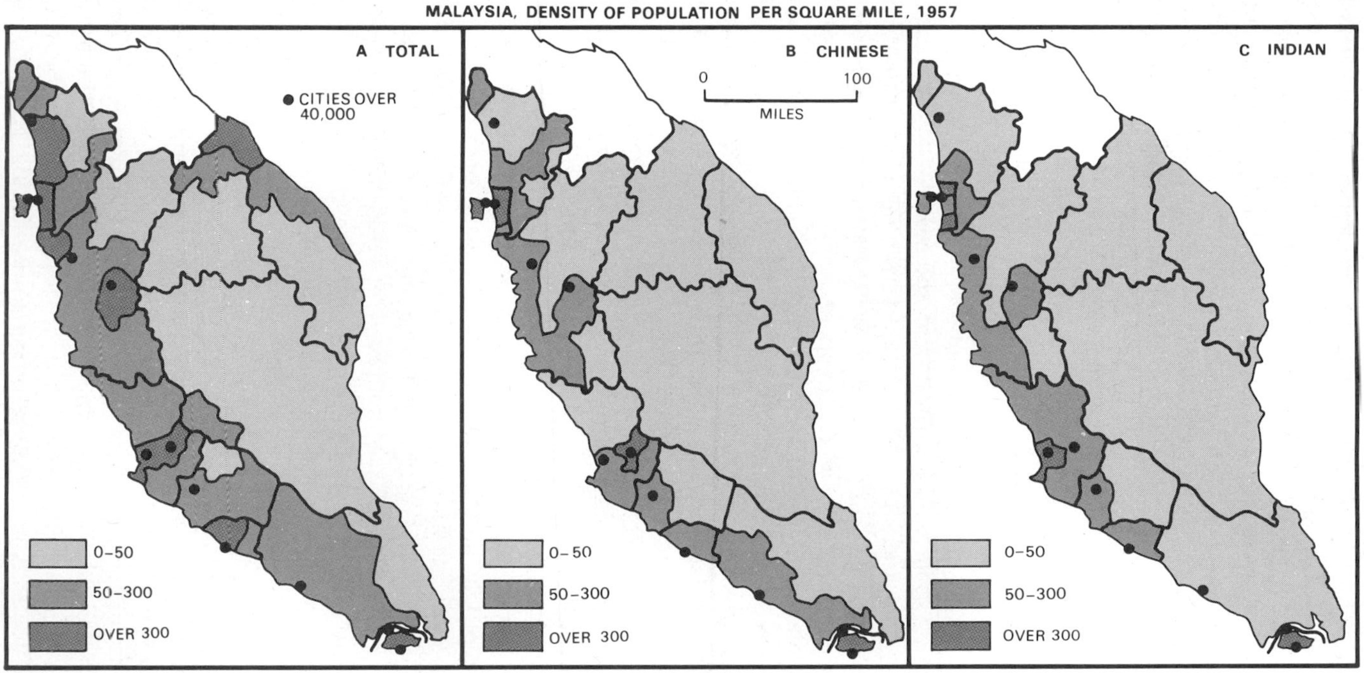

MALAYSIA. DENSITY OF POPULATION PER SQUARE MILE, 1957

Fig. 11.4. Malaya—density of population. After Ooi Jin-Bee, *Land, People and Economy in Malaya*, Longmans, Green and Co.

sheltered east side. In addition the Strait of Malacca is the main sea route between the Indian and Pacific Oceans. Moreover, the west side lies close to Sumatra from which many of Malaya's early settlers came. Besides, the sheltered west side affords more favorable conditions for the deposition of deltas and floodplains, whose fertile alluvial surfaces provide the country's best agricultural land. Only along the northernmost reaches of the eastern littoral are there deltas of noteworthy size.

During the last century or so, a new and prime factor tending to further concentrate population on the west side was the discovery there of large deposits of alluvial tin. It was this resource, either directly or indirectly, that influenced the establishment of British rule, which subsequently initiated and promoted the modern commercial period in Malaya. Tin and British initiative in turn share the credit for the development of modern transportation facilities, both land and water, and these were almost exclusively on the west side. And so when rubber plantations were established somewhat later, it was only natural that they too were concentrated on the west side where efficient transport facilities in the form of ports, shipping lines, and road and rail nets had already been developed. The effects were cumulative, since the huge successes in tin and rubber exploitation furnished the revenues for additional extensions of port, rail, and road facilities, which in turn further concentrated later developments in rubber and other commercial crops. And since the Malay population was disinterested in the hard, regularized labor required in mines and on plantations, alien labor on a vast scale was attracted to western Malaya. These immigrants came in such numbers that they not only swelled the total population but also greatly reenforced the west side's earlier population superiority and in addition radically altered the country's mix of people. Thus, on the western lowland of Malaya, there came to exist in close juxtaposition tiny subsistence paddy farms, large commercial plantations, and extensive tin-mining operations, and these in turn supported a plural society composed of small-farm Malays and Chinese and Indian laborers and tradesmen. Because the non-Malay element predominantly dwells in towns, here on the western plain are concentrated three quarters of all urban places with 5000 or more inhabitants.

Within the west-side population belt are four main areas with population densities well above the regional average. The first of these is situated close to the northern extremity of the belt, and extends both north and south of Penang. It is an area of old settlement and long-time commercial development, with an economy based on intensive fishing and agriculture (paddy rice, rubber, and coconuts) and of trade carried on through the port of Georgetown, second largest city of Malaya. A second cluster of settlement is in the Kinta Valley, prime tin-producing region, with

Ipoh, the third-ranking city, as its focus. It is now a center of plantation rubber as well. A third area of population concentration, with an economy based chiefly on tin and rubber, is situated in the vicinity of Kuala Lumpur, the national capital, metropolis, and industrial center. The fourth, southernmost, and oldest of the western population clusters, developed around Malacca, is based on an agricultural economy combining rubber, fruit, and coconuts.

Distribution of the Main Racial Groups. *Malays (Native Malays Plus Immigrants from Indonesia).* The basic precolonial pattern of Malay concentration in the form of strips along rivers and coasts has been altered somewhat as their numbers have multiplied and pressure on resources increased. Two general shifts may be noted, one to locations further inland and the other toward the towns. The latter, more often than not, has resulted less from a push associated with rural population pressure and more from general dissatisfaction with the dullness of rural living and an eagerness to enjoy the amenities of urban life. But in spite of some drift toward the towns, a great majority of the Malays are still predominantly subsistence farmers, hence rural in residence, and most concentrated in those districts least affected by a commercial type of economy. Eighty-seven percent of the Malay population is classed as rural and live either in the open countryside or in villages having fewer than 5000 inhabitants. About 76 percent are employed in primary industry, half in paddy and a third in rubber.

As the Malays increased in numbers, the procedures involved in occupying new agricultural lands differed in various parts, but it included at least the following. One very common form of expansion involved a thrust of the ribbonlike riverine settlements farther inland along the levees of the main streams and tributaries. A similar development of strip settlement took place along rail lines and new roads. Many of the latter were at right angles to the rivers, resulting in a lattice pattern of occupance. The penetration of ribbonlike strips of settlement farther inland often carried Malay subsistence farming beyond the coastal lowland and into the foothills, where rubber and tin were being exploited.[21] Another form of Malay expansion on to new lands involved only a broadening of the original filaments of riverine settlement. Still another was in the nature of an advance of settlement inland from the coast along a broad front. This type very shortly encountered the interior swamplands.

The chief areas of Malay concentration, all of them peripheral, are five in number: (1) a long strip in the northwest, extending both north

[21] Ooi, *Land, People and Economy in Malaya,* pp. 141–142.

and south of Penang; (2) about midway down the west coast in latitudes 3–4°N; (3) a long coastal strip in the southwest, from about Malacca southward; and (4) the Kelantan and (5) Trengganu deltas along the northeast coast. If Singapore island is included, that comprises a sixth area of Malay concentration.

Chinese. The composition of the Chinese labor force provides clues to the distribution of that ethnic group. About 46.7 percent (1957) are engaged in primary industry (mainly mining and cash-crop agriculture), 13.4 percent are in secondary industry, and 35.9 percent are in the tertiary sector. Thus, 53.3 percent are in the secondary and tertiary sectors combined, which is almost the identical percentage of Chinese living in towns. Of the Chinese labor force in primary production, 57 percent are associated with growing rubber, 17 percent are in mixed agriculture, mainly market gardening, and 10 percent are in tin mining, while only 2.7 percent cultivate paddy.[22]

The Chinese in Malaya are overwhelmingly concentrated on the west side, facing the Strait of Malacca, the region of commercial agriculture, tin mining, urban development, and trade (Fig. 11.4). Three main areas of relatively high Chinese density may be noted: (1) the states of Penang and Province Wellesley in the north, where Chinese employment is both old and varied; (2) the Kinta Valley, inland from the coast, where the attraction is both tin and rubber; and (3) the area around Kuala Lumpur, with similar employment opportunities. A fourth area, and one of extraordinary Chinese concentration, is the state of Singapore, where about two thirds of the urban population are Chinese.

Indians. The general distribution pattern of this ethnic group resembles that of the Chinese (Fig. 11.4). Almost all are located on the west side. But the Indians are far more rural in residence than are the Chinese, although less so than the Malays. Only a third live in urban places. The main concentration is in the northwest in the Penang-Province Wellesley area, which was the main entrance point for the early stream of Indian immigrants. Employment there is largely in cash-crop agriculture—rubber, coconuts, and oil palm. The only other Indian concentration is in the Klang Valley near Kuala Lumpur, which has long been a region specialized in rubber growing. Expectably, Indians are also numerous in the new state of Singapore.

Urban Places. Malaya's towns and cities are chiefly the creations of the immigrant populations and the commercial economies whose labor requirements they provided. Of 84 communities classed as urban (1957 census), all but 10 are situated in the western belt. Thirty-one percent

[22] Ooi, *Land, People and Economy in Malaya*, p. 151.

of western Malaysia's total population is locally classed as urban; 24 percent reside in localities with 20,000 or more inhabitants. Of the 21 largest cities, 18 had populations in which more than 50 percent were Chinese, 13 more than 60 percent, 5 more than 70 percent, and 2 more than 80 percent. Only two cities had populations with more than 50 percent Malays.

INDONESIA[23]

The immense Indonesian Archipelago (735,000 sq mi and an estimated 121 million people in 1970) is a region of unbelievable population complexity and diversity. Among the native peoples 25 different languages and 250 lesser dialects are spoken. In addition there are immigrant Chinese, European, Indian, and Arab peoples. Three great religions—Islam, Hinduism, and Christianity—are represented. Extreme population contrasts prevail between coasts and interiors and between Java-Madura and the Outer Provinces, while the cultural spread between the headhunters of New Guinea and the relatively advanced civilization of Java is profound indeed.

The unusual complexity of population patterns, both of numbers and characteristics, stems from a variety of causes, among them the succession of ethnic and cultural incursions and the immense size and fragmentation of the land area. As a consequence the evolution of peoples and cultures has tended to develop in a variety of isolated centers.[24]

Java Versus the Outer Provinces. Of commanding importance in the population geography of Indonesia is the staggering contrast in number and density of people between Java, the core area, and the remainder of the archipelago, commonly designated the Outer Provinces (Table 11.4). Of the country's estimated total population of 121 million in 1970, Java-Madura, with only 8–9 percent of the land area, supports about 65 percent. This resulted (1961) in a density of 51 per sq km for the whole country, 477 for Java-Madura, and only 19.2 for the outer islands. The overall pattern, then, is one of a congested core made up of Java-Madura, together with the two small islands of Bali and Lombok just to the east, and a far less developed periphery (Fig. 11.5). This unbalanced situation is by no means a recent feature resulting from the impact

[23] Attention here is on the state of Indonesia, including the territory of Western New Guinea, or West Irian.
[24] On this topic of heterogeneity of indigenous peoples, see Fisher, *South-east Asia*, Table 16, pp. 240–243. See also Figs. 35 and 36.

TABLE 11.4   Population of Indonesia, 1961

Province	Population (1000)	Density (Per Sq Km)
Java (Djawa) and Madura	63,059[a]	477
Outer Provinces	34,026[b]	19.2
Sumatra (Sumatera)	15,739	33.0
Borneo (Kalimantan)	4,102	7.6
Celebes (Sulawesi)	7,079	37.0
Bali and Nusatenggara	5,558	76.0
Moluccas	790	11.0
West Irian	758	1.8
Indonesia	97,085 (1968 est., 115,100)	51.0

SOURCE: *Population Census 1961*, Republic of Indonesia.
[a] 1968 estimate, 74,400.
[b] 1968 estimate, 40,700.

of Europeans and their commercialization of the economy, although these have further intensified it. Crawfurd estimated that, as early as 1830, small Java supported 6 million of the 11 million people in all Indonesia, or nearly 55 percent. Thus, Java over its modernization period of 140 years since 1830 may have raised its proportion of the country's total population only from 55 to 65 percent (74.5 percent in 1905). The fundamental question, then, both for the premodern and the modern periods, is why Java has consistently supported such a disproportionate share of the country's total population, and at present is burdened with roughly 25 times the population density of the Outer Provinces.

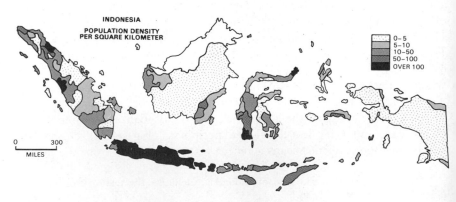

Fig. 11.5. Indonesia—population density. Modified from *Focus*, (American Geographical Society), May 1971.

The Premodern Period. There is some merit in examining the causes for Java's population predominance as of about 1830, before the modernization under Dutch supervision had appreciably affected either the economy or the vital processes.

A prime factor relating to Java's early preeminence in population within the archipelago was the fact that in that island agricultural skills, involving paddy-rice tillage, had reached a higher level than elsewhere. Consequently Java was able to support many more people per unit area of land. A great range of cultural levels with varying population potentials existed among the native societies in the different islands. At the lowest level were the primitive gathering and hunting societies. Somewhat higher were these engaged in shifting dry-crop cultivation. At the highest level was paddy-rice culture, a type largely confined to Java. By far the most widespread form of tillage throughout the Outer Provinces was that of shifting cultivation. This was an extensive type of farming that required at least 25 acres to support an average family; it precluded high rural densities. Only in a few spots in the Outer Provinces were there restricted areas of crowding among native peoples, and these were characteristically paddy lands.

The more space-efficient and fruitful agriculture of Java, in turn, stemmed partly from that island's earlier position as the main center of a more advanced type of Indianized civilization within the archipelago. Variations in the cultural levels of indigenous peoples were commonly related to the degree and kind of alien influence experienced.[25] Within the Indies, only nearby Bali may have equaled Java in its agricultural intensification, and hence in its density of population.

In its fertile volcanic soils Java had yet another asset that set it apart from the Outer Provinces and indirectly operated to swell the numbers of its peasant cultivators. While this physical factor may have functioned even more efficiently during the later period of intensive Dutch exploitation, it was not without influence even prior to about 1830. Pelzer[26] comments on the close relationship between soil fertility and numbers of people within the Indies, the chain of events being from rich soils to high yields, more abundant food supply, increased intensification of labor inputs, and hence greater crowding. The most fertile soils of the Indies are associated with volcanoes. But not all volcanic materials and their derived soils are fertile. If the ash or lava is relatively old, it is leached and infertile; only the fairly recent volcanic ejecta are rich in

[25] Fisher, *South-east Asia*, p. 87.
[26] Karl J. Pelzer, *Pioneer Settlement in the Asiatic Tropics*, The American Geographical Society, New York, 1945, p. 162.

soluble mineral plant foods. Thus, it is around young and active volcanoes—at their bases, on their slopes, and on adjacent alluvial lowlands where water and silt are derived from such volcanoes—that productive soils are concentrated. The young ash soils are recognized as being so rich that peasants will risk the dangers associated with new eruptions in order to cultivate the fresh upper slopes of volcanoes. On active Merapi Volcano in Java, native tillers push their settlements to within a few miles of the crater, even though occasional eruptions cause heavy losses to life and property. But after each catastrophe the peasants press back once more onto the devastated slopes, whatever the risk, so great is the native fertility of the recent deposit.[27]

However, not even all fresh, unleached volcanic materials are rich—it depends as well on the chemical composition of the ejecta. It is the basic lava and ash, containing a larger proportion of the soluble base elements—calcium, magnesium, potassium, and phosphorus—that are especially fertile. By contrast, acidic lavas, high in silica and low in lime and the other base minerals, produce soils that are not only chemically infertile but also physically inferior, since they are heavy, sticky, and less friable. Thus the richest volcanic soils are likely to be basic in chemical reaction as well as recent in origin.

Java has some 120 volcanoes strung out along the length of the island, 17 of them still active. In addition, most of the ejecta are basic or neutral in composition, and repeated replenishment with new basic ejecta is widespread. Here, then, ash and ash-derived alluvial soils are more fertile than those in the Outer Provinces, where volcanoes are fewer and the ejecta are both older and more acidic in composition. Only in a few scattered areas of restricted extent in the Outer Provinces are rich volcanic soils present. Even in all parts of Java the soils are not equally fertile, since in the Priangan region of western Java much of the volcanic material is acidic in character, and this feature is reflected in the less productive agriculture and in the generally lower density of population.

Other physical handicaps than infertile soils afflicted the several Outer Provinces in varying degrees. Most of them suffered from inhospitable coast lines; New Guinea and other eastern islands were handicapped by remoteness; Celebes suffered from a meagerness of lowland.

Doubtless Java also profited by the focal location of the Java Sea with respect to the interisland sea routes of the Indonesian Archipelago. For through traffic between the Indian and Pacific oceans the main route was via the Strait of Malacca and the China Sea. But even such shipping made some use of the secondary route by way of Sunda Strait, the Java

[27] Dobby, *Southeast Asia*, p. 221.

Sea, and Makasar Strait. From relatively early times Java's highly accessible north coast was able to capitalize on the island's position as a maritime focus for sea routes, both local and transoceanic.

Beginning in the early 17th century, Holland at nearly all times was the dominant European influence within the Indonesian Archipelago. But down to the early 19th century Dutch influence was exerted largely through the agency of the United East India Company, exclusively a profit-making organization concerned with collecting native products from eastern and southern Asia and exchanging them for Dutch manufactures. Although collecting centers, called factories, were maintained at various points, the company's headquarters was located on Java, at what was later Batavia. This fact of location focused a widely-ranging and profitable trade at that entrepôt. Such centrality with respect to sea routes and trading operations favorably affected the eventual growth of population. Toward the end of the 17th century, as the Asian coastal trade of the United East India Company began to decline, alternative sources of income were sought.

Period of Intensive Dutch Exploitation (After About 1830). During the 18th century small beginnings were made in the development of such commercial crops as sugarcane, coffee, tea, pepper, and indigo. This represented the initial stages of an exploitive system that gradually transformed Java from what earlier had been an entrepôt into a huge producer of tropical export products in the 19th and 20th centuries.[28] Thus Java developed into the administrative, military, and economic focus of the Dutch East Indian empire. To a high degree Dutch attention was lavished on Java, so much so that a lack of economic balance developed between the several parts of the Indies. An important consequence of this imbalance was an ever-widening population gap between the earlier and more intensively developed Java and the neglected Outer Provinces. Java came to be the showroom of the Dutch Indies.

The Occident's impact on population growth in the Indies was in direct proportion to the duration and intensity of Dutch influence. This influence operated mainly through a reduction of the death rate, and it worked in several ways: (1) by providing the natives with additional means of earning a livelihood, (2) by reducing the incidence of various diseases, (3) by subduing internal strife and maintaining law and order, and (4) by reducing the frequency and virulence of famine, mainly through transportation improvements. As far as these affected the Indies during most of the 19th century, they applied almost exclusively to Java. As a result, that island's population swelled from an estimated 4.5 to

[28] Fisher, *South-east Asia*, p. 138.

8 million in 1815 to over 30 million in 1905, or a 4 to 6-fold increase. By contrast, growth in the Outer Provinces during the same period may have only doubled—from an estimated 4.7 million to 9.7 million.[29] By 1815 only a modest part of Java was under cultivation; by the second quarter of the 20th century the proportion reached the astounding figure of nearly two thirds. Population growth during the 19th century paralled the expansion of the tilled area.

If it was Dutch influence that caused Java's greater 19th century population growth compared to that in the Outer Provinces, the question still must be answered as to why Java was singled out for such unusual attention while the rest of the Indies were relatively neglected. Doubtless there were involved many of the same factors previously invoked to explain Java's population preeminence in the premodernization period. These, it will be recalled, included (1) the unusual fertility of Java's soils, (2) the focality of Java and the Java Sea, and, especially, (3) that island's already much larger and culturally more advanced population, which was able to furnish the size and quality of the labor force necessary for the expanding commercial agriculture as well as an important market for Dutch manufactures.

But while it is understandable why the Dutch first concentrated their development efforts on Java, it seems obvious that they carried this policy too far. By 1930 and probably earlier, excessive overcrowding in Java was beginning to show harmful effects. The average native diet, already barely adequate at the turn of the century, had clearly deteriorated by the 1930's. Moreover, while 90 percent of the population was classed as rural, only 65 percent of the working population was engaged in subsistence agriculture, while the remaining 25 percent depended on occasional or irregular employment.[30]

The Dutch sought to solve the Java population problem in at least three ways. Beginning early in the 20th century, they had tried to increase the local food supply through an improved agriculture. This involved land reclamation, irrigation, new crops, improved seeds, and the application of science to all aspects of farming. The results were amazingly successful, and Indonesia's rice yield per acre became the highest in Southeast Asia. A second attempted solution was sought through increased industrialization. This involved a revival of handicrafts, a multiplication of workshop industries, and an expansion of factories. It is estimated that by 1939, 2.5 million workers were employed in small-

[29] Fisher, *South-east Asia*, p. 289; *Census of Indonesia, 1961*.
[30] J. H. Boeke, "Economic Conditions for Indonesian Independence," *Pacific Affairs*, Vol. 19, 1946, p. 399.

scale industries. A third solution was sought through emigration of Javanese to the Outer Provinces. Before the 1930's the voluntary migration of Javanese laborers to the Outer Territories greatly exceeded in volume the small stream of government colonists. But in the later 1930's government colonization was greatly expanded, so that between 1936 and 1940 the number of Javanese colonists living in the Outer Provinces rose from 68,000 to 206,000.[31] The Dutch had set as their goal the moving of 100,000 colonists out of Java each year, and genuine progress had been made toward achieving that goal when the Pacific War halted emigration. Most of the colonists came from congested eastern and central Java. About 82 percent of the migrants were settled in Sumatra (mainly in the Lampung district in the south), over 16 percent went to central Celebes, and 2+ percent went to southern and eastern Borneo. But even if the goal of 100,000 out-migrants from Java each year had been reached, even this large figure would have been grossly inadequate to solve the population problem, since the island's annual population growth was around 600,000 in the 1930's. The government estimated that an annual out-migration of 250,000–300,000 per year, mainly of young people in the reproductive ages, would have been required to halt population growth in Java. It is dubious whether such a figure ever could have been attained, much less maintained.[32] At the time the Pacific War began in 1941, the success of the measures adopted by the Dutch for alleviating Java's population problem were inconclusive but dubious.

Comparative Growth rates of Java and the Outer Provinces. It was pointed out earlier that population growth rates in Java exceeded those of the Outer Provinces during the 19th century. But during the first half of the 20th century the situation was reversed; Java's growth rate slowed perceptibly, while that of the peripheral regions quickened. The result was a trend toward a slightly better balance between the different parts of the Indies. Slowing of growth in Java reflected an increasing population pressure. Accelerated growth in the Outer Provinces denoted the tardy application to mortality there of the same techniques of Western science and medicine that had been applied in Java much earlier. Supplementing the effects of a declining death rate on population growth was an important immigrant element. As a result, the Outer Provinces, which represented only 24 percent of the Indies' population in 1905, had climbed to 33–34 percent in 1950 and nearly 35 percent in 1961. Java more and more was attempting to exploit its favored position as the core area of the Indies and to increasingly support its dense population

[31] Fisher, *South-east Asia*, p. 294.
[32] Pelzer, *Pioneer Settlement*, p. 211.

by means of services rendered as the administrative, managerial, and industrial focus of the whole archipelago.

Distribution Features. To be sure, there are within Java, and within each of the Outer Provinces as well, important regional contrasts in numbers and densities of inhabitants as well as population characteristics. However, much of this detail must be sacrificed in a survey book of this kind. Omitting the two main urban subdivisions of Java containing Djakarta and Jogjakarta, the island is divided into three provinces, west, middle, and east. West Java has an average density of 380 per sq km (1961), which is well below the island average (477), while central Java, the island's ancient cultural core, is distinctly above (538). East Java's average density is intermediate (455) between those of the west and central parts and not far from the island average (Fig. 11.5). Since Java's is so predominantly a rural population, expectedly areal variations in settlement density reflect mainly differentials in the agricultural potential of the land—chiefly the percentage of land in steep slopes and the soil quality. The markedly lower density of West Java reflects two physical handicaps of that region, (1) the greater height, ruggedness, and compactness of the western highlands, making them more formidable barriers to communications and more serious handicaps to agricultural land use, and (2) the generally poorer soils, reflecting a reduced prevalence of basic volcanic ejecta.

The more detailed patterns of settlement in Java are particularly difficult to generalize. Except in the west, where the compact mass of highland is formidable, the larger volcanic peaks are widely spaced at about 20–30-mi intervals, and are separated from each other by broad basins and valleys usually covered with fine volcanic debris. But while the range of relief in the center and east is impressive, the terrain system affords neither a serious obstacle to communications nor as much of an impediment to tillage as might be expected. This is suggested by the fact that although only 36 percent of the island is estimated to be below 500 feet in elevation and hence to be genuine lowland, some 60 to 70 percent is under cultivation. This may be compared with hilly Japan, where only 14–16 percent is tilled. Along the south side of Java, where in most parts the highlands approach close to tidewater, the population is relatively sparse. Only in three localities where there are breaks in the highland wall are there small coastal lowlands with dense clusters of population. Along the island's north exposure facing the Java Sea, where the belt of lowland is much more continuous as well as wider, the area of high population density is far more extensive. A similar but really less continuous concentration of settlement occurs in the intervolcanic basins of the central and eastern interior. Java's history reveals an alternation of the main centers of settlement and of political and economic power between the northern coastal plain and the interior basins.

The Outer Provinces, with 35 percent of the nation's population, show an overall density of only 19.2 persons per sq km, or about 1/25 that of Java-Madura. But as Table 11.4 reveals, there is a considerable variation in population density among the several Outer Provinces (Fig. 11.5). Well in the lead is the archipelago of small islands (including Bali) lying eastward from Java, with an average density of 76 per sq km. Celebes and Sumatra are next with 37 and 33 respectively, followed by the Moluccas with 11, Borneo with 7.6, and West Irian at the bottom with only 1.8 persons per sq km. Of course, all of these are only averages of extensive areas within which there are wide variations in density of settlement. For example, Bali, with a density of 321 per sq km, resembles Java more than the outer islands, and the same is true of Lombok Island just east of Bali. A few other areas such as southwestern Celebes, Padang, and Medan in Sumatra, and several islands in the Java Sea, have estimated densities of 50–150 per sq km. All of the above are favored by young basic volcanic soils. By contrast, Borneo and West Irian, lacking a single active volcano, are regions of unusually low densities. Emphatically, the correlation between young volcanic soils and relatively high population density is strong in Indonesia.

PHILIPPINES

A dozen major islands and over 7000 minor ones constitute this archipelagic state, whose estimated population of about 38 million (1970) make it, after Indonesia, the most populous country in Southeast Asia.

The process of racial mixing going on in these islands over millenniums of time has created a Filipino blend derived mainly from Mongoloid racial types. The earliest inhabitants were small Negrito peoples, remnants of whose offspring still persist as primitive mountain folk. These were followed by proto-Malay migrants, largely mainlanders originally from the Mongloid racial hearth. After about 500 B.C. the influx of peoples and cultures was chiefly from the Indonesian archipelago who brought with them a partially Indianized culture. Ninety-nine percent of the present population is a brown-skinned blend of basic Malayan stock. The small minorities are chiefly Chinese, Indians, and Europeans. A few hundred thousand, easily indentifiable, recent Chinese are especially active in trade, banking and transport activities.

Indian and Arab Moslems arrived in sufficient numbers in the 14th to the 16th centuries to significantly change some features of the social and political life. Islam became firmly established in southern parts, especially Sulu, Mindanao, and Palawan. It was at this time that the islands became less of a cultural backwater than formerly. As the Spanish began to arrive in force in the last half of the 16th century, a more thorough cultural transformation resulted than the one that followed the preceding Moslem infiltration. A Roman Catholic priesthood, acting hand in glove with Spanish civil officials, succeeded in infusing some new forms of architecture, dress, crops, food habits, social customs, language, and religion. One relic of the Spanish period is the overwhelmingly Christian composition of the population—a unique feature for Asiatic countries. Some 94 percent of the Filipinos are Christians and nearly 80 percent are nominal Roman Catholics, the latter feature providing a bond making for national unity. When the United States displaced Spain after 1898, still another set of cultural influences was added to the mix, leading to further important changes. A significant one was an expansion of health and educational services, the former having important effects on death and population growth rates. Some 60–70 percent of the adult Filipino population is literate; about 37 percent speak English, although few speak it in the home. Tagalog, English, and Spanish are the three official languages taught in the schools. In the lower grades instruction is in the local language.

Within Southeast Asia the Philippines tends to stand apart. Its Western traditions, as expressed in religion and language; its more literate population; its surviving military and commercial ties with the United States; and its stratified society composed of a small elite and a great mass of peasantry existing at a much lower standard of living—all these tend to make the country somewhat suspect among the neighboring nations.

Population Growth. The regime of law and order instituted by Spain may have had the effect of quickening the tempo of population growth. From an estimated only half a million inhabitants in the early 1600's, the numbers rose to about 1.6 million by 1800, 3.9 million by 1850, and 7.6 million at the time of the first American census in 1903.[33] From church records of baptisms and deaths, it appears that the crude birth rate in the last 19th century may have been as high as 45–50 per 1000; the death rate was also high (30–40) and variable from year to year. Under American influence, mortality fell from 28 per 1000 in 1905 to under 19 in 1939. The birth rate has remained unchanged since the beginning of the century and even today may approach 50. This high fertility combined with an estimated death rate of about 10–15 indicates an annual

[33] Irene B. Taeuber, "The Bases of a Population Problem: The Philippines," *Population Index*, Vol. 26, April, 1960, p. 98.

growth rate of 3.2–3.5 percent. Such an unusually high rate will double the population in 20–21 years.

Overall density of population at present exceeds 320 per sq mi. This is a high figure for most of Southeast Asia—two to three times that of Burma, for example. But on the other hand, it is only a quarter that of Java. Because so much of the land is unfit for tillage, the physiologic density approaches 1200–1300 persons per sq mi of cultivated land.

Distribution. The spread of population over the archipelago is highly uneven, while the pattern of distribution is so exceedingly complex as to almost defy description. It is also difficult to rationalize. Part of the complexity derives from the insular nature of the country, since most coastal strips are likely to show crowding.

Since about 70 percent of the economically active population are engaged in farming, inequalities in density will, to a considerable degree, reflect differences in inherent agricultural potentials. It is therefore of the greatest importance that hill and mountain lands greatly predominate; sizeable lowlands are few and alluvial lands represent only about 15 percent of the land area. Thus, with population concentrated on these most productive lowland sites, it is understandable why the distribution pattern is a fragmented one composed of small clusters and linear strips of dense population (Fig. 11.6). But for a variety of reasons, not all Philippine lowlands are closely settled; the fairly extensive Cagayan Valley in northeastern Luzon is a prime example.

However, the concentration of people is as much regional as topographic, since cultural as well as physical factors have left a strong imprint. Throughout most of the modern period, prolonged and substantial population growth has occurred mainly in focal areas of Spanish colonization and control, and more recently in those feeling the stimulating effects of American influence. For the most part, it is the southern sections of the country—in Mindanao, Palawan, and Sulu—situated peripheral to the focus of Spanish influence in Luzon and outside the circumference where Spanish civil government was effective, that are more sparsely settled. These same regions are also more strongly Moslem and pagan in culture. The bulk of the population is in the northern and central parts, particularly in western and in southeastern Luzon and in some of the centrally located Visayan islands. These parts lay relatively close to the center of administration and power and benefited also by proximity to the main routes of transport, both rail and ocean. The single greatest compact cluster of dense population is coincident with the largest lowland, the Luzon Central Plain, at whose southern end is Manila, the national capital and metropolis. Hinterland zones located off the main lines of communication on large islands, and medium and small islands

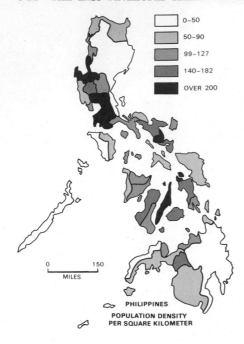

0-50

50-90

99-127

140-182

OVER 200

Fig. 11.6. Philippines—density of population per square kilometer, 1960. After R. E. Huke, *Shadows on the Land*.

0   150
MILES

PHILIPPINES
POPULATION DENSITY
PER SQUARE KILOMETER

at some distance from the central island groups, usually have fewer people. About 46 percent of the total population are located in the large northern island of Luzon, which has 35 percent of the area. Nearly 30 percent of the inhabitants are in the centrally located Visayan Islands, with only 19 percent of the area. Some 19 percent are on or near Mindanao, the large southern Island that has 31 percent of the area.[34]

By 1960 the average density of population per square mile of cultivated land had reached nearly 1000, but of course there were great regional and local variations. Along the Ilocos coast and on the Central Plain in Luzon densities rise to above 1500 per sq mi. Saturation is near, or even exceeded, in many of the localities of high density. Large parts of the agricultural labor force are unable to find adequate employment on the land. One fifth of the Filipino farmers are either fully or partially unemployed.[35] The largest areas of good unused or underused lowland

[34] Frederick L. Wernstedt and J. E. Spencer, *The Philippine Island World: A Physical, Cultural and Regional Geography*, University of California Press, Berkeley, 1967, pp. 138–139.

[35] Paul D. Simkins and Frederick L. Wernstedt, "Growth and Internal Migration of the Philippine Population, 1948–1960," *Journal of Tropical Geography*, Vol. 17, 1963, p. 198.

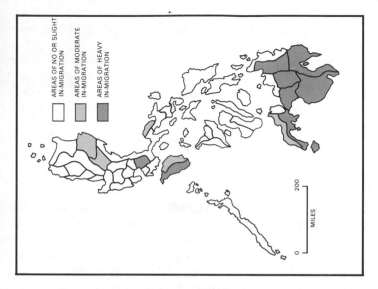

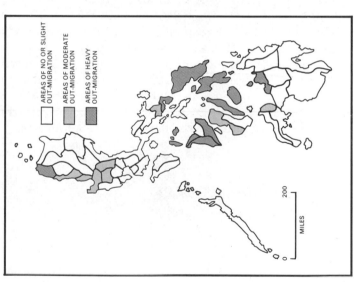

Fig. 11.7. Philippines—regions of internal migration during the period 1948–1960.

are in Mindanao, where an estimated 11 million acres are so classified. Other smaller areas exist in Mindoro, Palawan, and the upper Cagayan Valley in Luzon.

But in spite of the strong rural population gradients, little migration and redistribution actually took place before the Pacific War. By contrast, the postwar period has seen large-scale relocation of peasant farmers— perhaps as many as two million over the period 1948–1960. The movement has involved an especially large emigration from the densely settled Luzon and Visayan regions, where as a result the overall rate of population growth has been well below the country average (Fig. 11.7). In Luzon the out-migration has been largely to less-dense parts of the same island. Main regions of new settlement were southern Mindanao, which absorbed 30 percent of the national population growth in the period 1948–1960, and the island of Mindoro. Both islands grew at rates more than double the national average, indicating heavy in-migration. Almost all of the new settlers in Mindanao came from the crowded Visayan region.

Urban Population. Most LD countries have, over recent decades, shown higher rates of population growth in their urban than in their rural components. But rapid urbanization has not been characteristic of the Philippines. Only greater Manila experienced a growth rate (1946–1960) substantially greater than that of the whole population. Growth in other urban places was about on a par with that of the total population. And since fertility ratios in the cities other than Manila do not depart greatly from those of rural areas, it appears that city growth has been largely due to natural increase. In 1960 only about 15 percent of the total population lived in places with 20,000 or more inhabitants.

REFERENCES

General

Dobby, E. H. G. *Southeast Asia*, Eighth ed., London, University of London Press, 1964.
Fisher, Charles A. *South-east Asia: A Social, Economic and Political Geography*. Methuen, London, 1964.
Le Bar, Frank M., Gerald C. Hickey and John K. Musgrave, *Ethnic Groups of Mainland Southeast Asia*. Human Relations Area Files Press, New Haven, 1964.
Robequain, Charles. *Malaya, Indonesia, Borneo and the Philippines*. Trans. by E. D. Laborde. Longmans, Green and Co., London, 1954.

Mainland Southeast Asia

Barton, Thomas F. "Thailand's Population Density and Distribution." *Transition*, A. J. Nystrom and Co., Chicago, Vol. 3, No. 2, no date.

Blanchard, Wendell, et al. *Thailand: Its People, Its Society, Its Culture.* Human Relations Area Files, New Haven, Conn., 1966.

Buchanan, Keith. *The South-east Asian World*, New York: Taplinger, 1967.

Credner, Wilhelm. *Siam: Das Land der Thai.* J. Engelhorns Nachf., Stuttgart, 1935.

Dobby, E. H. G. *Southeast Asia.* Eighth ed., London, University of London Press, 1964, 147–195, 259–318.

Fisher, Charles A. *South-east Asia: A Social, Economic and Political Geography.* Methuen, London, 1964, pp. 407–580.

"French Indo-China: Demographic Imbalance and Colonial Policy," *Population Index*, Vol. 11, No. 2, April, 1945, pp. 68–81.

Goldstein, Sidney. "Urbanization in Thailand, 1947–1967," *Demography*, Vol. 8, 1971, pp. 205–223.

Louka, K. T. *The Role of Population in the Development of South-east Asia.* Population Research Project, George Washington University, 1960.

Ng, Ronald C. Y. "Recent Internal Population Movement in Thailand," *Annals of the Association of American Geographers*, Vol. 59, 1969, pp. 710–730.

Purcell, V. *The Chinese in South-east Asia*, 2nd ed., under the auspices of the Royal Institute of International Affairs, London, Oxford University Press, 1965.

Siampos, George S. "The Population of Cambodia 1945–1980," *Milbank Memorial Fund Quarterly*, Vol. XLVIII, July 1970, pp. 317–360.

Sternstein, Larry. "A Critique of Thai Population Data," *Pacific Viewpoint*, Vol. 6, 1965, pp. 15–35.

Thailand. National Statistical Office. *Report: The Survey of Population Change, 1964–1967*, E-SuR-No. 3-69 (Bangkok, 1969).

Zelinsky, Wilbur. "The Indochinese Peninsula: A Demographic Anomaly." *The Far Eastern Quarterly*, Vol. 9, 1950, pp. 115–145.

Malaysia

Caldwell, J. C. "Malaysia's Population Problem," in S. Chandrasekhar (ed.), *Asia's Population Problems.* Frederick A. Praeger, New York, 1967, pp. 165–188.

Chapman, F. Spencer. "The Chinese in Malaya," *Geographical Magazine*, Vol. 23, 1951, pp. 401–411.

Cho, Lee-Jay, et al. "Recent Fertility Trends in West Malaysia," *Demography*, Vol. 5, No. 2, 1968, pp. 732–744.

Dobby, E. H. G. *Southeast Asia.* Eighth ed., London, University of London Press, 1964, pp. 87–146.

Fisher, Charles A. *South-east Asia: A Social, Economic and Political Geography.* Methuen, London, 1964, pp. 583–661.

Ginsburg, Norton, and Chester F. Roberts, Jr. *Malaya.* University of Washington Press, Seattle, 1958.

Wang Gungwu (ed.), *Malaysia: A Survey.* Frederick A. Praeger, New York, 1965.

Ho, R. *Environment, Man, and Development in Malaya,* Kuala Lumpur, 1962.

Hodder, B. W. "The Population of Malaya," in *Man in Malaya.* University of London Press, London, 1959, pp. 32–44.

Jones, L. W. "Malaysia's Future Population," *Pacific Viewpoint,* Vol. 6, 1965, pp. 39–51.

McTaggart, W. D. "The Distribution of Ethnic Groups in Malaya, 1947–1957," *Jour. of Tropical Geography,* Vol. 26, 1969, pp. 69–81.

McTaggart, W. D. "Urbanization in Malaya—The Small Towns," in *Modernization of the Pacific Region,* Inter-Congress Meeting of the Standing Committee on Geography, Pacific Science Association, University of Malaya, Kuala Lumpur, 1969, pp. 25–31.

Ooi, Jin-Bee. *Land, People and Economy in Malaya.* Longmans, Green and Co., London, 1963.

Purcell, Victor. *The Chinese in Malaya.* Oxford, 1948.

Robequain, Charles. *Malaya, Indonesia, Borneo and the Philippines.* Trans. by E. D. Laborde. Longmans, Green and Co., London, 1954, pp. 118–125.

Siampos, George S. "The Population of Cambodia, 1945–1980," The Milbank Memorial Fund Quarterly, Vol. 48, 1970, pp. 317–360.

Skinner, G. William. "Chinese Assimilation and Thai Politics," *Journal of Asian Studies,* Vol. 16, 1957, pp. 237–270.

Swee-Hock, Saw. "Fertility Differentials in Early Postwar Malaya," *Demography,* Vol. 4, 1967, pp. 641–656.

Indonesia

Central Bureau of Statistics. *Statistical Pocketbook of Indonesia,* 1963.

Dobby, E. H. G. *Southeast Asia.* Eighth ed., London, University of London Press, 1964, pp. 196–258.

Fisher, Charles A. *South-east Asia: A Social, Economic and Political Geography.* Methuen, London, 1964, pp. 205–404.

Hawkins, Everett D. "Indonesia's Population Problem," in S. Chandrasekhar (ed.), *Asia's Population Problems.* Frederick A. Praeger, New York, 1967, pp. 119–143.

Jones, L. W. *The Population of Borneo: A Study of the Peoples of Sarawak, Sabah and Brunei.* The Athlone Press, University of London, London, 1966.

Keyfitz, Nathan. "Indonesian Population and the European Industrial Revolution." *Asian Survey,* Vol. 5, October 1965, pp. 503–514.

Milone, Pauline D. "Contemporary Urbanization in Indonesia," *Asian Survey,* Vol. 4, No. 8, August 1964, pp. 1000–1012.

Pelzer, Karl J. "Physical and Human Resource Patterns," in Ruth McVey (ed.), *Indonesia.* Southeast Asia Studies, Yale University, HRAF Press, New Haven, Conn., 1963, pp. 1–23.

Peper, Bram. "Population Growth in Java in the 19th Century: a New Interpretation," *Population Studies,* Vol. 24, 1970, pp. 71–84.

Widjojo, Nitisastro. *Population Trends in Indonesia.* Ithaca, Cornell University Press, 1970.

Withington, William A. "The Distribution of Population in Sumatra, Indonesia, 1961," *Journal of Tropical Geography*, Vol. 17, May 1963, pp. 203–212.

Withington, W. A. "The Population of Java, Indonesia: A Study in Contrasts," in Paul H. Griffin (ed.), *A Geography of Population: a Teacher's Guide*, The 1970 Yearbook of the National Council for Geographic Education, Feardon Publishers, Palo Alto, California, 1969, pp. 227–254.

The Philippines

Concepcion, Mercedes B. "The Population of the Philippines," *First Conference on Population, 1965*, Quezon City, Philippines, 1966, pp. 185–199.

Dobby, E. H. G. *Southeast Asia.* Eighth ed., London, University of London Press, 1964, pp. 319–344.

Fisher, Charles A. *South-east Asia: A Social, Economic and Political Geography.* Methuen, London, 1964, pp. 691–736.

Lorimer, Frank W. "Analysis and Projections of the Population of the Philippines," *First Conference on Population, 1965*, Quezon City, Philippines, 1966, pp. 200–314.

Madigan, F. C. "Some Recent Vital Rates and Trends in the Philippines; Estimates and Evaluation," *Demography*, Vol. 2, 1965, pp. 309–316.

Pascual, Elvira M. "Internal Migration in the Philippines," *First Conference on Population, 1965*, Quezon City, Philippines, 1966, pp. 315–353.

Pascual, Elvira M. *Population Redistribution in the Philippines.* University of the Philippines, Manila, 1966.

The Philippine Economic Atlas. Philippines: Program Implementation Agency, Manila, 1966.

Robequain, Charles. *Malaya, Indonesia, Borneo and the Philippines.* Trans. by E. D. Laborde. Longmans, Green and Co., London, 1954, pp. 286–296.

Simkins, Paul D., and Frederick L. Wernstedt. "Growth and Internal Migration of the Philippine Population, 1948–1960." *Journal of Tropical Geography*, Vol. 17, 1963, pp. 197–202.

Simkins, Paul D. "Migration as a Response to Population Pressure: The Case of the Philippines," in *Geography and a Crowding World*, Wilbur Zelinsky et al. (eds.), Oxford University Press, New York, 1970, pp. 259–268.

Taeuber, Irene B. "The Bases of a Population Problem: The Philippines." *Population Index*, Vol. 26, April 1960, pp. 97–115.

Vandermeer, Canute, and Bernardo C. Agaloos. "Twentieth Century Settlement of Mindanao," *Papers of the Michigan Academy of Science, Arts and Letters*, Vol. 47, 1962, pp. 537–548.

Wernstedt, F. L., and Paul D. Simkins. "Migrations and the Settlement of Mindanao," *The Journal of Asian Studies*, Vol. XXV, 1965, pp. 83–105.

Wernstedt, F. L., and J. E. Spencer. *Philippine Island World: A Physical, Cultural and Regional Geography.* Berkeley, University of California, 1967.

CHAPTER

12

South Asia

South Asia is essentially the gigantic tongue-shaped peninsula that thrusts southward from Asia proper. Often designated the Indian subcontinent, it includes not only the state of India but also Pakistan, Ceylon, and the Himalayan states of Nepal, Sikkim and Bhutan. With a total area approaching two million square miles, the subcontinent in 1970 had an estimated 716 million inhabitants (India, 555; Pakistan, 137; Ceylon, 12.6; Nepal, 11.2; Bhutan, 0.8, and Sikkim, 0.2), or about 19 percent of the earth's total. This is 200 million more people than in the whole Western Hemisphere, and twice the number in Africa. It comprises one of the earth's trilogy of great population groupings; smaller than the East Asian concentration but similar in size to that of Europe, including the U.S.S.R.

THE SUBCONTINENT AND INDIA: CULTURAL ORIGINS AND RACIAL STOCKS

Like China, the Indian subcontinent is a region of great cultural antiquity. Evidence exists that paleolithic peoples with food-producing techniques involving sedentary agriculture dwelled in the Indus region as far back as 5000–7000 years ago. The subcontinent probably was once inhabited by Negroid peoples who subsequently were overrun by Australoids. Over long periods of time these pre-Dravidian stocks mixed with peoples from the northwest and northeast to form the dominant Dravidian type, characterized by many Australoid features, including short stature and dark skins. Perhaps as far back as two to three millenniums B.C. the Indus plains witnessed the development of a sophisticated urban civilization whose ancestral Dravidian people constructed the great capitals of Harappa and Mohenjo-daro. Later invasions into the subcontinent, beginning in the second millennium B.C., came mainly from the northwest and resulted in a thrusting of Caucasoid Mediterranean peoples across the Indus and Ganges plains and well to the south

350

into peninsular India. These later Indo-Aryan intruders (Sanskrit speakers), taller and having lighter skins than the Dravidians, were crude farmers who both tilled the soil and grazed animals; their culture was altogether less sophisticated than that of the more urbanized society which they displaced. It is mainly from the blending of these two peoples, the ancestral Dravidians and the Caucasoids, that the present inhabitants and the Hindu culture of the subcontinent have developed.

The bulk of the people of South Asia represent a Caucasoid mixture whose people differ from those of Southwest Asia chiefly in their darker skins. For gradually the Caucasian invaders darkened in color as they became a part of the Indian landscape, with the strongest pigmentation among the peoples of southern India where the Dravidian element is less diluted. The darker skins of the Caucasians in India probably resulted from intermarriage with the earlier dark-skinned inhabitants of South Asia. The south Indians, farthest removed from the portal areas of Caucasian entrance in the northwest, are of slighter build and darker skin than the average inhabitants; those of the Ganges Plain are taller and of an olive-brown complexion. Degree of pigmentation enters to some extent into the ancestry of the poorer classes and lower castes of modern Indian society. Peoples of Mongoloid racial stock are located mainly in the highlands along the northern and eastern frontiers of the subcontinent, where juncture is made with China and Southeast Asia; on the plains, Mongoloid traits are confined to East Pakistan and Assam.

POPULATION NUMBERS

Evolution and Distribution in the Past. The Indian subcontinent is believed to have been one of the earth's early centers of population concentration. The most ancient period for which a population estimate is available is about the second century B.C., during the rule of the Emperor Asoka, when the numbers are thought to have been between 100 and 140 million.[1] This conjecture, while having slight statistical value, has been accepted by Davis[2] as being a reasonable one. But for about the beginning of the Christian era, Colin Clarke uses Usher's much smaller estimate of only 70 million.[3] He suggests that there may have been

[1] Pran Nath, "A Study of the Economic Conditions of Ancient India," *Proceedings of the Royal Asiatic Society,* London, 1929, Chapter 5.
[2] Kingsley Davis, *The Population of India and Pakistan.* Princeton University Press, Princeton, New Jersey, 1951, p. 24.
[3] Colin Clark, *Population Growth and Land Use.* Macmillan, London, 1967, pp. 64, 75.

massive losses of human life in the tumultuous period after Asoka. What the distribution was of the conjectured 100 to 140 million inhabitants is highly speculative. Cultures with an advanced technology are known to have existed in the Ganges and Indus valleys in the north, and there were almost equally advanced civilizations in southern peninsular India.[4]

Davis is of the opinion that India's population changed little over the 1.5 to 2 millenniums from the ancient period of Asoka to the beginning of the modern period, roughly 1650. Probably it experienced periods of gradual growth in more normal times, but inevitably catastrophes in the form of wars, epidemics, and famine followed in which the previous gains were wiped out. Thus, the long-time trend in numbers may have shown a relatively static condition.[5] Moreland's estimate of 100 million for India's population in 1605[6] has been used by several authors endeavoring to judge the increase of the subcontinent's population in modern times, but that figure has little basis of reliability and must be judged as of only a gross order of magnitude.

Moreland also provides some meager information concerning population distribution in the subcontinent as of the early 17th century.[7] One large concentration probably existed in the far south-central part where the Hindu state of Vijayanagar was located. Employing various yardsticks, Moreland conjectures that this southern concentration contained at least 30 million people and probably substantially more. North of the Hindu state but still mostly south of latitude 20°N and situated within the drainage basins of the Krishna and Godavari rivers were a number of Moslem kingdoms concerning whose populations information is extremely meager. But from the wars these kingdoms were able to wage, it would appear that the manpower base providing the required troops was moderately large.

In the Mogul Empire of Akbar located north of about parallel 20°, the population spread was very uneven but with the principal concentration in the Indo-Gangetic lowland, especially the part that included the upper Ganges and the eastern upper-Indus Plains. Here the area under cultivation may have been as much as 70 to 80 percent of that tilled at the time Moreland was writing in 1911.[8] This same source infers that

[4] Nath, "A Study of the Economic Conditions of Ancient India," p. 3.
[5] One source suggests that India's population may have increased from 73 million in 14 A.D. to 100 million by 1600 and 150 million by 1650. See Colin Clarke, Population Growth and Land Use, p. 64.
[6] W. H. Moreland, India at the Death of Akbar. Macmillan, London, 1920, pp. 9–22.
[7] Moreland, India at the Death of Akbar, pp. 11–22.
[8] Moreland, India at the Death of Akbar, p. 21. See population map of India for the 16th century in Abott Payson Usher, "The History of Population and Settlement in Eurasia," Geographical Review, Vol. 20, 1930, p. 130.

the northern plains, from about the present Multan on the west to the borders of Bengal on the east, may have supported 30 to 40 million people. Thus, the southern Hindu center plus this northern Mogul concentration together may have accounted for some 60–70 million people. In addition there were populous Gujarat, Bengal, and the Moslem states of peninsular India referred to earlier; hence, Datta judges that the total population of the subcontinent in 1605 my have been between 85 and 117 million.[9]

Datta's historical study indicates an increase in population during the 16th and 17th centuries, followed by a slowing down or even halting of growth during most of the 18th century as a consequence of political and economic troubles, including famines and other disasters. He believes that population growth was resumed in the 19th century, but wide margins of error must be allowed for any estimates of the population of the subcontinent during the 18th and early 19th centuries. The range involved in the "low," "medium," and "high" variants of estimates of population in India-Pakistan down to the time of the first census in 1871, as given by Durand, are shown below.[10]

	1750	1800	1850
Low	160	160	215
Medium	190	195	233
High	214	214	242

The first but incomplete census of 1871–1872 counted 206 million, and the more complete census of 1881 yielded a count of 256 million. The third and complete decennial census was taken in 1891, and from that year on the series are fairly reliable. Decennial growth of population from 1891 to 1961 is summarized in Table 12.1. Up to about 1921 growth was relatively slow and erratic; two decades actually showed absolute, although small, declines. But after 1921 the decennial rate of increase has been consistently positive and relatively high, with the decade 1951–1961 showing much the largest increment as well as the highest

[9] See Jatindra Mohan Datta, "A Reexamination of Moreland's Estimate of Population of India at the Death of Akbar," *Indian Population Bulletin*, Vol. 1, 1960, p. 166. By a variety of calculations employing different bases and methods, Datta arrives at not greatly different figures than Moreland for population in the subcontinent in 1605. His estimates range from a low of 85.5 million to a high of 117.2 million.

[10] John D. Durand, "The Modern Expansion of World Population," *Proceedings of the American Philosophical Society*, Vol. 111, June 22, 1967, pp. 136–159. See also Gohran Ohlin, "Historical Outline of World Population Growth," a paper contributed to the World Population Conference, 1965.

TABLE 12.1   Growth of the Subcontinent's and India's Population, 1891–1961 (in Millions)

Census Year	Subcontinent	India (Adjusted to Present Area)	Increase in Millions	Percent Change from Preceding Decade
1891	282	235.9	—	—
1901	285	235.5	−0.4	−0.2
1911	303	249.0	13.5	5.7
1921	306	248.1	−0.9	−0.4
1931	338	275.5	27.4	11.0
1941	389	314.8	39.3	14.2
1951	434	359.2	44.4	14.1
1961	532	438.0	78.8	21.5

SOURCE: *Census of India*, 1961, Provisional Population Totals, p. xii; Kingsley Davis, *The Population of India and Pakistan*, p. 27.

rate of increase. The striking contrast in rates of growth during the two periods 1891–1921 and 1921–1961 is overwhelmingly a consequence of the mortality patterns of the two intervals. In the earlier one high death rates (estimated at 43 to 49 per 1000) tended to cancel out high birth rates. During the four decades 1921–1961, estimated death rates declined from about 36 per 1000 to 22.0. No doubt during this latter period a falling off in deaths from normal causes was significant, but the main determinant of mortality decline was probably the waning effects of catastrophes—famines, famine diseases, epidemic diseases, and floods. And while, the last decade, 1951–1961, shows by far the highest rate of decennial population increase, still, even its 21.5 percent growth rate cannot be considered abnormally high, because although it does exceed the world average of about 17.0, it is well below that of most LD countries and is similar to the growth rates of even a few highly developed countries like Australia and New Zealand. It is because of the massiveness of India's population that the 2.1 percent annual rate of increase produced the enormous absolute increment of nearly 79 million people over the 10-year period. If the decade increment were spread evenly over the whole of India, the increase in numbers per square mile would be 66 persons, which is about the average density of the conterminous United States in the late 1960's. It is a dangerously large increase in an already overburdened land. Preliminary reports from the Indian census of April 1, 1971 indicate the latest decade growth rate of population was a discouraging 24.57 percent, the highest ever. The total number of inhabitants counted was 546.95 million, or an amazing increase of about 109 million during the 1961–1971 decade.

Intra-India rates of population increase by decades and longer periods indicate variable regional growth patterns (Table 12.2).[11] During the three decades 1891–1921 the growth patterns showed marked areal contrasts, signifying that the incidence of abnormal deaths differed markedly from region to region. In the later period 1921–1961 there was a somewhat greater regional consistency in rates of increase.[12] Rates above the country average were characteristic mainly of Assam in the northeast, a semi-frontier region where in-migration was large, in Kerala in the southwest, West Bengal which contains Calcutta, and also, in lesser degree, of the

[11] Glenn T. Trewartha and Gurdev Gosal, "The Regionalism of Population Change in India," *Cold Spring Harbor Symposia on Quantitative Biology*, Vol. 22, 1957, pp. 71–81; G. S. Gosal, "Regional Aspects of Population Growth in India, 1951–1961," *Pacific Viewpoint*, Vol. 3, September 1962, pp. 87–99.
[12] Gosal, "Regional Aspects of Population Growth," pp. 92–93.

TABLE 12.2   Rate of Population Growth in Different States of India in Various Decades and Periods (percent)

State	1941–51	1951–61	1921–61	1901–61
Andhra Pradesh	14.02	15.65	67.99	88.7
Assam	19.28	34.45	130.19	219.8
Bihar	10.20	19.78	65.16	70.1
Gujarat	18.69	26.88	102.78	126.9
Jammu and Kashmir	10.42	9.44	46.88	—
Kerala	22.82	24.76	116.66	164.3
Madhya Pradesh	8.67	24.17	68.85	92.0
Madras	14.66	11.85	55.75	75.0
Maharashtra	19.27	23.60	89.71	104.0
Mysore	19.36	21.57	76.32	80.7
Orissa	6.38	19.82	57.27	70.3
Punjab	0.21	25.86	62.91	53.1
Rajasthan	15.20	26.20	95.83	95.8
Uttar Pradesh	11.80	16.66	58.02	51.7
West Bengal	13.22	32.79	99.85	106.2
India	13.31	21.50	74.75	85.89

SOURCE: Variation in Population Since 1901, *"Census of India,"* Paper No. 1, 1962, p. 8.

dry and subhumid western parts where during this period serious droughts were relatively few.[13] (Regional growth rates for the decade 1951–1961 are discussed in a subsequent section dealing with demographic characteristics.)

DISTRIBUTION OF THE SUBCONTINENT'S POPULATION

Since the population of India-Pakistan is so overwhelmingly rural and agricultural, it is to be expected that the patterns of spatial distribution will be strongly influenced by the food-producing potential of the land. This involves mainly the availability of water (either rainfall or irrigation), the quality of soil, and the degree of slope. Dry lands, hilly lands, and areas of low-grade soils—all presenting discouraging features to subsistence agriculturists—are the usual physical types exhibiting overall sparse settlement. So it is not unexpected that the subcontinent's gross pattern of settlement exhibits a belt of high density, variable in width, that is peripheral to and wraps itself around the Deccan Massif that forms the hilly core of the Hindustan peninsula (Fig. 12.1). Within the massif the prevalence of slopes, the widespread occurrence of leached low-grade residual soils, and over large parts a deficiency of water, are the main deterrents to close agricultural settlement.

The Northern Plain. The single most populous segment within the enveloping peripheral belt of average high density is the one that coincides with the great northern lowland drained by the Indus-Ganges-Brahmaputra rivers. This immense lowland of some 300,000 sq mi, vastest of the earth's alluvial plains, is roughly 1900 miles long and averages 200 miles in width. It supports close to one half the subcontinent's population. Within the northern lowland population densities are generally high, but still there are noteworthy variations, both in gross and in local patterns of density (Fig. 12.1). In the former class is the general decline in density upstream in the Ganges lowland. Thus, over large areas of the middle and lower Ganges, densities exceed 1000 per sq mi, while the average probably is between 800 and 1000. A band of somewhat lower density (600± per sq mi), separates two core areas of unusually high density, one in the delta and the other in the middle Ganges. This band of less crowding coincides with a narrowing of the lowland where hill lands encroach, and where the coarse alluvial fan of the errant Kosi River reduces productivity. In the upper-Ganges lowland, or between about Delhi and Lucknow, overall density further declines, so that the

[13] Gosal, "Regional Aspects of Population Growth," p. 92.

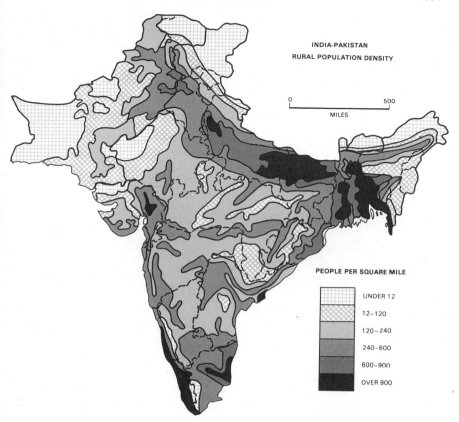

INDIA-PAKISTAN
RURAL POPULATION DENSITY

0   500
MILES

PEOPLE PER SQUARE MILE

UNDER 12

12–120

120–240

240–600

600–900

OVER 900

Fig. 12.1. Density of rural population in the Indian subcontinent. Modified and simplified from National Atlas of India (based on 1951 census), supplemented by changes based on later censuses of India and Pakistan.

average may be between 600 and 800 persons per sq mi. Farther to the northwest, in the trans-Ganges region of India, and beyond in the northern Indus Plains of West Pakistan, average density drops below 600. Beyond the confluence, where the Indus traverses the Thar Desert as a single stream, the overall lowland density is low indeed. Only the belt of irrigated floodplain has close rural settlement.

The interpretation of the gradual decline in population density upstream in the Ganges Valley is complex. Several physical factors are indirectly involved, among them water availability, drainage, soil quality, and terrain. Both rainfall amounts and reliability decline upstream, and this is reflected in a falling off in agricultural productivity. Annual rainfall in the delta amounts to 60–70+ in. In the middle Ganges it drops to about 40 in. on its western margins, and along with this subhumid amount there is increased variability from year to year. In the upper Ganges rainfall averages only 25 to 40 in., so that semiarid conditions prevail, at least in the western parts, while dependability also declines. In the trans-Ganges and upper-Indus Plains, annual precipitation varies from below 10 in. in the southwest to 25± in. in the east, so that it is nearly all dry, most of it steppe but part of it desert.

Within the Indus-Ganges Plain two kinds of alluvium may be recognized, the young and the old. The former is usually more fertile, both because it is newer and less leached of its soluble mineral plant foods and because it may be subject to annual inundation and hence receives frequent new accumulations of fertilizing silt. But inundation combines elements of both asset and liability, since losses from damaging floods are widespread on parts of the low new alluvium. The older alluvium, mainly forming the interfluves (doabs), is higher, less subject to inundation, and in humid climates likely to be more leached and hence less fertile. The new alluvium is typical paddy-rice 'country; the older alluvium is more often devoted to somewhat less-productive dry crops. As a general rule, in the drier wheat-growing parts of the plain population densities are higher on the interfluves than on the floodplains; in the rainier rice-growing sections a reverse situation prevails. With increasing distance from the mouth of the Ganges, the proportion of the lowland floor that is new alluvium declines, while that of the older alluvium increases. Hence, from the standpoint of soil quality and sites fit for paddy rice, the quality of the environment declines upstream in the Ganges Valley.

The progressive changes in the terrain characteristics of the northern lowland from the Ganges delta upstream result in variations in the agricultural practices. These in turn affect population-supporting potentials. In the amphibious delta, paddy rice occupies about three quarters of the cultivated area, with much smaller proportions in jute and a variety of lesser food crops. Even though multiple cropping is not common, such an agricultural system, based largely on paddy, is able to support a dense population. The less-humid middle Ganges, with less new and more old alluvium but also with less swampland, actually has a larger percentage of its surface under cultivation than is true of the delta. But the less-abundant water supply significantly reduces the proportion (35–38 percent) of the cultivated land in paddy, while at the same time favoring a much more diversified agriculture, with more unirrigated crops. Approximately 24 percent of the cultivated area receives supplementary irrigation water, and 15–20 percent is double cropped. Thus, in spite of a reduced rice monoculture, this middle-Ganges region is as densely populated as the somewhat rainier and generally more fertile delta. In the drier upper-Ganges Plain, paddy rice no longer is the crop of first importance, being greatly surpassed by less productive rain-fed dry crops of wheat, barley, and millet. Almost a quarter of the crop area is irrigated, and a similar proportion is double cropped. A less fruitful agriculture here results in a somewhat lower population density. In the still drier trans-Ganges and upper-Indus Plains, paddy rice has become only a minor crop (1–2 percent of the cultivated area), and drought-resistant, quick-maturing crops predominate; again population density declines.

Thus far the feature of population distribution on the great northern lowland that has been emphasized is the general decline in the density upstream from the lower and middle Ganges. But superimposed on this broad-scale pattern is another consisting of multitudes of local ones stemming from microdifferences in relief, soils, drainage and flood problems, available irrigation water, shifting of river channels, transport facilities, and the frequency of cities. The result is a complex mosaic consisting of great numbers of patches of varying population densities.

A clustered village-type settlement predominates. Dispersed settlement is most common in a few regions—areas where defense has not been a pressing problem, areas where physical conditions made compact settlement difficult, or very dry areas where the size of the cultivating group is limited by the water supply.[14]

The Lower Ganges-Brahmaputra Lowland. While overall population densities are exceptionally high in this deltaic region, still there are important areal variations of more than local magnitude. One such is the contrast that exists between the eastern and western parts of the delta. The western section, situated mainly south and west of the Ganges-Padma rivers and with the greater part in West Bengal, is known as the "moribund delta," because there the streams are heavily silted and decadent and carry little water. Interfluves are poorly drained and stagnant swamps are widespread. Even in flood season the land is not inundated, so that soil-reviving new silts are scarce. Here, although average rural densities are high (and overpopulation prevails), they are distinctly below those in the eastern, or active, part of the delta.

The eastern delta is the exit region of the main streams, so rivers are active, stagnant swamps are less extensive, and annual inundation is widespread in the flood season, resulting in a deposit of new silt with a consequent fructification of the soil. Rice and jute monopolize the cropped area, and such high-yielding crops support excessive crowding.

[14] K. II. Buschmann, "Settlements and Habitations in India," *Geographical Review of India*, Vol. 16, September 1954, p. 19.

Most severe rural crowding is restricted to a fairly compact block of territory in the southeastern part of the delta around Dacca and Comilla in East Pakistan, where densities exceed 2000 per sq mi of cultivated area. In some parts they are in excess of 3000.[15]

Areas of relatively low density within the lower Ganges-Brahmaputra region are of several physical types. One of the parts most empty of population is the Sundarbans, a belt of tidal swamps and forest 60–80 mi wide, fringing the seaward margins of the delta. Also modestly settled and utilized are the seasonal shallow lakes or *bhils*, which are especially common in the moribund western delta. A third block of relatively low density is in the far north of the Bengal Plain, near the base of the Himalayas, where the unruly Tista River, debouching from the mountain foothills, has built up an extensive, coarse-textured alluvial fan over which it has repeatedly swung back and forth. A fourth physical type of more modest density consists of three separate and fairly extensive areas of older alluvium (diluvium) (Fig. 12.2). These low, dissected uplands are sufficiently elevated to be above flood level and so do not benefit from recurrent deposits of new silt. Their soils—leached, red, and infertile—are hard to work when dry, and are low in water retentiveness. Large areas

[15] B. L. C. Johnson, "Rural Population Densities in East Pakistan," *Pacific Viewpoint*, Vol. 3, 1962, pp. 51–62.

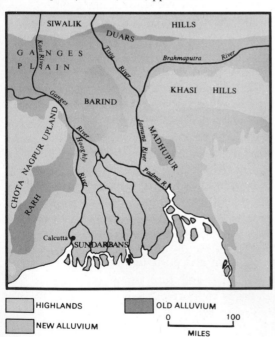

HIGHLANDS

NEW ALLUVIUM

OLD ALLUVIUM

0   100
└────────┘
      MILES

Fig. 12.2. The lower Ganges-Brahmaputra delta region in India-East Pakistan. Note especially the extensive regions of older alluvium; also the Tista River.

of these diluvial surfaces have a cover of inferior degraded forest, shrub, jungle, and grass. One such area of older alluvium, the Madhupur jungle, lies east of the Jamuna channel in East Pakistan. A second, the more extensive Barind, is located farther north and west between the Ganges and Jamuna rivers, and belongs to both India and East Pakistan. A third block of older alluvium, called the Rarh, flanks the westernmost side of the delta, in the form of a band of terrace some 50 miles wide at the base of the peninsular plateaus. In all three regions of older alluvium, forest destruction has brought serious erosion, giving the landscape the appearance of desolation. The lateritic interfluves mainly have a cover of poor short grass, inferior degraded forest, and shrub. Paddy fields occupy many valley floors, so population distribution tends to have a riverine pattern.[16]

The Middle-Ganges Region. This part of the great northern lowland between approximately Lucknow and the delta gains some distinction because it has what is probably the highest overall population density of any of the subcontinent's extensive geographical subdivisions, and at the same time one of the lowest per capita incomes (Fig. 12.1). Cities are unusually few, the rural population composing probably as much as 90–95 percent of the total. Most likely one third to one half of the total area boasts a density of 400–600 per sq km (1000–1600 per sq mi). Density is distinctly below the regional average in the narrow strip of poorly drained *terai* situated along the northern margins of the plain at the base of the highlands. The lowest density of all, however, is in a section in northeastern Bihar where the Kosi River, most rampaging and temperamental of India's mountain streams, has built a huge fan, characterized by poor sandy soils and subject to disastrous floods. Within the last 200 years these recurrent floods have converted extensive areas of fertile paddy lands into barren sand plains and grassy marshes. The Kosi River region has the lowest per capita income in all Bihar.[17] Excluding the two regional exceptions just mentioned, the general spread of rural settlement over the middle-Ganges region appears to be fairly uniform. However, in detail it shows intricate patterns of density contrasts, which reflect small-scale variations in drainage conditions, flood susceptibility, terrain irregularity, soil fertility, availability of subsurface water, and other local conditions affecting agricultural land utilization. In some parts there can be observed a degree of rural clustering around cities

[16] Johnson, "Rural Population Densities in East Pakistan," pp. 58–59. See also O. H. K. Spate and A. T. A. Learmonth, *India and Pakistan: A General and Regional Geography*, 3rd ed., Methuen, London, 1967, pp. 572, 582–583, 586–587.

[17] Enayat Ahmad, "The Rural Population of Bihar," *Geographical Review*, Vol. 51, April 1961, p. 265. See Fig. 12.2 for location of Kosi River.

and towns as focal points, where not only are markets close at hand, but also the land is more productive because it receives much fertilizer in the form of refuse and night soil from the settlements. Annually inundated strips along major streams are likely to have only sparse permanent settlement; the same is true of sand ridges and marshy tracts.[18]

The Upper-Ganges Lowland. Upstream from about Allahabad and Lucknow, in what is known as the upper-Ganges region, there is a perceptible falling off in population density. This in turn relates to a decline in rainfall and also a reduction in the proportion of readily irrigated fertile new alluvium. The upper-Ganges region is predominantly one of flattish old-alluvium surfaces (doabs), which are essentially undissected except along their margins where doab drops down to floodplain. In this subdivision isohyets trend northwest-southeast, so that the drier southwestern part experiences as little as 25 in. of annual precipitation, while the northeast has 40 in. or more. Irrigation is extensively developed, much more so than in the rainier middle Ganges. Because of the great demand for large amounts of artificially applied water under the prevailing cropping practices, the population distribution on the doabs has a significant linear pattern, as influenced by the courses of canals and minor streams. In the northwestern part of the Ganges-Yamuna Doab, particularly to the east and north of Delhi, the part east of the Yamuna River has an especially well-developed irrigation system. As a consequence rice paddy becomes more important and rural settlement thickens very perceptibly. Here also towns are numerous, so the proportion of nonfarmers is relatively high.

The Indus-Ganges Divide. Population density falls off abruptly westward from Delhi and the Yamuna River, where both rainfall and irrigation decline. Over the semiarid divide as a whole, designated the trans-Ganges, population density is less than half what it is in the upper-Ganges subdivision. Here, understandably, the main density variations are closely

---

[18] Ahmad, "The Rural Population of Bihar," p. 266. For details of regional population distribution in India, as a whole, see the following: (1) *National Atlas of India*, Preliminary Edition, 1957, Ministry of Scientific Research and Cultural Affairs, Government of India, New Delhi, Plate 21, Density of Rural Population. (2) S. P. Chatterjee, "Regional Patterns of the Density and Distribution of Population in India," *Geographical Review of India*, Vol. 24, June 1962, pp. 1–28. No population density map of India appears in the published paper. But in a xeroxed typescript copy of the same paper there is a density map similar to the one that appears in the *National Atlas of India*, 1957. (3) Population Maps for the Main English Edition of the *National Atlas of India*, scale 1:1,000,000, Plates 110–124 (4 not yet published), 1959–1962. Population is represented by proportional dots and circles. On the back of each map is a printed text describing spatial distribution of population for the area covered by that sheet.

related to the amount of water available for crops. Rural settlement is thickest on the northern submontane margins of the plain, where both rainfall and irrigation water are most abundant. It falls off southward as water becomes scarcer, and becomes sparse indeed as the Rajasthan Desert is approached and the canals are left behind.

The Upper-Indus Plains. The subdivision lies largely within West Pakistan. Annual rainfall, except in the submontane belt, averages only 10–15 in. Much of the dry upper-Indus Plain has been settled only recently—largely within the last century, or the period of British rule. Earlier, only the extreme north and east (where rainfall is appreciably above the regional average) or along the irrigated river floodplains had there been significant agricultural settlement. The broad interfluves between the six main rivers remained largely empty. But with the development of perennial irrigation systems associated with large-scale dams and reservoirs, the interfluves have been rapidly settled and population densities greatly increased, so that in parts they equal those of the upper Ganges. But in the western section, between the Jhelum and Indus rivers, where irrigation development has lagged, population still remains very sparse. Large parts of the Thal Desert and the Derajat are nearly empty of settlement. In the upper-Indus Plains where paddy rice is not an important crop, and wheat and millets are paramount, population densities on the floodplains are only about one third what they are on the interfluve plains of older alluvium.

Downstream from the confluence of the Indus and its several tributaries, the fructifying combination of Indus water and fertile floodplain soils has permitted a narrow riverine ribbon of dense rural settlement that carries across the otherwise barren Thar desert for some 450 mi. The pattern is strikingly Nilotic in character (Fig. 12.1). Variations in soil, drainage, and availability of water result in sharp density contrasts even within the floodplain ecumene.

The Western Littoral Lowlands. Of the two littoral plains flanking the Deccan Massif of peninsular India, that on the west side facing the Arabian Sea is narrower, except toward the north. For this reason the belt of high population density is also narrower on the west (Fig. 12.1).

In the extreme north, the region of Kutch and the Kathiawar peninsula, situated between the West Pakistan border and the Gulf of Cambay, is quite unlike the remainder of the Arabian Sea littoral. Kutch, lying north of the Gulf of Kutch, has two somewhat unlike sections. Its northern and eastern parts, known as the Rann of Kutch, is a part of the Great Indian Desert. Mostly it is a desolate landscape composed of tidal marsh, tidal mud flats, and salt efflorescence. Human life is scarce indeed. Southern Kutch is a degree better, because although it too is arid to semiarid, its terrain, consisting of flat-topped uplands and small alluvial basins, is less repellent. In the valleys and on the interfluves of the radially developed intermittent streams is a sparse population—pastoral, agricultural, and nonrural—whose average density is nearly 13 per sq km (34–35 per sq mi). The rate of population increase is very slow.

The broad Kathiawar peninsula, situated between the Gulf of Kutch and the Gulf of Cambay, provides a total environment that is somewhat more attractive for human settlement than that of Kutch. The climate is semiarid (15–30 in. of rainfall). Terrain features are those associated with a core made up of lava sheets, flanked by younger rocks and aeolian and alluvial deposits. Probably half or more of the area is utilized for agriculture, seemingly a high figure considering the low and unreliable rainfall. Irrigation water from wells and tanks supplements the inadequate precipitation. Overall population density is probably around 150 per sq mi, higher in the moister south and lower in the drier north. The proportion of the population that is urban is well above the national average.

At the head, and along the eastern margins of the Gulf of Cambay, are the Gujarat Plains, composed of the silts from a number of streams entering the Gulf, where they form an alluvial belt some 250 mi long and up to 60 mi wide. Rainfall varies from subhumid or semiarid in the north (29 in. at Ahmedabad) to 60–70 in. in the extreme south. Average population densities are high. One core area of unusually high density (600–800 persons per sq mi) is situated on the part of the lowland at the head of the Gulf, roughly between the cities of Ahmedabad and Baroda (Fig. 12.1). This is an important industrial area where the proportion of urban people approaches 50 percent of the total. Population densities continue high in a strip following the coast southward.

Farther south, between parallels 20° or 21° and 14°, the coastal lowland, 20–50 mi. in width, ceases to be a plain but instead exhibits a surface in which low hills predominate and flat alluvial plain is scarce. Overall population density is only moderate (300–400 per sq mi) by Indian standards. Nonagricultural settlements stud the seaward margins of the lowland. Associated with the main coastal irregularity is the metropolis of Bombay and a group of industrial satellite cities and towns. In the vicinity of Goa as well, where conditions are more deltaic, there is an intensifying and also a broadening of the coastal settlement belt. Dispersed rural settlement is common.[19]

Just south of about parallel 14°, in South Kanara, there is an embayment of alluvium where the lowland widens to approximately 45 mi and the belt of dense population similarly broadens. But it is not until

[19] C. D. Deshpande, "Settlement Types of Bombay Karnatak," *Indian Geographical Journal*, Vol. 17, 1942, p. 16.

about 12°N, in the state of Kerala, that abnormally high densities are to be found, and this situation continues to the southernmost part of the subcontinent (Fig. 12.1). Lowland Kerala is one of India's most distinctive regions, both physically and culturally. Somewhat isolated from the rest of the country, it is homogeneous in language, is strongly caste conscious, and has the highest percentage of Christians of any large subdivision of the country. The Kerala lowland in most parts is only 15–30 mi in width, but it expands to over 50 mi in the vicinity of the Palghat Gap, which marks an important break in the Western Ghats escarpment. Sandy beach ridges and new alluvium make up the seaward part of the lowland; farther inland, low lateric uplands and hills are common. An unusually intensive system of agriculture, involving rice and coconuts, supports population densities that are among the highest in the country, even rivaling those of regions of greatest crowding in the Ganges lowland. Overall densities on the Kerala Plain are between 1000 and 1500 per sq mi, and locally they reach 2000–4000 even in purely rural environments. Here the population problem is indeed grave. Close to the coast, where nonagricultural settlements are also numerous, a distinctly linear pattern of population distribution prevails, with the residences occupying dry sites on the sandy beach ridges, while paddy fields monopolize the intervening wet swales.

The Eastern Littoral Lowlands. The overall greater width of the eastern littoral lowlands reflects mainly the asymmetry of the Deccan watershed, whose crest is not far removed from the Arabian Sea. The longer east-flowing rivers provide more extensive delta surfaces on the east, and also a greater abundance of irrigation water, which in a region where annual rainfall is only modest is a critical factor in determining density of rural settlement (Fig. 12.1).

The gross morphology of the eastern lowlands involves two main elements: (1) a series of three extensive delta regions separated by (2) strips of true belted coastal plain with infacing escarpments. Largely because the deltas have more fertile soils and a more plentiful supply of irrigation water, efficiently distributed through a system of canals, they are also nodal areas of dense rural settlement. The intervening strips of coastal plain, handicapped by inferior soils and less irrigation water (the latter supplied mainly from inefficient wells and ponds rather than canals), are usually less crowded.

Northernmost of the three extensive alluvial surfaces and coinciding with a main population node that forms the heart of Orissa state, is the compound delta of the Mahanadi, Brahmani, and Baitarni rivers. Even though this northern section is the wettest part of the eastern littoral, 60 in. being an average, 36 percent of the cultivated area is irrigated.

Paddy rice occupies 80–90 percent of the net sown area, with a resulting high overall density of population. In the most crowded part it rises to 700–800 per sq mi; still, this is only half to two thirds the average density of large areas in the middle-and lower-Ganges Valley. Bordering the coast is an extensive belt of swamp and sand where agricultural settlement is relatively sparse. As a rule, density increases inland from the delta mouth to the apex. Also, it is higher in the irrigated and flood-protected tracts than where these beneficial features are lacking. Over the delta as a whole the proportion of population that is urban is far below the country average.

The second major alluvium surface, also coincident with a major population concentration, consists of the combined deltas of the Godavari and Krishna rivers situated at about 16–17°N. Annual rainfall is only around 35 in., so that irrigation must provide supplementary water for paddy rice, which is far and away the dominant crop. Overall densities seem to be only slightly lower than those in the Mahanadi delta.

The Cauvery delta in the extreme southeast, with its well-developed irrigation system, is the granary of southern India. Rural population density is high, with an average of over 700 per sq mi, rising in parts to over 1200.

The strips of coastal plain between and beyond the deltas have varying densities of rural settlement, depending in large measure on variations in such physical features as annual rainfall, available irrigation water, drainage conditions, and soil quality. The relatively wide, subhumid coastal plains south and west of the Cauvery delta, in what is southern Tamilnad, have average population densities well below the average for Indian lowlands; density is only one fourth to one third what it is on the Kerala lowland on the opposite coast. Scarcely 40 percent of the land is under cultivation; rice, watered mainly from artificial ponds, occupies barely one quarter to one third of the tilled area. Here the density pattern is an uneven one, reflecting mainly irrigation potentials. A degree of population concentration occurs along a series of small streams and an even more striking one along the inner margins of the lowland where it makes contact with the highlands, since there irrigation water is more abundant than elsewhere.

Northward from the Cauvery delta to about Madras the coastal plain is nearly as well occupied as the Cauvery delta itself. But beyond Madras, and north nearly to the Krishna delta, the broad coastal plain is much less crowded. Here a deficiency of both rainfall and irrigation water; shifting sand dunes; and stretches of saline soils intermingled with lagoons and backwaters provide a total environment that is relatively unproductive.

North of the Godavari the coastal plain narrows, but its densities are high, approaching those of the delta itself. On the coastal plain north and east of the Mahanadi densities are again lower.

The Peninsular Massif. The peninsular massif, composed mainly of old igneous and metamorphic rocks, is characterized by a hilly surface that is for the most part under 3000 feet in elevation. As a rule slopes are not unusually steep, but on the other hand plains are scarce. In a region of such complex terrain the patterns of population distribution at the meso-level expectably are complex. They appear even more so because they do not fit into a classification according to any well-recognized system of physical and cultural regions.

The North Deccan. The most distinctive subdivision of the massif is the north Deccan, which is essentially a tableland formed on basic lavas, with mesas and buttes rising above the general level and shallowly incised stream valleys cut below it. The whole surface slopes gently southeastward from the crest of the Western Ghats. A large share of the region is included within the Marathi linguistic area and the state of Maharashtra. Although the climate is subhumid or semiarid, irrigation is minor and crops depend largely on rainfall. Fortunately the dark regur soils are water retentive. Probably as much as two thirds of this extensive region is under cultivation, almost exclusively in dry crops, a very high figure considering the nature of the physical environment. A distinctive feature of the region's rural settlement is its remarkably even spread, in conjunction with only a modest average density of about 60–80 per sq km (160–210 per sq mi). Doubtless among all the large regional subdivisions of India the north Deccan exhibits one of the most uniform diffusions of rural population. Still, there is a perceptible thickening of settlement on the flatter, lower areas within the upland, where the accumulation of fertile regur soils is deepest. It is also denser within a north–south belt of variable width (some 50 mi wide in the vicinity of Kolhapur) and about 200–300 mi long, situated just eastward of the crest of the Western Ghats. Here water is more abundant, since there is some spillover of rain from the windward (in summer) side of the Ghats. In addition this is the headwater region of the north Deccan's main rivers and their alluvial basins. Population tends to concentrate along these waterways, resulting in a strongly linear pattern of distribution.

Along the northern margins of the north Deccan are the two large westward flowing rivers, the Narmada and Tapti, separated by the sparsely populated Satpura Range. Neither of the two great river valleys is as densely populated as might be expected in such a subhumid-semiarid environment where irrigation water is in great need. In neither valley is there a highly concentrated and continuous riverine belt of population, especially in the case of the larger Narmada. A partial explanation is to be found in the fact that this latter stream flows in a trough whose bottom is incised 20–40 feet below the valley-floor level, a feature that makes utilization of the river's water difficult. In addition an extensive floodplain is lacking, while the lowland floor is so badly gullied as to make it relatively unattractive to agriculturalists. The valley of the smaller Tapti has a more extensive floodplain and is somewhat more densely peopled. Modest-sized industrial cities, many of them specialized in cotton textiles, are fairly numerous.

The Old Crystalline-Rock Massif.   The peninsula's old-rock hill lands, which surround the north Deccan on the north, east, and south, are a region of intricate and disordered population patterns. Overall densities are characteristically above the massif's modest average along its northern margins where contact is made with the Indo-Gangetic Plain. In that transition zone there is an interdigitation of densely peopled valleys and more sparsely settled hilly interfluves.[20]

In the extreme northeastern part of the massif, in the Bihar section of what is called the Chota Nagpur, population is unusually dense for what is essentially a nonlowland region. In part this reflects the fairly abundant annual rainfall and the considerable amount of upland plain. On the rolling peneplain surfaces, even in the absence of irrigation, rural settlement is widespread and moderately dense. But it thickens in the valleys, and especially in the Damodar Basin and around Jamshedpur, which lie within the western part of the Bihar-Bengal manufacturing region. Here is produced by far the greatest part of India's coal, iron ore, and steel.

In those parts of the massif in eastern peninsular India south of Chota Nagpur and east of the north Deccan, population densities are generally lower and also regionally more variable than on the lava upland. This is predominantly a terrain consisting of low hills developed on granites and gneisses. Slopes prevail; soils are thin and of low grade. Two or three exceptional population regions may be noted. In the upper reaches of the Mahanadi system there has evolved the Chhattisgarh Basin, whose floor, some 10,000 sq mi in area, is underlain by nearly horizontal sedimentary beds. Annual rainfall amounts to about 55 in., but supplementary irrigation is provided to fructify the paddy fields that appear to nearly monopolize the plain's surface. Chhattisgarh stands out sharply on population maps because of its higher densities compared with those of the

[20] Nitya Nand, "Distribution and Spatial Arrangement of Rural Population in East Rajasthan, India," *Annals of the Association of American Geographers*, Vol. 56, 1966, pp. 205–219.

surrounding thinly wooded hills.[21] A tongue of higher density continues westward following the Tapti lowland.

The combined basins of the upper Godavari and Krishna rivers show a somewhat similar thickening of the rural settlement. In contrast, an extensive region of unusually low density is coincident with the hilly, forested region of the Eastern Ghats, which forms the watershed between Mahanadi and Godavari drainage. There average densities drop below 100 per sq mi.

In the narrowing southernmost part of the massif, south of about the latitude of Madras City, the overall population density is distinctly higher than it is over most of the Deccan. It is worth recalling that this southern extremity of India has been one of the subcontinent's two main centers of culture and population over two millenniums. Spatial distribution patterns of human settlements are exceedingly complex; areas of high density are intermingled with a few that are exceedingly low. The latter reflect mainly conditions of high and rugged terrain in portions of the Western Ghats. Medium to high densities are characteristic of the interior Mysore and Coimbatore plateaus, both of which are mainly nonrice regions even though there is some irrigation. The Mysore and Coimbatore settlement concentrations are not wholly isolated from the regions of still higher density in the Kerala and Tamilnad coastal lowlands to the west and east. On the west the formidable Western Ghats do form an almost complete barrier, except for the narrow isthmus of high density that follows the Palghat Gap separating the Nilgiri from the Cardamom Hills. On the east, the lower and more broken Eastern Ghats cause no comparable break in the continuity of population density between interior uplands and eastern lowlands. There the most conspicuous connecting strip of high density is the one that follows the Cauvery Valley.

CHARACTERISTICS OF THE INDIAN POPULATION

Demographic Characteristics. For all India, three different sets of calculated vital rates are shown in Table 12.3. Jain suggests that the decade birth rates as they appear in set (b) may be the most plausible.[22] Sets (a) and (b), which mutually support each other, clearly indicate

---

[21] Spate and Learmonth, *India and Pakistan: A General and Regional Geography*, pp. 709, 711. See also "Chhattisgarh Basin," in R. L. Singh (ed.), *India: Regional Studies*, 21st International Geographical Congress, India, 1968. pp. 275–280.

[22] S. P. Jain, "State Growth Rates and Their Components," in Ashish Bose (ed.), *Patterns of Population Change in India, 1951–1961.* Allied Publishers, New York, 1967, p. 30.

TABLE 12.3   Estimates of All-India Decennial Birth and Death Rates

Decennium	Set (a)		Set (b)		Set (c)
	Birth Rate	Death Rate	Birth Rate	Death Rate	Birth Rate
1901–10	49.2	42.6	52.4	46.8	44.9
1911–20	48.1	47.2	—	—	44.3
1921–30	46.4	36.3	50.8	40.4	43.9
1931–40	45.2	31.2	46.2	33.5	43.9
1941–50	39.9	27.4	43.1	30.0	43.5
1951–60	41.7	22.8	40.4	20.9	42.1

SOURCE: S. P. Jain, "State Growth Rates and Their Components," p. 30.

a decline in national birth rates from about 50 per 1000 early in this century to around 40 as of the decade ending with 1960. Over the same six decades the drop in death rates was far greater—from between 40–50 per 1000 early in the century to the low 20's half a century later.

Because of the inadequacy and unreliability of birth and death registrations in India, any spatial analysis of that country's vital rates is bound to have a weak base. We are obliged to resort to official computed estimates not only for the nation but for the individual states as well. It should be cautioned, however, that any official estimates, however carefully made, are based on certain unproved assumptions, which makes them poor substitutes for directly observed rates. When age-structure statistics, which suffer from dislocations and great limitations, must be used to compute vital rates, it is scarcely justifiable to read too much significance into small regional differentials in birth and death rates between individual provinces. Moreover, the value of any official statistics by states is greatly impaired as a consequence of territorial changes in state areas and boundaries during the intercensal periods, especially that of 1951–1961. And finally, any analysis of regional differentials in vital rates by states has only limited value because of the great size and internal diversity of most of the Indian states. Any generalization applied to such extensive regions can only be complex weighted averages of large numbers of areal and local differences, many of which serve to cancel each other out because they operate in opposite directions. Estimates of vital rates for the much smaller district subdivisions are lacking or incomplete.

Birth Rates. For what it may be worth, it can be pointed out that of the 14 principal states in 1960 (Jammu and Kashmir omitted), 7 had birth rates below the estimated national rate of 41.7 per 1000, while an equal number had rates above it (Table 12.4). The seven states with below-average birth rates represented about 56 percent of the total population. Values for individual states ranged from a high of 49.3 in Assam to a low of 34.9 in Tamil Nadu (Madras). Of the 14 states, 9 had estimated average birth rates that were within 2 points either way from the country average of 41.7, a departure that is probably lacking in significance, considering the poor quality of the data. Two states only, Madras (birth rate 34.9 per 1000) and Kerala (38.9), located in southernmost India, had crude birth rates that were significantly below the national average. Just why fertility should be lowest there has never been adequately explained. Nevertheless certain coincidences may be worth

TABLE 12.4   Computed Birth and Death Rates in Indian States (1951–1960)

States	Birth Rate	Death Rate
Andhra Pradesh	39.7	25.2
Madras (Tamil Nadu)	34.9	22.5
Uttar Pradesh	41.5	24.9
Assam	49.3	26.9
Bihar	43.4	26.1
Madhya Pradesh	43.2	23.2
Orissa	40.4	22.9
Gujarat	45.7	23.5
Kerala	38.9	16.1
Rajasthan	42.7	19.4
Maharashtra	41.2	19.8
Mysore	41.6	22.2
Punjab	44.7	18.9
West Bengal	42.9	20.5
All India	41.7	22.8

SOURCE: S. P. Jain, "State Growth Rates and Their Components," p. 25.

noting. One of these is that the general fertility rate (birth rate per 1000 women age 15–44) among the Indian states is also lowest in Tamil Nadu (Madras) and next lowest in Kerala. Another is that the proportion of married women ages 15–44 to total women in that age bracket is lowest in Kerala (68.7 percent) and Madras (78.3). Still a third observation is that the median age of marriage for wives is highest in Kerala and either second or third highest in Madras. And finally, the gross reproduction rate is lowest in Tamil Nadu (Madras state) and next lowest in Kerala.[23] As a general rule, it would seem that the causes of differential fertilities among the Indian states are more likely to be found in the social and cultural environment than in the economic one.[24]

Three states had crude birth rates that were significantly above the national average—Assam (49.3), Gujarat (45.7), and Punjab (44.7). Their locations within India lack any similarity. Assam is a semifrontier region with a particularly strong net in-migration whose selective effects, favoring young adult age groups, may help to account for its unusually high birth rate. Among the Indian states, Assam also had the highest general fertility rate, much the highest marital fertility rate, and the highest gross reproductive rate. Punjab and Gujarat rank either second or third in these same features.[25]

Death Rates. For the decade 1951–1960, India as a whole, as well as most of the states, showed a marked decline in the computed death rates over those of 1941–1950. This appears to have been the main reason for the acceleration of population growth during the decade 1951–1960. According to one set of estimates, the average all-India decade death rate declined from 27.4 per 1000 in 1941–1951 to 22.8 in 1951–1961, or 4.6 points. But another estimate sees it as declining from 30.0 to 20.9, or 9.1 points (Table 12.3).

The range in death rates for 1951–60 among Indian states was from an estimated low of 16.1 in Kerala to a high of 26.9 in Assam, a large differential indeed, amounting to 10.8 points (Table 12.4). Seven states had estimated rates above the national average (22.8), and 7 were below. If the states that are within 2 points of the national average are disregarded, then there are 4 states (Assam, 4.1 points above; Bihar, 3.3; Andhra Pradesh, 2.4; and Utter Pradesh 2.1) with rates sufficiently above the average to warrant comment. Similarly, there are 5 states (Kerala, 5.7 points below; Punjab, 3.9; Rajasthan, 3.4; Maharashtra, 3.0; and West Bengal, 2.3) with rates more than two points below the national death-rate

[23] Jain, "State Growth Rates and Their Components," p. 26.
[24] Jain, "State Growth Rates and Their Components," p. 28.
[25] Jain, "State Growth Rates and Their Components," p. 26.

average. In neither group do the states occupy contiguous blocks of territory, or have any overall environmental or cultural characteristic that
might in some way influence economic and social conditions and hence
mortality rates. No satisfactory explanation has been offered for the state
deviations in death rates noted above.

Regionalism of Population Growth Rates, 1951–1961. Some 80 million
people were added to the all-India population during the decade
1951–1961, or on the average more than 50 persons per sq mi in rural
areas. This represented a national growth rate of about 21.5 percent,
by far the largest in any of the last 7 decades. The variations in growth
rates among the Indian states were very largely a matter of natural increase resulting from differentials in fertility and mortality; net migration
was a less significant factor (Table 12.2). Migration was somewhat
more important when applied to districts, which are administrative subdivisions of the states. The regional analysis to follow is based largely
on Gosal's map and discussion of population growth, in which he makes
use of district data.[26]

On the Gosal map (Fig. 12.3) four different 1951–1961 rates of growth
are distinguished and their spatial distributions shown: (1) areas with
an abnormally high rate of decade increase, or over 30 percent, compared
with the national average of 22–23 percent; (2) areas with a high rate
of increase (20–30 percent), which for the most part is higher than the
national average; (3) areas with a moderate rate of increase (10–20 percent), or well below the national average; and (4) areas with a low
rate of increase (below 10 percent).

[26] G. S. Gosal, "Regional Aspects of Population Growth in India, 1951–1961,"
Pacific Viewpoint, Vol. 3, 1962, pp. 87–99.

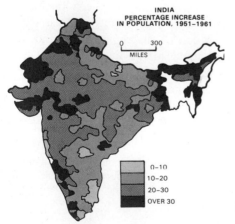

Fig. 12.3. Data by districts. After
Gurdev Singh Gosal.

With few exceptions, regions with abnormally high rates of population increase, in addition to showing large differentials between births and deaths and hence a large natural increase, have a considerable net in-migration. Usually responsible for this influx are one or more of the following factors: rapid expansion of industry and associated urbanization; improvement and enlargement of irrigation facilities; reclamation of new lands for agriculture, both on lowlands and uplands; and the entrance of refugees from East Pakistan.

Among the regions with a high rate of population increase are the following: (1) The Assam Plain, a region of continuing land reclamation and high birth rates; Assam state also had the largest net in-migration of any state, including an influx of nearly a million refugees from East Pakistan; (2) Tripura, adjoining densely populated East Pakistan on its eastern margins, which also received large numbers of refugees; (3) West Bengal (and adjoining parts of Bihar) and Orissa, which represent an area of expanding industry as well as a receiving region for numerous refugees from East Pakistan; (4) the Punjab Plain east of the Sutlej River and parts of adjacent Rajasthan, where, in addition to a large natural growth, there has been an important influx of new settlers attracted by the reclamation of waste lands and the extension of canal irrigation; (5) parts of Gujarat and adjoining areas of Rajasthan and Madhya Pradesh farther east, where rapid population growth is closely tied to increased industrialization and urbanization, with associated in-migration; and (6) upland areas in the states of Kerala, Tamil Nadu (Madras), and Mysore in the south, where the extension of plantation agriculture and general farming, together with increased industrialization, is mainly responsible for rapid population growth.

Regions with a high but not spectacular decade rate of increase (20–30 percent), cover a vast area, mainly in western and northern peninsular India. The greater part so characterized has a growth rate at least somewhat exceeding the national average. Much of the region is upland, the climate is subhumid or semiarid, rural standards of living are low, and population densities are, with a few exceptions, only medium or low. Large parts are even classed as underpopulated.[27] By far the greater share of the population increase is natural and is occasioned by a continuing high birth rate and a falling death rate as famines and epidemic diseases have been increasingly eliminated.

[27] P. Sen Gupta, "Population and Resource Development in India." Paper submitted for the Symposium on the Geography of Population Pressure on Physical and Social Resources, The Pennsylvania State University, September 17–23, 1967. Published subsequently, but in altered form in *Geography and a Crowding World*, Wilbur Zelinsky et al. (eds.), Oxford University Press, New York, 1970, pp. 424–441.

Also of vast extent and covering close to one half the area of the country are the regions characterized by a decade population increase of only 10 to 20 percent, or one generally well below the country average. Included are the following regions: (1) most of the Ganges Plain up-river from West Bengal; (2) the Punjab Plain west of the Sutlej River; (3) large parts of the states of Orissa and Andhra Pradesh and Tamil Nadu (Madras); and (4) scattered areas along the west coast. Most inland parts are characterized by high population densities, so that even the below-average rates of increase resulted in large absolute increments per unit area (Fig. 12.3). Nutritional densities are especially high, malnutrition and underfeeding are chronic, and death rates are usually above the national average. With few exceptions, the degree of urbanization is low. The economy is overwhelmingly one of subsistence agriculture. In view of the heavy pressure of the population on resources, it would appear that in many parts a saturation level has already been reached and overpopulation prevails. These have been classed as "problem regions."[28]

Areas with a very low rate of increase (less than 10 percent) constitute only a small fraction of the Indian territory. Composed mainly of widely scattered fragments of no great extent, the type has most of the characteristics just previously described for the areas with a 10 to 20 percent increase rate, but in an intensified form. Ordinarily areas of this type have been regions of net out-migration for many decades.

Rural-Urban Composition. According to the 1961 census, out of a total Indian population of 439.2 million, only 78.94 million, or about 18 percent, were living in urban places, as nationally defined. But although the urban sector is small relatively, its absolute size is enormous. In only seven of the world's countries do even total populations outnumber the urban dwellers of India. Only three countries have more urban people.

Prior to 1961 Indian censuses defined as "urban" essentially those settlements having a minimum population of 5000. But the 1961 census adopted a somewhat more restrictive definition that had the general effect of reducing the 1961 count of urban people below what it would have been if the earlier, looser definition had been followed.[29] It may be noted,

[28] Gupta, "Population and Resource Development in India."
[29] The new definition of urban is still only moderately precise, since it continues to include what local statutes regarded as towns—municipalities, cantonments, notified areas, and others having local administrations. For all others three tests were applied: (1) a population of not less than 5000, (2) a density of not less than 1000 per sq mi, and (3) at least three-quarters of the adult male population employed in nonagricultural pursuits. The less rigorous earlier definition required only a minimum population of 5000.

TABLE 12.5   Urban Population of India by Size Classes, 1961

Class of Urban Place	Number	Population (in Millions)	Percent of Total Urban Population
100,000 and over	107	35.13	44.50
50,000–100,000	139	9.53	12.07
20,000– 50,000	518	15.75	19.95
10,000– 20,000	820	11.30	14.32
5,000– 10,000	848	6.34	8.03
<5,000	268	0.89	1.13
Total	2700	78.94	100.00

SOURCE: Census of India, 1961, Vol. I, Part II-A.

also, that "rural population" (for the most part those living in places with fewer than 5000 inhabitants) is not synonymous with "agricultural population," since perhaps 17 percent of the rural people, or some 60 million, derive their livelihood from nonagricultural pursuits.

While nearly 18 percent of India's total population lives in urban places of all sizes, according to United Nations sources, only some 14 percent reside in settlements with 20,000 or more inhabitants, and 8 percent in cities of 100,000 or more. Or, shifting the base from total to urban population, some 44.5 percent of the latter live in 107 cities of 100,000 or more inhabitants and 76.5 percent dwell in 764 localities of 20,000 and more.[30] (See Table 12.5.) Seven Indian cities were metropolises of over one million inhabitants in 1961.

Growth of Urban Population. The urbanization process began late in India and has accelerated at only a slow or moderate pace, probably because of the country's laggard economic development. An increased rate of urbanization was first noticeable in the decade 1911–1921; during the previous decade the rate of urban growth lagged behind those of the rural and total populations. India in 1901 had nearly the same level of urbanization as did the United States about 1839. And in 1951, half a century later, India was farther behind the United States in urbanization than it had been in 1901.[31] But since 1911 the proportion of the total population that is urban has consistently risen, as have the decade growth

[30] Ashish Bose, "Six Decades of Urbanization in India," *Indian Economic and Social History Review* (Delhi), Vol. 2, January 1965, p. 32.
[31] Kingsley Davis, "Urbanization in India: Past and Future," in Roy Turner (ed.), *India's Urban Future*. University of California Press, Berkeley, 1962, pp. 7–8.

TABLE 12.6 Percentages of India's Population That are Rural and Urban,
and Their Decade Growth Rates

| | Percentage of Population | | Decade Growth Rates (Percent) | | |
| | Rural | Urban | Total Population | Rural Population | Urban Population |
Year					
1901	89.0	11.0			
1911	90.0	10.0	5.8	6.4	0.35
1921	89.0	11.0	−0.3	−1.3	8.3
1931	88.0	12.0	11.0	10.0	19.1
1941	86.0	14.0	14.2	11.8	32.0
1951	83.0	17.0	13.3	8.8	41.4
1961	82.0	18.0	21.5	20.6	26.4
				(19.0)[a]	(34.0)[a]

SOURCE: S. N. Agarwala, *Some Problems of India's Population*. Bombay, 1966,
pp. 23, 139.

[a] Adjusted for definitional change.

rates of urban population, at least down to 1951 (Table 12.6). At the
beginning of the 20th century, urban population comprised only 10–11
percent of the total population. By 1961 the urban fraction had risen
to over 18 percent, while the total number of urban dwellers had multiplied about three times.

More careful scrutiny of the urban growth trends in India (excluding
the present Pakistan area) during the 20th century shows a constantly
accelerating rate through the four decades ending in 1941 (Fig. 12.4).

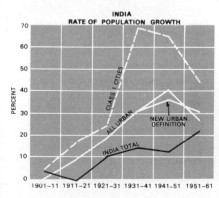

Fig. 12.4. Rates of population growth over
a period of six decades. Note that the rate
of urban growth has exceeded that of total
population growth over the five decades
from 1911–1961. Urban growth has been
most rapid in large cities of 100,000 or
more inhabitants. Data from *Census of
India*, 1961, Vol. I.

By contrast, there has been a deceleration of the rate during the two decades ending in 1961 and an actual decline in the rate during 1951–1961. For Class 1 cities, or those with 100,000 or more inhabitants in 1961, the decline in growth rate became evident as early as the 1941–1951 decade, as the rate dropped from 68 percent during 1931–1941 to 65 percent in 1941–1951 and only 44 percent in 1951–1961.

This recent slowing in the acceleration of the urbanization process, culminating very lately in a decline, came as a surprise to the Indian government. And coming as it did at a time when the rate of total population increase was the highest ever, it requires an explanation. A number of suggestions have been advanced—the slow pace of industrialization; a slowing rate of rural-urban migration; increasing unemployment in the cities, which acted to discourage in-migration from the rural areas; some improvement of economic conditions in the rural areas; a wider dispersion of industries leading to a more balanced regional development—but these are little more than conjectures, since no serious study of the problem has been made.[32] Brush[33] thinks that the extreme congestion and population pressure within the core areas of cities is an additional factor operating to slow up urbanization. Urban dwellers tend to crowd the city centers in order to profit by proximity to place of work and to markets. Consequently existing supplies of urban housing and amenities remain strongly focused within the old urban cores, where they have become highly inadequate to meet the current needs. According to this view Indian cities are experiencing a serious population implosion.

Since in India natural rates of increase are not greatly different in urban and rural places (urban birth and death rates are probably both a little lower), accelerated urbanization could have resulted only from a net in-migration. Probably somewhat more than half the urban growth results from natural increase in the resident population; the remainder is derived from net in-migration. It is estimated that in the 1941–1951 decade some 9 million persons originating in rural areas were added to urban places. In the decade following, this net rural in-migragion declined to only 5.2 million.[34]

Because the 1961 census count of India's urban population was based

[32] S. N. Agarwala, *Population*. National Book Trust, New Delhi, 1967, pp. 58–59.

[33] John E. Brush, "Some Dimensions of Urban Population Pressure in India," in *Geography and a Crowding World*, Wilbur Zelinsky et al. (eds.), Oxford University Press, New York, 1970, p. 299.

[34] D. J. Bogue and K. C. Zachariah, "Urbanization and Migration in India," in Roy Turner (ed.), *India's Urban Future*. University of California Press, Berkeley, 1962, p. 31.

TABLE 12.7   Total and Percent Urban Population, 1901–1961

Year	Total Urban (Millions)	Percent Urban	Increase in Each Decade (Millions)	Percent Increase in Each Decade
1901	25.85	10.8		
1911	25.94	10.3	0.09	· 0.35
1921	28.09	11.2	2.15	8.27
1931	33.46	12.0	5.37	19.12
1941	44.15	13.9	10.70	31.97
1951	62.44	17.3	18.29	41.43(35.2)[b]
1961	78.94(83.67)[a]	17.97(19.1)[a]	16.50(21.23)[a]	26.41(34.0)[a]

SOURCE: *Census of India*, 1961, Vol. I, Part II-A.

[a] Adjusted upward for definitional change in "urban" between 1951 and 1961.

[b] A part of the unusually large urban increase in the decade 1941–1951 was abnormal in that it involved a large influx of refugees following partition of the subcontinent into India and Pakistan. In the last column the figure in parentheses for 1951 indicates the much smaller percentage increase that would have occurred if the refugees are omitted.

on a more restrictive definition of "urban" than had been used earlier, it suffered a reduction by about 4.7 million—from 83.6 to 78.94—compared with what it would have been if the earlier definition of urban had been continued. If in Table 12.7 the 1961 urban figures are adjusted upward (numbers in parentheses) for the change in definition, then the differentials in various urban quantities between 1951 and 1961 are seen to be less unusual and particularly, the slowing of the urbanization rates appears less dramatic. The 1951–1961 decade gain in total urban numbers (column 1) becomes the largest ever, instead of lagging behind the 1941–1951 gain as the unadjusted figures suggest. The percent urban rose from 17.3 in 1951 to 19.1 in 1961 instead of to only the unadjusted 17.97, while the percent decade increase becomes 34.0 in 1961 instead of only 26.4. In addition, the 1951 urban figures are considerably inflated as a consequence of an abnormal condition resulting from a large influx of refugees from Pakistan because of partition. If this element is excluded, the increase in urban population in the 1941–1951 decade (column 4) becomes 35.2 percent (instead of 41.3), which is relatively close to the adjusted 34.0 percent for 1951–1961.

Distribution of Urbanization.   Analysis of spatial variations in urban intensity using state data represents only a crude method of measurement; still, it has modest significance. There is a considerable range among

TABLE 12.8   Percent of Urban Population in Indian States, 1961

State	Percent of Total Population in Urban Areas	Percent of Total Population in Towns of 20,000 and Above	Percent of Total Population in Cities of 100,000 and Above
Andhra Pradesh	17.43	13.00	7.06
Assam	7.67	4.38	0.84
Bihar	8.42	6.01	3.00
Gujarat	25.79	19.87	10.95
Jammu and Kashmir	16.57	11.52	10.96
Kerala	15.09	11.54	4.08
Madhya Pradesh	14.30	9.55	4.51
Madras (Tamil Nadu)	26.68	19.41	10.06
Maharashtra	28.22	23.34	17.07
Mysore	22.34	15.13	8.22
Orissa	6.32	3.42	0.85
Punjab	20.14	14.77	5.27
Rajasthan	16.27	10.66	6.15
Uttar Pradesh	12.85	10.48	6.48
West Bengal	24.45	21.39	13.57
India	17.97	13.75	8.00

SOURCE: Bose, Ashish, "Six Decades of Urbanisation in India," p. 32.

Indian states in the proportions of their populations that are urban—from a low of 6.3 percent in Orissa to a high of about 28 in Maharashtra (Table 12.8). Nine states had urban percentages below the national average of nearly 18 percent; six were above. But only nine deviated as much as four percentage points from the national average and therefore appear to warrant comment. Four states are weakly urbanized and show percentages of 14 percent or less—Uttar Pradesh, Assam, Bihar, and Orissa. The last three, where the urban percentages are less than 9 percent, are especially noteworthy. Three different kinds of regions are represented within this group: (1) the fertile, densely populated, non-industrial, and overwhelmingly agricultural middle- and lower-Ganges Plain (omitting the western delta containing the Calcutta conurbation) represented by Uttar Pradesh and northern Bihar; (2) the low-grade physical environment of the northern and northeastern part of the peninsular massif in southern Bihar and Orissa; and (3) the highly rural and agricultural Assam lowland, a region of strong in-migration and new settlement. All four states are relatively backward regions, characterized by small per capita income and subsistence farming, in which modern industry has made little headway.

Fives states have urban percentages well above the country average of about 18 percent; in fact, all five are recorded as having 22 percent or above. These most urbanized states are Maharashtra, containing the great Bombay conurbation and manufacturing concentration, and in addition Poona and Nagpur; Tamil Nadu (Madras), which includes the industrial metropolis of Madras; Gujarat, having the metropolis and manufacturing center of Ahmedabad; West Bengal, a prime manufacturing region, which includes the great cities of Calcutta and Howrah; and Mysore, with its metropolis of Bangalore. In all four of these states one and usually more of the following attributes are present: commercial crops are above average in importance, secondary industry supports a relatively large segment of the inhabitants, and densities of rural population are not suffocatingly high.

The national pattern of urbanization based on district (not state) data reveals that by far the greatest share of the northeastern part of the country, both in hill lands and lowlands, is less than 10 percent urban, or well below the national average (Fig. 12.5).[35] The main exception is the West Bengal industrial region, which includes the metropolis of Calcutta and its satellite cities. Particularly to be noted is the elongated strip of higher urbanization that reaches inland from the Damodar Valley west of Calcutta, along the upper Mahanadi and its tributary valleys to the Wainganga Valley and the city of Nagpur and even beyond. In general, the west and south are more urbanized than the north and east. Expectably, districts in which individual large cities are situated stand out prominently.

Distribution of Recent Changes in Urban Population. The all-India urban growth rate for the decade 1951–1961 was about 26 percent (34 percent if adjusted upward for definitional change). Among the individual Indian states, urban growth ranged from a high of 125 percent in Assam to a low of 10 in Rajasthan (Table 12.9). Seven of the 15 states experienced growth rates in excess of the country average; six of these reached six or more percentage points above the mean. It is recognized, of course, that Indian states are so large and often so diverse in character that their average urban growth rates may not be so meaningful, since the average may well be a mean of highly unlike district averages. It may be suggestive that the three states (Assam, Orissa, Bihar)

[35] See map in "India's Urbanization," *Focus* (American Geographical Society), Vol. 19, September 1968, p. 3.

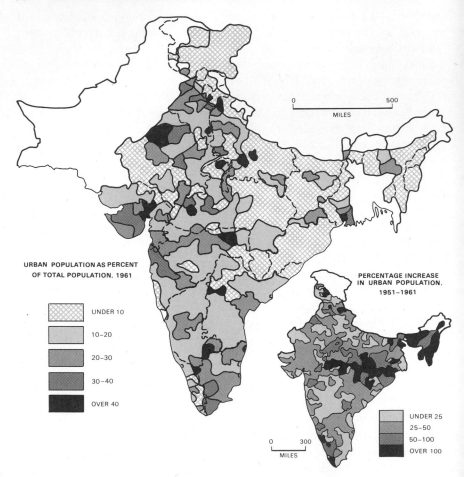

URBAN POPULATION AS PERCENT
OF TOTAL POPULATION, 1961

UNDER 10

10-20

20-30

30-40

OVER 40

PERCENTAGE INCREASE
IN URBAN POPULATION,
1951-1961

UNDER 25
25-50
50-100
OVER 100

Fig. 12.5. Data by districts. After Gurdev Singh Gosal. Inset map of urban population change, 1951-1961, after *Focus* (American Geographical Society), September 1968.

with the highest urban growth rates also have at present the lowest degree of urbanization, so their speed-up could be interpreted as a case of making up for a slow start. Significantly, Bihar and Orissa are showing evidence of important change, including programs for irrigation and rail development, active exploitation of minerals, and the establishment of heavy industry. Also distinctly above average in urban rate of growth are Madhya Pradesh in the northern Deccan, Kerala in the extreme southwest, highly industrialized West Bengal in the northeast, and Punjab in the northwest. The first two states are below average in intensity of urbanization; the last two are above.

TABLE 12.9   Total Urban Population by States of India,
1951 and 1961, and the Decade Rate of Growth

State	1961 (Millions)	1951 (Millions)	Growth 1951–1961 (Percent)
India	78.8	62.6	25.9
Andra Pradesh	6.3	5.4	16.6
Assam	0.9	0.4	125.0
Bihar	3.9	2.6	50.0
Gujarat	5.3	4.4	20.5
Jammu and Kashmir	0.6	a	a
Kerala	2.6	1.9	36.8
Madhya Pradesh	4.6	3.1	48.4
Madras (Tamil Nadu)	9.0	7.3	23.3
Maharashtra	11.2	9.3	20.4
Mysore	5.3	4.5	17.8
Orissa	1.1	0.6	83.3
Punjab	4.1	3.1	32.3
Rajasthan	3.3	3.0	10.0
Uttar Pradesh	9.5	8.6	10.5
West Bengal	8.5	6.2	37.1

SOURCE: Census of India, 1961, Paper No. 1 of 1962, Final Population
Totals, pp. 165–252.
a 1951 census not held.

On the map[36] showing recent urban change by districts, it is especially noticeable that it is in parts of the weakly urbanized northeast that rate of urban growth has been most rapid (Fig. 12.5, inset). The extreme southwest, mainly Kerala state, also stands out for the same reason.

Religious Composition.   In India religion strongly permeates the economic, political, and social fabric of the population. For this reason an understanding of the spatial attributes of religious composition, as expressed in the relative numerical importance of various religious groups in India, has geographical significance.

Hindus comprise a vast majority (83.5 percent) of the Indian population. Except in the few districts where Christians and Sikhs predominate, Hindus are everywhere a majority. Among the minority religious groups, Moslems form 10.69 percent of the population, followed in order by Christians (2.44), Sikhs (1.79), Buddhists (0.74), and Jains (0.46). In

[36] "India's Urbanization," p. 3.

contrast to the nearly ubiquitous Hindus, the minority religions are concentrated in particular regions. The very fact that Hindus are both so predominant numerically and so widely distributed is of the highest political and social importance.

The most distinctive feature of Hinduism as a religion and way of life is the symbiotically related socioeconomic institution of caste. Doubtless Indian caste represents the most intense hierarchical organization of society known anywhere. The system is so complex as to defy easy definition, but it will suffice to say that its fundamental tenet is that the accident of birth determines a person's caste and hence his position in society. Exclusivism is carried to such extremes that caste determines whom a person may marry, with whom he may eat, and which occupations he may enter. Brahmins (priests) represent the top strata of Hindu society and untouchables the lowest, with the latter restricted to the most menial and ritually unclean occupations. Within cities there has been a weakening of caste rules relating to food and occupations, but among rural Hindus they still remain strong as features of the social organization.

From Fig. 12.6 showing distribution of Hindus as a percentage of the total population in 1961, the regions where this majority group represents less than 84 percent, the country average, are mainly peripheral in location except for a few scattered inland tracts.[37] The peripheral regions of reduced Hindu dominance include a fairly continuous belt of districts along the northwestern, northern, and northeastern margins, and another along the southwestern coast, mainly in the state of Kerala. In the latter region, long subjected to outside influences coming by sea, conversion to Islam and Christianity has been widespread. The Indian regions bordering the strongly Moslem state of Pakistan expectably have a somewhat reduced Hindu majority. In some of the more isolated hill lands of Assam where tribal peoples prevail, Hindus are actually in the minority. These same regions have witnessed a large-scale conversion to Christianity.

Although Moslems constitute only 10–11 percent of the total population, they number about 47 million, even after the large exodus at the time of partition in 1947. This largest of the minority religious groups is appreciably concentrated in only a few regions; elsewhere Moslems are widely but sparsely distributed (Fig. 12.6). The areas of highest Moslem concentration border East Pakistan. This focus is one of long

---

[37] G. S. Gosal and A. B. Mukerji, "The Religious Composition of India's Population: A Spatial Analysis," *Tijdschrift voor Economische en Sociale Geografie*, Vol. LXI, 1970, pp. 91–100.

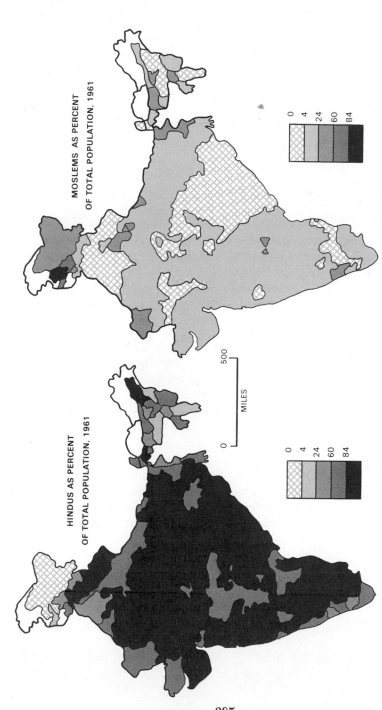

Fig. 12.6. India—religious composition. Distribution of (*a*) Hindus and (*b*) Moslems as percentages of the total population, 1961, by districts. After maps by Gurdev Singh Gosal.

385

standing, going back many centuries, and it has been renewed and in-creased by recent infiltration from the vast reservoir of Moslems in East Pakistan. A second region of Moslem concentration is the northwest in the parts bordering West Pakistan. Some increase of the Moslem element has also occurred in certain districts of Rajasthan and Gujarat bordering on Islamic West Pakistan, from which there had been an important in-filtration during the census decade 1951–1961. A third is in the state of Jammu and Kashmir, in parts of which Moslems represent an important majority. The strong predominance of Moslems in the Vale of Kashmir has its origins in the large-scale conversion to Islam beginning in the 15th century.

The 10 to 11 million Christians in India live mainly in rural areas, with their principal concentration in the southwestern coastal zone from Goa southward. In Kerala Christians represent as much as 21–22 percent of the total population. They are also relatively numerous among the tribal hill peoples of Assam.

Sikhs, numbering nearly eight million, are overwhelmingly concen-trated in Punjab, where they comprised about one third of the total population in 1961.

Sex Composition. India's population has a relative deficiency of fe-males, with only 941 women for every 1000 men. This shortage of women was observed in the results of the first complete census, that of 1891, and it has continued to persist down to the present. Indeed, the deficiency is more striking today than it was at the beginning of the present century. At first the relative scarcity of females was attributed to their under-enumeration; subsequently, after a succession of censuses it has been established as a reality.[38]

The unbalanced sex composition of India results from such extremely complex processes that as yet no adequate explanation has been forth-coming. It is known that more male infants are born than females, but offsetting this, deaths are more frequent among boys than girls up to the age of 11. Significantly, the most important decline in the proportion of females, and so seemingly the one that most affects the overall sex composition of the country, occurs during the female reproductive years (15–44). This is especially true in the later years of the maternity period, or between the ages of 35 and 44. It is estimated that 10 percent of Indian wives die in childbirth.[39] Thus it is likely that at least one factor leading to a relative scarcity of adult females is the toll taken by frequent

---

[38] G. S. Gosal, "The Regionalism of Sex Composition of India's Population," *Rural Sociology*, Vol. 26, 1961, pp. 122–123.

[39] Gosal, "The Regionalism of Sex Composition," p. 124.

childbearing and the physical exhaustion and related ailments associated with it. Less commonly now, but frequently in earlier decades, recurrent famines and epidemics were also sex selective in that they caused more deaths among women than among men.

For the country as a whole, the relative proportion of females to males is smaller in cities and towns (845 per 1000) than in the rural villages (963). (See Table 12.10.) It is also smaller in the larger cities of over 100,000 where housing is especially acute than it is in the smaller ones. In Delhi, for example, there are only 786 females per 1000 males (1961). The proportionately fewer females in cities reflects, for one thing, the scarcity of urban employment opportunities for women; consequently they enter less into rural-urban migration. It also denotes the higher costs of living in cities, especially in the metropolises, a fact that discourages the movement of whole families from rural to urban areas. In the face of these handicaps, males moving to the cities for employment may decide to leave wives and families behind in their home villages.

TABLE 12.10   Sex Ratios by States, 1961 (Females Per 1000 Males)

State	Total Population	Urban Population	Urban Population in Cities Over 100,000	Rural Population
India	941	845		963
Andra Pradesh	981	951	941	988
Assam	876	677	530	895
Bihar	994	811	787	1012
Gujarat	940	896	NA	956
Jammu and Kashmir	878	844	844	884
Kerala	1022	991	NA	1027
Madhya Pradesh	953	856	813	970
Madras (Tamil Nadu)	992	963	923	1003
Maharashtra	936	801	742	995
Mysore	959	913	900	973
Orissa	1001	807	725	1015
Punjab	864	814	807	878
Rajasthan	908	882	912	913
Uttar Pradesh	909	812	801	924
West Bengal	878	701	640	943

SOURCE: Columns 1, 2, and 4 are from *Census of India*, 1961, Vol. I. Part II-A(i), General Population Tables, p. 67. Column 3 on cities over 100,000 is from *Census of India*, 1961, Provisional Population Totals, p. xxxiii.

Somewhat puzzling is the fact that the proportion of women in urban places is higher in Tamil- and Telegu-speaking southern India than elsewhere. Possibly this reflects the greater prevalence there of cottage industries in which the opportunities for female employment are better than they are in large-scale factory industries. Also in these same southern regions women enjoy a somewhat higher status in society than they do in most other parts.

Regionalism of Sex Composition.[40] While eight of the 15 states in 1961 had female/male ratios below the country average of 941, only 4 (Assam, Punjab, West Bengal, and Jammu and Kashmir) were below 900 and hence represent a sufficient departure from the mean as to be genuinely meaningful. These 4 were all concentrated in either the northwest or the northeast (Table 12.10).

The more refined map of sex ratios, making use of data by districts, also emphasizes the female deficiency in these same general regions. The area of female scarcity in the northwest includes the western half of the Ganges Plain, much of Punjab, large parts of highland Jammu and Kashmir, and some eastern and western parts in Rajasthan (Fig. 12.7). Explanations for the marked deficiency of females in India's northwest are tenuous. Gosal suggests the following features: (1) a greater male excess at birth, (2) the low status of women in a part of the country where the patriarchal system of society has favored males, and (3) the

[40] Note that in India it is the ratio of females to males that is used. The reverse of this, with females as the denominator, is more common.

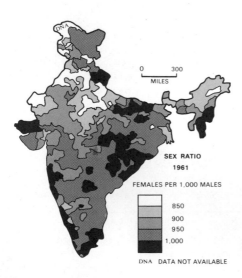

SEX RATIO
1961

FEMALES PER 1,000 MALES

850
900
950
1,000

DNA   DATA NOT AVAILABLE

Fig. 12.7. Data by districts. After a map by Gurdev Singh Gosal.

concentration here in earlier decades of this century of such forces of "abnormal mortality" as epidemics and famines, which bore more heavily on females than on males.[41]

In the northeast, the Assam Plain's low proportion of females is largely attributable to the male-selective in-migration stimulated by the expansion of the cultivated area on the fertile lowlands, and by the labor demands of the tea plantations. In West Bengal, which includes the Calcutta conurbation, and in the Damodar Valley of Bihar, the female deficiency relates chiefly to the male-selective migration into these areas of increasing industrialization. A similar explanation holds for the industrialized districts of Greater Bombay and Ahmedabad in western India. In Coorg and Shimoga districts, far to the south in Mysore state, it is the extension of upland commercial agriculture that has stimulated an important male-selective in-migration.

The only other category of sex composition to be analyzed in terms of its regionalization is one in which the ratio of females to males is not only above the country average of 941 but is even in excess of 1000. Females therefore predominate, a condition that is quite unusual for India. While seven Indian states have sex ratios above the country average, in only two, Kerala in the extreme southwest and Orissa (which includes the northeastern part of the peninsular massif together with adjacent coastal lowlands), does the ratio exceed 1000. Gosal's sex-ratio map (Fig. 12.7), based on district instead of state data, shows much more precisely the regions where female numbers predominate. While such regions are widely scattered, nearly all have one feature in common: they have experienced a male-selective out-migration. This results in a concentration of females being left behind in the regions of exit.

Occupational Structure. *Population Engaged in Agriculture.* In a country where nearly 70 percent of the total working force in 1961 was employed in agriculture, either as cultivators or agricultural laborers, the other occupational sectors of necessity must be only moderately represented. As in most LD countries, India's population is thoroughly rural and agricultural.

Among the 15 major states of India, there is, nevertheless, a large range in the percentages of the total labor force that is agriculturally employed—from a high of 79.3 to a low of 38.3. Of course the range becomes even greater if district data are considered. Only the states that depart as much as 5 percentage points from the national average of nearly 70 percent are considered worthy of comment.

Five of the major states have more than 75 percent of their labor

[41] Gosal, "The Regionalism of Sex Composition," pp. 130–131.

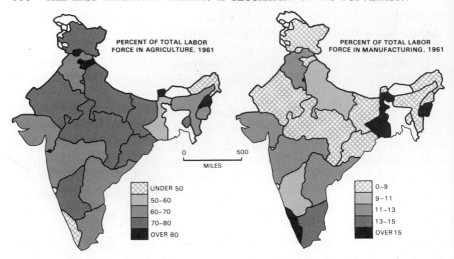

Fig. 12.8. India—percentage of total labor force engaged in agriculture (cultivators and laborers) and manufacturing, both household and factory. Data from *Census of India*, 1961, Paper No. 1 of 1962.

forces engaged in agriculture, as either cultivators or laborers (Fig. 12.8). One of these, Jammu and Kashmir, is situated in the Himalayan mountain system. The other four (Rajasthan, Uttar Pradesh, Madhya Pradesh, and Bihar) form a contiguous block of territory in northern India. They include most of the middle and upper Ganges lowland as well as the northern part of the hilly massif north of the Satpura Range. Despite the diverse nature of the regions included, there are, however, some common features that interrelate with the fact that such large proportions of their labor forces are engaged in agriculture. One such is that all five states have a low degree of urbanization, a situation that points to meager opportunities for employment in the secondary and tertiary economic sectors. Inefficient, submarginal, subsistence farming predominates, so that the processing of raw materials and associated household industries, which ordinarily flourish in regions of cash crops, are here meagerly developed. In some of the hill and mountain lands even a tribal culture still prevails.

In four states the percentage of the labor force that is engaged in agriculture is more than 5 percent below the country average of about 70. Two of these, Punjab (63.9 percent) and Tamil Nadu (Madras) (60.5 percent) are within 10 percentage points of the country average and so are not especially unusual. The other two, however, West Bengal (53.8 percent) and Kerala (38.5 percent), exhibit such wide departures from the normal as to be genuinely exceptional. In Kerala state, located in the far southwest, fishing and commerce provide employment for a goodly number. Here, too, specialized commercial crops, including coconuts on the coastal lowland and tea and coffee in the hill lands to the rear, require a variety of different kinds of nonagricultural labor, as do the thriving small-scale processing plants. In West Bengal state the great Calcutta-Hooglyside complex of commercial and industrial development provides unusual opportunities for nonagricultural employment. Within this same region as much as 25–55 percent of even the rural population is employed in nonagricultural activities, including homecrafts, as well as cottage and factory industries.[42]

Population in Manufacturing. As might be expected, a map showing distribution of workers in household and factory industries as a percentage of the total labor force is somewhat of a reverse image of one that does the same for agricultural workers (Fig. 12.8). For all-India, workers engaged in processing goods make up only 10.6 percent of the labor force. The states are equally divided between those whose proportions are above and below the national average. But only three states show values that are more than three percentage points above the national average; in only two states are they more than three percentage points below, and in these two they are only slightly so. Of the two states where the proportion of workers employed in manufacturing is distinctly above the all-India average, Kerala (18.08 percent) and West Bengal (15.62 percent), the former's processing plants are typically small-scale, including much that would be classed as household industry. Specialization is in products that derive mainly from local raw materials from the farms, including coir, copra, soap, and cosmetics from the coconut; the weaving of cotton; and the fabrication of tile made from local clay. By contrast, factory employment, especially in jute mills and engineering establishments, is more characteristic of West Bengal, although household industries are also of signal importance.

Literacy. In spite of recent forward strides in education, India is still a highly illiterate nation. As of 1961, counting people of all ages, only 24 percent (29 percent in 1971) could read and write with understanding. If only persons 10 years old and over are considered, the figure (calculated) rises to 33.9 percent. Growth rates in literacy were especially slow down to about 1931; over the 4 decades 1891–1931 the proportion of literates in the part of the population age 10 and over rose only from

[42] G. S. Gosal, "The Occupational Structure of India's Rural Population—A Regional Analysis," *The National Geographical Journal of India*, Vol. 4, September 1958, map on p. 140.

TABLE 12.11   Literacy Rates in India Among Persons 10 Years of Age and Over
From 1891 to 1961

| Census Year | Percent Literate | | |
	Persons	Males	Females
1891	6.1	11.4	.5
1901	6.2	11.5	.7
1911	7.0	12.6	1.1
1921	8.3	14.2	1.9
1931	9.2	15.4	2.4
1941	15.1	27.4	6.9
1951	22.2	32.2	10.1
1961	33.9	48.8	18.3

SOURCE: Gurdev S. Gosal, "Literacy in India," *Rural Sociology*, Vol. 29, September 1964, p. 263.

6.1 to 9.2 percent (Table 12.11). By contrast, during the 3 decades 1931–1961, they increased from 9.2 to 33.9 percent, a remarkable accomplishment indeed. But even these figures scarcely do full justice to the actual educational gains, since they fail to take into consideration the magnitude of the population growth and the number of deaths among literate persons in each of the three decades. The number of literates increased from 59–60 million in 1951 to 103 million in 1961 a *net* increase of 44 million. But during that decade the population grew by 77 million, while the estimated deaths were 68 million; the number of new literates required to compensate for the literates dying was 8.2 million. Adding this figure to the *net* number of new literates, the estimated *gross* increase in literates for the decade was nearly 52 million.[43] It is encouraging to note that the proportion of literate persons to total population in 1961 was about 3.5 times what it was in 1931, whereas the increase in actual number of literates was more than 5.5 times—from 18.5 million in 1931 to 105.3 million in 1961. The net increase of 44 million literates between 1951 and 1961 exceeded the combined increase of the two preceding decades. Yet due to the unprecedented growth of population between 1951 and 1961, the total number of *illiterates* has increased by 34 million.[44]

[43] Joseph Schwartzberg, "Observations on the Progress of Literacy in India, 1951–1961," *Indian Population Bulletin* (New Delhi), No. 2, August 1961, pp. 295–300.
[44] G. S. Gosal, "Literacy in India: An Interpretative Study," *Rural Sociology*, Vol. 29, No. 3, September 1964, p. 264.

Literacy differentials between urban and rural populations are striking—nearly 47 percent are literate in the former as against only about
19 percent in the latter.

Until recently, literacy in India meant largely male literacy. In 1931
the male-female literacy ratio was 6 or 7 to 1. This reflects the long-time
prejudice against the education of women and also against their employment outside the home. In recent decades the male-female literacy ratio
has gradually been improving, and in 1961 it was about 2.7 to 1. The
ratio is about 8:5 in urban places; it is still only 7:2 in the rural villages.[45]

Before 1948, when there was no uniform national policy for the extension of educational facilities to all parts of the country, there were wide
regional variations in literacy. Since then the regional contrasts have declined, and male-female and rural-urban differentials have narrowed. State
regional variations in urban literacy are considerably smaller than in rural
literacy.

Figure 12.9 shows the spatial distribution of literate persons as a percentage of the total population, including children, in 1961. Data are
by districts. Important regional disparities are conspicuous. One of the
broadest generalizations to be made is that regions with literacy rates
above the national average (24 percent) are, with few exceptions, located
on the seaward margins of the country. Below-average literacy is characteristic of much the greater share of the interior, in both peninsular
India and the broad northern part. The concentration of literates in regions not too far removed from the sea appears to have some connection

[45] Gosal, "Literacy in India," p. 261.

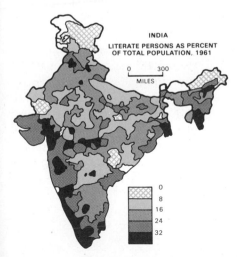

INDIA
LITERATE PERSONS AS PERCENT
OF TOTAL POPULATION, 1961

0   300
MILES

0
8
16
24
32

Fig. 12.9. Data by districts. After
Gurdev Singh Gosal.

with one or more of the following factors: (1) the longer contacts there with foreigners in general, and with foreign missionaries in particular; (2) the earlier inception of educational institutions, both state and private; and (3) a higher degree of urbanization, and a relatively well developed system of communication between coastal settlements via the sea.[46]

Above-average literacy is especially characteristic of the west side of peninsular India, which has had a longer and more continuous contact with Europeans and their Christian missions than have most parts along the east side. In the latter region the spots of higher literacy are fairly coincident with the principal delta areas, where prosperity is greater and there is a larger proportion of urban dwellers. In West Bengal, containing the large Calcutta conurbation, literacy rates are especially high. So are they along the west side in the industrialized and urbanized parts of Gujarat and Rajasthan in the north and in the coastal lowlands of Kerala and Mysore in the south. In Kerala nearly 47 percent of the people can read and write, a rate by far the highest for any Indian state. If young children below 5 years of age are excluded, the Kerala literacy figure rises to 55 percent. This same state also leads all others in male, female, urban, and rural literacy, while at the same time it has the lowest rural-urban and male-female differentials in literacy. All the more remarkable is the fact that Kerala's first rank in all features pertaining to literacy exists in spite of its population being more rural than the all-India average. Partially compensating for the state's rurality as it influences literacy is the fact that about one third of Kerala's people are classed as Christians, reflecting intensive Western missionary activity. Doubtless some weight also attaches to the fact that the former native states of Travancore and Cochin had long pursued an enlightened educational policy and concurrently established a climate of law, order, and political stability even prior to the period of British rule.[47]

Core areas of especially low literacy (under 16 percent) include the mountain regions in the northeast and the northwest, a large part of the middle and upper Ganges Plain in Uttar Pradesh, and extensive regions within the hill lands and plateaus of interior peninsular India both to the north and south of the Narmada and Tapti troughs. These same regions with low literacy in the total population are even more strikingly low in female educational attainment. In all regions where overall literacy is below 16 percent, that for females is under 6 percent and in some sections even less than 2 percent. The male-female literacy differential is largest in these same regions.

A relatively strong coincidence exists between regions of low literacy

[46] Gosal, "Literacy in India," p. 45.
[47] Gosal, "Literacy in India," p. 274.

and those of meager urbanization. And outside of the Bihar and Uttar Pradesh sections, a large majority of the districts with low literacy are situated within territories of what were former native states, where education was neglected. As a general rule, also, literacy is lower in what were the former princely states than in the earlier British provinces.

Languages. Within India there are powerful forces, some of which have a centripetal influence and work for unification; others have a centrifugal bent and favor regional interests and fragmentation. One influential unifying force making for cultural integration is Hinduism or Indian nationalism. Of the opposite kind is the prevalence of strong regional linguistic communities, which have a divisive effect. The linguistic fragmentation in India involves 12 main languages (13 if Kashmiri is included), each confined to a fairly compact block of territory, which together comprise the mother tongues of more than 95 percent of the population.

Hindi, including Urdu, the language of the Moslems of northern India, is spoken by nearly a third of the over 550 million inhabitants. Not only is Hindi spoken by the largest number of people; it is also the official language under the constitution, is common to the largest area, is the current language of the dynamic culture-hearth of the subcontinent (the Ganges Plain and south to the Narmada River) and is the base of the greatest political power. Four northern states—Rajasthan, Uttar Pradesh, Madhya Pradesh, and Bihar—represent the core Hindi region; in them there is a vigorous switching to Hindi in their provincial administrations. It also has wide currency throughout most other parts of India, chiefly in commercial circles. Although the decision to make Hindi the sole official language by January 26, 1965 had been taken while Nehru was still prime minister, he realized that there was no easy solution to the problem of imposing a common language on India's polyglot society. The process would have to be slow and evolutionary. But when the deadline date approached and the Shastri Government refused to promise that Nehru's plan for gradual change would be followed, such a violent anti-Hindi upsurge occurred in the less Hindu southern states, accompanied by serious rioting, that a retreat was called for. At that time Nehru's earlier assurance of a more gradual approach to the imposition of Hindi was given legal form. English, although spoken by only 2 percent of the population, has remained the second official language, since in practice it is still the language of government, higher education, and the professions. The existing linguistic dilemma may even compel English to be kept as the language of the Federal administration until Hindi can be made more acceptable to the two thirds who are non-Hindi speakers.

As a result of intense regional agitation by a number of non-Hindi language groups, there has occurred a widespread revision of state boundaries in order to make them conform approximately to linguistic groupings. Of course the linguistic plan cannot be complete; some inconsistencies are bound to remain. The first of the linguistic states came into being as early as 1935, when the boundaries of the new state of Orissa were drawn to coincide with the distribution of the Oriya language. This action set a precedent for other similar demands. In 1953 the central government yielded to intense regional pressure and set up the new southeastern state of Andhra Pradesh, thereby emphasizing the partial autonomy of the Telegu-speaking people. Subsequently there has been a large-scale reorganization of the internal political boundaries, resulting in the foundering of some of the former provinces, the emergence of a number of new states, and a modification of the boundaries of most of the others. A consequence of all this internal boundary reshuffling is that a great majority of the present states and territories are reasonably coincident with well-defined linguistic regions (Fig. 12.10). Among the new and reorganized states, established after November 1965, Kerala is identified with the Malayalam speakers, Maharashtra with the Marathi, and Gujarat with the Gujarati. Tamil Nadu is identified with the Tamil language, Mysore with Kannada, and Punjab with Punjabi. Thus, while the Hindi states in the north (Bihar, Madhya Pradesh, Uttar Pradesh, and Rajasthan and the new state of Hariana) are aggressively changing to Hindi, the Bengali, Oriya, Assamese, Telegu, Tamil, Kannada, Malayalam, Marathi, and Punjab linguistic states are at the same time zealously becoming more parochially monolingual.

The problem of a common language for India remains a serious one, because the linguistic weapon is a potent threat in the hands of forces bent upon disunity. To be sure, there are just arguments for linguistic states; certainly a common tongue among the mass of a state's people, and between the people and those who govern, is to be desired. Yet the principle of linguistic states carries with it the real risk of separatism. In this respect, the quite opposite situations in India and China are striking.

Internal Mobility. Although this section on population mobility is concerned almost exclusively with internal migration in India, it may not be out of place at the beginning to remark briefly on external migration. The single most massive recent migration across the national boundaries occurred late in the 1941–1951 decade and was occasioned by the partition of the subcontinent into the two states of Pakistan and India. At that time it is believed that over 7 million persons crossed from India to Pakistan, while roughly an equal number were involved in a reverse flow. More normal was the entrance of 9 to 10 million

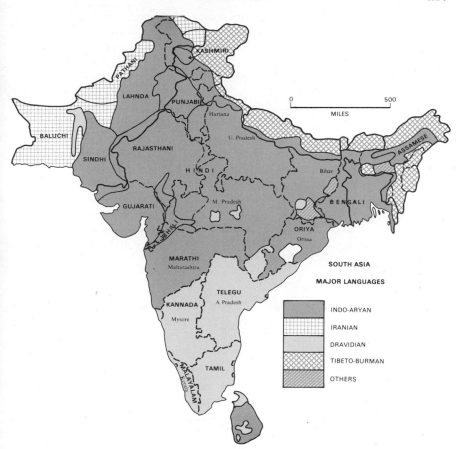

Fig. 12.10. Major language groups and main linguistic regions of South Asia. Within the subcontinent, Indo-Aryan languages dominate in the north and central parts and Dravidian languages in the south. Both are represented in Ceylon. Note that the Indo-Aryan language group also prevails in both West and East Pakistan. The linguistic regions' boundaries on the map may not precisely coincide with the international or state boundaries. Where the linguistic-region name is relatively similar to the linguistic state name, the latter has not been added; where such is not the case, the state name has been added in smaller type. Only approximate coincidence between linguistic region and state can be expected. Based mainly on *Karta Narodov Indostana*, Ethnographic Institute of the Soviet Academy of Sciences, Moscow, 1956.

foreign migrants into India during the decade 1951–1961, almost exclusively from the nearby countries of Pakistan, Nepal, and Ceylon. Nearly 66 percent of these outlanders concentrated in two general regions, the northeast (mainly West Bengal and Assam) taking 43 percent and the northwest (Punjab) 23 percent.

TABLE 12.12   Trend in Internal Interstate Migration, 1901–1961

Year	Percentage of Migrants to Total Population	Decennial Growth Rate of Total Population (Percent)	Decennial Growth Rate of Migrants (Percent)
1901	3.30		
1911	3.59	+5.75	+14.87
1921	3.97	−0.31	+10.39
1931	3.59	+11.00	+0.25
1941	N.A.	+14.22	N.A.
1951	3.00	+13.31	+8.39
1961	3.31	+21.51	+33.87

SOURCE: Gupta, "Some Characteristics of Internal Migration in India," p. 2.

Of much greater magnitude, however, is the country's internal migration, although India's is far from being a mobile population. Including both long-range interstate and short-range intrastate movements, during the decade 1951–1961 there was a total of 65.9 million people classed as mobile. In an absolute sense this is a vast number, but in comparison with the total population it amounts to only about 16 percent. Moreover, of the mobile group, 87 percent restricted their movements to within state boundaries, while only 13 percent represented an interstate movement.

In 1961, out of a total population of 439 million, only 14.5 million, or 3.3 percent, were enumerated outside the state or territory of birth. In all the decennial years from 1901 to 1961 the growth rate of interstate migrants was more rapid than that of the total population, except in 1931 and 1951 (Table 12.12). Especially noteworthy is the sharp increase in mobility of population that occurred in the 1951–1961 decade, when the decennial growth of interstate migrants reached 33.87 percent, by far the highest for any of the previous six decades.[48] This is to be compared with a decennial growth rate in total population of 21.51 percent. Reasons for the recent increase in India's population mobility include

[48] P. Sen Gupta, "Some Characteristics of Internal Migration in India." Paper submitted to *ECAFE Expert Working Group on Problems of Internal Migration, Urbanization and Settlement*, Bangkok, May–June, 1967, Office of the Registrar General of India. See also *Census of India*, Part II-C (iii) and (iv), Migration Tables, 1961.

the following: (1) a strong push factor in many rural areas because of population saturation, a dearth of new arable land and a high rate of unemployment or underemployment, (2) the steadily growing pull factor of employment opportunities in the cities, (3) the extension of the area under irrigation, and (4) the reorganization of the country's states.

Among the factors either stimulating or damping migration in India, the economic element is paramount. Regions with high proportions of immigrant population are usually those where (1) new agricultural settlement has been occurring or (2) rapid urbanization has been spurred on by the development of industry, trade, and other important urban functions. In contrast, regions with small proportions of immigrant people are characteristically those where (1) intensity of urbanization is low and cities are of small size, (2) industry and commerce are meagerly developed, (3) the economy is prevailingly of the subsistence type, or (4) there is presently little reclaimable new land for agriculture. The latter situation may include fertile regions that are already overcrowded, as well as poorly endowed regions with only sparse populations.[49]

Of the short-range intrastate migration during 1951–1961, 73 percent was from one rural area to another; only 15 percent was from rural to urban locations. Of the longer-distance interstate migration, 33.4 percent was between rural areas, 35.2 percent was from rural to urban environments, and 26.2 percent was from one urban place to another. Thus 61.4 percent of the migrants who crossed a state boundary moved toward urban areas, compared with only 22.8 percent in the case of migrants moving within a state. Of the total internal migration-flow (intrastate plus interstate) of nearly 66 million people during the decade 1951–1961, 72 percent moved to rural areas and 28 percent to urban centers. The net result of this rural-urban mobility was an overall loss to rural communities of 8.6 million persons or 2.9 percent and a gain to urban places of 13.8 percent.[50]

Regionalism of Internal Migration. Prior to partition, the predominant net movement of people within India was from west to east and mainly toward the nation's prime industrial region in western Bengal, centered in Calcutta, and to the plantation agricultural region in lowland Assam. In the period since partition (1947) not only has there been a marked increase in the mobility of the population, but also the movement has undergone considerable change as the flow patterns have increased in complexity, and directions of movement have become more varied.

[49] Gurdev Singh Gosal, Internal Migration in India—A Regional Analysis," *India Geographical Journal*, Vol. XXXVI, 1961, p. 121.
[50] Gupta, "Some Characteristics of Internal Migration," pp. 3–5.

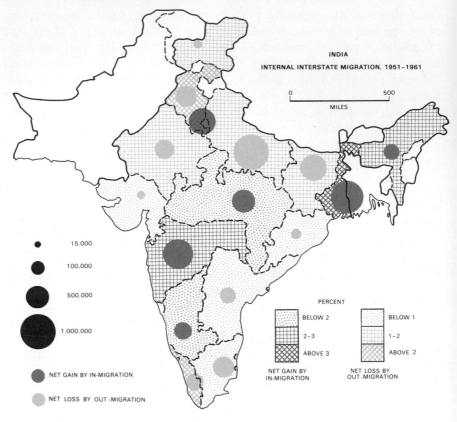

Fig. 12.11. India—internal interstate migration, 1951–1961. After P. Sen Gupta.

TABLE 12.13   Direction of Internal Migration in India, 1951–1961

Movement Toward	Net Immigrants	Percent of Total
Northeast (West Bengal, Assam)	1,172,425	35.22
West (Maharashtra)	842,692	25.32
Northwest (Delhi)	541,812	16.28
Center (Madhya Pradesh)	518,443	15.58
South (Mysore)	252,909	7.60
Total	3,328,281	100.00

SOURCE: Gupta, "Some Characteristics of Internal Migration in India," p. 13.

During the decade 1951–1961 the northeast continued to exert the strongest pull on internal migrants, attracting 35 percent of the total (Fig. 12.11, Table 12.13). Attraction was to two regions, mainly that of industrial West Bengal, but secondarily the plantations of the Assam Valley. It should be noted that immigrants from outside the country were also at a maximum in this eastern region, where they were three to four times as numerous as were the net internal migrants. Next in its attractive power for net immigrants was the west, represented by the state of Maharashtra containing the industrial metropolis of Bombay. In this region also, immigrants from outside the country were numerous, more than half as many as the net immigrants from within. Together the northeast and west, where are located the two great industrial magnets of the country, Calcutta and Bombay, accounted for nearly 61 percent of the total number of net internal immigrants. Population movements toward the northwest (Delhi) and center (Madhya Pradesh) are of recent origin. The pull of Delhi is related to its employment opportunities associated with services, trade, commerce, and construction. Immigration from abroad to the Delhi center was nearly equal to that from internal sources. Madhya Pradesh, an interior state in central India, does not boast a dense population and there is only a modest industrial development. Yet it is the expansion of its industrial and mining activities that provided the chief pull for in-migration.

Gross out-migration is at a maximum in three states (Uttar Pradesh, Bihar, and Punjab) that occupy the crowded middle and upper parts of the Ganges lowland. They are followed in order by Tamil Nadu (Madras) in the extreme southeast and dry-subhumid Rajasthan in the northwest. If migrant outflow is measured against inflow to obtain a *net* out-migration, the first four of the states named above are again included among the highest, but in somewhat different rank order, while small but crowded Kerala, in the extreme southwest, ranks fifth. When intensity of net out-migration (proportion of net out-migration to total population) is considered, the order of importance is Kerala, Punjab, Bihar, Rajasthan, and Uttar Pradesh. The push tendency was strong in the rural areas of all five of these states.

PAKISTAN

Pakistan, with an estimated 137 million people in 1970, obviously is one of the earth's population giants, ranking fifth among the nations in total number of people. Perhaps the obscurity of Pakistan's high rank in population numbers may derive from the fact that it is located in the midst of other population giants. Five of the earth's seven nations with inhabitants in excess of 100 million lie along the margins of eastern and southern Asia, where the two supergiants, China and India, greatly dwarf all the others.

Because of the long history of political unity that the subcontinent enjoyed before partition in 1947, it is to be expected that in many of its population characteristics and most of its population history Pakistan will resemble India. Accordingly, some features of modern population growth and distribution in Pakistan have been included in the preceding survey of the subcontinent as a whole and of India in particular. A briefer separate analysis will therefore suffice for Pakistan.

Pakistan's crude birth rate in 1970 is believed to have approached 50 per 1000, one of the earth's highest, and considerably exceeding that of its neighbor, India. Its estimated death rate of 18 is also high, but in spite of such a mortality the differential between natality and mortality is so great that it provides a current annual growth rate of about 3.3 percent, which will double the population in about 21 years. Accordingly, soaring population numbers and accompanying widespread poverty are the current hallmarks of Pakistan, while the outlook for a significant prompt improvement is gloomy. Religion is the prime unifying force, for this new Moslem state was carved out of the Indian subcontinent when that region gained independence from Britain in 1947, and simultaneously underwent political fission into India and Pakistan. This unfortunate separation, which weakened both states, had its roots in the socioeconomic conflicts stemming from religious differences and jealousies between Hindus and Moslems.

As might be expected from the spectacularly high fertility rate, a very young dependent population is characteristic of Pakistan, with all the attendant economic and social burdens that such an age structure entails. The average age is between 22 and 23 years, while 45 percent of the inhabitants are less than 15 years old. Oldsters are relatively few. Roughly 8 out of 10 inhabitants who are 15 years of age and over are unable to read in any language, and the illiteracy rate is 2 to 3 times as high for females as for males. Only 1 percent has a high school education. As in India, there is a fairly strong male predominance, with about 110 males per 100 females. Population is overwhelmingly rural, while 75 percent are engaged in the primary economies, mainly agriculture; only 13.1 percent are classed as urban.[51] The per capita annual national income of about $90 is very low indeed, but still rather similar to that of India. Moslems greatly predominate representing 81.1 percent of the

---

[51] Defined as places with not less than 5000 inhabitants.

SOUTH ASIA   403

population, followed in order by Hindus (10.7 percent) and Christians
(0.8 percent).

Working to the serious disadvantage of Pakistan is the fact that its
national domain is severed into two far-removed parts, East Pakistan
(52,000 square mile) and West Pakistan (310,000 square mile) separated
by more than 900 land miles of Indian territory, and 2600 miles as measured by the sea route. Other than their common Moslem religion, the
two far-separated sections of Pakistan have almost nothing in common;
they differ ethnically, culturally, linguistically, and politically. East Pakistan is humid and deltaic; West Pakistan is largely dry. In the East they
eat rice and fish, not wheat and mutton as in the West. East Pakistanis
speak Bengali, and the educated people use the Bengali script; their second
language is English, not Urdu, with its foreign Persian-Arabic script,
which prevails in West Pakistan. Bengali has been accepted as the official
language of East Pakistan and as the alternate national language to the
Urdu of West Pakistan. East Pakistanis dress as do the Hindus; the men
wear the draped breech cloth (*dhoti*); the women wear the *sari*, consisting
of a long piece of cloth wrapped around the body with one end over
the head.

Other significant contrasts are revealed in Table 12.14. From it can
be noted the fact that greatly smaller East Pakistan, with only 15 percent
of the national area, supports about 54 percent of the total population.
A result is that the humid and fertile East, a large part deltaic lowland,
boasts the astoundingly high density of 922 per sq mi (1961), compared
to only 138 for dry, West Pakistan. However, the somewhat larger population of East Pakistan has been kept from exerting political power in
the national government in proportion to its numbers. The flame of
resentment has been further fanned by the belief that the eastern province
has been exploited economically for the benefit of the western part.

From Table 12.14 it may also be noted that West Pakistan is far more
exclusively Moslem (97 percent) than is the East, where Hindus make
up an important 16 percent minority group. In addition, Pakistan reverses
the relationship that usually prevails between the two population characteristics of urbanization and literacy, since less-urban East Pakistan
(5.2 percent of inhabitants) has a higher proportion (21.5 percent) of
literate persons 5 years of age and over than does more urban West
Pakistan (22.5 percent), where only 16.3 percent are literate. Agriculture
dominates the economy of the East (85.3 percent of the labor force)
to a far greater extent than it does in the West (59.3 percent).

Spatial Distribution. In an earlier section, spatial distribution of inhabitants within the entire subcontinent was sketched, so it is necessary
only to briefly supplement the earlier discussion as it relates to Pakistan.

TABLE 12.14 Comparisons of East Pakistan and West Pakistan, 1961

					Population			By Religions (Percent)		
	Area (Sq Mi)	Numbers (Thousands)	Density (Per Sq Mi)	Urban (Percent)	Literate, 5 Years and Over (Percent)	Labor Force in Agriculture (Percent of Total Labor Force)	Moslems	Hindus	Christians
East Pakistan	55,126	50,840	922	5.2	21.5	85.3	83.1	15.9	0.25
West Pakistan	310,403	42,880	138	22.5	16.3	59.3	97.2	1.5	1.4

SOURCE: *Pakistan Statistical Yearbook*, 1964. Government of Pakistan, Central Statistical Office.

404

Because so much of dry, and in parts hilly, West Pakistan is unfit for normal rain-fed agriculture, the predominantly rural population there is spatially distributed mainly with respect to available water for crops—either natural rainfall or irrigation. Thus the ecumene, or occupied land, of West Pakistan where the population density exceeds 100 persons per sq mi takes the shape of an hourglass (Fig. 12.12). Its broad section lies to the north, a region which not only has somewhat more rainfall, but where also there are 5 great mountain-fed rivers, widely spread but converging southward, which yield vast amounts of irrigation water.

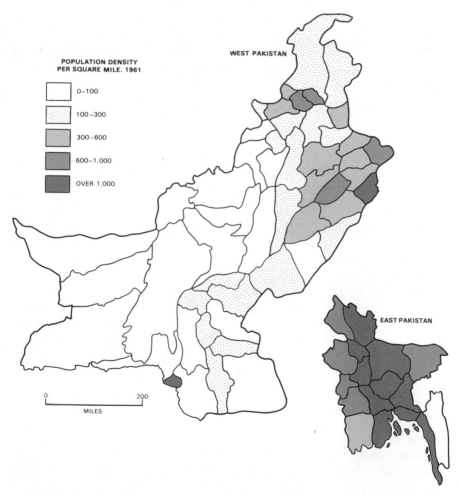

Fig. 12.12. Data from *Census of Pakistan*, 1961.

The constricted part of the hourglass ecumene is in the southern desert half, where the five tributary streams combine to form the single Indus channel. Here, because of nearly complete dependence on irrigation water, a Nilotic pattern of population distribution prevails.

In East Pakistan the lowest densities are in the Chittagong Hills in the extreme southeast where there are fewer than 100 persons per sq mi. *Relatively* low densities are also a feature of the extreme southwestern district, the southern half of which is included within the Sunderbans, the forested, poorly drained seaward margins of the tidal delta. Unusually high densities of over 1500 per sq mi characterize the eastern districts in the vicinity of Dacca and southeastward from that metropolis (Fig. 12.12). This is a region of intensive paddy culture, with double cropping common. Densities decline somewhat in the western tier of districts where physical conditions for rice culture are of lower quality—some parts of it moribund delta and others older alluvium and sandy alluvial fans, the latter mainly in the extreme northwest.[52]

CEYLON

Based on a 10 percent sample census, Ceylon had an estimated total population of nearly 10.6 million in 1963, and this may have grown to 12–13 million by 1970. The average population density of about 500 per sq mi in 1970 was appreciably higher than that of India. Resembling much of South and Southeast Asia, the island's population shows a male predominance, in the ratio of 1080 males to 1000 females.

With an estimated recent birth rate of about 32–33 per 1000 and a death rate as low as 8, vital rates in Ceylon are well below those of India and Pakistan. There has been a precipitous decline in the death rate during the last 15–20 years, largely as a consequence of the near elimination of malaria through spraying with DDT. Within a single year death rates declined by one third. Between 1946 and 1947 the reported malaria morbidity declined 77.5 percent and the mortality rate by 82.5 percent. And since malaria seriously debilitates and lowers the resistance of those infected persons it does not kill, its near elimination caused death from other causes to decline as well. The low death rates that prevail in Ceylon, as well as in Malaysia and Singapore, reveal how effective was British influence on mortality reduction in the instance of these relatively small national populations. It is worth repeating that scale is of the utmost importance in considering population problems,

[52] Johnson, "Rural Population Densities in East Pakistan," map, p. 6.

since British influence had no comparable effect on mortality in the much more populous Indian subcontinent.

While it is true that Ceylon's natality rate is low for Asia and apparently is lower now than it has been in the recent past, the downward trend has not been sufficiently clear and consistent to assure that the decline in birth rates is firmly established. Relatively late marriage is no doubt one factor that has reduced natality in Ceylon.

A noticeable feature of Ceylon's population is its plural ethnic-cultural communities, together with the potential for communal tensions that such a situation offers. To be sure, there are no very obvious physical differences between the ethnic groups, but still they are unlike in language, tradition, culture, and attitudes. Greatly predominating are the Sinhalese, who represent about 70 percent of the total population. They are Aryans who speak a tongue that is of the same family of languages as modern Hindi; it is totally different from the Dravidian languages, of which Tamil is one branch. The Sinhalese look upon themselves as the chosen people in Ceylon, an attitude resembling that of the Old Testament Jews in the eastern Mediterranean world. They are mainly peasant cultivators, although other occupations claim a fair number, and predominantly Buddhists. Their chief concentration is in the wet zone of the south and southwest, in both lowland and upland locations. They are far more thinly spread over the northern lowland "dry zone" and along certain stretches of the eastern and northern coasts.

Tamils, a strong minority of 20–25 percent, are composed of two distinct groups. One of these, representing an ancient in-migration, is the Ceylon Tamils who came from southern India to Ceylon in the 13th century. It was these invaders who destroyed the flourishing indigenous Sinhalese civilization that at that time spread over the northern lowland, forcing the displaced people to move southward into the more humid highlands. Hindu by religion but speaking Tamil, the Ceylon Tamils (11 percent of total population) are strongly segregated in the extreme north, both in and around the Jaffna peninsula.

The slightly more numerous Indian Tamils (12 percent) represent a much more recent 19th century migration from Dravidian southern India. It was the opportunities for employment on the rapidly expanding plantations in humid southwestern Ceylon that served as the pull factor attracting the Indian Tamils. Their main concentrations are still in the regions of commercial agriculture, chiefly in the wet zone of the southwest, both in the highlands and on the coastal lowland.

It was not for eight years or so after independence was attained in 1948 that the latent communal disharmony exploded into serious clashes and rioting between Sinhalese and Tamils. Expectably, the political strife adversely affected the island's economy. Bearing in mind the numerical predominance of the Sinhalese and their feeling of superiority as the favored natives compared with the outlanders, continuing friction can be expected, since the national identity of Ceylon is closely related to the language and religion of the powerful Sinhalese majority.

Over many centuries prior to the Tamil invasions of the 13th century, the almost exclusively Sinhalese population was concentrated on the extensive northern and eastern plains, in what is called the "dry zone," where the strongly seasonal total annual rainfall is under 75 in. and in parts under 50 in. This flourishing Sinhalese civilization was based on the cultivation of paddy rice, whose large water requirements demanded supplementary tank (pond) irrigation. Present spatial distribution of Ceylon's overwhelmingly rural population is quite different from what it was in the pre-Tamil period, since now the concentration is in the wet zone of the southwest, both in the central highlands and on the coastal lowlands (Fig. 12.13). Two other separate and smaller concentrations are to be noted, one in the vicinity of the Jaffna peninsula at the north end of the island and the other in a narrow east-coast strip that extends both north and south of Batticaloa. The Jaffna peninsula, densely peopled largely by Ceylon Tamils despite its porous limestone soils, supports an intensive garden type of agriculture specialized in rice, tobacco, and vegetables. Well irrigation makes such close rural settlement possible. An intensive paddy-rice culture on the fertile alluvial east-coast strip in the vicinity of Batticaloa explains the crowding in that location. The rainy southwestern lowland, largely undulating country, is the most crowded part of the island, with many sections having densities exceeding 1000 per sq mi. Rice and coconuts are the mainstays of this crowded region.

Much of the well-watered central hill country, especially that in the Kandy region, is also closely settled. In medieval times this knot of hill land came to be occupied by the Sinhalese who had been driven from their lands in the northern lowlands by the invading Tamils. Then in the 19th century the hill-country population was supplemented by an in-migration of modern Tamils from India seeking employment on the developing tea, rubber, and cacao plantations. Hence while Sinhalese and Indian Tamils are both important elements of the hill-land population, the Tamil latecomers continue to form the bulk of the estate labor.

The lowland "dry zone" of the north and east is for the most part sparsely occupied, except for the two areas previously mentioned. Although the region is scarcely dry, it does suffer from a strong seasonality of rainfall as well as a high degree of rainfall variability and frequent droughts. The cover of scrub forest reflects the water deficiency. Ample

CEYLON
RURAL POPULATION DENSITY

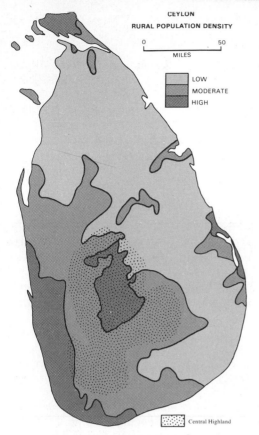

0   50
└──────────────────┘
MILES

LOW
MODERATE
HIGH

Central Highland

Fig. 12.13. Ceylon: generalized population-density regions.

evidence in the forms of ancient settlement ruins and remains of old irrigation ponds and channels testify that these northern lowlands in earlier centuries supported a flourishing civilization.

REFERENCES

Agarwala, S. N. "How Are We Doing in Family Planning in India?" *Demography*, Vol. 5, No. 2, 1968, pp. 710–713.

Allchin, Bridget and Raymond, *The Birth of Indian Civilization*, Penguin Books, Baltimore, 1968.

Bhat, L. S. "Regional Contrasts in Population Density and Growth in India, 1951–1961," *Geography*, Vol. 48, 1963, pp. 313 317.

Bogue, D. J., and K. C. Zachariah. Urbanization and Migration in India. In Roy Turner (ed.), *India's Urban Future*. University of California Press, Berkeley, 1962.

Bose, Ashish. "Internal Migration in India, Pakistan and Ceylon." *World Population Conference, Belgrade, 1965*, Vol. 4, United Nations, New York, 1966, pp. 483–486.

Bose, Ashish (ed.). *Patterns of Population Change in India, 1951–1961*. Allied Publishers, Bombay, 1967.

Bose, Ashish. "Six Decades of Urbanization in India," *Indian Economic and Social History Review* (Delhi), Vol. 2, January 1965, pp. 23–41.

Brush, John E. "Some Dimensions of Urban Population Pressure in India," in *Geography and a Crowding World*, Wilbur Zelinsky et al. (eds.), Oxford University Press, New York, 1970, pp. 279–304.

Brush, John E. "Spatial Patterns of Population in Indian Cities," *Geographical Review*, Vol. 58, No. 3, 1968, pp. 362–391.

Bulsara, J. F. *Problems of Rapid Urbanization in India*, Bombay, Popular Prakashan, 1964.

Census Atlas of India, 1961, Vol. 1, Part 1X, New Delhi, 1970.

Chandrasekhar, S. "India's Population: Fact, Problem and Policy," in S. Chandrasekhar (ed.), *Asia's Population Problems*. Praeger, New York, 1967, pp. 72–99.

Chandrasekhar, S. "How India Is Tackling Her Population Problem," *Demography*, Vol. 5, No. 2, 1968, pp. 642–650.

Chatterjee, S. P. "Regional Patterns of the Density and Distribution of Population in India," *Geographical Review of India*, Vol. 24, No. 2, June 1962, pp. 1–28.

Cook, Elsie K. "The Population of Ceylon," in *Ceylon: Its Geography, Its Resources, and Its People*, 2nd ed. Macmillan, London, 1951, pp. 223–232.

Davis, Kingsley. *The Population of India and Pakistan*. Princeton University Press, Princeton, New Jersey, 1951.

Davis, Kingsley. "Urbanization in India: Past and Future," in Roy Turner (ed.), *India's Urban Future*. University of California Press, Berkeley, 1962.

Farmer, B. H. *Ceylon: A Divided Nation*. Oxford University Press, London, 1963.

Gosal, G. S. "Internal Migration in India—A Regional Analysis," *Indian Geographical Journal*, Vol. 36, 1961, pp. 106–121.

Gosal, G. S. "Literacy in India: An Interpretative Study," *Rural Sociology*, Vol. 29, No. 3, September 1964, pp. 261–277.

Gosal, G. S. "The Occupational Structure of India's Rural Population—A Regional Analysis," *The National Geographical Journal of India*, Vol. 4, September 1958, pp. 137–148.

Gosal, G. S. "Regional Aspects of Population Growth in India, 1951–1961," *Pacific Viewpoint*, Vol. 3, September 1962, pp. 87–99.

Gosal, G. S. "The Regionalism of Sex Composition of India's Population," *Rural Sociology*, Vol. 26, June 1961.

Gupta, P. Sen. "Population and Resource Development in India." Paper submitted for the Symposium on the Geography of Population Pressure on Physical and Social Resources, The Pennsylvania State University, September 17–23, 1967. Published subsequently in altered form in *Geography and a Crowding World*, Wilbur Zelinsky et al. (eds.), Oxford University Press, New York, 1970, pp. 424–441.

Gupta, Sen. *Some Characteristics of Internal Migration in India*, Office of the Registrar General, India, New Delhi, 1967.

Jain, S. P. "Indian Fertility—Our Knowledge and Gaps," *Journal of Family Welfare*, Vol. 10, No. 4, June 1964, pp. 16–32.

Jain, S. P. "State Growth Rates and Their Components," in Ashish Bose (ed.), *Patterns of Population Change in India, 1951–1961*. Allied Publishers, New York, pp. 13–32.

Johnson, B. L. C. "Rural Population Densities in East Pakistan," *Pacific Viewpoint*, Vol. 3, March 1962, pp. 51–62.

Karan, P. P. "Population of South Asia," in Paul F. Griffin (ed.), *Geography of Population: a Teacher's Guide*, 1970 Yearbook of The National Council for Geographic Education. Feardon Publishers, Palo Alto, California, 1969, pp. 163–176.

Kuriyan, George. "India's Population Problem," *Focus* (American Geographical Society), Vol. 5, No. 2, October 1954.

Lal, A. "Patterns of In-migration in India's Cities," *Geog. Rev. of India*, Vol. 23, No. 3, 1961, pp. 16–23.

Lall, Amrit, and Ranjit Tirtha. "India's Urbanization," *Focus* (American Geographical Society), Vol. 19, September 1968, pp. 1–7.

Learmonth, A. T. A. "Selected Aspects of India's Population Geography," *Australian Journal of Politics and History* (St. Lucia), Vol. 12, No. 2, 1966, pp. 146–154.

Mauldin, W. Parker. "The Population of India," in Ronald Freedman (ed.), *Population: The Vital Revolution*. Anchor Books, New York, 1965, pp. 191–205.

National Atlas of India. Preliminary Edition, 1957. Ministry of Scientific Research and Cultural Affairs, Government of India, New Delhi.

Querishi, Anwar I. "Pakistan's Population Problems," in S. Chandrasekhar (ed.), *Asia's Population Problems*. Praeger, New York, 1967, pp. 146–164.

Rajan Sundara. "India's Linguistic Dilemma," *The Reporter*, May 6, 1965, pp. 31–32.

Robinson, W. C. (Ed.). *Studies in the Demography of Pakistan*, Karachi, Pakistan Institute of Development Economics, 1967.

Robinson, W. C. "Urban-Rural Differences in Indian Fertility," *Population Studies*, Vol. 14, 1961, pp. 218–234.

Sarkar, N. K. *The Demography of Ceylon*, Colombo, Ceylon Govt. Press, 1957.

Schwartzberg, J. E. "Agricultural Labour in India: a Regional Analysis with Particular Reference to Population Growth," *Econ. Develop. and Cultural Change*, Vol. 11, 1963, pp. 337–352.

Schwartzberg, Joseph. "Observations on the Progress of Literacy in India, 1951–1961," *Indian Population Bulletin* (New Delhi), No. 2, August 1961.

Singh, R. L. *India: Regional Studies*. Twenty-first International Geographical Congress, India, 1968, pp. 9–15, 41–54, 74–86, 114–122, 197–205, 275–280, 294–298, 316–323.

Sopher, David. "India's Languages and Religions," *Focus* (American Geographical Society), Vol. 6, February 1956.

Spate, O. H. K., and A. T. A. Learmonth. *India and Pakistan: A General and Regional Geography*, 3rd ed. Methuen, London, 1967, pp. 121–149, 150–172.

Trewartha, Glenn T., and Gurdev Gosal. "The Regionalism of Population Change in India," *Cold Spring Harbor Symposia on Quantitative Biology*, Vol. 22, 1957.

Visoria, P. M. "Migration Between India and Pakistan," *Demography*, Vol. 6, 1969, pp. 323–334.

Visaria, Pravin M. "Mortality and Fertility in India, 1951–1961," *Milbank Memorial Fund Quarterly*, Vol. 47, No. 1, Part 1, January 1969, pp. 91–116.

CHAPTER
13

Southwest Asia

By Southwest Asia is meant the extensive and diverse region lying west of the subcontinent of India-Pakistan as far as the Mediterranean and Red Seas and bounded by the U.S.S.R. on the north. It embraces much of what is ordinarily included under the somewhat ambiguous terms, Near East and Middle East. In this largely dry or subhumid region, predominantly upland and covering some 2.5 million sq mi, there dwell probably 122 million people, representing an overall density of about 45–50 per sq mi. Of the more than a dozen states comprising Southwest Asia, Turkey (which includes a very small sector in Europe) is the most populous, with nearly 36 million inhabitants, followed by Iran with 28 million and Afghanistan with 17 million. All others have fewer than 10 million, while 6 have less than 5 million. Of all the LD regional populations of the world, those in Southwest Asia are probably subjected to the cross currents of international politics to the greatest degree. Considering the region's strategic geographic location, its richness in oil, and the impoverished condition of its people, Southwest Asia resembles the lightning rod that attracts the thunderbolt.

Three main groupings of population are recognized—the settled peasant agriculturists, the nomads, and the townspeople. In spite of the deficient and variable rainfall, most of which falls in the winter half year, agriculture provides a livelihood for about three quarters of the population and its products represent some 40 percent of the national income. Seven to 8 percent of the inhabitants may be nomads. Perhaps 10 percent live in urban places having 25,000 or more inhabitants.[1] Deserts, which make up more than half the total area, often have little or no sedentary population.

Vital Rates. Reliable demographic data for Southwest Asia are scarce. Registration of births and deaths is so incomplete and of such low reli-

[1] Joanne E. Holler, "Population Growth and Social Change in the Middle East," Publication of the George Washington University Population Research Project, Washington, D.C., 1964, pp. 1–2.

ability where it exists at all that the published data often are of little use. Resort must be made to estimates based on census counts, but even respectable censuses are lacking for most countries.[2] Such a data situation precludes any but the most rudimentary treatment of the population geography of the Middle East.

Average birth rates in this predominantly Moslem region are assumed to be high, probably about 44 per 1000, a rate that is higher than the average for tropical Latin America (estimated 40) but lower than that for Africa (47). The exceptions are non-Moslem Israel and Cyprus, both with crude birth rates not far from 25 per 1000. Israel unquestionably should not be included among the LD group of countries, while Cyprus is somewhat transitional in character. Registered or estimated death rates vary widely from country to country, but the average is probably intermediate between the estimated 9–10 per 1000 for Latin America and the 20 for Africa. Western influence in the forms of sanitation and medicine began earlier here than it did in Africa, so that its effects on mortality reduction have been greater. As a consequence of high fertility and intermediate but declining death rates, the natural increase is relatively high, probably averaging between 2 and 3 percent per year. This is not as high as in Latin America, where death rates are lower. At current rates of increase, the population will double in about 25–30 years, and with the probability of a further decline in the death rate, this time span is likely to be shortened. The impressive resistance of Moslem peasant culture to European influence, including birth-control measures, augurs against any immediate decline in birth rates. Indeed, this is one of the earth's hard-core regions of high fertility, apparently fairly well removed from the threshold of fertility decline. The crude birth rate projections of the United Nations to the year 2000, implied in its "medium estimates," indicate that Southwest Asia's estimated crude birth rate probably will decline to only 38 by 1980, but could shrink to 30 by 1995–2000.[3] By comparison, Africa's is expected to decline from an estimated 1960–1965 rate of 46 to only 40 over the same period. But it must be pointed out that even a birth rate of 30, in conjunction with anything like modern mortality rates (such as 10 per 1000), still represents an annual growth rate of 2 percent per year, or a doubling of the population in about 35 years. Southwest Asia obviously faces a serious population growth

[2] M. A. El Badry, "Trends in the Components of Population Growth in the Arab Countries of the Middle East: A Survey of Present Information," *Demography*, Vol. 2, 1965, p. 140.

[3] United Nations, *World Population Prospects as Assessed in 1963*, New York, 1966, p. 34.

problem even if it should succeed in reducing births to 30 over the next quarter century.

Population Characteristics. Like most of the LD world, Southwest Asia is a region of low educational attainments and meager per capita national incomes. Except in Israel and Cyprus, literacy rates are low; of the population aged 15 years and over, 60–65 percent are illiterate in Turkey and 85–95 percent in Iran and Afghanistan, the three most populous countries.

Only in Kuwait, Israel, and Cyprus does the per capita annual national income (as of about 1970) exceed $600. In five of Southwest Asia's countries it is below $200. In the three most populous countries, Turkey, Iran, and Afghanistan, the estimates are $290, $280, and $70 respectively.

A number of the population characteristics of southwest Asia have their roots in the region's great antiquity and long duration of human settlement. Within it ancient states and empires flourished and three of the earth's great religions had their origins. Because it served as a transit land of ancient commerce between three continents, successive waves of immigration poured into the region. These and other associated historical events throw light on the astounding heterogeneity of Southwest Asia's population characteristics in race, language, religion, and social customs. Viewed broadly, Southwest Asia has served as a route for the migration of people ever since the dispersion of earliest man. The result has been a mixing of cultures on a grand scale.

Earliest tillage culture, involving agricultural-village settlements, is believed to have originated in the hill lands flanking the Mesopotamian lowland on the north, while the lowland itself may have been the cradle of earliest urban culture. The powerful pre-Christian states of Assyria, Babylon, and Persia left the first imprints; later came the effects of Macedonian and Roman rule. Of particular importance as it affected the population traits of the Middle East was the Arab conquest of the 7th century. This brought a rough, uncultured desert people, mainly pastoralists and caravan traders, into contact with the sophisticated cultures of Rome and Iran. The fusion of the two produced an extraordinary cultural and intellectual revival.

Southwest Asia's present population represents an intermingling of several racial stocks. Two racial strains, the long-headed Mediterranean and the round-headed Armenoid, form the dominant elements. But Iranian, Indo-Aryan, and Turki elements are also present. For the most part the Middle Asian peoples are of swarthy complexion, with dark hair and small-to-moderate stature.

Languages. Two large language subdivisions may be recognized: (1) a very extensive southern region, lying south of the folded mountain

SOUTHWEST ASIA
MAIN LANGUAGE GROUPS

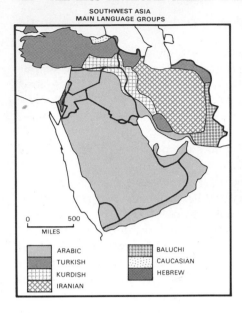

ARABIC
TURKISH
KURDISH
IRANIAN

BALUCHI
CAUCASIAN
HEBREW

0   500
MILES

Fig. 13.1. Modified from a map by W. B. Fisher, *The Middle East*, Methuen, 6th ed.

zone in Anatolia and Iran, where Arabic so predominates that it almost excludes all others, and (2) a northern and far more populous zone, coinciding with the belt of northern highland, in which there is a composite of various languages, both recent and ancient. In the latter are to be found people speaking Turkish, Greek, Persian, Kurdish, Hebrew, Armenian, Baluchi, Central Asiatic, and Aramaic (Fig. 13.1). The Arabic zone is more or less confined to the Arabian peninsula, Mesopotamia, and the eastern Mediterranean countries, or the Levant.

Kinship Culture. The extended family system in which property is held in common and controlled by the eldest male is traditional throughout Southwest Asia. Indeed, the whole civilization is so saturated with family loyalty that it has been called a "kinship culture." Under this system the extended family operates as an economic and social unit; the authority of the elders is pervasive. Early marriages are the rule, and large families are greatly desired. Education is directed toward making the child an obedient member of the kinship group. Although these traditional attitudes are gradually weakening (mainly among the urban people and the middle and upper classes), they are still strong among the rural inhabitants and especially so among the nomads. But even in rural society, increasingly the young adults are restive under the strictures imposed by the kinship culture.

Religions. Four of the world's great monotheistic religions—Judaism,

Christianity, Islam, and Zoroastrianism—had their origins within Southwest Asia. The geographic significance of the different religions and their distributions stems from the fact that many features of social, political, and economic life in the region originate from religious beliefs and practices. They also have served to divide Southwest Asia into rival groups and regions. Doubtless the current frictions between the Arab states and Israel partly derive from the religious conflict between Judaism and Islam. And the same is true between the several rival subdivisions of Islam. Unification of the Arab world against Israel has not thus far been successful because of the rivalries between states professing Islam or because of adherence to different subdivisions and sects of Islam by the peoples of different states. Christians too are divided into a number of independent and rival churches—Greek Catholic (Orthodox), Roman Catholic, Coptic, Jacobite, Armenian Orthodox, Nestorian, and Protestant.

During medieval times religious rivalries and influences were much stronger in Southwest Asia than they are today. But they are far from absent even yet. Under the *millet* system, adopted as the basis of civil administration in the Turkish Empire after 1229, the religious community and its Moslem leader had important legal and civil functions as well. Thus, *millets* became states within states. During periods of Moslem persecution of Christians such an organization opened the way for interference by the Western powers, with France championing the cause of Roman Catholicism and Russia interceding in behalf of the Greek Christians. And while admittedly religion today has less influence in political, social, and economic affairs than formerly, clericalism is still a more potent force in Southwest Asia than it is in most of Europe and Anglo-America. Party politics are all too often organized on a religious basis. Lebanon, Iraq, Jordan, and Israel represent states where clerical influence is still strong but scarcely dominant. In Turkey, Egypt, and to some extent Iran, nationalism has largely superseded religion as the mainspring of political activity and the principal socially cohesive factor. Yet even in Turkey, Islam is taught in state schools. At the opposite extreme are Yemen, Arabia, and Libya, where religious feeling is still a prime force in politics, while the nation's ruler derives great authority from his acceptance as a religious leader.

Nomads. An especially characteristic feature of the socioeconomic structure of Southwest Asia is that of nomadism, whose distinctive feature is its regular seasonal shifting of location in search of pasture for animals. Estimates of the proportion of nomads in the general population of Southwest Asia usually range from 7 or 8 up to 12 percent. Nomadism is characteristic of areas of scanty rainfall and therefore meager pasture in many parts of the Old World, with Southwest Asia as one of the earth's prime regional examples. True nomadism probably should be thought of as involving mainly horizontal movement; transhumance is more a change in altitude following the seasons and belongs to the New World as well as to the Old. Patriarchal tribal organization, with unusual emphasis on group solidarity and discipline, are distinguishing features. The supreme leader is the sheik. Somewhat different forms of nomadism can be distinguished, involving such items as extent of seasonal movement, kinds of animals grazed, and the degree to which tillage and transhumance are practiced. On the whole there appears to be a tendency for nomads to become increasingly settled.

The mountain foreland is the zone of nomadism in its fullest development. Hence it is in the northern parts of Southwest Asia, where highlands prevail, that the main concentrations of nomadic population occur. But in the drier south and east, although numbers are fewer, nomads represent a relatively larger proportion of the total population.

Urbanization. While Southwest Asia conforms to the standard pattern of the LD world in having a large proportion of its population engaged in agriculture and herding and living in small rural villages and hamlets, still the fact that as many as one third of the inhabitants are usually classed as urban is somewhat unusual. Probably only Afghanistan has less than 30 percent of its population living in places of over 5000 population. First and foremost of the factors that have contributed to the growth of urban places in Southwest Asia is the remarkable degree to which commerce has been traditional to this region over millenniums of time. Since far back in antiquity trading relations operating through caravans not only have linked the various regions of Southwest Asia itself but, even more important, have joined the Middle East with regions beyond—China, India, Europe, and northern Africa. Accordingly, a large and rich merchant element has been a feature of the region's culture structure since early times. Commerce was a main factor in the growth of towns because of its need for fixed nodal points possessing a measure of security, where exchange could take place.

A second factor contributing to the remarkable development of towns in Southwest Asia was the restricted supply of fresh water. Consequently dense populations have been forced to collect in a few favored spots where adequate supplies of water were available. And quite naturally the oasis-centered urban place came to dominate extensive areas of surrounding countryside.

Religion also played a role in the region's urban growth, since its spread and development were most striking among urban peoples. So religious tradition came to be associated with urban places, and the growth of religious tradition in turn fostered commercial activity, especially through pilgrimages. We think immediately of Mecca and Jerusalem in connection with religious centers, but there are numerous others as well.

Thus, as centers of trading activity, defense, administrative control, and religious association, many of the region's cities have persisted over millenniums of time, often outlasting its states and empires. Urban places are most numerous and closely spaced in the western parts where the overall population is denser. Here too are numerous port cities fostered by Mediterranean and Black Sea trade, and others stimulated by religious association and by the refining and shipment of petroleum.

DISTRIBUTION OF PEOPLE

Considering the antiquity of Southwest Asia's culture and its fame in trade, it does not seem unusual that this region has supported a goodly number of inhabitants from ancient times down to the present, in spite of its prevalent dryness. Of the 54 million inhabitants estimated by Beloch to have lived within the Roman Empire in 14 A.D., he attributes 19.5 million, or 36 percent, to the Asiatic sector, mainly Southwest Asia.[4] For about the same date Russell estimates the population of Asia Minor and Syria to have been 13.2 million, and 16 million by 350 A.D. Six million of these were assigned to the Province of Asia (western Anatolia), 6 million to Syria at the eastern end of the Mediterranean, 7 million to the rest of Asia Minor, and 500,000 to Cyprus.[5] Subsequently, plagues and wars took their tolls, so that Russell conjectures that by 1500 the region's population may have been reduced to only 8 million. At all times the chief concentrations of people were in the Mediterranean, Aegean, and Black Sea coastal lands.

The present distribution of population numbers in Southwest Asia shows strong regional and local contrasts. The gross pattern reveals the highest overall densities to be in the northern and western parts and the lowest ones to the south and east (Fig. 13.2). Thus there is a general falling off of numbers and densities both from north to south and from west to east. The most obvious feature controlling this large-scale pattern is the distribution of annual rainfall amounts, since precipitation too declines from the north and west to the south and east. Such a situation arises from the fact that all of Southwest Asia except the Arabian

[4] J. Beloch, *Die Bevölkerung der griechisch-römanischen Welt*, Duncker and Humbolt, Leipzig, 1886, p. 507.

[5] J. C. Russell, "Late Ancient and Medieval Populations," *Transactions of the American Philosophical Society*, New Series, Vol. 48, Part 3, 1958, p. 148.

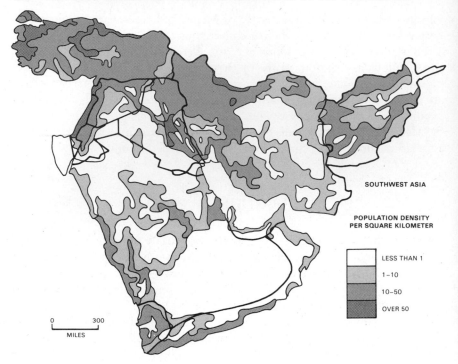

Fig. 13.2. Greatly simplified and otherwise modified from *Map of the Peoples of Southwest Asia* (ethnic and density), scale, 1:5,000,000, Institute of Ethnography, Academy of Sciences, U.S.S.R., Moscow, 1960.

peninsula falls within the westerly-wind circulation; consequently the portal region, both for atmospheric moisture and the rain-bringing cyclonic storms, is on the Mediterranean-Black Sea side.

But although fresh water, either in form of rainfall or irrigation, may be the primary factor influencing population numbers in this dry subtropical land, other factors are not inconsequential. Certainly historic antecedents have a way of leaving both positive and negative imprints on populations, in numbers as well as characteristics. For example, Moslem culture, while showing no religious prejudice for or against birth control, does indirectly in a variety of ways aid and abet high birth rates and large families. But, on the other hand, Islam remains a stubborn obstacle to westernization and modernization, influences that in turn affect population growth, especially through reducing mortality. Thus a stronger Western impact in the Mediterranean rimlands has doubtless favored a greater population increase and higher densities there. The same influence in these westernmost parts bordering navigable seas was largely responsible for the development there of trade and port cities, which very appreciably expanded the urban population. Moreover, where strong political organization has maintained a greater degree of peace and security, population growth usually has been stimulated.

Even a cursory glance at a population map of Southwest Asia discloses certain prominent facts of spatial distribution, as described below.

Major concentrations, with resulting high relative density, are observed along the coastlands of Turkey bordering the Black Sea, the land margins of the easternmost Mediterranean (especially in Israel and Lebanon), the southern shores of the Caspian in Iran, and certain oasis spots in northeastern Afghanistan. All of these except the last have benefited in their population growth by trade and port development. They all profit from above-average rainfall as well. All are relatively restricted in extent.

Intermediate densities are characteristic of the remainder of Anatolia, much of westernmost highland Iran, the part of the Levant between the coastal strip and the Syrian Desert, lower Mesopotamia and its northeastern plains, northern and eastern Afghanistan, and Yemen in southwestern Arabia. All of these regions of moderate concentration benefit either from modest rainfall sufficient for rain-fed agriculture, as in Anatolia, inland Levant, western Iran, and Yemen, or from irrigation water as in lower Mesopotamia, parts of western Iran, and northeastern Afghanistan. One important sector of this fragmented region of moderate population density has been designated the Fertile Crescent. It exists in the form of a great northward-bending arc that loops around the Syrian Desert. This arc of fairly level and subhumid grassland, situated intermediately between desert and mountains, links the head of the Persian Gulf and Mesopotamia (via the north Syrian steppe and the Levant) with Egypt. Over the centuries communication between Egypt and Mesopotamia occurred via the Fertile Crescent, so that it became one of the earliest international highways. The Crescent includes, in addition to the Levant (which is the great semicircle's western limb), western and northern Syria and adjacent parts of southeastern Turkey, northern and eastern Iraq, and western Iran. Mosul and Aleppo are situated within the northern reaches of the arc. Along most of the Fertile Crescent rain-fed agriculture is possible, but in some places rainfall is supplemented by irrigation water, and in these there is a thickening of the settlement pattern. In lower Mesopotamia agriculture is almost completely of the irrigated type .

Very low densities, or even near absence of population, are characteristic of most of the Arabian and Syrian deserts and those of interior eastern Iran and western and southern Afghanistan. But in a fair number of desert regions, nodes and lines of close settlement testify to the presence of intensive irrigated agriculture and of towns and cities dependent thereon. Certain unusually high and rugged areas likewise have meager settlement. But the fact that highlands induce more rainfall is an important offsetting factor to the terrain handicap, so that in general highlands in this dry land support more people than would ordinarily be expected.

Significantly, population nodes in Southwest Asia do not show much correspondence with present political units. This is quite at variance with the situation in Latin America, where international boundary lines uncommonly cut across important population clusters. There the settlement cluster characteristically is the core area of a state or of a province. But in Southwest Asia, with its long and complicated political history, national boundaries have changed frequently. Moreover, many of the present states and their boundaries are of relatively recent origin, a fact that helps to account for the general lack of coincidence between political units and population clusters.

Turkey.   The most populous (35–36 million, 1970) and one of the most secularized and westernized of the Moslem states of Southwest Asia, it has very recently adopted a national policy of family planning, signifying its concern over the country's rapid population growth and its eagerness to do something about it. But as yet population pressure is not a serious problem in Turkey, since there is still potentially productive dry-farming and grazing lands that can be brought into use. With an estimated birth rate of about 43 per 1000 in 1970, and a death rate of about 16, Turkey's annual rate of natural growth probably approaches 2.7 percent. This means a doubling of the present population in about 26 years. Vital rates vary widely within the country, and steep fertility and mortality gradients prevail. Crude death rates are lowest in the metropolitan areas (10–11 per 1000) and highest in the rural areas (15–21 per 1000). The rural rates vary regionally as well, from a high of 21 in the central part of the interior plateau down to 15 in the northern and western lowlands. Crude birth rates exhibit even greater variations. Metropolitan areas had birth rates of only 23.7 in 1960 and "other" urban areas 35.1, but for rural areas they attained the high average of nearly 49. Regional fertility within Turkey forms a pattern such as might be expected if European fertility norms and practices were in the process of diffusion. In other words, it is lowest at the western end of the country where European contacts have had a long and varied history and where economic and social development reaches the highest levels. Fertility, both general and rural, is highest in the less developed central and eastern sectors.[6]

Turkey's average per capita income is about $290, a figure that is well above the Asian average. The population is predominantly young, with 44 percent under 15 years of age. Some 60–65 percent of the inhabitants who are 15 years of age and over are illiterate; this is above the Asian average but below that for Southwest Asia.

Overall density of population is nearly 2.5 times that of the entire Southwest Asian region; this positive departure from the mean reflects, for one thing, Turkey's *relatively* more favorable physical environment. Located in the extreme northwestern part of Southwest Asia and flanked by large seas on its northern, western, and southern sides, Turkey has no deserts. To be sure, much of the country is a subhumid-semiarid plateau having only a modest population potential, while not more than a fifth of its area can be cultivated, although twice that amount is suitable for grazing. Still, only modest amounts of the national area—some too dry and some too rugged—would be classified as empty lands. About three quarters of the people depend on the land for a livelihood, and 80 percent live in rural areas. During the past half century genuine progress in modernization has been accomplished. Both public and private life have been secularized, Islam has been disestablished, polygamy has been abolished, women have been enfranchised, and economic improvement and birth-control programs have been started.[7] But while the transformation has been striking, the rural areas especially continue to show a traditional reluctance to change.

Highest densities of population are coastal and toward the west; lowest densities are chiefly interior and to the east, but also along parts of the south coast where highlands approach close to the sea. About 41.5 percent of the population dwells on the 17.5 percent of the country's surface that is under 500 meters in elevation. These are the littoral plains and adjacent lower slopes of the plateau. Nearly half (49.6 percent) live at elevations between 500 and 1500 meters on 57 percent of the surface. This is mainly the Anatolian plateau. So only about 9 percent must live on the highland quarter of the surface lying above 1500 meters.[8]

Concentration of population along the coasts involves not one but several causes. That such locations are often the most humid regions is

[6] Frederic C. Shorter, "Information on Fertility, Mortality and Population Growth in Turkey," *Population Index*, Vol. 34, January-March 1968, pp. 3–14.

[7] Holler, "Population Growth and Social Change," pp. 21–26.

[8] Ali Tanoglu, "Die Verteilung der Bevolkerung in der Turkei," *Review of the Geographical Institute of the University of Istanbul*, International Edition, No. 5, 1959, pp. 9–102.

of the greatest importance. But their accessibility to navigable seas, their lowland character, and the opportunities that they provide for more varied sources of income are also involved. These factors almost always act in combination.

Although the coastal margins contain a disproportionately large part of the population and hence the highest overall densities of the country, still there are wide variations in the closeness of settlement along different coastal stretches. Highest densities are along the Black Sea coast and especially its eastern part, or from about Samsun eastward, a region that Tanoglu speaks of as the most fruitful subdivision of Turkey. There the combination of abundant rainfall (40 to 60+ in.), a lowland with rich soils, and maritime interests associated with fishing and trade have provided the chief attractions for settlement. The belt of dense population on the eastern Black Sea coast is relatively compact; high mountains to the rear terminate it fairly abruptly on the land side.

The northern coastal population belt continues westward from about Samsun in somewhat changed form. Densities are reduced appreciably, and the populous belt is also less compact. This is because the mountains to the rear are not as high as those farther east and they contain depressions and valleys into which population has penetrated. Where the coastline trends NW by SE, rainfall drops to 25–30 in. (60–80 cm) which offers some handicaps, but on the whole this is a humid coast with ample moisture for rain-fed agriculture. Coal fields in the western part have added their influence to that of a fruitful mixed agriculture in supporting an overall dense population.

The Marmora-Thrace section of the littoral is somewhat transitional in character between the Black Sea and Mediterranean coasts, showing considerable variety in relief, climate, and vegetation in its different parts. As a consequence population distribution has an irregular pattern, and a compact coastal belt of high density is lacking. Still, this littoral is well populated and cities are numerous. This is especially true along the Bosporus and in the vicinity of Istanbul.

The Aegean margins of Turkey are one of population contrasts. There is no conspicuous band of high population density paralleling the coast, since this is an elevated and much indented littoral without significant lowland, except at the heads of some of the bays, where settlement does thicken somewhat. Indeed, the most conspicuous pattern of population in this Aegean section is one that is orientated at nearly right angles to the coast, following a similar terrain pattern. Here there is a series of tectonically depressed lowlands, occupied by streams and floored by alluvium, separated from each other by spines of hilly interfluves. Settlement is concentrated in these east-west depressions—less on the poorly drained alluvial floodplains and deltas and more along the valley margins or at the base of the limiting hills.[9] This western side is a somewhat decadent region that has seen more prosperous days. It would be capable of supporting larger populations, comparable to those of the coast lands in Greece and Italy, if swamps were drained, floods controlled, and irrigation systems developed.

The south coast in its western and central parts, where the formidable Taurus Mountains approach close to tidewater, is the least populated of the main littorals of Turkey. The southern mountains themselves are empty regions indeed. Along the bays lowlands expand somewhat and settlement thickens. By far the largest population concentration along the south coast is at its easternmost extremity, where the mountains recede farther inland and extensive lowlands have developed at the bay heads. Adana is located on one such lowland, the largest and one of the most productive in Turkey, and Antakya is on another. Floods, swamps, and deficient irrigation hinder these eastern plains from attaining their production and population potentials.

Eastward from the Adana Plain, and hence beyond the Mediterranean littoral, the mountains continue to recede northward, leaving to the south an extensive interior upland plain whose average elevation is between 500 and 1000 meters. It represents the northernmost sector of the Fertile Crescent. A modest rainfall of 16–24 in. has permitted the development of an agricultural system that combines the raising of crops (wheat, barley, legumes), and the pasturing of animals, mainly sheep and goats. Such an economy is able to support a rural population density that is distinctly above the national average; indeed, over considerable areas the closeness of rural settlement rivals that on the Adana littoral lowland.

In contrast to the peripheral coastal zone with its well-populated strips and clusters, interior plateau-Anatolia is a land of overall weaker and generally more uniform densities. A more severe and drier climate causes this upland to be less productive agriculturally, so the landscape is a relatively monotonous one combining grain fields and natural grazing lands. Below-average densities are characteristics of several subdivisions, among them the following: (1) the higher mountains along both the northern and southern margins; (2) the higher, more rugged, and climatically more severe east, where the Kurdish population emphasizes animal raising more than crops; and (3) the drier west-central part of the plateau, especially west and south of Lake Tuz, where rainfall drops below 40 cm (15 in.).

Iran. Second most populous state in Southwest Asia, Iran is, like

[9] Tanoglu, "Die Verteilung der Bevölkerung in der Turkei," pp. 103–104.

Turkey, a non-Arab Moslem country. Its estimated 28–29 million inhabitants give it an overall density of about 45 per sq mi, which is just slightly under the average for Southwest Asia but not much more than one third that of Turkey, a feature that reflects the greater extent of dry land in Iran and also the greater intensity of the aridity. Some 17 percent of the national area is classed as barren desert.

Birth rates (estimated 48 per 1000) and death rates (estimated 18) are both high. The inferred present natural increase of 3 percent per year will result in a doubling of population in about 24 years. Significantly, the government very recently has shown an interest in initiating family-planning activities as a part of the nation's five-year development program. Iran's population is heavily loaded with young dependents, some 46 percent being under 15 years. Seventy-five to 85 percent of the population aged 15 and over is illiterate. In spite of the fact that Iran is an important oil producer, the per capita national income is still only $280. A meager 8 percent of the area is under cultivation, while 67 percent of the cultivated land is irrigated. Agriculture provides about half of the gross national income. An estimated 25 percent of the population is judged to be nomadic. Two thirds make their livelihood from agriculture and herding, while 70 percent live in rural villages. Some 30 percent are believed to reside in urban places of 5000 or more inhabitants and the ratio is increasing.

A degree of ethnic and cultural unity is characteristic of Iran, since a majority of the population speaks various Persian dialects. But Arabic is spoken by some two million people living in the southwestern plains, and a similar number living in the northwest speak Armenian; Kurdish, Baluchi, and Turkish are spoken by numerous others.

The people are desperately backward and poor. Only about 5 percent of the farmers own the land they till, since most crop land is in the possession of wealthy absentee landowners who live in cities, many of these feudal aristocrats never having even seen much of the land they possess. Unfortunately the landlord class is able to dominate Parliament and so make it difficult to improve the position of the landless peasant farmers.[10] In Iran wealth and poverty exist in close juxtaposition.

In a land characterized by such climatic and terrain variety, a very uneven distribution of the people is to be expected. The gross pattern is one that has its roots in the distribution of water, either rain or irrigation, which in turn is largely a function of terrain. Iran is essentially an upland encircled on almost all sides by folded mountain chains. The central upland, with an average elevation of 2000–3000 feet, is basinlike

[10] Holler, "Population Growth and Social Change," p. 27.

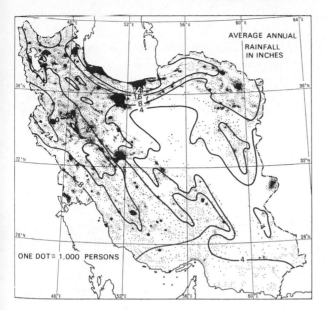

Fig. 13.3. Iran—population distribution and annual rainfall. Population after map in *National and Province Statistics of the First Census of Iran,* November 1956, Vol. 1.

in configuration and characterized by intense aridity. Greater, but still modest annual rainfalls typify most parts of the surrounding highlands. Accordingly, the gross population pattern shows a general density maximum coinciding with the node of fused highlands in the northwest and with the two chains of highland that diverge eastward from this node, with the dry near-empty upland basin between (Fig. 13.3). The emptiness is complete in the sections of the upland basin where saline swamps prevail, but there is a sprinkling of sedentary oasis people and nomads where the environment is slightly less adverse.

A somewhat more refined pattern within the highland environments reveals several clusters of higher population density, a majority of them having one or more cities. Thus there is one band of high density coinciding with the Caspian borderlands to the north of the Elburz mountains, and another just to the south around Teheran. A third is in the vicinity of Tabriz, Ardabil, and Rezaiyeh in the extreme northwest, and still a fourth is around Hamadan, Arak, and Kermanshah in the Zagros mountains farther south.

Details of settlement distribution patterns in the highlands show extreme irregularity to be sure, but on the whole linearity of form is most conspicuous. This is not unusual, since the highlands are of folded origin, containing structural valleys and basins, many of them with rivers and hence irrigation possibilities. The linear population concentrations sometimes show a degree of parallelism.

A noteworthy feature of the Iranian population is the importance of tribal groups, many of which practice varieties of nomadism. It is estimated that as many as 25 percent of Iran's people follow a degree of nomadic existence. Their concentration is in the peripheral highland sections of the country. In the Zagros highlands the broken character of the terrain has retarded the consolidation of the tribes, with the result that intertribal warfare, raiding, and disorder are rife, a disunity which has been further exacerbated by the contrasting social and cultural characteristics of the tribes. For example, the Kurds are of Armenian racial stock, speak an Aryan language, and are moderately strict Sunni Moslems; the Qashqai are Mongoloid people who speak a Turki language; and the powerful Bakhtiari are only very nominal Moslems.[11]

Afghanistan, third most populous (17 million) of Southwest Asia's states, it is also one of the most backward. Population data, even estimates, are largely lacking, but the vital rates are judged to be high. Eighty-five to 95 percent of the adult population is believed to be illiterate, while the per capita national income may be no more than $70, the lowest in all Southwest Asia.

The population distribution of the Afghan people resembles that of the Iranians, except that it is reversed in direction. Thus, highlands with modest rainfall and moderate population densities encircle the country on the east and north, while the west and south are a part of the same arid and empty upland basin to be found in eastern Iran. The very high and snow-covered parts of the Hindu Kush are without settlement, but on the other hand, population is strikingly concentrated in the radially oriented stream valleys descending from these mountains. The meager population of the dry western and southern upland region is similarly linear or riverine in pattern, being confined to the proximity of a few main streams.

Iraq.   With only about 9–10 million inhabitants, Iraq is only one fourth to one third as populous as Iran or Turkey, but it resembles them in its high vital rates and in most other population characteristics as well. Its area of 170,000 sq mi presents such a difficult habitat, mostly dry, that only 3 percent is presently farmed. The estimated per capita national income of $230 is low to be sure, yet it is scarcely indicative of the deep and widespread poverty that prevails. For while as many as 75 percent of the people are believed to derive their living from agriculture

---

[11] W. B. Fisher, *The Middle East: A Physical Social and Regional Geography,* 6th ed. Methuen and Co., London, 1971, pp. 295–296.

and grazing, that economic sector provides only about 25 percent of the country's income. Oil has become the main source of national wealth, but only a mere trickle of the gains from its sale filters down to the impoverished masses. Seventy-five to 85 percent of the population over 15 years of age are estimated to be illiterate.

Iraq is composed of a mosaic of religious, ethnic, and linguistic groups, whose loyalities often are more to the group than to the state. But unlike the two more populous countries just described, Iraq is an Arab state, so that there is an overall pervading Arab-Moslem identity that operates as a centripetal force to appreciably unify the culture. Some 95 percent of the Iraqis are Moslems, but the Moslem majority itself is split between two major Islamic sects, the Sunni and the Shi'a. Most numerous of the several minority groups is the Kurds, numbering some 800,000, who are concentrated on the northeastern frontier. They are tied to the Iranians by a language similarity, and to the Turks and Arabs by their Sunni Moslem religion. Ambitious to create a compact Kurdish state that would include parts of Iran, Iraq, and Turkey, this minority opposes being integrated into the political and social structure of the nation.

Four unlike geographical subdivisions, each with its own population individuality, compose Iraq. The first is the unirrigated arid land, which is almost without sedentary population. It includes the extensive region situated west of the Euphrates, which is a part of the great Arabian Desert, and in addition the territory that extends beyond the Euphrates north of Hit and eastward to the Tigris between Mosul and Samarra. Enclaves of meagerly settled dry country exist farther south, both the area between the two great rivers and their main distributaries and a large section east of the Tigris below Baghdad that reaches to the Iranian border. This is nomad land.

Of the three remaining subdivisions, containing mainly sedentary population, most important is the dry one composed of scattered strips of irrigated alluvial plain—that watered by the Tigris below Samarra, a wider belt along the Euphrates below Hit, and strips bordering distributaries, artificial canals, and the Diyala (an eastern tributary of Tigris) from the point where it debouches on to the plains, downstream as far as Baghdad. This arid irrigated region, with its strongly riverine settlement pattern, may contain as much as 70 percent of the country's total sedentary population.[12]

The two remaining regions, located in the extreme northeastern part of the country, have population densities that are intermediate between

---

[12] J. H. G. Lebon, "Population Distribution and the Agricultural Regions of Iraq," *Geographical Review,* Vol. 43, April, 1953, p. 224.

those of the floodplains and the deserts. One of these is a piedmont plain developed on only slightly disturbed Tertiary formations that are mantled with loess and older alluvium. On the plain settlement is widely spread. Closer to the Turkish and Iranian borders the piedmont gives way to the Zagros mountains, where the dissident Kurd population is concentrated in broad valleys and intermontane basins. In both of these regions the modest winter rainfall of some 15 in. is sufficient to nourish a nonirrigated agriculture that combines the cultivation of winter wheat and barley and the grazing of livestock. This is one sector of the Fertile Crescent.

The Arabian Peninsula. Covering more than a million sq mi, it probably supports fewer than 16 million inhabitants. Some 14 to 15 million of these are within the states of Saudi Arabia (7.7 million), Yemen (5.7 million), and Southern Yemen (1.3 million), formerly Aden. The region is almost all desert except for the Yemen highlands. Of the Saudi Arabian population about two thirds are believed to be nomadic and 12 percent are estimated to be sedentary oasis agriculturists, while 22 percent may be town dwellers.[13] Some of the driest parts are empty of people, nomadic or otherwise. A modest concentration of sedentary inhabitants coincides with the oases of the interior parts of the peninsula and with others along its western, or Red Sea, margins.

Highland Yemen, the only humid part of the peninsula, is the most densely settled. Some 90 percent of the population are farmers engaged mainly in rain-fed agriculture. In arid Southern Yemen most of the small population is concentrated in Aden City, or along the floor and sides of the Wadi Hadramawt. There is also a slight thickening of settlement in the Muscat-Oman region of the southeast, where highlands induce a modest increase in rainfall. Both rain-fed and oasis agriculture are represented.

The Levant (Syria, Jordan, Lebanon, and Israel). This region consists of the four states at the eastern end of the Mediterranean Sea that together contain some 14 million people, or nearly as many as in the whole Arabian peninsula, a fact that points to a far greater congestion of people within the restricted Levant littoral region than is typical elsewhere in Southwest Asia.

Only within a belt extending about 100 mi inland from the Sea is it sufficiently humid to permit natural tillage; beyond that, to the east, is the largely unoccupied desert, which isolates the Levant states on their land frontiers. But within that 100-mi strip is the single largest, fairly compact bloc of high-density population in all of Southwest Asia. As a rule the highest densities are along the coast. In part this reflects the

---

[13] Holler, "Population Growth and Social Change," p. 40.

dense agricultural population that inhabits the littoral plains of Israel, Lebanon, and Syria. And because the plains, everywhere restricted in width, are considerably wider in Israel than elsewhere, high coastal concentrations of population are more conspicuous in that section than farther north. But an equally important factor in the coastal concentration of people is the fact that the Levant has since ancient times specialized in maritime activities, resulting in the development of numerous port cities.

Inland from the coastal plains population patterns are to a considerable degree affected by the complex terrain. An outstanding feature is a north-south linear arrangement of two parallel chains of hills separated by a long structural depression, varying in width from 2 to 15 mi, parts of which are occupied by the Jordan and Orontes rivers and by the Dead Sea and other lakes. Minor cross faults in the western range have created two significant east-west lowlands, that of Akkar-Bukeia near the boundary between Syria and Lebanon, and the Esdraelon Plain just north of Haifa in Israel. Both east-west corridor lowlands are densely settled in most parts, although malaria in the past has been a deterrent to full utilization. The longitudinal lowland separating the twin north-south highlands is by no means a continuous strip of intensive cultivation and dense population. In fact, the opposite is true more often than not because of handicaps in the form of saline and stony soils, floodings, and reed-covered swamps. Parts of the Orontes lowland have been reclaimed and irrigation schemes completed, with new settlements resulting. Other projects along the Orontes and Jordan rivers are contemplated.

One of the most developed sections of the structural depression is the rich alluvial plain, 6 to 10 mi wide, of the Litani River in Lebanon, most parts of which are a productive granary that forms the country's main agricultural core. Another noteworthy section of close settlement lies in the Jordan Valley north and south of Lake Kennert (Sea of Gallilee).

The highlands vary greatly in elevation, slope, and degree of ruggedness, and consequently in population as well. But considering their harsh environment, they are generally well peopled. The Lebanon mountains, at intermediate elevations, are especially so.

Eastward from the innermost of the two ranges of highland, rainfall for a short distance continues to be precariously sufficient for rain-fed agriculture, although where possible it is usually supplemented by irrigation. This interior strip of rain-fed, relatively extensive agriculture is coincident with a band of modest population density that decreases in intensity eastward toward the desert. Within it are such urban nodes as those around Damascus, Homs, Hama, and Aleppo. All of this inner section is a part of the Fertile Crescent that continues on northward into Turkey.

REFERENCES

Awad, M. "Nomadism in the Arab Lands of the Middle East," in UNESCO, *The Problems of the Arid Zone,* 1962.

Baer, Gabriel. *Population and Society in the Arab East.* Frederick A. Praeger, New York, 1964.

Clarke, J. I. and W. B. Fisher (Eds.). *Populations of the Middle East and North Africa,* 1971.

Cressey, George B. *Crossroads: Land and Life in Southwest Asia.* J. B. Lippincott Co., Chicago, 1960.

El-Badry, M. A. "Trends in the Components of Population Growth in the Arab Countries of the Middle East: A Survey of Present Information," *Demography,* Vol. 2, 1965, pp. 140–186.

Fisher, W. B. *The Middle East: A Physical, Social and Regional Geography.* 6th ed. Methuen and Co., London, 1971, pp. 101–141.

Holler, Joanne E. *"Population Growth and Social Change in the Middle East."* Population Research Project, The George Washington University, Washington, D. C., 1964.

Kingsbury, Robert C., and Norman J. G. Pounds. *An Atlas of Middle Eastern Affairs.* Frederick A. Praeger, New York, 1963.

Longrigg, Stephen H. *The Middle East: A Social Geography.* Aldine Publishing Co., Chicago, 1963.

The Middle East: A Survey and Directory of the Countries of the Middle East, Tenth ed. Europa Publications, London, 1963.

Planhol, Xavier de. *The World of Islam.* Cornell University Press, Ithaca, New York, 1959.

Regional

Bharier, Julian. "A Note on the Population of Iran, 1900–1966," *Population Studies,* Vol. 22, No. 2, July 1968, pp. 273–279.

Brice, W. C. "The Population of Turkey in 1950," *Geographical Journal,* Vol. 120, 1954, pp. 347–352.

Brice, William C. *South-West Asia.* University of London Press, 1966, pp. 56–65.

Dakot, Besrim. "Sur les mouvements demographiques en Turkie," *Review of the Geographical Institute of the University of Istanbul,* International Edition, No. 2, 1955, pp. 37–44.

Fişek, Nusret H. "Fertility Control in Turkey," *Demography,* Vol. 5, No. 2, 1968, pp. 578–579.

Fisher, W. B. (ed.). *The Land of Iran.* Cambridge History of Iran, Vol. 1. Cambridge University Press, Cambridge, England, 1968.

Goblot, H. "La structure de la population de l'Iran," *L'Ethnographie*, New Series, No. 57, 1963, pp. 33–54. Map.

Hazard, Harry W. "Size and Distribution of Population," in *Saudi Arabia*. Subcontractor's Monograph HRAF50, Human Relations Area File, New Haven, 1956, pp. 18–26.

Lebon, J. H. G. "Population Distribution and the Agricultural Regions of Iraq," *Geographical Review*, Vol. 43, April 1953, p. 224.

Longrigg, Stephen H. *The Middle East: A Social Geography*. Aldine Publishing Co., Chicago, 1963, pp. 88–121 especially.

Louis, Herbert. "Die Bevölkerungskarte der Türkei," *Berliner Geog. Arbeiten*, Vol. 20, 1940, pp. 1–43.

Rousseau, R. "La population de la Turquie en 1960," *L'Information géographique*, 27, No. 4, September–October 1963, pp. 154–157. Map.

Selen, Hamid Sadi. *Population Distribution in Turkey* (in Turkish, English summary). Dogus Ltd., Ankara, 1957. Population density map, scale 1:2,500,000.

Shorter, Frederic C. "Information on Fertility, Mortality and Population Growth in Turkey," *Population Index*, Vol. 34, January–March, 1968, pp. 3–21.

Stauffer, Thomas R. "The Economics of Nomadism in Iran," *The Middle East Journal*, Vol. 19, No. 3, 1965, pp. 284–302.

Taeuber, Irene. "Population and Modernization in Turkey," *Population Index*, Vol. 24, 1958, pp. 101–122.

Tanoglu, Ali. "Die Verteilung der Bevolkerung in der Turkei," *Review of the Geographical Institute of the University of Istanbul*, International Edition, No. 5, 1959, pp. 94–106.

Tümertekin, Erol. "The Distribution of Sex Ratios with Special Reference to Internal Migration in Turkey," *Review of the Geographical Institute of the University of Istanbul*, International Edition, No. 4, 1958, pp. 9–16.

Tümertekin, Erol and Necdet Tuncdilek. *Population Map of Turkey* (In Turkish, English summary). University of Istanbul, Geographical Institute Publication No. 37, Istanbul, 1963.

Tuncdilek, Necdet and Erol Tümertekin. *The Population of Turkey; Population Density, Population Increase, Internal Migration, and Urbanization* (In Turkish, English summary). University of Istanbul, Geographical Institute, Monograph Series, No. 25, Istanbul, 1959.

Wilber, Donald N. "Size and Geographical Distribution of Population," in *Afghanistan*, Vol. 1, Subcontractor's Monograph HRAF53, Human Relations Area File, New Haven, 1956, pp. 35–66.

Index